P9-DNR-039

Perennial All-Stars

The 150 Best Perennials for Great-Looking, Trouble-Free Gardens

Rodale Press, Inc.
Emmaus, Pennsylvania

OUR PURPOSE

"We inspire and enable people to improve their lives and the world around them."

©1998 by Jeff Cox
Illustrations ©1998 by Elayne Sears

All rights reserved. No part of this publication may be reproduced or transmitted in any form or by any means, electronic or mechanical, including photocopy, recording, or any other information storage and retrieval system, without the written permission of the publisher.

The information in this book has been carefully researched, and all efforts have been made to ensure accuracy. Rodale Press, Inc., assumes no responsibility for any injuries suffered or for damages or losses incurred during the use of or as a result of following this information. It is important to study all directions carefully before taking any action based on the information and advice presented in this book. When using any commercial product, always read and follow label directions. Where trade names are used, no discrimination is intended and no endorsement by Rodale Press, Inc., is implied.

Printed in the United States of America on acid-free ∞, recycled ♲ paper

Library of Congress Cataloging-in-Publication Data

Cox, Jeff
    Perennial all-stars : the 150 best perennials for great-looking, trouble-free gardens / Jeff Cox.
        p.   cm.
    Includes bibliographical references and index.
    ISBN 0-87596-780-9 (cloth : acid-free paper)
    1. Perennials. I. Title.
Sb434.C67 1998
635.9'32–dc21   97-33811

Distributed in the book trade by St. Martin's Press

2 4 6 8 10 9 7 5 3   hardcover

PERENNIAL ALL-STARS EDITORIAL AND DESIGN STAFF

Editor: Deborah L. Martin
Technical Editor: Barbara Kaczorowski
Interior Book Designer: Barbara Field
Design Assistance: Diane Ness Shaw
Interior Illustrator: Elayne Sears
Cover Designer: Nancy Smola Biltcliff
Photography Editor: James A. Gallucci
Copy Editor: Liz Leone
Senior Research Associate: Heidi A. Stonehill
Manufacturing Coordinator: Patrick Smith
Indexer: Ed Yeager
Editorial Assistance: Jodi Guiducci, Sarah Wolfgang
        Heffner, Rebecca S. McElheny

RODALE HOME AND GARDEN BOOKS

Vice President and Editorial Director: Margaret J. Lydic
Managing Editor, Garden Books: Ellen Phillips
Director of Design and Production: Michael Ward
Associate Art Director: Patricia Field
Studio Manager: Leslie M. Keefe
Copy Director: Dolores Plikaitis
Book Manufacturing Director: Helen Clogston
Office Manager: Karen Earl-Braymer

On the cover: Photos by Connie Toops; Robert Cardillo; Richard Shiell; John Glover

WE'RE HAPPY TO HEAR FROM YOU.
    For questions or comments concerning the editorial content of this book, please write to:

    Rodale Press, Inc.
    Book Readers' Service
    33 East Minor Street
    Emmaus, PA 18098

    For more information about Rodale Press and the books and magazines we publish, visit our World Wide Web site at:
    http://www.rodalepress.com

For Carol and Buddy

Contents

Acknowledgments

Introduction

I'D LIKE TO THANK MAGGIE LYDIC, editorial director of Home and Garden Books at Rodale Press, and Ellen Phillips, managing editor of Garden Books, for their guidance in developing this book. Special thanks to my editor, Deb Martin, to copy editor Liz Leone, and to Barbara Field, the book's designer. I'd also like to thank Becky McElheny, Barbara Kaczorowski, and Jim Gallucci. Thanks to Brian Carnahan for ideas that helped make the book more practical. And very special thanks to Tom Gettings, Anne Cassar, and the folks in Rodale Photography Support.

I received strong support and help from Louise Hole and Bob Stadnyk at Hole's Greenhouses and Gardens in Alberta, Canada. Landscaper and true friend Larry Korn of Mu Landscaping in Oakland, California, gave me the benefit of his extensive knowledge. David B. Lellinger of The American Fern Society and Sue Olsen, editor of "The Hardy Fern Foundation Newsletter" in Bellevue, Washington, deserve my thanks. Mary Lou Gripshover of The American Daffodil Society went to great trouble to help me understand this genus. Ann Lunn of The American Primula Society and Robin Parer of The International Geranium Society gave me generous help. And Jacques Mommens of The North American Rock Garden Society in Millwood, New York, lent me his help and insight.

A heartfelt and special thanks is reserved for Dr. Steven Still of The Perennial Plant Association in Columbus, Ohio, who from the outset pointed me in all the right directions.

WELCOME

It's easy to think up features that would make a perennial "perfect." The perfect perennial would be covered in showy flowers for most of the growing season. When it wasn't flowering, its foliage would be an attractive addition to the garden, and it would never look tatty. It would have gorgeous leaf color in fall and striking berries or seedpods.

This perfect perennial would take very little work to maintain. It wouldn't need staking or a lot of pinching and fussing over. In addition, it would be drought resistant—yet, if grown in a rainy area, it would tolerate wet conditions. Diseases wouldn't bother it and pests would pass it by.

It also would grow well in a wide variety of soils, from the acid, humusy soils of the Northeast to the alkaline, low-humus soils of the Southwest. It would be able to thrive in a variety of climates, too, from hot to cold, from sea level to the mountains, and from the humid East to the arid West. It would do equally well in sunny or shady conditions.

Our perfect perennial would look good in the front or back of the bed and would make a good-looking combination with any other plant in the garden. It would be well behaved and noninvasive, so the gardener wouldn't have to spend a lot of time digging out unwanted shoots or inferior volunteer seedlings.

And, of course, its flowers would be delightfully fragrant.

Finding this perfect perennial is a bit harder. When I asked one perennial grower which plant she thought would fill all these bills, she thought for a moment and said, "A plastic plant." She meant that no single perennial will do and be everything. But some perennials do come remarkably close. Among all the most cherished garden perennials, a select few outperform all the others across the wide spectrum of traits that make a perennial an all-star.

To write this book, I embarked on a search for these all-stars. Some were recommended to me by plant growers, landscapers, or nurserypeople who have worked with these plants and who know them by their many positive attributes. Others I know because I've grown them in my gardens both in Pennsylvania and in California—dissimilar conditions indeed—and have seen them perform admirably in both places.

In *Perennial All-Stars*, I've brought together 150 true perennial stars of various sizes, colors, and functions in the garden so that they form a group of darn-near foolproof plants. These are the fundamental plants—the ones that will be growing vigorously when more finicky plants are struggling or have perished. I think that if you use them as the basis for your own perennial gardens, you'll be pleased at how they perform through the years.

This doesn't mean that these are the only plants that belong in your perennial garden. Your beds can and should include personal favorites, challenging plants, gift plants, or rare plants. But these all-stars are the proven and beautiful performers that will form the backbone of that most sought-after garden: the one that takes the least amount of work and gives the best and most reliable results, year after year.

Availability, as well as performance, were the major criteria in selecting the plants in this book. There's no use telling you about great plants that are virtually unobtainable. I've found that wide availability often goes hand-in-hand with sturdy performance. In other words, the really good plants are widely available because they are so reliable and beautiful.

So use these plants in large drifts or as accents, with the knowledge that they will become old friends that return reliably year after year to greet you with their cheery habits, forms, and colors. You will find, as I have, that the times of their appearance and

flowering will become milestones in the natural year, marking off the seasons in your garden. The day will come when the reddish spears of the emerging peonies show through their mulch, and that day will be perennially remarkable because of it.

How comforting when the spring ground is covered once again with phlox. And how exciting when the lilies are in season. How bittersweet when the blooming clouds of asters mark the beginning of autumn. How lonely when only the browned stalks of the heleniums and black-eyed Susans are left, sticking stiffly through the ice and snow.

But the glory and promise of perennials is that they will be back. And if the perennials in your garden are among the all-stars in this book, they will surely keep that promise.

Ten Steps to a Starring Perennial Garden

I REALLY ENJOY THE COLOR AND FRAGRANCE that seem to overflow from my perennial garden. But I find that there's also a lot to enjoy in the steps along the way. One part of perennial gardening that I think is really fun is choosing the plants. As I page through colorful catalogs or browse among plant-filled nursery benches, the potential of all those plants makes me feel that anything is possible. Their growth may turn out to be incredibly vigorous, their blooms exquisitely beautiful, their colors fantastically glorious—and they haven't required a lick of work…yet.

On the other hand, the choices can seem overwhelming. Without years of trial and error, how can you select the best perennials for your garden from the hundreds clamoring for your attention? Wouldn't it be great to have some expert advice to help guide your selections no matter where you garden?

Now you have it—in *Perennial All-Stars*. As a gardener with more than 25 years of experience, I know the investment that a successful perennial garden represents. So in this book, I've chosen 150 perennials that offer big returns on your gardening efforts. Each of these plants has the star-studded qualities that make perennials so popular: They're easy to grow, they have beautiful flowers and form, they're reliable in a variety of soil and climate conditions, and they're pest- and disease-resistant.

Since I wanted to make sure that these perennial all-stars represented the best perennials across the country, I consulted with the top perennial nurseries and experts in the United States and Canada before making my final choices. You can bet that I had a lot of fun talking with perennial experts, making my choices, and describing these familiar garden friends and new-found favorites for you. And I know you'll have fun reading about all these wonderful perennials and choosing your own favorites.

Once you've looked at some perennial all-stars and gotten really inspired, turn to the Perennial Plant Finder on page 8 to make sure the plants you're thinking about will grow well in your conditions. It's important to choose plants that will thrive where you plant them so you can spend time enjoying your lush, beautiful garden instead of fighting to keep struggling plants alive.

When you've narrowed down your all-star lineup, you're almost ready to order. But before you bring home your perennials,

The mixture of foliage textures at the front of the border enhances the flowers in this purple-themed garden.

remember that creating a garden is more than putting in plants. That's not to say that you need a whole complicated regimen to get your garden going. For me, it comes down to ten simple steps. These steps will guide you through the planning, preparation, and planting of great-looking, easy-care perennial gardens that shine with all-stars all season long.

1. SELECT THE RIGHT SITES.

Where do you need gardens in your landscape? Do your plans include flowering borders to flank a walkway, fence, or wall? Or do you plan to use freestanding island beds to create a much-needed focal point in your yard?

Place your gardens where you'll see them easily and often. Look out your kitchen window or out the main windows of your home and see if there's a spot in plain view where a flower garden might go. Think about where you walk in your yard or where you spend the most time outdoors, and put your gardens nearby.

Keep work to a minimum by choosing a location that's close to a water source and easy to get to with a wheelbarrow full of plants or compost. Look for visual advantages, too. For example, if you can plant your garden in front of dense evergreens, you'll have a wonderful dark backdrop to set off your perennials.

2. ASSESS YOUR SOIL.
It's no secret that the soil in which you plant can make or break your garden. If your soil is "good"—if it's right for the plants you've chosen—you'll save yourself a lot of headaches and a lot of work. Perennials have their soil preferences, too. You'll find out what each all-star prefers when you look at its entry; or for an overview, turn to the Perennial Plant Finder.

Most perennials like a loose, humusy loam that's moist but well drained. Loam is a soil

All-star perennials make it easier to have a great-looking garden. Showy selections of durable plants such as goldenrod and yellow-flowered sneezeweed add color to the garden for weeks—or even months—without requiring hours of care.

that has some clay, some silt, and some sand in it, plus enough organic matter to make it dark, crumbly, and easy to dig in. (Most of us have to improve our soil with lots of organic matter—compost, leaves, shredded newspapers, grass clippings, and the like—before it resembles this ideal state.) This kind of soil lets your perennials spread their roots with ease and keeps them well supplied with moisture and nutrients. It also makes it easy for you to plant, lift, and divide your perennials without having to take a pick to the soil. If you plant loam-loving perennials in poor, dry soil, they may struggle along, producing less growth and fewer flowers; they certainly won't look their best.

By comparison, some perennials like loose (almost gravelly), poor to average, dry, well-drained soil in a sunny, warm location such as on a south-facing bank. Plants such as coreopsis, mullein, thyme, and yarrow are in this group. In rich, moist garden soil, these plants tend to grow weak and leggy, tumbling over themselves and producing foliage at the expense of flowers.

Still other perennials can tolerate or even flourish in poorly drained sites or clay soils.

Sun-loving perennials like 'Moonshine' yarrow, violet sage, and daisylike lance-leaved coreopsis create a pretty, drought-tolerant combination for a bright spot in the landscape.

Some plants that can grow in wet soil include daylilies, Joe-Pye weed, obedient plant, and queen-of-the-prairie. But if your chosen site is in a low spot that often holds standing water, either stick with true bog plants or build a raised bed to lift your perennials above the water level.

Of course, there are those places (especially if your home has just been built) where all the soil is poorly drained, heavy clay. If that's all you have, start by working in as much organic matter as possible to help loosen it up. Adding sand helps improve drainage, too, but it takes a lot to make a difference: Spread at least 2 inches of sand over the top of your garden, then work it into the soil along with plenty of organic matter. Consider making raised beds of improved soil. By mounding the bed's soil above ground level, you immediately improve drainage. Don't worry too much about rocks, unless they're very big. They make it hard to dig but don't have much effect on drainage.

3. TAKE A LOOK AT THE LIGHT. While you're preparing the soil for your garden, look at how much sunlight it gets. If your garden gets eight or more hours of sun a day, it's considered to be in full sun. It's in partial sun if it's in direct sunlight for five to eight hours a day; and if it gets less sun than that, it's in partial shade. A garden that's open to the south and shaded from the north is usually hot and sunny. A garden that's open to the north, with trees or buildings to the south, will be cooler and more shady. As with soil, perennials have light preferences. You'll find the sun or shade preferences of each all-star in the individual entries.

It makes a big difference whether shade comes in the cool morning or in the hot part of the afternoon. That's because most perennials that are classified as plants for partial shade actually prefer morning sun and afternoon shade. For these plants, you'll want to arrange your garden with plenty of open space to the east and southeast and perhaps shade-casting shrubs, trees, or structures to the west and northwest

If you adore sun-loving perennials but don't have a site with eight-plus hours of sun each day, don't despair. Many sun-worshipping perennials will do just fine in partial shade if they get shade in the morning and full sun by midday and through the afternoon. That means siting your garden with open space to the west and southwest and shade from the east and northeast.

Some plants like what's called bright shade. It's just what it sounds like—a spot that gets a lot of reflected light from nearby walls or lawns or pavement, with a high overhead tree canopy providing light shade. For most plants, dappled shade amounts to the same thing as bright shade.

You can really heat up the already warm tones of 'Moerheim Beauty' sneezeweed (front) with the rich red flowers of 'Lucifer' crocosmia—if you garden in Zones 6 to 9, where crocosmia's hardy. In a cooler climate, use cardinal flower to supply an equally brilliant shade of red.

There aren't too many perennials that require full shade. Most are choice woodland plants such as European wild ginger, variegated Solomon's seal, and epimediums, that have made the transition to the garden. These plants prefer to grow where the hot light of the sun can't reach them, such as beneath the branches of evergreen trees and shrubs.

4. ZERO IN ON YOUR ZONE. Check the USDA Plant Hardiness Zone Map on page 344 to see which zone you live in. Your hardiness zone represents the average annual minimum temperature in your region. You can use the range of hardiness zones provided for each all-star to help you choose plants that can survive in your zone. That's because most plants have a definite winter survival range and will die if it gets colder than that.

However, keep in mind that other factors also contribute to a plant's hardiness. Certain features of your garden site may make it colder or warmer than the zone average for your area. For example, if your home is on a south-facing slope, your site may be a half-zone warmer than its surroundings. If you're in a deeply shaded valley, or in an area exposed to sweeping winds, it may be a half-zone colder.

Winter protection can affect hardiness, too. A plant listed as hardy in Zone 6 might have a hard time surviving in that zone without mulch or snow cover through the winter. Prolonged exposure to subzero temperatures and soil that alternately freezes and thaws and heaves the roots out of the ground both can spell doom for an unprotected plant. With a constant, deep snow cover, plants that are hardy to Zones 5 or 6 usually can withstand much colder winters. Similarly, with deep, careful mulching, you often can grow plants a full zone north of their usual hardiness zone. But if a perennial is listed for Zones 4 through 7 and you live in Zone 3, it will take heroic measures to get it through your very cold winters. Zone 4 means that plant is hardy only to Zone 4 and that the lower winter temperatures of more northern zones are likely to kill it. It may even be injured or killed by a particularly severe winter in Zone 4.

In the warm-winter zones of the South and coastal Northwest, perennials may struggle if planted in zones warmer (higher) than the upper end of their range. In Zone 9, the combination of summer heat and winter warmth can kill plants that have an upper hardiness limit of Zone 7. Some perennials need cold winters to thrive. For example, herbaceous peonies don't do well here in coastal California where winter temperatures rarely go below 20°F. Summer protection can make a garden more successful in the warmer zones. Most perennials that grow in full sun in the North (Zones 6 and lower) will appreciate some shade in the fierce summer heat of Zones 7 through 10.

5. DON'T LIMIT YOURSELF. Remember that your perennial garden can include plants besides perennials. Foliage plants, groundcovers, ornamental grasses, and vines can really perk up a bed or border.

They'll also add color to your garden at times when more of your perennials are out of bloom than in; so will choosing perennials that have brightly colored or variegated foliage. Even when they're not blooming, these plants give the effect of flowers in the garden. Don't overlook annuals, either. Although they require yearly installation, it's hard to beat plants like impatiens, petunias, and sweet alyssum for adding spring-to-frost color to your garden.

There's no law that says you can't include a few woody plants in your perennial garden. In fact, shrubs and trees are welcome additions because they give the garden year-round structure while transforming it into what's referred to as a "mixed border." Deciduous flowering shrubs and trees are useful for adding seasonal color, too, while evergreens supply color and contrast all year long

Some perennials perform useful functions beyond the confines of the garden bed. Clematis, for instance, is useful for softening the hard lines of a building or porch. Verbena is a handy plant for the tough growing conditions in the spaces between walks and driveways. Other all-stars look great spilling over walls or growing down a difficult slope. Use the Perennial Plant Finder lists to find all-stars that solve problem areas in your yard and garden.

6. LET YOUR GARDEN HAVE ITS UPS AND DOWNS. Choose plants of varying heights. A garden filled with only little plants, only medium-size plants, or only tall perennials quickly becomes monotonous, and no plant in it is able to shine. Instead, choose a variety of heights and mix them up in your garden. Obviously, the smallest plants go in front and so on, with the tallest plants filling in the back. But vary the rule now and then. Place a big floppy perennial right up near the path. Break things up. Don't be too predictable. Just don't hide a small plant behind a larger one.

7. CHOOSE A STAR FOR EACH SEASON. Pick a favorite perennial and plan a color scheme around it. Say, for instance, that you love the care-free yellow-orange flowers of heliopsis that reach their vibrant peak in August. You can use heliopsis as a keynote plant, then build the rest of your garden around it, choosing plants to bloom with it as well as plants to bloom before and after it. You might add black-eyed Susans to provide a richer, darker echo of the heliopsis flowers. To cool things down, you might have purple asters and white boltonia, or you might intensify things with the fall colors of helenium.

Use plants with white flowers or with silver or gray-green foliage to separate

Lenten rose is an easy choice if you want an all-star to bloom in late winter, when few other perennials dare to show their faces. And you can continue to enjoy its flowers into the spring, when it's joined by a chorus of snowdrops and other spring bulbs.

groups of perennials with clashing colors. In other words, you can use white flowers to separate a group of yellow- and blue-flowering perennials from a simultaneously blooming group of plants with a clashing pink-and-mauve theme.

8. PLANT IN DRIFTS. A garden of single plants is incoherent—more like a museum collection than a living perennial garden. Make drifts with at least 5—or 7, 11, even 15—plants of the same perennial. Interweave the drifts. This gives you large areas of the same plant (and the same flower color) so that your garden has substance, not just pinpoint dots of color.

A group of red bee balms looks good, but several groups scattered here and there look much better. Make the spacings of the groups irregular. Put two groups closer together and the third farther away. The repetition of plants draws the eye through the garden by tying one part to the next. It becomes a composition, instead of a hodge-podge where every group is a different color. And remember that simple is more elegant than complex. If 5 different perennials in a garden are good, 15 aren't necessarily better. Sometimes just two well-chosen partners are perfect—when they're each planted in drifts.

If you do use single plants, make them big, contrasty ones like plume poppy or Japanese silver grass. Or use intensely colored perennials as accents—for example, use a single specimen of fiery orange butterfly weed as an accent in a large drift of soft blue milky bellflower.

9. MOVE YOUR MISTAKES. Don't be shy about digging up and moving plants that don't look right, don't thrive, or otherwise seem out of place in your garden design. Gardens only improve when you are scrupulous about moving out the inferior plants and trying new plants in their place. It's tough to get a garden right the first time, and half the fun is in the tweaking that follows.

Lavish drifts of 'Ruby Glow' sedum and 'Goldsturm' black-eyed Susan add color and interest to the garden in late summer.

10. FIND A PLACE FOR YOUR EXTRAS. Most perennials will eventually need dividing. When they do, you can compost the extras, give them away, start new gardens, or—this is my strategy—plant them helter-skelter in an out-of-the-way place. I call this my cutting garden, and I don't care what it looks like. I go out there whenever the cut flowers in the house start to fade into mush. And I happily gather color-coordinated flowers and foliage to fill fresh vases.

The 150 perennials in this book are superb garden plants. I guarantee that you'll find in these pages the foundation plants for your best gardens ever. Many of these all-stars need such minimal care that you'll enjoy their flowers for years to come, even if you plant them and forget about them. So plan your gardens, fill them with all-stars, and above all, have fun.

The
Perennial
Plant Finder

*Your Guide
to the Stars*

▲ CRIMSON MOTHER-OF-THYME

▲ DOWNY CLEMATIS

▲ ROCK SOAPWORT

▲ 'CHATTAHOOCHEE' PHLOX

HOW TO USE THE PERENNIAL PLANT FINDER

Use these lists to identify the perfect perennial all-stars to suit your site, your soil, or your color scheme. Whether you're seeking a red-flowered summer bloomer, an easy-growing groundcover, or the right perennial to add color to a shady spot in your yard, this key will guide you to all the all-stars that fit the bill. If trouble-shooting's what you need, look for your problem and you'll find the all-stars that can cope with it—whether you've got hungry deer, dry soil, or a soggy spot. Then turn to the page number that precedes each plant name to get the complete story on how easy it is to grow and use these first-rate performers in your garden.

SPRING-BLOOMING ALL-STARS BY FLOWER COLOR

Blue to Lavender-Blue

32 ......'Burgundy Glow' ajuga
40 ......Arkansas amsonia
46 ......Music Series hybrid columbines
68 ......'Novalis Blue' aubrieta
72 ......Blue wild indigo
78 ......Siberian bugloss
86 ......Serbian bellflower
106 ....Downy clematis
220 ....Virginia bluebells
226 ....Forget-me-not
246 ....'Chattahoochee' phlox
254 ....Jacob's ladder
264 ....'Mrs. Moon' Bethlehem sage
318 ....'Bowles' Variety' periwinkle

Blue-Violet to Lilac

38 ......'Purple Sensation' Persian onion

46 ......Music Series hybrid columbines
90 ......Perennial cornflower
186 ....'Caesar's Brother' Siberian iris
262 ....'Mikado' Siebold's primrose
266 ....Pasque flower
312 ....'Homestead Purple' verbena

Pink

74 ......'Perfecta' bergenia
116 ....'Tiny Rubies' cheddar pinks
150 ....'Ingwersen's Variety' bigroot cranesbill
184 ....'Beverly Sills' bearded iris
238 ....'Degas' oriental poppy
268 ....Ornamental rhubarb
276 ....Rock soapwort

Red

46 ......Music Series hybrid columbines
48 ......'Düsseldorf Pride' sea-pink
182 ....Delavy incarvillea
298 ....Crimson mother-of-thyme
308 ....'Fusilier' tulip

White

46 ......Music Series hybrid columbines
108 ....Lily-of-the-valley
144 ....Sweet woodruff
146 ....White gaura
170 ....'Palace Purple' heuchera
180 ....'Snowflake' perennial candytuft
192 ....'White Nancy' spotted dead nettle
228 ....'Ice Follies' daffodil
234 ....Allegheny spurge
256 ....Variegated Solomon's seal
284 ....False Solomon's seal
300 ....Wherry's foamflower

Yellow

46 ......Music Series hybrid columbines
70 ......Basket-of-gold

SUMMER-BLOOMING ALL-STARS BY FLOWER COLOR

JOHNNY-JUMP-UP ▲

'CRIMSON STAR' PURPLE CONEFLOWER ▲

'NIOBE' CLEMATIS ▲

'PINK JEWEL' DAISY FLEABANE ▲

▲ 'Goblin' blanket flower

▲ 'Snow Lady' Shasta daisy

▲ 'Moonbeam' threadleaf coreopsis

▲ 'Mönch' Frikart's aster

FALL-BLOOMING ALL-STARS BY FLOWER COLOR

WINTER-BLOOMING ALL-STARS BY FLOWER COLOR

LONG-BLOOMING ALL-STARS

These all-stars typically bloom for more than six weeks.

'INGWERSEN'S VARIETY' CRANESBILL ▲

'GOLDSTURM' BLACK-EYED SUSAN ▲

'TAPLOW BLUE' GLOBE THISTLE ▲

'MOERHEIM BEAUTY' SNEEZEWEED ▲

▲ 'MAY NIGHT' VIOLET SAGE

▲ WHERRY'S FOAMFLOWER

▲ 'MIKADO' SIEBOLD'S PRIMROSE

▲ 'TINY RUBIES' CHEDDAR PINKS

ALL-STARS LESS THAN 2 FEET TALL

This group of all-stars ranges in height from just a few inches to about 2 feet tall. Use them for edgings and at the front of a bed or border, on top of terraced walls, and along pathways.

ALL-STARS 4 FEET OR TALLER

These are the tallest all-stars. Most look best in the back of a bed or border, but you can also add drama by bringing a few of these tall beauties to the front of the garden.

ALL-STARS FOR COLD CLIMATES

Some all-stars easily weather the winters in the North, some actually grow best in the cold of Zones 2 to 5, and some are cold-tolerant relatives of tender perennials. They're all here—choose your favorites.

ALL-STARS FOR THE DEEP SOUTH

Many perennials burn out or just don't do well in the Deep South or the hot regions of the West, but not these heat-tolerant all-stars.

JAPANESE SILVER GRASS ▲

'LORD BALTIMORE' HIBISCUS ▲

MONKSHOOD ▲

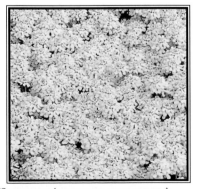

'SNOWFLAKE' PERENNIAL CANDYTUFT ▲

▲ Jerusalem sage

▲ 'Blue Danube' Stoke's aster

▲ Cardinal flower

▲ 'Bowles' Variety' periwinkle

ALL-STARS FOR DRY SITES

Some perennials can withstand long dry periods without damage. Among our all-stars, these are the most drought tolerant.

ALL-STARS FOR WET SITES

Most perennials can't tolerate wet or boggy soil. These all-stars can.

VARIEGATED SOLOMON'S SEAL ▲

PURPLE GAS PLANT ▲

'HAPPY RETURNS' DAYLILY ▲

BUTTERFLY WEED ▲

▲ 'CONNECTICUT KING' LILY

▲ 'FUSILIER' TULIP

▲ 'SUNNY BORDER BLUE' SPEEDWELL

▲ 'FAMA' PINCUSHION FLOWER

ALL-STARS THAT SELDOM NEED DIVISION

After a few years, most perennials need lifting and dividing, but these all-stars either rarely need such treatment or actually perform better without it.

DEER-RESISTANT ALL-STARS

These all-stars are unpalatable to deer. If deer are hungry enough, they'll eat almost anything, but they'll turn to these plants last.

150 ....'Ingwersen's Variety' bigroot cranesbill
166 ....Lenten rose
184 ....'Beverly Sills' bearded iris
190 ....'Royal Standard' red-hot poker
228 ....'Ice Follies' daffodil
244 ....Jerusalem sage
268 ....Ornamental rhubarb
322 ....Adam's-needle

GROUNDCOVERING ALL-STARS

These all-stars will spread to make attractive groundcovers.

32 ......'Burgundy Glow' ajuga
36 ......Lady's-mantle
54 ......European wild ginger
62 ......Dwarf Chinese astilbe
74 ......'Perfecta' bergenia
78 ......Siberian bugloss
86 ......Serbian bellflower
100 ....Goldenstar
108 ....Lily-of-the-valley
138 ....'Elijah Blue' fescue
144 ....Sweet woodruff
150 ....'Ingwersen's Variety' bigroot cranesbill
156 ....Golden variegated hakone grass
170 ....'Palace Purple' heuchera
172 ....'Bridget Bloom' foamy bells
176 ....'Krossa Regal' hosta
178 ....'Frances Williams' Siebold's hosta
192 ....'White Nancy' spotted dead nettle

208 ....'Majestic' big blue lilyturf
234 ....Allegheny spurge
258 ....'Superbum' Himalayan fleeceflower
276 ....Rock soapwort
288 ....'Silver Carpet' lamb's-ears
318 ....'Bowles' Variety' periwinkle

ALL-STARS FOR NATURALIZING

In a favorable site, some perennials will multiply or spread year after year to fill in any gaps in your gardens. These naturalizing all-stars are especially useful for bringing color to out-of-the-way places.

32 ......'Burgundy Glow' ajuga
40 ......Arkansas amsonia
58 ......'Mönch' Frikart's aster
76 ......'Snowbank' boltonia
78 ......Siberian bugloss
84 ......'Telham Beauty' peach-leaved bellflower
90 ......Perennial cornflower
100 ....Goldenstar
140 ....'Venusta' queen-of-the-prairie
144 ....Sweet woodruff
168 ....'Happy Returns' daylily
214 ....Gooseneck loosestrife
220 ....Virginia bluebells
224 ....'Marshall's Delight' bee balm
228 ....'Ice Follies' daffodil
250 ....'Vivid' obedient plant
262 ....'Mikado' Siebold's primrose
276 ....Rock soapwort
284 ....False Solomon's seal
302 ....'Zwanenburg Blue' spiderwort
304 ....'Miyazaki' toad lily
308 ....'Fusilier' tulip
318 ....'Bowles' Variety' periwinkle

HIMALAYAN FLEECEFLOWER ▲

'ICE FOLLIES' DAFFODIL ▲

DWARF CHINESE ASTILBE ▲

'BURGUNDY GLOW' AJUGA ▲

▲ JAPANESE PAINTED FERN

▲ RED BARRENWORT

▲ 'HOMESTEAD PURPLE' VERBENA

▲ 'BOWL OF BEAUTY' PEONY

ALL-STARS WITH EVERGREEN OR SEMIEVERGREEN FOLIAGE

In warm-winter regions (Zones 8 to 11), these all-stars are evergreen. Where winters are colder Zones 5 to 7), they tend to be semievergreen.

26 ......'Coronation Gold' yarrow
32 ......'Burgundy Glow' ajuga
74 ......'Perfecta' bergenia
86 ......Serbian bellflower
100 ....Goldenstar
128 ....Red barrenwort
138 ....'Elijah Blue' fescue
166 ....Lenten rose
172 ....'Bridget Bloom' foamy bells
180 ....'Snowflake' perennial candytuft
196 ....'Hidcote' English lavender
198 ....'Barnsley' tree mallow
208 ....'Majestic' big blue lilyturf
234 ....Allegheny spurge
244 ....Jerusalem sage
258 ....'Superbum' Himalayan fleeceflower
288 ....'Silver Carpet' lamb's-ears
294 ....Prostrate germander
298 ....Crimson mother-of-thyme
312 ....'Homestead Purple' verbena
322 ....Adam's-needle

ALL-STARS WITH COLORFUL OR VARIEGATED FOLIAGE

These all-stars have uniquely colored, textured, or variegated foliage that adds contrast in the garden and extends their season of interest.

32 ......'Burgundy Glow' ajuga
50 ......'Silver Brocade' beach wormwood
64 ......'Sprite' star astilbe

66 ......Japanese painted fern
74 ......'Perfecta' bergenia
128 ....Red barrenwort
138 ....'Elijah Blue' fescue
156 ....Golden variegated hakone grass
162 ....Blue oat grass
170 ....'Palace Purple' heuchera
176 ....'Krossa Regal' hosta
178 ....'Frances Williams' Siebold's hosta
192 ....'White Nancy' spotted dead nettle
196 ....'Hidcote' English lavender
216 ....'Coral Plume' plume poppy
234 ....Allegheny spurge
240 ....'Husker Red' foxglove penstemon
242 ....Russian sage
256 ....Variegated Solomon's seal
264 ....'Mrs. Moon' Bethlehem sage
268 ....Ornamental rhubarb
274 ....Lavender cotton
288 ....'Silver Carpet' lamb's-ears
296 ....'Lavender Mist' meadow rue

FRAGRANT ALL-STARS

The flowers of these all-stars have appealing fragrances.

92 ......Red valerian
108 ....Lily-of-the-valley
116 ....'Tiny Rubies' cheddar pinks
134 ....'Gateway' Joe-Pye weed
144 ....Sweet woodruff
184 ....'Beverly Sills' bearded iris
196 ....'Hidcote' English lavender
220 ....Virginia bluebells
224 ....'Marshall's Delight' bee balm
228 ....'Ice Follies' daffodil
230 ....Catmint
232 ....Missouri evening primrose
236 ....'Bowl of Beauty' peony
248 ....'David' summer phlox
256 ....Variegated Solomon's seal

ALL-STARS THAT ATTRACT BUTTERFLIES

Plant these all-stars in your garden and enjoy the brightly colored butterflies that will come to sip their nectar.

ALL-STARS THAT ATTRACT HUMMINGBIRDS

Hummingbirds just love the color red and tubular or long-throated flowers. These all-stars are some of their favorites.

'KOBOLD' SPIKE GAYFEATHER ▲

'CROWN OF RAYS' GOLDENROD ▲

MUSIC SERIES HYBRID COLUMBINES ▲

'VIVID' OBEDIENT PLANT ▲

Perennial All-Stars Hall of Fame

The 150 All-Time Top Performers

BROADLEAVED BEAR'S-BREECH

Acanthus mollis 'Latifolius'

BROADLEAVED BEAR'S-BREECH IS A FIRST-RATE foliage plant, unfurling 36- to 48-inch-wide, waist-high clumps of huge leaves up to 24 inches long and 12 inches wide. This broadleaved cultivar of bear's-breech is an all-star because it's a bit hardier and more robust than plain old *Acanthus mollis*. And most gardeners prefer *A. mollis* over other *Acanthus* species, most of which have leaves tipped with sharp, skin-puncturing spines.

A native of the Mediterranean region from Portugal to Greece, bear's-breech was a favorite of the Greeks during their classic period.

Its handsome foliage provided the pattern for the leafy decorations that top Corinthian columns.

Beyond Broadleaved Bear's-Breech

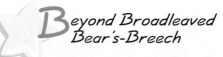

While broadleaved bear's-breech is the all-star of the genus, spiny bear's-breech (A. spinosus, also called A. spinosissimus) is a durable plant with attractive (but spiny) darker green foliage. A. perringii (also called A. dioscoridis var. perringii) is a smaller, more compact plant with rosy red flower bracts.

Spotlight on Broadleaved Bear's-Breech

USDA Plant Hardiness Zones: 7 to 10

Season of Bloom: June to August

Height × Width: 3 to 6 feet × 4 feet

Flower Color: Pinkish white and mauve

Light Requirements: Partial shade to full sun

Soil Requirements: Sandy, well-drained soil amended with limestone

Place of Origin: Mediterranean region

Plant Sources: Kurt Bluemel, Carroll Gardens

In some parts of the South and especially on the West Coast, where it finds the hot, dry Mediterranean conditions of its origins, bear's-breech blooms from June to August, sending up sturdy, long-lasting, 4- to 6-foot-tall flower spikes of pinkish white florets covered by attractive mauve hoods.

HOW TO GROW BEAR'S-BREECH This all-star prefers a sandy, well-drained soil sweetened with ground limestone. In Zones 8 to 10, bear's-breech performs best in moist, partially shaded sites. With good drainage and a protective winter mulch, it grows well as far north as Zone 6 and into the southern parts of Zone 5, although it rarely blooms in these colder areas. Except for slugs and snails, which may eat holes in the big leaves, most pests ignore bear's-breech.

PROPAGATING BEAR'S-BREECH In Zones 8 to 10, divide the fibrous roots of bear's-breech during the winter months. Spring division is more successful in Zones 6 and 7. Pieces of roots left behind as you divide bear's-breech will sprout and form new

Although its spikes of mauve and white flowers are attractive, most gardeners grow broadleaved bear's-breech for its glossy, dark green foliage.

plants. Place divisions 3 feet apart when replanting. You can grow bear's-breech from seed, but plants are so easy to divide that seed-starting seems unnecessarily slow.

THE RIGHT SITE FOR BROADLEAVED BEAR'S-BREECH
Use this all-star to give a dramatic, dignified, architectural structure to the shady part of the garden. It will also grow in full sun in all but the very sunniest, hottest regions of its range, where it requires partial shade.

Because of their dark color, bear's-breech leaves form an ideal backdrop for colorful flowers planted in the foreground. Its bold texture makes it perfect for breaking up a boring bed of little green leaves. Bear's-breech makes an excellent specimen plant in the garden and is bold enough to hold its own when placed against brick walls or stonework.

CO-STARS FOR BROADLEAVED BEAR'S-BREECH
Combine the big, bold leaves of bear's-breech with the lacier foliage of bamboo, ornamental grasses, and large-leaved ferns. Plant it behind spires of white or pale pink hollyhocks (*Alcea* spp.).

A Stellar Idea

Although the flowers of bear's-breech are beautiful, its foliage declines after the plant blooms. But if you remove the spent flower spikes, new leaves will appear with the fall rains. Western gardeners who grow bear's-breech for its foliage often remove the flower spikes as they appear, thus preserving the leaves' good looks until winter. In the Southeast and East, where bear's-breech tends to flower poorly, the foliage remains handsome all season.

'CORONATION GOLD' YARROW

Achillea 'Coronation Gold'

YARROW HAS BEEN CALLED THE QUEEN of the summer garden, but I reserve that title for the all-star hybrid known as 'Coronation Gold'. Topping the list of its positive qualities is how easy it is to grow. This is one perennial you can pretty much neglect and still get excellent results. And because its 24- to 36-inch-tall flower stems are shorter and more robust than those of its parents, 'Coronation Gold' yarrow is less prone to toppling over when grown in moist, rich soil. The plants begin blooming in June, bearing masses of bright gold florets in flat, 3- to 5-inch-wide flowerheads. If you remove the spent flowerheads, 'Coronation Gold' yarrow will continue blooming for two to three months. And its finely divided, fragrant, gray-green leaves are always handsome. In warmer climates flowering begins earlier, and in cooler climates it continues into fall.

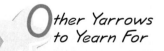

Other Yarrows to Yearn For

If you yearn for flowers in shades other than yellow, take a look at the many yarrow selections that share the easy-care attributes of 'Coronation Gold'. Hybrids such as 'Summer Shades Mix' include subtle pastel hues, while the flowers of 'Fireland' are a reddish color. 'The Pearl' sneezewort (A. ptarmica 'The Pearl') is a lovely white yarrow with a looser habit than 'Coronation Gold'.

Spotlight on 'Coronation Gold' Yarrow

USDA Plant Hardiness Zones: 3 to 9

Season of Bloom: June to September

Height × Width: 24 to 36 inches × 24 to 36 inches

Flower Color: Yellow-gold

Light Requirements: Full sun

Soil Requirements: Average to poor, well-drained soil

Place of Origin: A hybrid of the species A. filipendulina and A. clypeolata

Plant Sources: Kurt Bluemel, Bluestone Perennials, Carroll Gardens, Crownsville Nursery, Forestfarm, Garden Place, Milaeger's Gardens, Van Bourgondien, André Viette Farm & Nursery, Weiss Brothers Perennial Nursery, White Flower Farm

HOW TO GROW 'CORONATION GOLD'

This yarrow will perform like a star in just about any kind of soil, provided it's well-drained. Where it receives constant moisture, 'Coronation Gold' blooms prolifically all summer long. But it also puts on a good show in droughty conditions and poor soil, even though you won't get quite as many flowers.

PROPAGATING 'CORONATION GOLD'

Divide 'Coronation Gold' in the spring. You also can take root cuttings from around the plant's base then. If you prefer to divide your plants in the fall, do it early enough to allow the newly planted divisions to establish their roots before winter.

A drift of 'Coronation Gold' in full bloom creates a stunning effect in the garden. Its showy flowerheads look great in fresh or dried arrangements, too.

The rich yellow-gold flowers of 'Coronation Gold' yarrow help to warm up blue flowers like those of 'Cambridge Blue' edging lobelia.

THE RIGHT SITE FOR 'CORONATION GOLD'

'Coronation Gold' yarrow's handsome, fern-like gray-green leaves are one of its finest features. In warmer regions, the foliage persists in basal rosettes through the winter. The leaves are fragrant, too—pluck a leaf and crush it to release its strongly herbal aroma. Use clumps of 'Coronation Gold' to break up the monotony of darker greens and as a foil for plants with larger leaves.

CO-STARS FOR 'CORONATION GOLD' One of the best companions for 'Coronation Gold' yarrow is deep blue 'East Friesland' sage (*Salvia* × *superba* 'East Friesland'). Blue delphiniums, red and orange red-hot poker (*Kniphofia uvaria*), fresh white Shasta daisies (*Chrysanthemum* × *superbum*), the frosty violet hues of amethyst sea holly (*Eryngium amythestinum*), and the light and airy flower clouds of dusty meadow rue (*Thalictrum speciosissimum*) all look great combined with this all-star. You can also try it with red flowers: 'Gibson's Scarlet' cinquefoil (see page 260) and bronzy red 'Bishop of Llandaff' dahlia (*Dahlia* 'Bishop of Llandaff') are two good red-flowered companions.

A Stellar Idea

An added bonus to this all-star is that it makes a long-lasting, colorful cut or dried flower. Fresh-cut bunches will last for a couple of weeks in a vase. To dry 'Coronation Gold' yarrow, strip the leaves from its stems and hang the stems upside down in a warm, dark, dry room until they're brittle. The dried flowerheads retain their color and just-picked look for months and months, so you can enjoy them through the winter in dried arrangements. To keep both fresh-cut and dried yarrow flowers looking their best for as long as possible, wait until the florets show some pollen before you harvest.

'MOONSHINE' YARROW

Achillea 'Moonshine'

IF YOU NARROWED THE LIST of perennial all-stars down to the top dozen plants, 'Moonshine' yarrow would still make the cut. Its muted lemon yellow flowers, an inheritance from *Achillea taygetea*, look wonderful combined with almost any other flower color. From its other parent, *A. clypeolata*, 'Moonshine' yarrow gets handsome, gray-green, fernlike leaves. In fact, the foliage is so pretty that it would make this plant garden-worthy even without its outstanding flowers.

'Moonshine' yarrow is never out of flower for long. In most of its hardiness range, it begins to bloom in June with a big flush of flat, 3-inch-wide flowerheads. Flowering continues at a somewhat reduced rate until September, when 'Moonshine' often puts on another flush

Spotlight on 'Moonshine' Yarrow

USDA Plant Hardiness Zones: 4 to 9

Season of Bloom: June to September

Height × Width: 16 to 24 inches × 24 inches

Flower Color: Pale yellow

Light Requirements: Full sun

Soil Requirements: Average to poor, well-drained soil

Place of Origin: Hybrid of A. clypeolata and A. taygetea found by Alan Bloom in England

Plant Sources: Ambergate Gardens, Kurt Bluemel, Bluestone Perennials, Busse Gardens, Carroll Gardens, Crownsville Nursery, Forestfarm, Garden Place, Milaeger's Gardens, Powell's Gardens, Sunlight Gardens, André Viette Farm & Nursery, Weiss Brothers Perennial Nursery

A Pair of Shorter Yellow Yarrows

To enjoy the great foliage, long bloom time, and tough-as-nails durability of yarrow in a site where a lower grower is needed, try one of the following diminutive selections. Woolly yarrow (A. tomentosa) has aromatic grayish green leaves that are more finely divided than those of 'Moonshine'. It grows only 6 inches tall and makes a good, mat-forming plant for the rock garden. 'King Edward' yarrow (A. × lewisii 'King Edward') produces small (1- to 2-inch) light yellow flowerheads on 6-inch-tall plants.

of flowers before frost. Removing the spent flowerheads encourages ongoing blooming. 'Moonshine' yarrow's sturdy, 16- to 24-inch stems keep the flowers erect even in the kind of enriched garden soil that makes other yarrows leggy and prone to toppling over.

HOW TO GROW 'MOONSHINE' 'Moonshine' yarrow prefers rather dry, unimproved soil and definitely dislikes heavy, soggy soils. It succeeds in the difficult conditions of the seashore, where its sturdy stems resist wind damage and the poor, sandy soil suits it well. But in the hot, humid conditions of south Florida or the Gulf, it may languish and become short lived.

'Moonshine' yarrow's pale yellow flower clusters provide a handsome contrast to the rosy purple spires of 'Kobold' spike gayfeather.

PROPAGATING 'MOONSHINE' In the spring, 'Moonshine' yarrow sends out underground rhizomes. Cut some of these into 1½-inch pieces and plant them 1½ inches deep. Keep the soil moist until the plants show good growth. Then divide the central clump if needed. You also may divide clumps of 'Moonshine' yarrow in early October. Dividing then still gives the divisions enough time to establish their roots before winter arrives.

THE RIGHT SITE FOR 'MOONSHINE' 'Moonshine' yarrow makes a great middle-of-the-border plant for a sunny site. Its pale yellow flowerheads look good with a wide range of other flower colors. And when it's not blooming, 'Moonshine' yarrow's aromatic, finely divided leaves make a neat 24-inch mound of gray-green foliage that works well as a neutral separator for stronger-colored flowers or foliage. Like 'Coronation Gold' yarrow, 'Moonshine' makes an excellent fresh-cut flower and dries well for winter arrangements.

CO-STARS FOR 'MOONSHINE' Light lemon yellow 'Moonshine' yarrow looks particularly beautiful with the dusty blue-violet of

In the sunny garden, use 'Moonshine' yarrow's muted lemony flower color and ferny gray-green foliage to soften bolder colors and textures.

globe thistle (*Echinops ritro*) and amethyst sea holly (*Eryngium amythestinum*), and with the rosy pink of purple coneflower (*Echinacea purpurea*).

MONKSHOOD

Aconitum napellus

FROM THE MID-ATLANTIC STATES NORTH and in the Pacific Northwest, monkshood earns the right to be listed as an all-star since the plant is one of the most beautiful for the back of the border. On a trip to Alaska, I was surprised to find monkshoods growing wild not more than a mile from a large glacier—which gives you some idea of the conditions these gorgeous perennials need. They are not for hot, southern gardens. In fact, the farther north you go, the better their color and the better they perform.

From July through August, monkshood's intense purplish blue to indigo flowers bloom

Spotlight on
Monkshood

USDA Plant Hardiness Zones: 2 to 7

Season of Bloom: Late July to September

Height × Width: 3 to 4 feet × 3 feet

Flower Color: Violet-blue

Light Requirements: Partial shade

Soil Requirements: Rich, constantly moist soil

Place of Origin: Northern Europe

Plant Sources: Busse Gardens, Milaeger's Gardens, Shady Oaks Nursery, Van Bourgondien

Seed Source: Thompson & Morgan

on upright spikes. Flower color varies somewhat in the species and may not be as rich where the summers are hot and the soil is droughty. The dark green leaves are deeply lobed and divided like the fingers of a hand.

Monkshood's flowers are unique: An upper helmet-shaped hood covers a lower, pealike flower, creating the effect of a hooded monk. The flowers' unique shape and dark, intense color give them a rare beauty that few other perennials can match.

HOW TO GROW MONKSHOOD This plant is a good choice for the rich soil under trees, but be careful not to let it dry out. It's also at home in a full-sun planting as long as it gets a steady supply of moisture. Once established, monkshood is a trouble-free plant with few pests or diseases. Reliably hardy even through the coldest winters, it returns year after year, slowly increasing the size of its clumps.

More Monkshoods of Merit

A pinkish white–flowered selection, A. napellus 'Album', blooms in August and September, mixing nicely with the soft lilac pink of 'Franz Schubert' garden phlox (Phlox paniculata 'Franz Schubert').

Also noteworthy, 'Sparks Variety' autumn monkshood (A. henryi 'Sparks Variety') has rich dark blue flowers on spikes emerging from many-branched plants. It blooms in August and September. The fall-blooming azure monkshood (A. carmichaelii) has lovely dark blue helmeted flowers on compact 3-foot plants. Bicolor monkshood (A. × cammarum 'Bicolor') has purplish blue and white flowers.

This all-star perennial is pretty but poisonous! Always wash your hands thoroughly after you finish planting or dividing monkshood.

Monkshood gets its common name from the shape of its flowers. Each violet-blue blossom resembles the figure of a hooded monk.

PROPAGATING MONKSHOOD Monkshood spreads slowly to fill in its spot in the garden. It performs best when its brittle, fleshy roots remain undisturbed. However, flowering may become sparse as the plant grows into a crowded clump over the years. When this happens, divide monkshood in the fall. Use the sharp edge of a spade to divide the clumps of tuberous roots into sections with at least two or three shoots or stems emerging from them. Replant the divisions immediately in rich, moist soil.

THE RIGHT SITE FOR MONKSHOOD Plant monkshood in a moist, shady part of the garden. All parts of the plant are extremely poisonous (hence another of its common names, "wolf's bane"), so it's obviously not a plant for a spot where children might get hold of it or a passing dog might chew it. Monkshood is an excellent substitute for delphiniums in shady places where delphiniums won't bloom.

CO-STARS FOR MONKSHOOD Monkshoods are great back-of-the-border mixers and look stunning with Japanese anemones (*Anemone × hybrida*), great bellflowers (*Campanula latifolia*), and 'Autumn Joy' sedum (see page 280). They also mix nicely with long fronds of ferns, the big leaves of hostas, and the light airiness of columbine meadow rue (*Thalictrum aquilegifolium*). Mix them with other woodland perennials such as goat's beard (see page 52) and black cohosh (see page 102) or with fellow moisture lovers like late-blooming astilbes.

'BURGUNDY GLOW' AJUGA

Ajuga reptans 'Burgundy Glow'

'BURGUNDY GLOW' AJUGA is a garden workhorse, a plant that will quickly cover the ground in semishade or full sun where there is sufficient moisture. At 4 to 8 inches tall, it's not the most striking plant in the garden, but it's a wonderful spreader and can quickly make a colorful groundcover. Plants spread by underground stolons to produce a dense stand of attractive leaf rosettes. It excels in acid soils where grass won't grow, although it may compete with grass if it grows into the lawn.

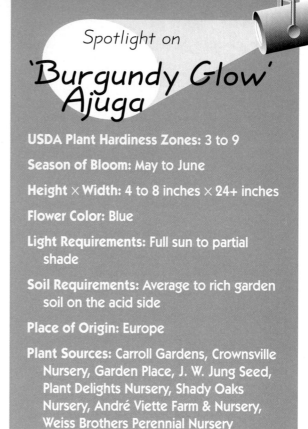

Spotlight on 'Burgundy Glow' Ajuga

USDA Plant Hardiness Zones: 3 to 9

Season of Bloom: May to June

Height × Width: 4 to 8 inches × 24+ inches

Flower Color: Blue

Light Requirements: Full sun to partial shade

Soil Requirements: Average to rich garden soil on the acid side

Place of Origin: Europe

Plant Sources: Carroll Gardens, Crownsville Nursery, Garden Place, J. W. Jung Seed, Plant Delights Nursery, Shady Oaks Nursery, André Viette Farm & Nursery, Weiss Brothers Perennial Nursery

Additional Ajugas to Acquire

Besides 'Burgundy Glow', there are other cultivars of A. reptans worth adding to your garden. 'Giant Bronze' has deep bronzy metallic leaves and grows to 9 inches tall in shade. 'Purpurea' (sometimes called 'Atropurpurea') has pretty purplish foliage. 'Variegata' has leaf margins splotched with yellow, and 'Jungle Bronze' and 'Jungle Green' are extra-big ajugas with flower spires to 10 inches tall.

Other useful species include Geneva bugleweed (A. genevensis), a rock garden favorite that ranges from 6 to 12 inches in height and does not produce stolons, and upright bugleweed (A. pyramidalis), a lowgrowing plant that also does not spread. The cultivar A. pyramidalis 'Metallica Crispa' is a popular selection, with deeply crinkled, metallic, reddish brown leaves.

In May and June, short flower spires arise from the centers of the rosettes if the plants get enough sunlight. Flowering continues into July in more northern regions. Deep blue blossoms whorl around these spires.

Although ajugas come in many leaf colors and textures, 'Burgundy Glow' stands out for its thick mats of lustrous, multicolored foliage. The oblong leaves have wavy margins, and each leaf features pink to pinkish rose and green areas with white margins. The new growth is usually wine red. In fall, the older leaves take on a bronzy hue, while the younger leaves have a rosy color.

In the warmer regions, ajuga is evergreen, but severe cold will nip back its top growth. Because they expand to capture more light, ajuga's leaf rosettes tend to be slightly larger (3 to 4 inches across) when grown in semishade than they are (at 2 to 3 inches) when grown in full sun.

Multicolored 'Burgundy Glow' ajuga makes a handsome groundcover that echos the colors of red-leaved shrubs like barberry or purple smokebush.

In addition to its colorful foliage, 'Burgundy Glow' ajuga bears spires of pretty blue flowers in late spring and early summer.

HOW TO GROW AJUGA Ajuga does best if you sprinkle an inch or so of loose compost over it in early spring or late summer. It needs regular water to perform at its peak. In most of the country, summer rainfall is enough to keep it going, although the occasional supplemental watering will refresh a tired, dry bed. Except for rare occurrences of root-knot nematodes, no pests or diseases of any consequence bother this vigorous grower.

PROPAGATING AJUGA You can divide ajuga at any time during the growing season. Plantings expand as underground stolons spread out and send up many new plants. Using a shovel or trowel, simply lift clumps of plants and replant the divisions about 8 to 10 inches apart. Five to seven plants in an area will send out many stolons over the growing season to fill the area completely. Use peat or finished compost between the newly planted divisions to encourage stolon production.

THE RIGHT SITE FOR AJUGA Invasive is too strong a word for ajuga, but it is a vigorous grower and spreader, so plant it where you can confine it easily. Or plant it in an area that needs an extensive groundcover and let it ramble!

The rounded leaves and low-growing habit of 'Burgundy Glow' ajuga provide a nice contrast for spiky, upright plants such as ornamental grasses and the foliage of spring bulbs. Use it to echo the foliage colors of other purple-leaved plants or as a groundcover to set off blue, pink, or white flowers.

CO-STARS FOR 'BURGUNDY GLOW' This ajuga makes a fine underplanting for early spring bulbs, such as snowdrops (*Galanthus nivalis*) and looks handsome during the summer with other vigorous, semishade-loving perennials. It's exceptional for carpeting the ground under red-leaved woody plants.

HOLLYHOCKS

Alcea rosea

Of all the old-fashioned cottage garden plants, none is more beloved than hollyhocks. They have a nostalgic charm that's unsurpassed, especially when they're growing against a brick or stone wall, along the side of a house, or by a picket fence.

Their sturdy stalks have large, hairy, coarse leaves at the bottom that get smaller toward the top of the stalk. The lovely crinkly petalled flowers open from the middle of the

Spotlight on Hollyhocks

USDA Plant Hardiness Zones: 3 to 9

Season of Bloom: July to September

Height × Width: 4 to 6 feet × 3 feet

Flower Color: Pink, red, yellow, and dark maroon, plus pastel shades of these

Light Requirements: Full sun

Soil Requirements: Rich, moist, deep soil

Place of Origin: China

Plant Sources: Bluestone Perennials, Busse Gardens, Carroll Gardens, Park Seed, Wayside Gardens, White Flower Farm

stalk upward over the course of the bloom season, with 18 to 24 inches of stalk in bloom at any one time. There are many double-flowered forms, but these never seem quite so prettily old-fashioned as the singles.

Most hollyhocks are biennials/perennials—that is, they flower the second year after sowing, like true biennials, but they may live for years when they find a good rich soil with adequate moisture. And at least some of their "perennial" tendencies come from hollyhocks' ability to self-sow in a favorable site.

Hosts of Other Hollyhocks

A. rosea 'Nigra' is a single hollyhock with maroon flowers so dark that they appear black, making a striking statement in the garden.

Besides the single hollyhocks, there are many fine doubles. 'Chater's Double' is a popular 6-foot-tall double-flowered selection in shades of scarlet, yellow, pink, and white. 'Chater's Double Apricot' grows to 6 feet tall and produces lovely peonylike blooms in subtle apricot shades.

The species *A. ficifolia* is a true perennial from Siberia with yellow flowers. It's most often found as a hybrid with *A. rosea*, where it keeps its perennial habit and single form and has many rust-free varieties.

To enjoy perennial hollyhocks in the South, choose *A. rugosa* and its cultivars—selections of *A. rosea* tend to be biennial in hot, humid southern climates.

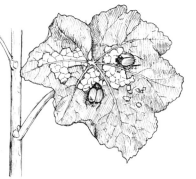

Handpick Japanese beetles into a jar of soapy water to keep them from devouring your hollyhocks' foliage.

Hollyhocks' stately flowerstalks provide a charming vertical accent in the garden. Plant a cluster of hollyhocks where they'll brighten up a wall or fence, or use them to add height to a cottage garden.

PROPAGATING HOLLYHOCKS While you can take cuttings from hollyhocks' new growth in early to midspring to perpetuate a favorite flower color, these plants are usually grown from seed. Seedlings of double-flowered hollyhocks are more likely to repeat the flower colors of their parents; flower color in single-flowered seedlings tends to vary from that of the parent plants.

THE RIGHT SITE FOR HOLLYHOCKS Because they grow to 6 feet tall or more (the oldest single strains can reach a towering 9 feet tall), hollyhocks provide a sought-after vertical accent in the yard and garden. They're delightful in a cottage garden or at the back of a flowerbed or border.

HOW TO GROW HOLLYHOCKS Plant hollyhock seeds in early summer by lightly pressing them into the soil surface. Hollyhock seeds need light to germinate, and some seeds sprout much later than others. Before mid-October, set the plants where you want them to bloom, watering them well so they get established before winter. Space the young plants about 24 inches apart—they'll grow large in their second year.

Some gardeners uproot hollyhocks after their second-year bloom, treating them as biennials—but hollyhocks may perennialize in a good site, *and* they self-sow readily. Once you have a stand in a place they like, your hollyhocks will return reliably year after year. These seedlings may not match their parents' flower colors exactly, but they will contribute charming, old-fashioned blooms to the display at the back of the border.

CO-STARS FOR HOLLYHOCKS Hollyhocks' big leaves and multicolored flowers look especially good combined with baby's-breath (*Gypsophila paniculata*), globe thistle (*Echinops ritro*), and balloon flower (see page 252). Hollyhocks can also stand alone as specimens that anchor a wall or corner of a building.

A Stellar Idea

You can get your hollyhocks to bloom twice a year if you cut them down to the ground when their main bloom is finished in July. Feed them with compost and water them well, and they'll produce a second flush of growth that will bloom heavily in September.

LADY'S-MANTLE

Alchemilla mollis

FEW PLANTS ARE AS USEFUL in the perennial garden as lady's-mantle, yet this is a plant that doesn't always get the attention it deserves. Its subtle beauty and easy-care attitude often hide other virtues that make lady's-mantle an all-star. Once you get to know this handsome, vigorous, ground-covering plant, you'll recognize it as a garden essential and will never be without it.

Lady's-mantle has masses of soft gray-green leaves, which give the plant its rounded outline. The leaves are quite elegant and feel like buttery-soft suede when you touch them. They emerge in April, folded fan-like, then open into pleated kidney shapes. Leaves reach as much as 6 to 8 inches across. This attractive foliage is the origin of the plant's common name—each leaf is said to resemble the cloak, or mantle, worn by ladies in bygone times. In the morning when the dew has fallen or after a sprinkling of rain, tiny leaf hairs hold droplets of water like glittering drops of quicksilver on the surface of the leaves, giving a charming effect.

Another Lovely Lady's-Mantle

A. ellenbeckii is an interesting species that trails along the ground on creeping stems, opening miniature versions of the leaves of A. mollis as it goes. It makes a fine choice for mixing in with small, low-growing perennials in moist, shady spots.

Spotlight on
Lady's-Mantle

USDA Plant Hardiness Zones: 3 to 9

Season of Bloom: June to August

Height × Width: 12 to 24 inches × 12 to 24 inches

Flower Color: Greenish yellow

Light Requirements: Sun to shade

Soil Requirements: Well-dug, humus-rich soil

Place of Origin: Greece to Turkey and east through Caucasus to Iran

Plant Sources: Kurt Bluemel, Bluestone Perennials, Busse Gardens, Carroll Gardens, Daisy Fields, Forestfarm, Weiss Brothers Perennial Nursery, White Flower Farm

Seed Source: Thompson & Morgan

Lady's-mantle blooms in late spring and into the summer but not with bright and bold blossoms. Instead it produces clouds of diminutive, soft chartreuse flowers carried above the foliage to create a nice contrast with the gray-green leaves. Florists prize lady's-mantle flowers for their unique chartreuse color. 'Improved Form' lady's-mantle is said to be a bit neater than the species and holds its flowers more upright, but the species is far from sloppy.

HOW TO GROW LADY'S-MANTLE Lady's-mantle originally made its home by streams and in high meadows and in the fir and beech forests of the upland Caucasus. It still prefers the humusy, moist, foresty soils of its native region. For that reason it may struggle

A mass of lady's-mantle looks handsome at the front of the perennial garden where it helps to weave together bolder colors and textures.

in the hot, dry heat of parts of the South and Southwest, or in the very cold-yet-dry (no snow cover) conditions found in the high deserts and parts of the Great Plains. It's wonderfully at home in most other conditions and locales, from sun to shade, from the Midwest to the Northeast, in the Pacific Northwest, and in northern California if it gets water and shade. Pests and diseases rarely bother this plant, and it's hardy everywhere in the lower 48 states.

PROPAGATING LADY'S-MANTLE You can divide lady's-mantle in the spring if you need plants for another part of your garden. But most gardeners find division unnecessary since lady's-mantle self-sows with ease. Removing the spent flowerheads will prevent unwanted seedlings.

THE RIGHT SITE FOR LADY'S-MANTLE Besides providing groundcover and mixing into perennial beds and borders, lady's-mantle is great for softening the lines of pathways and edgings in the garden. In situations where a space for a plant has been left in stone steps, lady's-mantle is a perfect choice. Lady's-mantle looks best in masses covering the ground in and around other plants with more visual punch. And its gray-green foliage makes it excellent for uniting the bolder flower colors of other perennials.

CO-STARS FOR LADY'S-MANTLE The soft gray-green and pale yellow of lady's-mantle make an attractive combination with purplish foliage and many white, yellow, blue, pink, or purple flowers. Siberian iris, pink azaleas, pink roses, many lilies, tulips in the cream to yellow range, blue bellflowers (*Campanula* spp.), and even hot orange crocosmias look good with it.

Lady's-mantle's soft gray-green leaves and chartreuse flowers make it a delightfully different groundcover for a shady site.

'PURPLE SENSATION' PERSIAN ONION

Allium aflatunense 'Purple Sensation'

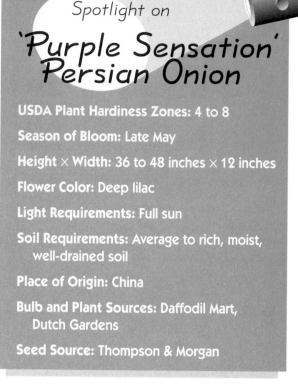

Spotlight on 'Purple Sensation' Persian Onion

USDA Plant Hardiness Zones: 4 to 8

Season of Bloom: Late May

Height × Width: 36 to 48 inches × 12 inches

Flower Color: Deep lilac

Light Requirements: Full sun

Soil Requirements: Average to rich, moist, well-drained soil

Place of Origin: China

Bulb and Plant Sources: Daffodil Mart, Dutch Gardens

Seed Source: Thompson & Morgan

THE ALLIUMS OR ORNAMENTAL ONIONS are a remarkably pretty, pest-free group of plants; of all of them, 'Purple Sensation' Persian onion is probably my favorite. This cultivar's flowerheads are perfectly round, 4-inch spheres made up of many star-shaped flowers of rich violet-lilac. Its flowerheads bloom atop 3- to 4-foot hollow stalks. These flowerstalks arise from a group of six to eight handsome, 1½- to 3-inch-wide, straplike leaves that fade away after flowering is finished.

HOW TO GROW 'PURPLE SENSATION'

Think of 'Purple Sensation' and other ornamental alliums as the onions they are, and you'll know how to start them from seed. Sow seeds in flats kept at room temperature until

Other Honorable Ornamental Onions

Giant onion (<u>A. giganteum</u>) is similar to Persian onion but larger, with 5-inch flower balls on 5-foot stalks in June and July. Lily leek (<u>A. moly</u>) is a small, 15-inch allium with yellow starlike flowers, while large-flowered Naples onion (<u>A. neapolitanum</u> 'Grandiflorum') has showy flattened clusters of fragrant, starlike white flowers with dark eyes.

they sprout, then move them to a cool (35° to 45°F) room for four to six weeks. Then bring them back to room temperature, and harden them off until you're ready to plant them out in the garden. But because alliums self-sow freely, you may not even have to start them.

Plant 'Purple Sensation' in a sunny spot in compost-amended soil. If the soil is heavy, dig in plenty of sand as well. Plant bulbs 5 inches deep and 12 inches apart in drifts of a dozen or more.

Ornamental onions do well in just about any sunny, well-drained site. The greatest hazard to their well-being is dense, heavy, waterlogged soil. In the warmest regions, their flowering may be variable—copious some years and sparse in others.

PROPAGATING 'PURPLE SENSATION'

'Purple Sensation' and other Persian onions produce ample amounts of seeds that are easy to sow and grow. In a favorable site, your plants will literally sow themselves.

A drift of ornamental onions helps bridge the floral gap between earlier spring-flowering bulbs and summer-blooming perennials. They're great cut flowers, too—if you don't mind their oniony scent!

You also can increase your planting by digging up some bulbs in the fall and separating and replanting the bulblets that have formed around their bases.

THE RIGHT SITE FOR 'PURPLE SENSATION'

When these all-stars flower in late May, most spring bulbs are finishing and later perennials are just getting going; so 'Purple Sensation' makes a striking show just when it's needed. Indoors, it will last as a cut flower for two weeks.

Plant 'Purple Sensation' in borders close to a walkway because their globe-shaped flowerheads merit close inspection. But don't brush the flowers—a pinch of their florets yields a distinctive oniony smell. Mix 'Purple Sensation' with later-blooming plants—these ornamental alliums will form a bridge between early bulbs and midseason perennials, so you'll have nonstop garden color.

CO-STARS FOR 'PURPLE SENSATION'

Plant this ornamental allium among daffodils, crocuses, snowflakes (*Leucojum* spp.), and other early bloomers. Mix all these bulbs in a spot where daylilies, phlox, yarrows, purple coneflowers (*Echinacea purpurea*), and other midseason plants are present to take over when the bulb display is finished.

Each of 'Purple Sensation' Persian onion's globe-shaped, 4-inch flowerheads holds a starry galaxy of rich violet-lilac flowers.

ARKANSAS AMSONIA

Amsonia hubrectii

THIS FINE MIDWESTERN NATIVE is not nearly well known enough in American gardens, a situation that I hope to change by including it here as an all-star. With many positive features to recommend it, Arkansas amsonia truly deserves the title perennial all-star.

Arkansas amsonia's flowers are exquisitely shaped, ¾-inch stars with slender petals of a showy, dusty sky blue. The flowers' characteristic blue color and starry shape earn Arkansas amsonia and other amsonia species the widely used common name blue star. The flowers bloom in loose clusters over the plants during May and June. After flowering

Spotlight on
Arkansas Amsonia

USDA Plant Hardiness Zones: 5 to 9

Season of Bloom: May to June

Height × Width: 24 to 36 inches × 36 to 48 inches

Flower Color: Sky blue

Light Requirements: Full sun to partial shade

Soil Requirements: Average, moist soil

Place of Origin: Midwestern United States

Plant Sources: Carroll Gardens, Crownsville Nursery, Milaeger's Gardens, Plant Delights, Shady Oaks Nursery, Sunlight Gardens, André Viette Farm & Nursery, Wayside Gardens, We-Du Nurseries

Other Shining Blue Stars

Another species, willow blue star (A. tabernaemontana), is more widely available from retail and mail-order nurseries, but it's not as showy as Arkansas amsonia. However, it is just as easy-growing and trouble-free and is a very pretty plant in its own right. Willow blue star is native to the eastern United States, from New Jersey to Florida and west to the Mississippi River. It has willowlike leaves and loose clusters of pale blue, star-shaped flowers in late spring.

Southern gardeners may also find downy amsonia (A. angustifolia) in nurseries. It's a native of the southeastern United States, with hairy foliage and pale blue flowers in spring, and is hardy only to Zone 7.

is finished, the fine-textured, threadlike, deep green leaves make a wonderful contrast with larger-leaved plants. In the fall, the whole plant turns a bright, rich golden-yellow.

Arkansas amsonia thrives in most gardens with little care. Like many of our other native plants, it is low-maintenance, easy to grow, and trouble-free. Pests rarely bother Arkansas amsonia, and its built-in drought resistance keeps it looking handsome even where summers tend to turn hot and dry.

HOW TO GROW ARKANSAS AMSONIA

Plant amsonia in full sun to light shade in evenly moist, well-drained soil of average fertility. The plant grows fairly big—reaching about 24 to 36 inches tall in a clump about 36 to 48 inches across—so it's easy to divide to increase your plantings. Shade-grown plants benefit from being pruned to about 12 inches tall after flowering to keep them compact.

In the fall, Arkansas amsonia adds late-season interest to the garden when its feathery, fine-textured foliage turns a bright golden-yellow color that echoes the fall colors in the trees.

PROPAGATING ARKANSAS AMSONIA

Division is the usual method of increasing this perennial. Divide clumps in spring or fall, and replant the divisions about 24 inches apart.

THE RIGHT SITE FOR ARKANSAS AMSONIA

Place Arkansas amsonia at several intervals in the perennial border so that its choice blue flower color is repeated and so that its bright golden autumn theme is echoed down the border in fall. Or naturalize it with other Midwestern natives in a prairie garden. Arkansas amsonia is substantial enough to use as an informal hedge to direct kids and dogs away from more fussy plants. You can plant it out in full sun, where it's right at home, or in partial shade mixed with other perennials or woody border shrubs.

CO-STARS FOR ARKANSAS AMSONIA

Since Arkansas amsonia is a native, it naturalizes well, and its lovely sky blue flowers combine nicely with other spring bloomers, especially with woody natives like mountain laurel (*Kalmia latifolia*), in a semishady spot. It also looks great with red valerian (see page 92), late-flowering tulips, Shasta daisies (*Chrysanthemum × superbum*), and peonies. Its feathery foliage looks especially good with the bold whitish leaves of dusty miller.

Arkansas amsonia and other amsonias are also called blue stars, because of their spring clusters of star-shaped, sky-blue flowers.

'SEPTEMBER CHARM' ANEMONE

Anemone hupehensis
'September Charm'

ALTHOUGH THERE'S SOME DOUBT among botanists as to how to classify 'September Charm' anemone (some sources list it as a cultivar of *A.* × *hybrida*), there's no question among gardeners: Place it at the top of any list of late-flowering perennials.

This all-star blooms for months, not weeks.

Additional Admirable Anemones

Many of the cultivars of Japanese anemone (A. × hybrida) offer care-free late-season beauty like 'September Charm'. 'Honorine Jobert' blooms for three months with pure white flowers; 'Queen Charlotte' bears bright pink blossoms, and the flowers of 'Prince Henry' are a deep rose color.

Other species of anemone include delightful spring bloomers, usually grown from bulblike corms. Low-growing wood anemone (A. nemorosa) naturalizes its white flowers in woodsy settings, and the blue flowers of Grecian windflower (A. blanda) rival crocuses for early color in March. In warmer zones, 'De Caen' hybrid poppy anemones (A. coronaria 'De Caen') produce scads of red, white, pink, and violet single flowers early in the year.

Spotlight on 'September Charm' Anemone

USDA Plant Hardiness Zones: 5 to 9

Season of Bloom: Late August to late October

Height × Width: 30 inches × 36+ inches

Flower Color: Bright rose pink

Light Requirements: Partial shade to full sun

Soil Requirements: Most soils, although it prefers a heavy, moist soil

Place of Origin: Hybrid of species native to area from Himalayas to Japan

Plant Sources: Kurt Bluemel, Busse Gardens, Carroll Gardens, Forestfarm, Garden Place, Milaeger's Gardens, Shady Oaks Nursery, André Viette Farm & Nursery, White Flower Farm

In most regions, 'September Charm' anemone starts blooming in early September and continues until late October, while in warmer regions it blooms in late August. My drift of 'September Charm', planted three years ago as five little starts spaced 18 inches apart, is now a well-established clump about 5 feet across and 3 feet deep. It's as pretty and welcome a part of my garden as the roses in June.

The plant starts being beautiful as soon as it leafs out in spring, for the foliage is rich green, resembling a small grape leaf, and can be oddly asymmetrical the way epimedium foliage is. The leaves are held 12 inches or so off the ground, making a fine groundcover.

In the late summer, flower stems that need no staking arise from among the leaves and branch at their tips, soon producing little ball-shaped buds that open out into inch-wide (or bigger) single blossoms of remarkable beauty. Each petal of 'September Charm' is a winning rose pink, crinkly above with a silvery sheen underneath. The center of each flower is a half-inch circle of fringelike golden stamens surrounding green, buttonlike pistils. The flowers nod and arch gracefully on their stems.

How to Grow 'September Charm'

Plant 'September Charm' in moist, humusy soil in full sun or partial shade. Because it likes plenty of water, it even prospers in heavier clay soils that stymie other plants. In light-textured soils, it can spread quite rapidly; so give it room to grow, or plan on dividing it frequently.

Propagating 'September Charm'

It's easy to increase your planting of 'September Charm' anemone by dividing the fibrous-rooted clumps in early spring or in the fall. You can also take root cuttings from dormant plants in late fall. In nursery boxes filled with sandy loam, bury 3- to 4-inch cuttings horizontally an inch or so below the soil surface. Keep the soil moist until roots and leaves form.

'September Charm' anemone spreads vigorously to form an attractive clump of grapelike foliage topped by pretty pink flowers on 30-inch stems.

The Right Site for 'September Charm'

'September Charm' anemone's late-season beauty, at a time of year when much of the garden looks tired, makes it an indispensable addition to nearly every border, bed, and informal garden space. Although this perennial is a vigorous spreader, it's so pretty and so trouble-free that I refuse to use the pejorative term "invasive" to describe it.

Co-Stars for 'September Charm'

Rhododendron foliage provides a good, dark backdrop for the pale pink flowers of 'September Charm'. Alternate clumps of 'September Charm' with clusters of white-flowered 'Honorine Jobert' Japanese anemone. Azure monkshood (*Aconitum carmichaelii*), pitcher's sage (*Salvia azurea* var. *grandiflora*), blue flax (*Linum perenne*), and purple-flowered asters are also fine companions.

The elegant rose pink blossoms of 'September Charm' anemone are a welcome sight in the fall.

'E. C. BUXTON' MARGUERITE

Anthemis tinctoria 'E. C. Buxton'

Spotlight on

'E. C. Buxton' Marguerite

USDA Plant Hardiness Zones: 4 to 9

Season of Bloom: June to August

Height × Width: 24 inches × 24 to 36 inches

Flower Color: Off-white with lemon yellow centers

Light Requirements: Full sun

Soil Requirements: Average to good garden soil, well-drained

Place of Origin: Central and southern Europe

Plant Sources: Bluestone Perennials, Garden Place, Milaeger's Gardens

NO LESS AN AUTHORITY than England's Graham Stuart Thomas says of 'E. C. Buxton' marguerite, "Invaluable in the garden and for picking, this variety stands out as the most useful of all the [very few] light yellow summer-flowering plants, and a summer border without it is difficult to conceive." A close look at the plant reveals why Thomas is full of praise and why I've picked it as a perennial all-star.

In spring, 'E. C. Buxton' marguerite emerges as a 24-inch clump of 3-inch long, finely divided, rich green leaves with slightly downy undersides. The foliage gives off an aromatic herbal scent when crushed.

As summer arrives, so do masses of single, 1- to 2-inch daisylike flowers, held aloft on stiff stems with their faces turned up to the sun. If you keep the soil moist and deadhead the spent flowers, 'E. C. Buxton' will repay you by

More Marguerites for Masses of Flowers

Depending on your color preferences, there are several other desirable selections of golden marguerite (A. tinctoria) to add bountiful blooms to your garden. 'Beauty of Grallagh' has deep golden, daisylike flowers. 'Moonlight' marguerite's light yellow flowers rival the beauty of 'E. C. Buxton', while the petals of 'Pale Moon' are the palest yellow fading to ivory.

blooming for several weeks—usually into August, but sometimes as late as September.

The color of 'E. C. Buxton' marguerite's flowers is showy and remarkable, the best of the cultivars of this species. The rayed petals are a soft ivory, with cool, lemon yellow centers giving a delicious lemon meringue effect to the sheaves of flowers that cover the plant.

HOW TO GROW 'E. C. BUXTON' Neither insects nor diseases bother 'E. C. Buxton' marguerite, and it gets along fine in average soil, so it doesn't even need yearly feeding. Rich soil, in fact, simply forces extra-long stems that may require staking, so it's best not to feed it. In the coldest regions of its range, a deep mulch may help the plants survive.

PROPAGATING 'E. C. BUXTON' Marguerites are easy to start from seed, but you'll want to divide established plants every two

Give 'E. C. Buxton' a sunny spot in average, well-drained soil and deadhead its spent flowers, and you'll get profuse bloom for several weeks during the summer.

'E. C. Buxton' marguerite's lemony daisies add a bright note to a patch of dark foliage. Their cool yellow color mixes elegantly with silvery leaves.

CO-STARS FOR 'E. C. BUXTON' Blue-flowered perennials such as bellflowers (*Campanula* spp.), balloon flowers (see page 252), pincushion flower (see page 278), and ladybells (*Adenophora confusa*) combine well with the lightly lemony shades of 'E. C. Buxton'. Its masses of pale flowers also look fine next to the pinks, lavenders and reds of garden phlox (*Phlox paniculata*) or bee balms (*Monarda* spp.).

A Stellar Idea

Its tendency to bloom and overbloom can get 'E. C. Buxton' marguerite into trouble. The plant actually can die from sheer exhaustion within a few years unless the gardener takes pity and cuts away the flower stems when the bloom is finishing up. This allows the plant to put its fall energy into the leaves and roots for good bloom the following year. The few minutes of work are a small price to pay for the beauty, usefulness, and long season of bloom of this cherished perennial.

to three years to keep them healthy and looking their best. Long-standing clumps tend to develop dead centers and benefit from division in either spring or fall.

THE RIGHT SITE FOR 'E. C. BUXTON'

'E. C. Buxton' marguerite is at home in any sunny perennial border or cutting garden. And since it's a bona fide dye plant, it's even at home in the herb garden, where it looks wonderful with gray-leaved plants like sage and lavender.

MUSIC SERIES HYBRID COLUMBINES

Aquilegia × *hybrida* Music Series

COLUMBINES AS A GROUP are so attractive that my affection for this or that kind has wandered over the years. For many years I loved the McKana Hybrids the most because of their lovely pastel colors and strong, robust growth. But having seen the small, red-and-yellow-flowered wild columbine (*A. canadensis*), I thought for a while that I loved it best. And

Classic Columbines to Collect

*The Music Series doesn't begin to exhaust the charms of this genus. Golden columbine (*A. chrysantha*) blooms nonstop all summer through the hottest weather. It has lemon yellow, fragrant flowers. Rocky Mountain columbine (*A. caerulea*) bears lovely sky-blue blossoms with a white corolla. Longspur columbine (*A. longissima*) has pastel yellow flowers with very long (4-inch) spurs.*

*Among the hybrids, Songbird Mix is very floriferous and may be purchased in its separate colors. Among the prettiest are 'Blue Jay', a selection of *A. caerulea*, and 'Robin', which has rose pink and white flowers. The McKana Hybrids are still widely planted and are lovely with their extra-large blossoms. 'Kristall' is a pure white cultivar with extra-long spurs. And there are many more to choose from.*

Spotlight on

Music Series Hybrid Columbines

USDA Plant Hardiness Zones: 3 to 9

Season of Bloom: May to June

Height × Width: 18 to 24 inches × 18 to 24 inches

Flower Color: Bicolors in shades of lavender, yellow, red, and white

Light Requirements: Partial shade to full sun

Soil Requirements: Average to rich, well-drained soil

Place of Origin: North America

Plant Sources: Carroll Gardens, Powell's Gardens, Wayside Gardens

Seed Source: Park Seed

now my fickle heart is set on the Music Series.

Like the birds for which they are named, columbine flowers dip and nod with every whisper of wind atop graceful, branched stalks that arise from dainty clumps of bluish green, lobed leaves. Botanists call columbines *aquilegia* after *aquila*, the Latin word for eagle. The common name, columbine, is from *columba*, the Latin word for dove. When the rich colors and charming pastels of hybrid columbines—of which the Music Series is an outstanding example—are combined with the graceful form of the flowers, I find it easy to think of columbines as the most beautiful perennial of them all.

Desirable features of the Music Series hybrids include larger flowers with extra-long spurs that add even more grace to each blossom, a compact and neat appearance, and a

You'll get lots of colorful, long-spurred flowers on compact plants from Music Series hybrid columbines.

PROPAGATING COLUMBINES

All columbines self-sow profusely, but hybrid colors seldom come true to the parent type. Dividing columbines requires great care, as established plants don't like being divided or moved.

harmonious mix of colors that includes intense hues as well as pretty pastels. Their beauty is long lasting, too—they bloom for four to six weeks in late spring and early summer.

HOW TO GROW MUSIC SERIES COLUMBINES

Plant Music Series hybrid columbines, as well as all other columbine species and hybrids, in well-drained soil in full sun to partial shade. Make sure that the crown of the plant's taproot doesn't become exposed in succeeding years. Individual plants aren't terribly long lived, but all columbines hybridize promiscuously and self-sow prodigiously, so you will never be in short supply. Since these offspring may or may not resemble their parents, you may need to buy new seeds or plants every few years to maintain your preferred garden color scheme.

Not much bothers columbines, but leafminers can invade the leaves and worm their wiry way through the leaf tissue. If you see their tracks undulating through the leaves, pick off and destroy the affected foliage. Sometimes mildews affect the leaves, but they rarely do much harm.

THE RIGHT SITE FOR MUSIC SERIES COLUMBINES

Plant Music Series columbines at the front of the border where you can enjoy their delicate beauty at close range. Or plant them outside a window where you can watch the hummingbirds that will flock to them.

CO-STARS FOR MUSIC SERIES COLUMBINES

Catmint (see page 230), common foxglove (*Digitalis purpurea*), peach-leaved bellflower (*Campanula persicifolia*), bearded irises (*Iris* hybrids), Siberian iris (*Iris sibirica*), peonies, lupines (*Lupinus* spp.), and oriental poppies (*Papaver orientale*) all combine well with columbines. But perhaps a clump of beautifully colored hybrid columbines among the broad foliage of hostas makes the prettiest picture.

Bright bicolors and soft pastels make Music Series columbines as appealing to gardeners as they are to hummingbirds. Seedlings from these hybrids probably won't resemble their pretty parents, so buy new plants to keep the colors going.

'DÜSSELDORF PRIDE' SEA-PINK

Armeria maritima 'Düsseldorf Pride'

Spotlight on

'Düsseldorf Pride' Sea-Pink

USDA Plant Hardiness Zones: 5 to 9

Season of Bloom: May to June

Height × Width: 8 inches × 12 to 18 inches

Flower Color: Wine red

Light Requirements: Full sun

Soil Requirements: Sandy, light, well-drained soil

Place of Origin: Coastal northern Europe

Plant Sources: Kurt Bluemel, Bluestone Perennials, Carroll Gardens, Garden Place, Powell's Gardens, Wayside Gardens

ALONG WITH THE UNRELATED PINKS of the genus *Dianthus*, sea-pink is perhaps the most commonly grown low edging plant in the perennial garden—and with good reason. Even if it had no flowers, sea-pink's 4- to 5-inch tufts of evergreen, grassy, grayish green foliage would earn it a place along the edge of many a perennial garden path. But of course it does flower—in mid-May and through June—producing sweet little ball-shaped flowerheads, each perched atop a single slim stalk, and held 3 to 4 inches above the mat of foliage.

'Düsseldorf Pride' sea-pink stands out as the star selection of this worthy species because of its extra-large flowerheads and strong wine red color. It's extra floriferous, too, producing masses of blossoms at the

height of its flowering season. 'Düsseldorf Pride' was developed in Germany in 1957 as one of a series of large-flowered cultivars that followed the introduction of the lilac-pink selection called 'Laucheana'.

HOW TO GROW SEA-PINK Sea-pinks grow wild in the coastal regions of the northern hemisphere from Iceland to northern Russia. This gives you an idea of the conditions they prefer: sandy, dry, well-drained soil, lots of sunshine, and rocky, cliffside spots on which to perch. Don't despair if your garden lacks rocky cliffs to grow your sea-pinks on—focus on those conditions you can control. This is not a plant for soggy soils or hot, humid climates. I've seen sea-pinks growing and blooming quite happily on the coastal cliffs of northern California where, during the summer, they get moisture only from the wet fogs that roll in off the Pacific. In such mild climates, they bloom nearly year-round.

Six Select Sea-Pinks

Other garden-worthy cultivars of A. maritima, which is also called common thrift, include white-flowered 'Alba' and lilac-pink 'Laucheana'. 'Robusta' bears 3-inch pink flowers on 12-inch-tall stems, and 'Splendens' has bright rose-colored flowers. Among other sea-pink species, 'Bevan's Variety' sea-pink (A. juniperifolia 'Bevan's Variety') is a more compact plant with pastel pink flowers. The hybrid 'Bee's Ruby' has large, bold pink flowers on extra-long stems that make it useful for cutting.

Fine-textured, tidy foliage and showy wine red flowers make 'Düsseldorf Pride' a favorite for the front of the border. Its ability to withstand drought makes this all-star a great choice for containers, too.

In your garden, sea-pink will thrive in average, well-drained soil. While it normally grows in full sun, sea-pink likes afternoon shade in hot-summer regions.

PROPAGATING 'DÜSSELDORF PRIDE'

Although sea-pink, or thrift, as it is sometimes called, grows easily from seed, you will not get 'Düsseldorf Pride' from its seeds. To increase your planting of this cultivar, divide its clumps in spring or fall. After a few years, you'll notice the clumps' centers getting brown and dying out. Divide them and replant the divisions about 8 inches apart to give them room to fill in. You also can take stem cuttings of 'Düsseldorf Pride' in the spring.

THE RIGHT SITE FOR 'DÜSSELDORF PRIDE'

Sea-pink probably looks its best growing in a bed on top of a dry wall, where its foliage and flowers are elevated and more easily seen by passersby. Use it between rocks in the rock

Sea-pink blooms happily in the crevices of a stone wall and supplies an upright contrast to the prostrate growth of sedums and rock cresses.

garden and to fill around the stones that edge a path. Place it at the front of the border. Its grasslike foliage is extremely welcome as a contrast to the many busy, broader leaves of other perennials. Its ability to endure droughty conditions makes sea-pink an excellent potted plant.

CO-STARS FOR 'DÜSSELDORF PRIDE'

The wine red flowerheads of 'Düsseldorf Pride' look great next to the white globes of 'Alba' sea-pink. Combine 'Düsseldorf Pride' with the blue flowers of 'Johnson's Blue' cranesbill (*Geranium* 'Johnson's Blue') and catmint (see page 230) and the creeping, rounded foliage of thymes. In the rock garden, its grassy leaves make a nice contrast to the rounded foliage of succulents.

A Stellar Idea

When your sea-pinks finish blooming, take a moment to snip off the spent flowerheads. It only takes a second with a string trimmer or a pair of garden shears, and it lets the plant put more of its energy into developing stronger roots and foliage.

'SILVER BROCADE' BEACH WORMWOOD

Artemisia stelleriana 'Silver Brocade'

THE ARTEMISIAS ARE NOT GROWN for their flowers but for their excellent gray-green to almost silvery white foliage. In the case of 'Silver Brocade', not only is the foliage color beautiful, but it makes neat 24-inch mounds of the most exquisitely shaped leaves. Their silvery green, deeply divided, rounded lobes could be the pattern for a leafy tapestry design. In the garden, 'Silver Brocade' is the perfect perennial replacement for the silvery white, similarly shaped foliage of frost-tender annual dusty miller (*Senecio cinerarea*).

HOW TO GROW 'SILVER BROCADE'
'Silver Brocade' is a superb wormwood for the Northeast and for the Pacific Coast states. In

A Trio of Admirable Artemisias

For those in areas where 'Silver Brocade' won't thrive, the genus Artemisia has many other cultivars to choose from. I recommend hybrid 'Powis Castle' Artemisia for the South's hot, humid climate. It has feathery, filigreed foliage of shiny, silky silver and forms a mound 24 to 36 inches tall and about as wide. In the colder regions of the North, 'Valerie Finnis' white sage (A. ludoviciana) and 'Silver Mound' artemisia (A. schmidtiana 'Silver Mound') will thrive happily.

Spotlight on 'Silver Brocade' Beach Wormwood

USDA Plant Hardiness Zones: 4 to 8

Season of Bloom: August to October

Height × Width: 12 to 18 inches × 18 inches

Flower Color: Soft yellow

Light Requirements: Full sun

Soil Requirements: Poor to average, well-drained soil

Place of Origin: Northeastern North America

Plant Sources: Bluestone Perennials, Busse Gardens, Carroll Gardens, Crownsville Nursery, Garden Place, Powell's Gardens, Weiss Brothers Perennial Nursery, White Flower Farm

the Southeast and in the central Midwest it may suffer in the heat and humidity. A deep leaf mulch is useful in helping 'Silver Brocade' endure winters in the cold upper Midwest and Great Plains states.

Like most artemisias, 'Silver Brocade' does best in a dry, sunny, well-drained site. It's perhaps a bit more sensitive to being overwatered than some of its more aggressive kin but, as its name indicates, 'Silver Brocade' beach wormwood is a good choice for tough seaside conditions.

PROPAGATING 'SILVER BROCADE'
Divide 'Silver Brocade' in spring and replant the divisions about 20 inches apart. Division is especially useful if the plant starts to die out from the center, which artemisias may do in

high heat or humidity. You can also increase your planting by taking stem cuttings in the early summer and rooting them in a mixture of peat and perlite. Artemisia also spreads via self-sown seedlings.

THE RIGHT SITE FOR 'SILVER BROCADE'

Artemisias perform a valuable role in the garden: They're perfect for setting off and separating many colors in the flower border. Their silver, gray, or white foliage brings light to green-heavy gardens and keeps warring color schemes from clashing.

'Silver Brocade' is especially useful because it's one of the brightest light grays and has that lovely foliage shape as well. It's at home in the rock garden and as an edging for perennial borders and beds. It's also a great companion for flowering shrubs. Its bright, light color helps define the edges of its companions so their shapes are easier to see.

CO-STARS FOR 'SILVER BROCADE'

Place 'Silver Brocade' in front of the blue flowers of Frikart's aster (*Aster* × *frikarti*), and let the dark chocolate blooms of chocolate cosmos (*Cosmos atrosanguineus*) display themselves

'Silver Brocade' weaves a rich tapestry of lobed foliage that helps blend other colors in the garden. It's especially pretty with the rich blues of salvias.

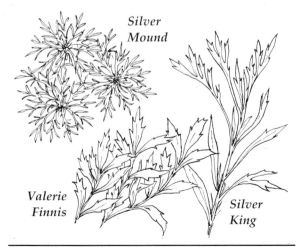

Silvery artemisias come in different shapes and leaf textures. 'Silver Mound' forms a rounded mound of feathery foliage, while 'Valerie Finnis' and 'Silver King' are upright with pointy leaves.

against its silvery whiteness. The value of this plant is that it looks good with all colors and, because of its interesting foliage shape, it even works well with other gray to silver-white plants.

A Stellar Idea

Artemisias generally aren't bothered by insects and diseases. In fact, some species' leaves are crushed and used as insect repellents. If you crush a leaf of any of the cultivars mentioned here, you'll notice artemisia's characteristic, somewhat medicinal, herbal aroma. Try putting some dried, crushed artemisia leaves in your drawers and linen closet to repel silverfish and moths.

GOAT'S BEARD

Aruncus dioicus

GOAT'S BEARD IS A SMASHINGLY HANDSOME plant that makes a 3- to 4-foot-high, shrub-size mound of ferny divided foliage. From June through July, the plant is topped with many long-lasting, 6-foot-tall, feathery plumes of tiny whitish florets on slender brown stems. In and out of flower, goat's beard is an all-star for beauty, usefulness, ease of cultivation, and reliability. Goat's beard grows wild in the eastern United States. It's also native in northern Europe and in Russia, northern China, and Japan.

HOW TO GROW GOAT'S BEARD Goat's beard will grow in any fertile soil, dry or moist, although it's at its best in moist, humus-rich soils such as those found in its

Great (Not Gargantuan) Goat's Beards

If space constraints in your garden dictate that you seek a more diminutive form of goat's beard, take a look at the cultivar 'Kneiffii'. This widely available selection has very finely divided leaves, and thin, nodding shoots. Its ivory flower plumes reach only to 36 inches, making it resemble a rather husky astilbe. Smaller still is dwarf goat's beard (A. aethusifolius), which reaches only 12 inches tall with 3- to 4-inch clusters of white flowers and glossy, dark green leaves.

Spotlight on Goat's Beard

USDA Plant Hardiness Zones: 3 to 9

Season of Bloom: June to early August

Height × Width: 3 feet × 3 feet

Flower Color: White

Light Requirements: Full sun to full shade

Soil Requirements: Any good soil, dry or moist

Place of Origin: Northern hemisphere

Plant Sources: Kurt Bluemel, Bluestone Perennials, Busse Gardens, Carroll Gardens, Crownsville Nursery, Dutch Gardens, Forestfarm, Garden Place, Milaeger's Gardens, Park Seed, Shady Oaks Nursery, Van Bourgondien, André Viette Farm & Nursery, Wayside Gardens, We-Du Nurseries, Weiss Brothers Perennial Nursery, White Flower Farm

Seed Sources: Park Seed, Thompson & Morgan

native woodlands. Still, it's not finicky. Goat's beard thrives in full sun in the northern part of its range or in partial shade, but it likes the protection of partial or full shade in the southern part of its range. Plants growing in heavy shade will tend to flower more sparsely than those that get some sun.

Insects and diseases don't seem to bother goat's beard, and once established, it will put on a show year after year. Plants grow slowly, so they seldom need division.

PROPAGATING GOAT'S BEARD Goat's beard is easy to grow from seed, or you can divide it to increase your planting. Lift and divide

At the front of a semishaded garden, dwarf goat's beard raises its flower clusters against a background of bergenias, phlox, and tall black cohosh.

A spot beneath the trees suits goat's beard just fine. Its shrublike stature and creamy flowers make it a great backdrop for shorter shade-loving perennials.

clumps in the spring, leaving at least one bud per division. Goat's beard roots are thick and woody, so bring a well-sharpened knife or shovel when you tackle this task.

THE RIGHT SITE FOR GOAT'S BEARD Goat's beard is so dramatic that a large specimen will occupy a space by itself quite nicely. For a solid drift in the back of the border, place plants 18 inches apart in groups of three to five.

Because of its shade tolerance, goat's beard makes the perfect plant for a shady spot where its tall plumes will appear bright in the dim light. Its height makes it a standout when it's used as the highest centerpoint of a free-standing island bed.

CO-STARS FOR GOAT'S BEARD Goat's beard makes a fine backdrop for almost any perennial you plant in front of it. For the front and middle of your garden, choose colorful

perennials to stand out against the leaves of goat's beard. Combine it with other woodland plants that enjoy the same growing conditions. Siberian iris (*Iris sibirica*), monkshood (see page 30), common foxglove (*Digitalis purpurea*), peach-leaved bellflower (*Campanula persicifolia*), shrub roses, astilbes, and bleeding hearts (*Dicentra* spp.) are all exquisite partners for this plant.

A Stellar Idea

Goat's beard is dioecious, meaning male and female flowers appear on separate plants. The female flowers are slightly yellowish white in color, while the male flowers are a brighter, more attractive ivory. The female flower clusters tend to nod and droop more than the upright male plumes (which are actually the pollen-bearing structures). The female flowers also produce viable seed. If you'd like showy flowers but don't want to weed out seedlings, grub out females when young plants bloom and reveal their gender.

EUROPEAN WILD GINGER

Asarum europaeum

ALMOST EVERY GARDEN has a shady, moist spot that's just right for delicate forest plants like ferns and dogtooth violets. It's in these places that the all-star groundcover European wild ginger finds a home.

While there are native wild gingers in the United States and Canada, notably Canada

A Generous Selection of Wild Gingers

The various species of wild ginger are all wonderful groundcovers for the shady, woodland garden. Canada wild ginger is a quick spreader with 4- to 6-inch, heart-shaped, deciduous foliage. It is among the hardiest (to Zone 3) of the wild gingers, and is more tolerant of alkaline soils than the other species. British Columbia wild ginger bears 2- to 6-inch semievergreen leaves.

Beyond the shiny green of European wild ginger are three other evergreen species notable for their silver-marked foliage. Virginia wild ginger (A. virginicum) has somewhat larger leaves with silvery markings like those of cyclamen foliage, but without European wild ginger's attractive glossiness. Mottled wild ginger (A. shuttleworthii) has attractive dark green and silver leaves of about 2 to 3 inches across. A. hartwegii is a western species with similarly silvery foliage. These species spread more slowly than European wild ginger, so they're less useful as groundcovers.

Spotlight on European Wild Ginger

USDA Plant Hardiness Zones: 4 to 9

Season of Bloom: May

Height × Width: 6 inches × 18 inches

Flower Color: Reddish brown, inconspicuous

Light Requirements: Full to partial shade

Soil Requirements: Humusy, moist, woodsy soil

Place of Origin: Europe

Plant Sources: Kurt Bluemel, Busse Gardens, Carroll Gardens, Crownsville Nursery, Forestfarm, Shady Oaks Nursery, Wayside Gardens, White Flower Farm

wild ginger (*A. canadense*) in the East and British Columbia wild ginger (*A. caudatum*) in the West, none has the gorgeous dark green, glossy, perfectly kidney-shaped leaves of the European species. The beauty of a large stand of European wild ginger on a woodland floor makes it obvious why this plant is an unquestionable all-star for the shade garden.

In most of its range, European wild ginger's leaves are evergreen, even where snow cover flattens them to the ground over the winter. In warmer zones, the foliage keeps its rich, deep green color for most of the year.

European wild ginger bears small, brownish to reddish brown flowers that are more interesting looking than pretty.

Few woodland groundcovers can compare with the glossy, kidney-shaped evergreen leaves of European wild ginger. In moist, humusy soil and full to partial shade, it makes a perfect companion for the arching, divided leaves of ferns.

European wild ginger is grown for its foliage not its unusual flowers, which bloom in May and hide down below the leaves. If you crush a root of European wild ginger, you'll notice a strong aroma like that of true ginger but slightly more medicinal.

How to Grow European Wild Ginger

When planting European wild ginger as a groundcover, space the plants about 12 inches apart in all directions in well-worked soil that's been amended with humusy compost. Choose a site that's at least partially shaded, such as beneath the canopies of deciduous and evergreen trees and shrubs, and keep the soil moist and cool—conditions wild gingers enjoy in their native ranges. European wild ginger will spread its rhizomes in the bare soil and, within a year, will fill in to make a carefree, pest- and disease-resistant groundcover that's reliably perennial and always beautiful.

In northern areas, such as Zones 4 and 5, you can grow European wild ginger in partial shade or even out in the sun. But the plants will need reliable snow cover or deep mulching in the winter to protect them from cold injury.

Propagating European Wild Ginger

European wild ginger spreads by sending out rhizomes that root as they go. Digging up and replanting some of these is an easy way to produce more plants. You can lift and divide entire clumps in spring before their May flowers appear or in the fall.

The Right Site for European Wild Ginger

European wild ginger goes great with many shade-loving perennials, but probably looks its best with the finely cut leaves of ferns. It's especially lovely with the lighter-colored Japanese painted fern (*Athyrium niponicum* 'Pictum'). Enjoy its glossy, rounded leaves as a superb groundcover under flowering shrubs, or as an excellent counterpoint to the spiky, upright foliage of spring-flowering bulbs.

Co-Stars for European Wild Ginger

European wild ginger enhances spring shade plants such as wild blue phlox (*Phlox divaricata* var. *laphamii*), hostas, sweet woodruff (see page 144), ferns, astilbes, epimediums, bleeding hearts (*Dicentra* spp.), and spring bulbs, especially dwarf daffodils.

BUTTERFLY WEED

Asclepias tuberosa

A MEADOW SURROUNDED MY GARDENS in Pennsylvania, and one year several wild butterfly weeds surprised me when they opened their big orange flowerheads. I hadn't known they were there, and in their natural setting, they put many of my carefully cultivated perennials in the nearby beds to shame.

Of Monarchs and Milkweeds

Butterfly weed gets its name from its attractiveness to monarch butterflies. In fact, butterfly weed has co-evolved with the monarchs, which feed exclusively on plants of the genus Asclepias, and use the poisonous alkaloids in the sap that they eat as a defense against predators. It makes them taste bad, and birds know it—or else they learn it after eating only one monarch butterfly and never try it again.

Common milkweed (A. syriaca) is the plant whose silky parachuted seeds are so much fun for kids to play with. Swamp milkweed (A. incarnata) has pink or white flowers and grows in moist lowlands.

Look carefully at your milkweeds and butterfly weeds and you may discover one of nature's most beautiful treasures—the chrysalis of a monarch butterfly. This milky gray-green capsule hangs under the leaves and has a series of raised points that look as though they are dipped in pure gold.

Spotlight on Butterfly Weed

USDA Plant Hardiness Zones: 3 to 8

Season of Bloom: July through September

Height × Width: 24 to 36 inches × 24 to 36 inches

Flower Color: Orange

Light Requirements: Full sun

Soil Requirements: Poor to average, sandy, well-drained, dry soil

Place of Origin: Eastern North America

Plant Sources: Kurt Bluemel, Busse Gardens, Carroll Gardens, Crownsville Nursery, Forestfarm, J. W. Jung Seed, Milaeger's Gardens, Powell's Gardens, Sunlight Gardens, Van Bourgondien, André Viette Farm & Nursery, Wayside Gardens, We-Du Nurseries, Weiss Brothers Perennial Nursery, White Flower Farm

Seed Sources J. W. Jung Seed, Park Seed, Thompson & Morgan

Of all the plants in the Milkweed Family, butterfly weed is the all-star for beauty. Its long, pointed, medium green leaves are arranged alternately on erect-to-sometimes-sprawling stems. The clusters of bright orange florets are exquisitely intricate, with five nectar cups each with incurved horns. When a pollinator lands on a milkweed flower, its foot slips between the cups, and bags of pollen attach themselves to the insect's legs. At the next flower, its foot slips again and the horns pull off the bags of pollen. Butterfly weed blooms from July through September, and its ripe seedpods are an attractive reddish color.

Heat up your summer garden with a drift of fiery colored butterfly weeds. You'll enjoy the bright flowers and the pretty butterflies that flock to them.

In spite of its name, once you've seen butterfly weed's brilliant orange flowers, you'll never again think of this showy perennial as a weed.

HOW TO GROW BUTTERFLY WEED Plant butterfly weed in a sunny site in average, well-drained soil. Good drainage is especially important during the winter months, and a winter mulch also helps keep the plant thriving. Established plants are relatively drought tolerant.

Unless you count the occasional yellow-, black-, and white-striped caterpillar of the monarch butterfly as a problem, butterfly weed is untroubled by pests and diseases. Butterfly weed emerges late in the spring, so be patient and perhaps mark where it's located so you don't inadvertantly dig it up when cultivating perennials that arise earlier.

PROPAGATING BUTTERFLY WEED Butterfly weed is notoriously difficult to divide once it's in the ground, because it forms a deep taproot and objects to being transplanted. However, you can take root cuttings in late winter from young plants growing in pots. The plant is easy to grow from seed sown outdoors in the fall or started indoors in the winter. To avoid injuring the sensitive taproot, transplant seedlings as soon as the second set of true leaves appears. Seedlings may take two years to reach flowering size.

THE RIGHT SITE FOR BUTTERFLY WEED Butterfly weed's wild origins make it a great choice for mixing with other wildflowers and native grasses in a sunny meadow planting where its hot orange flowers help it stand out amid the foliage. Yet it is equally at home in the middle of a more formal perennial border, and is well behaved enough to hobnob with perennials of much more distinguished breeding.

CO-STARS FOR BUTTERFLY WEED Use butterfly weed's bright orange flowers to brighten up ornamental grasses during the summer months. It also adds interest when set against the attractive foliage of perennials such as Arkansas amsonia (see page 40) or broadleaved bear's-breech (see page 24). In the border, let butterfly weed's fiery orange blossoms add a little heat to a cool-colored planting of blue- or lavender-flowered plants like balloon flower (see page 252), violet sage (*Salvia* × *superba*), or asters.

'MÖNCH' FRIKART'S ASTER

Aster × *frikartii* 'Mönch'

HERE WE HAVE ONE OF THE ALL-STARS of the all-stars! Great British gardener and plant authority Graham Stuart Thomas (not one to gush) says, "'Mönch' is not only the finest perennial aster; it is one of the six best plants, and should be in every garden."

For starters, 'Mönch' aster begins flowering in early July and continues right into October—an enormously long season of bloom for any perennial. And what flowers! Each blossom is a 2½-inch, slender-petaled, daisylike flower with lavender blue rays jutting out briskly from around a central disk of golden yellow. They bloom in profusion in

Spotlight on 'Mönch' Frikart's Aster

USDA Plant Hardiness Zones: 5 to 9

Season of Bloom: July to October

Height × width: 24 to 36 inches × 24 inches

Flower Color: Lavender-blue

Light Requirements: Full sun

Soil Requirements: Average, moist, well-drained soil.

Place of Origin: Hybridized in Switzerland circa 1920 from A. amellus and A. thomsonii

Plant Sources: Kurt Bluemel, Carroll Gardens, Crownsville Nursery, Forestfarm, Garden Place, Milaeger's Gardens, Powell's Gardens, Sunlight Gardens, André Viette Farm & Nursery, Wayside Gardens, Weiss Brothers Perennial Nursery, White Flower Farm

Asterisks for These Asters

Another popular selection of Frikart's aster is 'Wonder of Staffa'. Its flowers are pretty but less emphatically blue than those of 'Mönch' and the plant's shape is more open. Despite its height of only 18 to 24 inches, 'Wonder of Staffa' aster sometimes becomes top-heavy enough to need staking.

'Flora's Delight' (A. 'Flora's Delight') is another hybrid aster—an Alan Bloom introduction—that resembles a dwarf Frikart's aster. Its leaves are gray-green and its flowers are lilac with prominent yellow centers. 'Flora's Delight' aster blooms for weeks and weeks, although not for the impressive four months typical of Frikart's aster cultivars.

loose panicles at the ends of sturdy, well-branched, upright stems that don't need staking. Beneath this exuberant floral display, the rough-textured, lance-shaped leaves add a touch of refinement.

HOW TO GROW 'MÖNCH' You'll find that 'Mönch' is a trouble-free plant, needing only decent soil, full sun, and regular water to do its best. It performs pretty well in partial shade, too, and outright thrives in rich garden soil.

Few pests and diseases bother 'Mönch', but if conditions turn too hot and dusty dry, red spider mites may invade it. In the Deep South, where heat and humidity are intense, mildew can get going on the leaves, although it usually doesn't harm the plant. The long southern growing season may mean it needs annual division. In the North, plant 'Mönch' where winter drainage will be good, and if you love it as I do, you'll pamper it with a deep leaf mulch to protect it from the cold.

PROPAGATING FRIKART'S ASTER Like chrysanthemums, most asters benefit from regular division, and that's true of Frikart's aster. Divide it with some care in the spring by carefully lifting the plant and pulling the rootball apart with your fingers. Retain the young outer growth that shows both roots

'Mönch' Frikart's aster spreads via slow-creeping stems to form clumps of branched, upright stems topped by masses of pretty lavender-blue daisies.

For long-lasting summer-to-fall beauty on durable, easy-care plants, few perennials can compare with 'Mönch' Frikart's aster.

and growing points, and discard any old, woody material in the center. Replant the divisions 18 inches apart.

THE RIGHT SITE FOR 'MÖNCH' The color of 'Mönch' aster is a wonder. It's the coolest shade of lavender-blue, a subtle hue that blends well with just about every color imaginable: Yellows, reds, purples, blues, and amethysts. Place 'Mönch' aster anywhere in the border, and it will continue to please until frosts cut it down. But it also naturalizes beautifully in a prairie garden, meadow garden, or along the edge of a woodland.

CO-STARS FOR 'MÖNCH' What sunny border perennial doesn't go with 'Mönch' aster? Try this versatile and showy plant with just about anything—and anyplace where your garden needs some long-lasting, late-season color. However, if you need a specific reason to use 'Mönch' aster in your garden, it's a good plant to follow and cover over the fading foliage of earlier spring-blooming bulbs and plants.

'ALMA PÖTSCHKE' NEW ENGLAND ASTER

Aster novae-angliae 'Alma Pötschke'

WITH MORE THAN 600 SPECIES OF ASTERS in the world and thousands upon thousands of hybrids and their cultivated varieties, there's a lot to choose from when trying to select one as an all-star. While many plantspeople like this aster or that one, almost everyone mentions the New England aster 'Alma Pötschke'.

The Tall and the Short of the Asters

New England aster grows like a weed—to 6 feet tall and 3 to 4 feet across from small starts in spring. Its relative, New York aster or Michaelmas daisy (A. novi-belgii), is another tall, large-flowered aster that's native to eastern North America. Both of these substantial late-season bloomers have a remarkable array of excellent cultivars to choose from.

Look also for the neat and tidy Italian aster (A. amellus) and East Indies aster (A. tongolensis). These two mat-forming aster species and their cultivars bear large lavender daisies in summer.

'Purple Dome' is a short (to 24 inches tall) selection of New England aster that will bloom unstaked in your fall garden. This exceptionally pretty aster covers itself with purple flowers in September and October.

Spotlight on 'Alma Pötschke' New England Aster

USDA Plant Hardiness Zones: 4 to 9

Season of Bloom: Late August into October

Height × Width: 3 feet × 3 feet

Flower Color: Bright warm pink

Light Requirements: Full sun to light shade

Soil Requirements: Average, slightly acid, moist soil

Place of Origin: United States from Eastern Seaboard to Rocky Mountains

Plant Sources: Kurt Bluemel, Bluestone Perennials, Busse Gardens, Carroll Gardens, Garden Place, Klehm Nursery, Milaeger's Gardens, Powell's Gardens, André Viette Farm & Nursery, We-Du Nurseries, Weiss Brothers Perennial Nursery, White Flower Farm

Its chief charm is its color—a stunning, bright pink that's vivid without shouting, warm without being hot, giving a dazzling display to help warm up cool fall days. Like most asters, the flowers of 'Alma Pötschke' New England aster are daisylike, but these are big—2 inches wide—with many slender, ray-like pink petals and yellow-gold centers.

On dreary, wet days, and at night, the flowers droop and close as though mourning the absence of the warm sunlight. But as soon as the sun shines again, they perk up and continue their display from late August or early September onward for the next six weeks into October. For a long-lasting, late-season floral display, it's tough to top 'Alma Pötschke'.

Among the many excellent asters that are available, 'Alma Pötschke New England aster stands out for its summer-into-fall bounty of bright pink daisies. This warm shade of pink lets 'Alma Pötschke' get along easily with a wide range of flower and foliage colors. Warm it up with yellow companions or use blue flowers and silvery foliage to create a cooler combination.

How to Grow New England Aster

New England asters perform best in average, evenly moist soil. Plants growing in rich soil may become floppy and require staking or support from other plants. While you don't have to pinch back New England aster's tips in late June or early July, such pinching will stimulate the formation of secondary shoots and many more clusters of 40 to 50 flowers each on stiff stems. A benefit of growing 'Alma Potschke' is that this is one aster that does not need pinching to be covered with flowers literally from head to toe.

Insect pests don't bother New England aster, although it may develop mildew in humid conditions where the foliage remains damp for long periods of time. Drought-stressed plants are also susceptible to mildew problems. However, 'Alma Pötschke' is more mildew-resistant than the species.

Propagating 'Alma Pötschke'
Divide 'Alma Pötschke' and other asters regularly to keep the clumps from dying out in the centers. Division every other year or so refreshes the plants and maintains their ability to produce masses of flowers. Divide in the spring, leaving three to five growing points on each division. You also can take stem cuttings in the spring.

The Right Site for 'Alma Pötschke'

Plant 'Alma Pötschke' aster in the middle to back of the border with neutral foliage or cool blue-to-purple colors around it. In rich soil, stiff-stemmed companions help keep floppy asters upright—although 'Alma Pötschke' usually stands without staking.

Co-Stars for 'Alma Pötschke'
Use 'Alma Pötschke' to add pizzazz to foliage plants such as fountain grass (*Pennisetum alopecuroides*), pampas grass (*Cortaderia selloana*), or artemisias. For a great color combo, mix it with the blues of mid- to back-of-the-border companions such as azure monkshood (*Aconitum carmichaelii*), garden mums (*Chrysanthemum × morifolium*, hardy ageratum (*Eupatorium coelestinum*), or azure sage (*Salvia azurea*).

'Alma Pötschke' looks right at home in a cottage garden planting between a carpet of 'Silver Brocade' artemisia and a backdrop of azure sage.

DWARF CHINESE ASTILBE

Astilbe chinensis var. *pumila*

IT WAS ON MY FIRST WALK with renowned perennial plantsman Fred McGourty, in his Connecticut garden one August, that he pointed out a striking, spiky-looking, raspberry pink–flowered groundcover filling a bed beneath larger shrubs. It turned out to be an astilbe—dwarf Chinese astilbe to be exact—that I've loved ever since. Even as I write, my stand is blooming in the side garden, and this plant certainly is one of my personal favorite all-stars.

The dense tufts of finely cut leaves grow only to about 6 inches tall, and make an exceptionally beautiful groundcover on their

Spotlight on Dwarf Chinese Astilbe

USDA Plant Hardiness Zones: 4 to 9

Season of Bloom: Late July to September

Height × Width: 8 to 15 inches × 24 to 36 inches

Flower Color: Raspberry pink

Light Requirements: Partial shade

Soil Requirements: Moist, humusy soil

Places of Origin: China, Japan

Plant Sources: Kurt Bluemel, Bluestone Perennials, Busse Gardens, Carroll Gardens, Crownsville Nursery, Dutch Gardens, Garden Place, Klehm Nursery, Milaeger's Gardens, Shady Oaks Nursery, André Viette Farm & Nursery, White Flower Farm

Seed Sources: J. W. Jung Seed, Thompson & Morgan

Assorted Astounding Astilbes

In addition to the variety pumila, *several cultivars of* A. chinensis *are available from nurseries. These plants bloom late in the season, with flowers that resemble those of dwarf Chinese astilbe and, like their parent, they tend to be more drought tolerant than the more widely grown summer-flowering hybrid astilbes (*A. × arendsii *cultivars). 'Finale' has pale mauve-rose flower spikes that reach 14 to 18 inches tall and is the last of all the astilbes to bloom. 'Serenade' is another late-bloomer with rose red flowers that grow to about 12 inches tall. Rosy purple-flowered 'Veronica Klose' reaches 20 inches tall and blooms late in August or September.*

own. But in August and September, the plants send up stiff, narrow spikes with knobby inflorescences of a vivid raspberry pink. These resemble tiny pink evergreens that reach only 10 to 15 inches tall.

Dwarf Chinese astilbe is a stoloniferous plant, meaning it spreads by horizontal, underground stems. This makes it a well-behaved groundcover that's easy to increase by division in spring or fall. It's the only astilbe with that groundcovering habit.

HOW TO GROW DWARF CHINESE ASTILBE

Astilbes, in general, like rich, humusy soil that's kept consistently moist, and a shady or semishady spot. But dwarf Chinese astilbe has advantages here: It tolerates some

Use dwarf Chinese astilbe's upright raspberry pink plumes to provide a vertical accent amid the many rounded shapes in the perennial garden.

summer dryness and even full sun better than any of the other species. However, like other astilbes, dwarf Chinese astilbe prefers a sheltered, moist, rich spot in the garden. Give it an annual feeding of compost spread over its site in early spring, and it will reward you by remaining attractive and trouble-free all season long. This is a supremely self-reliant plant with no insect or disease problems.

PROPAGATING DWARF CHINESE ASTILBE

Although dwarf Chinese astilbe will spread out on its own, division is the way to go if you want to increase your planting or get plants for another spot in your garden. Divide plants in spring or fall, and replant the divisions in rich, moist, well-amended soil.

THE RIGHT SITE FOR DWARF CHINESE ASTILBE

Dwarf Chinese astilbe's late-season, vivid rose pink blooms are a great benefit when you want an early fall garden that's just as colorful and flower-filled as it was in the spring and early summer months.

Planted about 12 inches apart, it will fill in and become one of the finest of all perennial groundcovers. Intersperse swaths of this astilbe with darker-leaved evergreens or hostas for a nice undulating effect. Dwarf Chinese astilbe is also good for edging beds and borders where strong color is needed.

CO-STARS FOR DWARF CHINESE ASTILBE

Not every plant looks good next to dwarf Chinese astilbe's raspberry pink plumes, so plan accordingly. It's great for livening up the foliage of plants that have bloomed earlier in the season, such as lungworts and Bethlehem sage (*Pulmonaria* spp.), Christmas rose (*Helleborus niger*), and Japanese iris (*Iris ensata*). Dwarf Chinese astilbe also makes a

Dwarf Chinese astilbe makes a great groundcover for sites where you want something more interesting than the usual vinca or euonymus ground huggers.

nice combination with the blue, late summer flowers of azure monkshood (*Aconitum carmichaelii*), and it's a fine companion for plants that are grown mostly for their foliage, such as hostas, Allegheny spurge (see page 234), blue lilyturf (*Liriope muscari*), bigleaf ligularia (*Ligularia dentata*) and small ferns.

'SPRITE' STAR ASTILBE

Astilbe simplicifolia 'Sprite'

ONE OF THE PRETTIEST GARDEN SCENES I've ever seen was in upstate New York where a massed planting of 'Sprite' astilbe bordered a clump of dark evergreens and low green grasses. From overhead, a beam of sunlight fell through the trees and touched the astilbes' plumes, giving the woodsy floor of the garden a soft, luminous, pink glow—a fitting home

Some Other Stellar Astilbes

Star astilbe (A. simplicifolia) is the parent of many fine cultivars in addition to 'Sprite'. 'Bronze Elegance' has clear pink blooms touched with salmon; 'Dunkellachs' is German for "dark salmon," an apt description for the rich salmon-pink flowers of this cultivar, which also has coppery leaves. Some think the prettiest sibling of 'Sprite' is 'Aphrodite', which grows to 20 inches tall and has dark foliage, reddish new growth, and clusters of red flowers in July and August.

The old standbys among astilbes are the A. × arendsii hybrids—larger than star astilbe and somewhat coarser and shaggier in leaf and flower—which bloom early in the summer. Selections are available with flower colors in shades of pink, red, salmon, and white. 'Rheinland' has clear pink flowers in early summer on 24-inch-tall plants. 'Superba' fall astilbe (A. taquetii 'Superba') is big—48 to 60 inches—with rosy purple flower clusters in August and September.

Spotlight on 'Sprite' Star Astilbe

USDA Plant Hardiness Zones: 4 to 9

Season of Bloom: Early July to August

Height × Width: 12 inches × 18 to 24 inches

Flower Color: Shell pink

Light Requirements: Full sun in cool North to partial shade or shade in hot, sunny regions

Soil Requirements: Plant in moist, woodsy, humusy soil of average fertility

Place of Origin: Probable hybrid of A. chinensis var. pumila and A. simplicifolia found and introduced by Alan Bloom in England

Plant Sources: Ambergate Gardens, Kurt Bluemel, Bluestone Perennials, Busse Gardens, Forestfarm, J. W. Jung Seed, Klehm Nursery, Milaeger's Gardens, Powell's Gardens, Shady Oaks Nursery, André Viette Farm & Nursery, Wayside Gardens

for a fairy queen if I ever saw one.

Of all the astilbes, 'Sprite' is the choicest. Jacqueline Heriteau, author of *The National Arboretum Book of Outstanding Garden Plants*, writes, "If you had to choose a single astilbe, this would be the one." And in recognition of its many fine qualities, the Perennial Plant Association named 'Sprite' astilbe its 1994 Plant of the Year.

Its 8- to 10-inch sprays of simple leaves (rather than compound, as with most astilbes) are glossy, bronzy green, as well as deeply divided and ferny. The combination of color

'Sprite' star astilbe's soft shell pink flowers look pretty next to the white flower plumes of 'Bridal Veil' astilbe, as well as with other pale pink flowers.

and form works beautifully under the branching, slightly pendulous clusters of tiny, lovely, shell pink flowers that appear in early July and continue into August.

HOW TO GROW 'SPRITE' Like other astilbes, 'Sprite' prefers evenly moist, rich soil and shady conditions. 'Sprite' is a vigorous grower that's rarely bothered by pests or diseases.

PROPAGATING 'SPRITE' As with all astilbes, division is the best way to get more plants and to maintain the vigor of existing plants. You can divide 'Sprite' in spring or fall, making sure that each division has several growing points. Replant the divisions in well-prepared soil.

In a moist, shady garden, plant airy 'Sprite' amid bold bergenias and hostas. Fragrant August lilies will add their flowers to the astilbe's display.

THE RIGHT SITE FOR 'SPRITE' 'Sprite' is at its best used as a bedding perennial in masses and drifts in the front of the border and in low pools of groundcover in the shady garden. One cluster of its irresistable pink flowers just doesn't do it. Start with five to seven plants, placed about 10 inches apart in every direction and, when this drift fills in, divide the clumps and extend the planting until you have a drift about 3 to 4 feet deep and 7 to 8 feet wide. The effect is exquisitely beautiful.

CO-STARS FOR 'SPRITE' STAR ASTILBE Combine 'Sprite' astilbe with hybrid columbines (*Aquilegia* hybrids), columbine meadow rue (*Thalictrum aquilegifolium*), fragrant hosta (*Hosta plantaginea*), and heartleaf bergenia (*Bergenia cordifolia*) in the shade. In partial shade to full sun, plant it with peonies, delphiniums, and Japanese iris (*Iris ensata*).

JAPANESE PAINTED FERN

Athyrium niponicum 'Pictum'

FERNS ARE AN ESSENTIAL PART of the shady perennial garden. They help separate flower colors that might otherwise clash and they provide a fine-textured contrast for the more substantial foliage of perennials such as hostas. So many excellent ferns are available that I turned to the experts for help in choosing an all-star.

The American Fern Society, a group associated with the U.S. National Herbarium of the Smithsonian Institution in Washington, D.C., took my query to Dr. John T. Mickel at the New York Botanical Garden. Dr. Mickel is the nation's foremost fern specialist.

"He suggests," the Fern Society said, "that the one fern to choose is *Athyrium niponicum* 'Pictum', the Japanese painted fern. It's hardy in the North (from New York to Illinois to Washington) and also in the South. Although it's heat tolerant, it must be planted in some shade in the South to avoid bleaching of the fronds."

I also asked Sue Olsen, editor of the Hardy Fern Foundation newsletter out of Bellevue,

Another Fetching Fern

A similar, but evergreen, fern is the Japanese shield fern (Dryopteris erythrosora). It's a shade lover, hardy to Zone 4 with protection, and its 24-inch-long fronds are rose-brown when young, turning to glossy green, with scarlet spore capsules underneath.

Spotlight on Japanese Painted Fern

USDA Plant Hardiness Zones: 4 to 9

Season of Bloom: Not applicable

Height × Width: 18 inches × 18 to 24 inches

Flower Color: Not applicable

Light Requirements: Best in dappled shade but tolerates full sun in northern part of its range; must have shade in southern zones

Soil Requirements: Prefers moist, humusy, well-drained loam but tolerates a variety of soil types

Places of Origin: Manchuria, Korea, Taiwan, and Japan

Plant Sources: Ambergate Gardens, Kurt Bluemel, Busse Gardens, Carroll Gardens, Forestfarm, Milaeger's Gardens, Plant Delights Nursery, Shady Oaks Nursery, Sunlight Gardens, André Viette Farm & Nursery, Wayside Gardens, We-Du Nurseries, White Flower Farm

Washington, to recommend the perfect fern. "My recommendation," she wrote, "would be *Athyrium niponicum* 'Pictum'. The plant does well in many areas of the United States, is colorful, popular, and adaptable."

Besides being an all-star performer in just about every part of the country, the Japanese painted fern is in my opinion the most beautiful of all the ferns. Its slowly creeping rootstock sends up many fronds with long, wine red stems. This color goes beautifully with the color of the leaflets, each of which is purplish at the base, then lavender, then metallic

Japanese painted fern's feathery, silver-green foliage makes it a handsome groundcover for a moist, shady part of the garden.

gray-green at the tips. The pinnae—the divisions of the leaflets—are metallic gray-green with a gray bar, and red veining is apparent upon close inspection. The overall effect is one of subtle gradations of silver, from gray to reddish pinkish lavender. It's exquisite.

HOW TO GROW JAPANESE PAINTED FERN

Japanese painted ferns are reliably hardy, perennial, and deciduous. Leave the frost-killed fronds on the plant overwinter to protect the crowns and tender shoots in spring. When the new crosiers—the tightly curled fiddleheads of new growth—reach 6 inches tall, remove last year's fronds. In Zone 4, mulch the crowns with leaves for the winter.

PROPAGATING JAPANESE PAINTED FERN

Dividing Japanese painted fern's clumping roots in spring is the preferred way to increase a planting. Replant the divisions 12

You may also find Japanese painted fern identified as <u>Athyrium</u> <u>goeringianum</u> 'Pictum'. It's beautiful no matter what you call it.

inches apart to create a massed effect, or 24 inches apart to allow each fern its own space.

THE RIGHT SITE FOR JAPANESE PAINTED FERN

The subtle silver shading of the leaves is particularly strong when the fronds open in the spring and makes Japanese painted fern a stand-out in the quiet shade of evergreen trees and shrubs. The whole plant has a graceful arching habit that displays the painted fronds in just the right position for garden visitors to see as they look down.

I find that Japanese painted ferns look best when grown against a dark mulch and evergreen background. I have mine planted under some redwoods and mulched with decayed bark for a superb shade-garden effect.

CO-STARS FOR JAPANESE PAINTED FERN

Japanese painted fern is the perfect fern to shine in front of dark green rhododendron leaves. It's equally wonderful mixed with columbines (*Aquilegia* spp.), and looks excellent in a trio with white-variegated curled leaf hosta (*Hosta crispula*) and red-leaved Japanese maple (*Acer palmatum* 'Atropurpureum'). Or mix its feathery fronds with the rounded, shiny foliage of European wild ginger (see page 54) and the matte finished leaves of solid-color hostas like 'Krossa Regal' hosta (see page 176).

'NOVALIS BLUE' AUBRIETA

Aubrieta deltoidea 'Novalis Blue'

IN 'NOVALIS BLUE' AUBRIETA you'll find a true perennial garden workhorse—an all-star that fills (literally) some unique niches in the garden. Here's the ideal perennial for planting between stepping stones or flagstones, in soil-filled crevices in rock walls, in low-growing beds of plants to tumble over a terrace wall, between steps in the garden, in strawberry jars and planters, and around rocks in the partial-shade rock garden.

Each plant expands into a compact 12- to 18-inch-wide mat of gray-green, small-leaved, toothed foliage. When 'Novalis Blue' aubrieta is in bloom, a profusion of 1-inch-wide, single (more rarely double), four-petaled, deep violet-blue flowers covers the leaves.

An Array of Aubrietas

While 'Novalis Blue' aubrieta's flowers are a deep violet-blue, other cultivars of aubrieta bloom in shades of pink and purple. One of the best, probably equal to 'Novalis Blue' in vigor and beauty, is 'Schloss Eckberg'—a selection that bears darker violet-blue flowers. 'Tauricola' aubrieta's flowers are lavender-lilac. 'Bressingham Pink' is the most commonly available pink-flowered cultivar, while the flowers of 'Red Carpet' are a strong begonia-red color. 'Purple Cascade' is a compact, purple-flowered hybrid.

Spotlight on 'Novalis Blue' Aubrieta

USDA Plant Hardiness Zones: 4 to 9

Season of Bloom: Late April to June

Height × Width: 4 to 6 inches × 18 inches

Flower Color: Rich violet-blue

Light Requirements: Partial shade to full sun

Soil Requirements: Sandy, well-drained, average soil

Place of Origin: Mediterannean region to Middle East

Seed Source: Park Seed

HOW TO GROW AUBRIETA Like many rock garden plants, aubrieta enjoys a sunny site in well-drained, neutral to alkaline soil. Where nights are cool and humidity's low, aubrieta will thrive with little care and almost no soil around its slender, rhizomatous roots. Just before it's about to bloom, and during bloom, aubrieta is most in need of adequate moisture, so give it a good soaking if the rain doesn't.

Immediately after bloom and before the plants set seed, cut back aubrieta by about half, but not too close to the roots. This encourages new growth that keeps the plant looking good for the rest of the year, and it keeps seed production to a minimum. Feed your plants with a bit of bonemeal after this shearing.

In the Deep South, aubrieta may be short lived, as it succumbs to heat and dryness. This plant really loves the cool, moist Pacific Northwest, New England, and the Rocky Mountain states. I've grown it very successfully in the mid-Atlantic region. Although aubrieta is a member of the Mustard Family it's not usually plagued by pests, such as flea beetles, that bother other mustards.

Plant 'Novalis Blue' aubrieta where it will spill prettily over the top of a wall. It's also at home between the pavers at the edge of a path, and it looks fine with miniature daffodils or with other small spring bulbs growing up through it.

THE RIGHT SITE FOR 'NOVALIS BLUE' In spite of its diminutive size, where it likes its conditions, aubrieta puts on a stunning garden display. The flower colors of some aubrieta cultivars are rather strident and visually aggressive, but 'Novalis Blue' is a well-behaved selection, easily grown from seed, that coexists nicely with almost any other of the stars of the spring color show. This plant is ideal for tucking into the crevices of a stone wall or letting spill over the top of a retaining wall.

CO-STARS FOR 'NOVALIS BLUE' Create a carpet of flowers by planting 'Novalis Blue' aubrieta with rock cresses (*Arabis* spp.), basket-of-gold (see page 70), perennial candytuft (*Iberis sempervirens*), moss pink (*Phlox subulata*), or any of the other low-growing, mat-forming spring bloomers. The deep violet-blue flowers of 'Novalis Blue' also look beautiful blooming amid stands of pastel tulips. If you choose other aubrieta cultivars, consider combinations with care to avoid creating clashes with their bold magenta-colored flowers.

PROPAGATING AUBRIETA Clumps of aubrieta are difficult, but not impossible, to divide in spring. It's easy to take cuttings from the new growth that appears when the plants are sheared back after they bloom. You can grow aubrieta from seed, sown in late spring for bloom the following year.

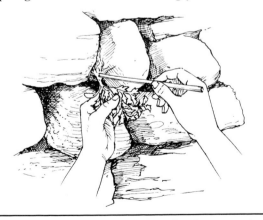

Aubrietas need just a little bit of soil to grow in the crevices of a rock wall. In spring, the aubrietas' bright flowers will cascade down over the stones.

A Stellar Idea

If your aubrietas seem prone to rotting, try amending their location to match the rocky sites they prefer. Where the stems emerge from the ground, replace the soil with a few handfuls of gritty soil or sand to improve drainage at the base of the plant. Rot problems usually are limited to plants growing in wet, heavy soil.

BASKET-OF-GOLD

Aurinia saxatilis

EVERY GARDENER NEEDS AT LEAST ONE PLANT that's supremely easy to grow. One that stays low and well-behaved, that isn't fussy or prone to diseases or insect attacks; one that gives a simple yet decorative look to the garden. Basket-of-gold is just such a plant. And although its identity may be in question—it's often sold as *Alyssum saxatile* or as *Alyssum* 'Basket of Gold'—this is one all-star that knows its place in the garden and fills it well. Basket-of-gold is a member of the mustard family and its loose, open, floppy habit, its gray-green leaves, and its cheery clusters of yellow flowers make it one of the best-loved of the spring-blooming perennials.

Several Solid-Gold Selections

Whether it's labeled <u>A. saxatilis</u> or <u>Alyssum saxatile</u>, basket-of-gold is almost always sold as the species. But there are <u>Aurinia</u> cultivars worth noting. 'Citrinum' (a.k.a. 'Lutea') has pale yellow flowers. As its name suggests, 'Compacta' is a dwarf form, reaching only 4 to 8 inches tall with small leaves and golden flowers. 'Plena' (a.k.a. 'Flore Pleno') is a double-flowered yellow cultivar. 'Sunny Border Apricot' has light yellow flowers with an apricot cast to them. It's best grown in warmer regions, for if its topgrowth freezes off, its flowers revert to the yellow color of the species.

Spotlight on Basket-of-Gold

USDA Plant Hardiness Zones: 4 to 9

Season of Bloom: April to May

Height × Width: 6 to 12 inches × 12 to 18 inches

Flower Color: Bright yellow

Light Requirements: Full sun

Soil Requirements: Poor to average, well-drained soil

Place of Origin: Eastern Mediterranean

Plant Sources: Bluestone Perennials, Busse Gardens, Forestfarm, Garden Place, Weiss Brothers Perennial Nursery

Seed Sources: Thompson & Morgan

HOW TO GROW BASKET-OF-GOLD Basket-of-gold spreads quickly to fill its spot in the garden. A 4-inch potful, planted in late summer, will grow to the size of a basketball by the following June. But don't plant basket-of-gold in really rich soil, or it gets too leggy. This all-star does best in gravelly, well-drained soil of just average fertility.

Once established, basket-of-gold needs very little care. If it outgrows its spot, just cut it back hard—a procedure that will renew it and improve its flowering the following spring.

PROPAGATING BASKET-OF-GOLD The easiest, and therefore preferred, way to start new plants of basket-of-gold is from seed, sown in either spring or fall. Established plants self-sow quite readily. Division in the fall is an option, although not always a successful one, or you can take stem cuttings in the summer to propagate a favorite cultivar.

Top a dry stone wall with basket-of-gold and enjoy its masses of cheery yellow flowers as they tumble over the sides.

THE RIGHT SITE FOR BASKET-OF-GOLD

Basket-of-gold is the perfect plant for edging walkways or for planting atop a dry stone wall. On top of a wall, it tends to grow out and spill over in the most charming way. Then, in April and May, amid the spring colors of tulips and pansies and mat-forming phlox, basket-of-gold opens its frothy, bright yellow puffs of many small flowers. It also stars in the rock garden, growing from stone crevices, and looks perfect coupled with red tulips beside the garden path.

CO-STARS FOR BASKET-OF-GOLD

Basket-of-gold truly shines when planted with other richly colored spring flowers. Try it with tulips, pansies, Johnny-jump-ups, 'Novalis Blue' aubrieta (see page 68), perennial candytuft (*Iberis sempervirens*), wall rock cress (*Arabis caucasica*), or moss pink (*Phlox subulata*).

A Stellar Idea

After basket-of-gold finishes blooming, many gardeners take a moment to grab the flowers up in a bunch and cut them off. Since this plant is a known self-sower, this is a good idea if you don't want it to spread beyond its given spot. If you do want it to fill in, rub the dry flowerheads between your hands over the surrounding area after you trim them off.

Basket-of-gold's bright yellow blossoms and gray-green foliage make an eye-catching spring combination with the rich rosy purple flowers of 'Red Wings' moss pink.

BLUE WILD INDIGO

Baptisia australis

BLUE WILD INDIGO IS ONE OF THE LONGEST-LIVED perennials. This plant makes a big, substantial, and very reliable clump of fresh, blue-green, three-lobed foliage on gray stems that reach 3 to 4 feet tall and sometimes higher. Its foliage looks good from spring until frost cuts it down late in the year. Blue wild indigo has an upright, vase-shaped habit.

In late spring or early summer, blue wild indigo opens loose, 12-inch-tall spikes of soft, blue-tinted indigo flowers. Each floret on the spike is shaped like a sweet pea blossom. The flower spikes rise above the foliage and persist for weeks, keeping the plant in bloom almost until July.

HOW TO GROW BLUE WILD INDIGO

Blue wild indigo will thrive and bloom even in light shade, but plants growing in less than full sun

Wild Indigos in White

White-flowered wild indigo makes a pretty companion for blue wild indigo and shares its cousin's pretty blue-green foliage and tap-rooted drought tolerance. You may find as many as three or four different species identified as white wild indigo—B. alba (or lactea), B. leucantha, and B. pendula—but these are believed to be regional variations of the same native species. All three bear 12-inch-long spikes of white, pealike flowers in late spring and early summer.

Spotlight on
Blue Wild Indigo

USDA Plant Hardiness Zones: 3 to 9

Season of Bloom: Late May to July

Height × Width: 3 to 4 feet × 3 to 4 feet

Flower Color: Indigo blue

Light Requirements: Full sun

Soil Requirements: Prefers moist, deep, humusy, acid soil

Place of Origin: Eastern United States

Plant Sources: Ambergate Gardens, Kurt Bluemel, Bluestone Perennials, Busse Gardens, Carroll Gardens, Crownsville Nursery, Forestfarm, Garden Place, Milaeger's Gardens, Plant Delights Nursery, Powell's Gardens, Shady Oaks Nursery, Sunlight Gardens, André Viette Farm & Nursery, We-Du Nurseries, Weiss Brothers Perennial Nursery, White Flower Farm

Seed Source: Thompson & Morgan

tend to stretch toward the sunlight and then need staking. For best results, find a sunny spot in the garden for this worthy all-star.

PROPAGATING BLUE WILD INDIGO

Blue wild indigo starts easily from seed, although seedlings take two or three years to bloom and three years to grow to full size. Deep roots make division difficult, but not impossible. In fall, use a sharp knife to cut the tough clumps into divisions with at least one bud apiece. Expect some losses if you try to divide.

THE RIGHT SITE FOR BLUE WILD INDIGO

You can use blue wild indigo in the middle of the border amid shrubs and taller perennials,

You'll enjoy blue wild indigo's upright vase shape all the more if you plant shorter, mounding perennials at its base to hide its bare "ankles."

but I find it charming moved out to the front of the border, where it interrupts the smaller edging plants that grow there. An occasional larger plant makes the border edge more interesting than if one low-growing plant after the other is lined up by the path. Blue wild indigo is one of the best perennials for this job because it's large but not coarse, and it stays pretty throughout the growing season.

CO-STARS FOR BLUE WILD INDIGO

Carolina lupine (*Thermopsis caroliniana*) looks like a slightly larger, yellow-flowered version of blue wild indigo. This cousin makes a handsome combination with blue wild indigo and enjoys the same growing conditions. Use shorter perennials such as columbines (*Aquilegia* spp.) and cranesbills (*Geranium* spp.) to dress up the base of a clump of blue wild indigo. Miniature red roses look beautiful with blue wild indigo's flowers. Or let its blue-green foliage provide a backdrop for late season asters or chrysanthemums.

A Stellar Idea

Blue wild indigo's persistent flowers are excellent and long lasting when cut for a vase. You can leave the inflated, black seedpods that follow the flowers on the plant to add interest to your winter garden, or harvest them for use in dried arrangements. However, cutting off the spent flowers may promote a second bloom, so you'll have to choose between ornamental seedpods or a second display of indigo blue flowers.

Blue wild indigo's pretty flowers are shaped like pea blossoms for good reason—it's a member of the legume family. Its nitrogen-fixing ability keeps it green and healthy even in average soil.

'PERFECTA' BERGENIA

Bergenia cordifolia 'Perfecta'

BERGENIA MAKES AN EXCELLENT, usually evergreen groundcover. Its big, rounded, cabbage-like leaves are leathery and rich green, and they perform the same groundcovering function as large-leaved hostas, but bergenia will thrive in those dry soils and sunny spots where hostas can't grow.

Other Beguiling Bergenias

Besides 'Perfecta' there are other bergenia cultivars and hybrids worthy of a spot in your garden: 'Rotblum' has red flowers. The flowers of 'Bressingham White' start out pinkish and bleach to white, while 'Silver Light' has flowers that start out white and change to pink. 'Alba' bears white flowers.

Other species of bergenia are useful, too. One of the best is leather bergenia (B. crassifolia), with leaves slightly smaller than heartleaf bergenia's, and pretty sprays of light lavender-pink flowers. Cold weather turns the leaves to a rich mahogany color.

B. purpurascens has rich pink flowers, red stems, and wonderful winter foliage color. Cold and frost turn the summer green leaves to beet red on top and mahogany red underneath. These look stunning in the winter garden growing beneath the yellow stems of golden-twig dogwood (Cornus sericea 'Flaviramea') and the red stems of Tatarian dogwood (C. alba).

Spotlight on 'Perfecta' Bergenia

USDA Plant Hardiness Zones: 3 to 9

Season of Bloom: April to May, earlier in warmest zones

Height × Width: 12 inches × 18 to 24 inches

Flower Color: Lilac-red

Light Requirements: Full sun to full shade

Soil Requirements: Prefers moderately heavy soil, moist or dry

Place of Origin: Siberia

Plant Sources: Busse Gardens, Klehm Nursery, Shady Oaks Nursery

Our all-star selection, 'Perfecta' bergenia, has all those advantages going for it, along with leaves that have a purplish brown cast to them and purplish stems. It blooms in spring, bearing dense clusters of very showy, scentless but sturdy, lilac-red flowers. Here in my California garden, bergenia starts blooming in January and my first garden bouquet of the new year usually includes some of its welcome flower clusters. One of the plant's nicknames is "pig-squeak" from the sound your thumb and forefinger make when you pull them rapidly up the surface of the shiny leaves.

HOW TO GROW BERGENIA While tolerant of full sun, bergenias thrive in partial to full shade as long as they're not crowded by the low-hanging limbs of shrubs and evergreens. A moist, humusy, woodsy soil in partial shade suits them best, but they are not picky at all.

The foliage of bergenia is every bit as important as the flowers and appears in dense

'Perfecta' bergenia shines in early spring when it produces showy clusters of lilac-red flowers. Its evergreen leaves remain handsome year-round and turn bronzy green when cold weather arrives.

rosettes that spread slowly from underground rhizomes. By planting cuttings or divisions about 12 inches apart in all directions, you can fill in an entire area with maintenance-free bergenia in just one growing season. Many plants are said to be maintenance-free; bergenia really is.

PROPAGATING BERGENIA Divisions, made in spring or fall, are an easy way to increase your bergenia planting. You also can take 3-inch cuttings of the rhizomatous stems in late fall or winter, before the really heavy weather sets in. Make sure each cutting has an eye (bud) in the axil above a leaf scar, and plant it upright so that the topmost part is just below the soil surface. Keep the cuttings moist and most of them will leaf out in the spring.

THE RIGHT SITE FOR 'PERFECTA' Bergenia provides a great contrast for small-leaved groundcovers such as spotted dead nettle (*Lamium maculatum*). Its bold leaves stand out against a backdrop of fine-textured shrubs and keep their landscape value through the winter. Plant 'Perfecta' bergenia where you can enjoy the bronzy color that cold weather brings to its evergreen leaves and where you'll catch sight of its showy flowers in early spring.

CO-STARS FOR 'PERFECTA' Bergenia makes a nice groundcover. In your perennial garden, combine it with the blue forget-me-not–like flowers of navelwort (*Omphalodes verna*) and Siberian bugloss (see page 78), ferns, Japanese anemones (*Anemone × hybrida*), lamiums, blue oat grass (see page 162) and other specimen grasses, and blue, pink, purple, or red spring-flowering bulbs.

In the moist soil next to a small water garden, 'Perfecta' bergenia raises its rosy flowers next to the forget-me-not blue blossoms of Siberian bugloss.

'SNOWBANK' BOLTONIA

Boltonia asteroides 'Snowbank'

To look at 'Snowbank' boltonia, you'd swear you were seeing an aster, but it's just a very asterlike plant with plenty of charm of its own. And while other boltonia cultivars tend to grow longer stems and need staking, 'Snowbank' has the great virtue of being able to hold itself erect without help from the gardener. It also produces slightly larger flowers of a clearer white than other cultivars. And while the species is weedy looking, 'Snowbank' is always trim. These many attributes tip the scales in favor of 'Snowbank' as our all-star in this useful group of plants.

'Snowbank' is an airy plant of 3 to 4 feet tall with small, gray-green leaves along stiff stalks. In late August or early September, it opens thousands of 1-inch, white daisies with diminutive raised yellow centers. The flowers stay on the plant throughout September and into October, making 'Snowbank' a sterling addition to the late border.

A Bonus Boltonia

Another boltonia cultivar, 'Pink Beauty' bears pretty, light pink flowers and looks very asterlike, resembling a floriferous 'Harrington's Pink' New England aster. It's often offered for sale in the catalogs, and it makes a nice companion for 'Snowbank', but its stems do grow to 4 to 5 feet and usually need staking, so be aware.

Spotlight on 'Snowbank' Boltonia

USDA Plant Hardiness Zones: 3 to 9

Season of Bloom: Late August to October

Height × Width: 3 to 4 feet × 3 to 4 feet

Flower Color: White

Light Requirements: Full sun

Soil Requirements: Average soil, moist or dry

Place of Origin: Eastern United States

Plant Sources: Ambergate Gardens, Kurt Bluemel, Bluestone Perennials, Busse Gardens, Carroll Gardens, Crownsville Nursery, Forestfarm, Garden Place, Milaeger's Gardens, Powell's Gardens, Sunlight Gardens, André Viette Farm & Nursery, We-Du Nurseries, Weiss Brothers Perennial Nursery, White Flower Farm

HOW TO GROW 'SNOWBANK' In warm regions, such as Zone 9 in the South and in California, keep boltonia adequately watered and fed or it will be stunted and bloom weakly on very short, thin stems. In consistently moist soil, it tolerates heat and humidity well.

In the temperate zones, rich soil and too much moisture will promote extra-long stems that may need staking. Give 'Snowbank' boltonia average soil and water only when there are droughty conditions and it will be trouble-free. Where alternate winter freezes and thaws are the rule and there isn't dependable deep snow cover, boltonia appreciates a winter mulch to keep its crowns from heaving and drying out.

PROPAGATING BOLTONIA 'Snowbank' boltonia is asterlike in more than appearance, and needs moderately frequent division (like asters) to look its best. In spring, divide large clumps into several smaller clumps and plant them 12 to 24 inches apart. Or you can separate each clump into little slips and replant each of these for the greatest increase.

THE RIGHT SITE FOR 'SNOWBANK' Plant 'Snowbank' among dark-leaved shrubs, and in the back of the border, where its airy-but-neat habit and bright white flowers are most effective. It always looks better massed into a drift than as a single plant, and it naturalizes well in out-of-the-way parts of the border.

CO-STARS FOR 'SNOWBANK' The soft lavender-blue flowers and upright form of Russian sage (see page 242) look especially lovely next to the white mounds of 'Snowbank' boltonia. And it looks equally good combined with the pink spikes of obedient plant (*Physostegia virginiana*) or with ornamental grasses. Asters are a natural companion, too, and 'Snowbank' makes a lovely family portrait next to its sibling, 'Pink Beauty' boltonia.

In late summer and into the fall, 'Snowbank' boltonia earns its name as it covers itself with thousands of 1-inch white daisies.

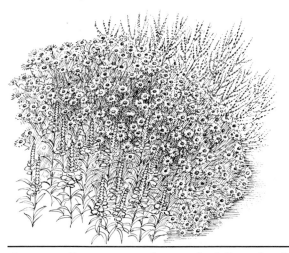

Accent a flower-covered mound of 'Snowbank' with the airy blue flowers of Russian sage and the stiffly upright, pink flower spikes of obedient plant.

SIBERIAN BUGLOSS

Brunnera macrophylla

WHAT IS IT ABOUT FORGET-ME-NOT BLUE that we find so charming? Maybe it's the color's sky blue promise of many fine summer days to come. Whatever it is, gardeners love it, and that's just one reason why I've chosen Siberian bugloss as a perennial all-star.

Foremost among its advantages are its abilities as a groundcover. Siberian bugloss naturalizes where it likes the spot and fills in to make a rather coarse-textured swath, 12 inches or so tall, of large, somewhat hairy, heart-shaped leaves. These leaves are lettuce green in the spring and turn darker as the summer progresses.

In late April, dark stems elongate and hang out loose clusters of sweetly diminutive, five-petalled sky blue flowers with pale eyes. These flowers bloom for a full six weeks, carrying the blue of forget-me-nots (*Myosotis* spp.) forward from their May display into the early summer.

A Siberian Bugloss with Something Extra

If fabulous forget-me-not–blue flowers and substantial heart-shaped leaves are not enough for you, try one of Siberian bugloss' variegated cultivars in your garden. 'Langtrees' has leaves that are very attractively spotted with silver, like a lungwort. The leaves of 'Hadspen Cream' have a wavy, creamy white margin, while 'Variegata' has wider, whiter margins on its leaves.

Spotlight on Siberian Bugloss

USDA Plant Hardiness Zones: 3 to 9

Season of Bloom: Late April into June

Height × Width: 18 inches × 18 inches

Flower Color: Blue

Light Requirements: Partial shade to full sun

Soil Requirements: Rich, moist soil

Place of Origin: Caucasus Mountains

Plant Sources: Ambergate Gardens, Kurt Bluemel, Bluestone Perennials, Busse Gardens, Carroll Gardens, Forestfarm, Garden Place, Milaeger's Gardens, Shady Oaks Nursery, Van Bourgondien, André Viette Farm & Nursery

HOW TO GROW SIBERIAN BUGLOSS

While Siberian bugloss tolerates full sun where the ground stays moist, it prefers rich soil in a cool, moist, semishady spot that doesn't get a lot of burning heat. In winter, the leaves turn black from the frost, but wait until spring to clean up the planting. The dead foliage protects the crowns—which will leaf out again in the spring—from the cold. If you are spreading mulch in the early winter, give some to your patch of Siberian bugloss, as alternate freezing and thawing can heave its roots out of the soil. Other than that, Siberian bugloss is a low-maintenance plant with few pest or disease problems.

PROPAGATING SIBERIAN BUGLOSS Siberian bugloss is a very easy perennial to propagate. In the springtime you can sow seed that has been given a few weeks in the freezer. Once established, the resulting plants will self-sow in a

In moist soil and partial shade, Siberian bugloss spreads happily to form a pretty groundcover of petite blue flowers and lettuce green leaves.

Siberian bugloss's clusters of forget me not like flowers provide a delicate contrast to the showy yellow daisies of leopard's bane.

favorable site. Although Siberian bugloss spreads to create groundcovering swaths, it rarely becomes overcrowded. Divide it in spring or early fall if you need more plants.

THE RIGHT SITE FOR SIBERIAN BUGLOSS

Besides its uses in the perennial bed or border, or with plantings of woody ornamentals, Siberian bugloss makes a fine stand in the natural conditions of the woods, much like Virginia bluebells do in the East. It likes the filtered light and moist humusy soil of the open woodlands. That's why it's so useful under ornamental trees and shrubs. In my Pennsylvania garden, I planted it under tall spicebush, where its blue flowers glowed prettily in the shade, and it happily reseeded itself naturally. Once it was established, I never had to do anything more with it.

CO-STARS FOR SIBERIAN BUGLOSS Siberian

bugloss makes an easy-care, informal groundcover that sets off the blossoms of spring flowering trees and shrubs like magnolias, forsythia, and evergreen shrubs. It's an agreeable plant and its flowers and foliage go well with many other perennials, including spring-flowering bulbs, leopard's bane (*Doronicum cordatum*), globeflowers (*Trollius* spp.), navelwort (*Omphalodes verna*), epimediums, bleeding hearts (*Dicentra* spp.), Jacob's ladders (*Polemonium* spp.), Virginia bluebells (see page 220), Boris avens (see page 152), barren strawberry (*Waldsteinia fragarioides*), and heartleaf bergenia (*Bergenia cordifolia*).

CALAMINT

Calamintha grandiflora

CALAMINT IS A RELATIVELY NEW PERENNIAL for American gardeners, although it's been a staple in European gardens for years. The calamints are closely related to the culinary herb savory (*Satureja* spp.), and some sources list calamint as *Satureja grandiflora*. Like savory, calamint's leaves have a fresh, minty or tutti-frutti aroma when they're crushed.

Calamint makes a dense, bushy plant of upright stems thickly covered by mintlike foliage. Plants typically grow to about 18 inches tall but may remain more compact where soil

Spotlight on
Calamint

USDA Plant Hardiness Zones: 5 to 9

Season of Bloom: July and August

Height × Width: 18 inches × 18 inches

Flower Color: Rose pink

Light Requirements: Full sun

Soil Requirements: Average, well-drained soil

Place of Origin: Southeastern Europe

Plant Sources: Carroll Gardens, Garden Place, Milaeger's Gardens, Powell's Gardens, Shady Oaks Nursery, White Flower Farm

Seed Source: Thompson & Morgan

Calling All Calamints

When you visit your local nursery, keep your eyes peeled for the variegated form of calamint. Its white-marked leaves make this hardworking plant even more useful in your garden.

Another calamint species, C. nepeta ssp. nepeta, produces white to pale lilac flowers, somewhat smaller than those of C. grandiflora, from August right up to frost and beyond. Its subtle coloring helps it mix well with other very late bloomers and adds a cool color to underpin the brightly colored flowers of taller perennials or late roses. It grows to about 18 inches on wiry stems. By planting the two calamints together, you can enjoy their fine form, clean fragrance, and lovely flowers in the garden for a full four months from midsummer into fall.

conditions are less favorable. Calamint's medium green, serrated leaves remain attractive throughout the growing season adding substance to the garden when the plant isn't flowering.

When calamint blooms, it will pleasantly remind you of its presence. Its inch-long flowers vary in color from rose to lilac-pink to reddish purple and resemble sage blossoms. Hummingbirds often visit calamint flowers, attracted by their tubular shape and rosy color. The flowers bloom in profusion amid the foliage on the upper half of the stems and will add their color to your garden over a good two months in midsummer.

HOW TO GROW CALAMINT Calamint is a supremely trouble-free plant with a sturdy, reliable constitution that lets it shine in your garden year after year. This is a perennial that performs in the South's hot and muggy

You can plant this durable perennial then forget about it! Care-free calamint puts on a pleasing midsummer floral display even in hot, dry conditions. Its tidy, toothed foliage remains attractive all season and has the same fresh, tutti-frutti fragrance as its culinary cousin, savory.

summers and north to the Canadian border. If the summer is hot and dry, it doesn't seem to affect calamint. You really can plant it and then do nothing more except enjoy it.

PROPAGATING CALAMINT Like many of its mint family relatives, calamint spreads via creeping roots, although not so vigorously as to be considered invasive. Its spreading habit makes calamint easy to divide in the spring if you want more plants for elsewhere in your garden. You also can propagate it by taking stem cuttings in early summer, and it grows easily from seed.

THE RIGHT SITE FOR CALAMINT Calamint's low, spreading habit

Watch for hummingbirds visiting calamint's tubular rose pink flowers. The inch-long flowers bloom amid the leaves on the upper half of the plant.

and soft colors make it an ideal plant for the middle to front of your perennial garden where it can help to unify stronger colors and textures. It will also thrive in hot, dry, rock garden conditions and is a natural for brightening up your herb garden.

CO-STARS FOR CALAMINT In the herb garden, mix calamint into a planting with lavender and sages. It's a fine-textured foil for taller, bolder perennials such as bear's-breech (see page 24) or hollyhocks (see page 34), and it looks good planted with showy stonecrop (*Sedum spectabile*), white-flowered pinks (*Dianthus* spp.), and catmint (*Nepeta* × *faassenii*). And it adds welcome midsummer color to rock gardens where it contrasts well with the fleshy leaves of sedums and sempervivums.

A Stellar Idea

If you plant calamint next to a path or at the front of your perennial border you can enjoy both its beauty and its pleasant scent. Its clean, minty fragrance will refresh you when you brush against it while walking in your garden.

'BLUE CLIPS' CARPATHIAN HAREBELL

Campanula carpatica 'Blue Clips'

WHETHER YOU FIND IT OFFERED AS 'BLUE CLIPS' or as 'Blue Chips', this Carpathian harebell cultivar is a true all-star that deserves a place in your perennial garden.

'Blue Clips' forms tidy tufts of 1½-inch, heart-shaped leaves with wavy edges. Their low, mounded shape and neat foliage make the plants interesting and pretty in their own

Spotlight on 'Blue Clips' Carpathian Harebell

USDA Plant Hardiness Zones: 3 to 9

Season of Bloom: June to September

Height × Width: 8 inches × 12 to 18 inches

Flower Color: Violet-blue

Light Requirements: Full sun to partial shade

Soil Requirements: Average, well-drained soil

Place of Origin: Carpathian Mountains of Eastern Europe

Plant Sources: Ambergate Gardens, Busse Gardens, Carroll Gardens, Garden Place, Greer Gardens, J. W. Jung Seed, Milaeger's Gardens, Shady Oaks Nursery, Van Bourgondien, André Viette Farm & Nursery, Weiss Brothers Perennial Nursery

Other Carpathian Harebells You Can Count On

Because of their attractive and compact form and their remarkable flower power, Carpathian harebells stand out as a favorite of gardeners amid the many popular and well-favored species of bellflowers (C. spp.). As a result of their popularity, there are many fine selections of Carpathian harebell from which to choose. 'White Clips' (a.k.a. 'White Chips') is a white-flowered sibling of 'Blue Clips'; 'Wedgewood White' is another fine, compact cultivar with white flowers. 'Karl Foerster' has deep, rich blue flowers, while 'China Doll' bears azure blue flowers. The novelty cultivar 'Jingle Bells' is slightly taller (to 12 inches tall) and produces both white and blue flowers on the same plant.

right, especially at the edge of the border. But then in June, 'Blue Clips' begins opening the first of its 1½- to 2½-inch-wide, bright violet-blue, cup-shaped flowers. In most of the country, early July brings the main flush of these open-faced, starry flowers, which bloom singly on short stalks and nearly cover the entire surface of the plant.

After the big show in July, flowering tapers off but doesn't quit completely. 'Blue Clips' typically continues to produce flowers through the late summer before coming back with a final flush of blue blossoms in September.

HOW TO GROW 'BLUE CLIPS' 'Blue Clips' does just fine in a semishaded spot, but can tolerate full sun as long as it receives adequate

If you remove its spent blossoms, 'Blue Clips' will cover itself with flowers in early summer and will keep blooming into early September.

moisture. Plants need well-drained soil in order to thrive and reseed themselves— 'Blue Clips' is rare among bellflower cultivars for its ability to come true to seed. And although 'Blue Clips' does self-sow in favorable sites, it's not the invasive sort and remains dainty, tidy, and well behaved in the garden.

Working a little ground limestone into the soil every few years will remind 'Blue Clips' of the soil in its limestone-based Carpathian Mountain homeland and will keep it happy. If your soil is already on the limy side, this won't be necessary, but if it's acidic, the treatment will help. Pests and diseases don't seem to bother 'Blue Clips'.

PROPAGATING 'BLUE CLIPS' 'Blue Clips' benefits from division in the spring every three to four years. Divide clumps from the newer growth around the outside of the plant and discard the older center. Replant the divisions about 12 inches apart. 'Blue Clips' is also easy to grow from seed.

'Blue Clips' produces oodles of starry, open-faced violet-blue cups on tidy, compact plants.

THE RIGHT SITE FOR 'BLUE CLIPS' 'Blue Clips' really stars as the perfect small companion for other blue- and white-flowered plants, and it makes a gorgeous underpinning for taller perennials with those color schemes. Its low, mounding habit works well at the front of a perennial border where its crisp, neat foliage looks good throughout the growing season and gives definition to the garden's edge. It's one of the best perennials for edging borders and also looks right at home in the rock garden. Its blue flowers are handsome next to light lemony yellows and most shades of pink, too.

CO-STARS FOR 'BLUE CLIPS' 'Blue Clips' sparkles beneath the tall, grassy foliage and light yellow flowers of lemon daylily (*Hemerocallis lilioasphodelus*). It also looks good planted amid the similarly shaped blossoms of blue- or white-flowered balloon flowers (see page 252). For contrasting textures, try it with the spiky flower balls of globe thistle (*Echinops ritro*), or mix its fine foliage with the bold leaves of hostas in a semishady location.

'TELHAM BEAUTY' PEACH-LEAVED BELLFLOWER

Campanula persicifolia
'Telham Beauty'

Spotlight on 'Telham Beauty' Peach-Leaved Bellflower

USDA Plant Hardiness Zones: 3 to 9

Season of Bloom: Late June to August

Height × Width: 24 to 36 inches × 18 inches

Flower Color: Powdery blue-violet

Light Requirements: Full sun to partial shade

Soil Requirements: Humusy, moist, well-drained soil

Place of Origin: Belgium and Holland to Russia and south to Turkey

Plant Sources: Busse Gardens, Daisy Fields, Forestfarm, Greer Gardens, Roslyn Nursery, White Flower Farm

I'VE HEARD PEACH-LEAVED BELLFLOWER referred to as the prettiest perennial in the garden. If that's true, then the cultivar called 'Telham Beauty' must be the fairest of the fair.

The plant makes a dense basal rosette of 8-inch, evergreen leaves. In June, it sends up thin, unbranched stems bearing sparsely spaced, 4-inch leaves. These upper leaves look a bit like the pointed, narrow leaves of a peach tree and give the plant the "peach-leaved" part of its common name and its species name—*persicifolia*—which means the same thing.

Along its stems, 'Telham Beauty' bears stunning, 3-inch, individual bell-shaped flowers. They appear to toss this way and that—some drooping, some horizontal—as though ringing some clear notes that only other bellflowers can hear. These floral bells (the Latin for bell is *campana*, hence the genus name *Campanula*) are the most pleasing shade of powdery blue-violet. 'Telham Beauty' continues blooming throughout July and will persist longer if you deadhead its spent blossoms.

Other Particularly Peachy Peach-Leaved Bellflowers

For a nice color combination in your garden, mix the wonderful blue of 'Telham Beauty' with the pure white flowers of 'Alba' peach-leaved bellflower (also sold as 'Grandiflora Alba'). Or you can simply grow 'Chettle Charm', a recent introduction with creamy white flowers that are blue at the petal margins. There are also double-flowered cultivars such as 'Blue Gardenia' and 'White Pearl', but I think the single bells are prettier.

HOW TO GROW 'TELHAM BEAUTY' Plant it in full sun or partial shade, but make sure you give it good drainage. If you have heavy clay soil, incorporate lots of compost and sand before planting peach-leaved bellflowers.

Once 'Telham Beauty' is established in your garden, you'll get the best results by digging it up and dividing it every year in early October (or in spring, if need be), and replanting the divisions in freshly worked soil.

You don't absolutely have to do this, but peach-leaved bellflower tends to die out after a few years if you don't, especially in Zones 7 to 9 where summers are hot and muggy.

PROPAGATING PEACH-LEAVED BELLFLOWER
Divide the basal clumps of peach-leaved bellflower in fall (or spring) at least once every three years. Replant the divisions 18 inches apart in small drifts or groups, where they will creep out to form mats.

THE RIGHT SITE FOR 'TELHAM BEAUTY'
Place it toward the front of the garden where visitors can fully enjoy its soft blue flowers. Planted amid shorter plants, its bell towers seem to ring silently above them.

It's worth planting a few divisions in a cutting garden to make sure you always have the option to bring some of these delightful flowers inside without diminishing their display in your yard.

Mix the showy blue-violet bells of 'Telham Beauty' with white or soft pink flowers. Its tall stems look good next to lower, mound-shaped perennials.

CO-STARS FOR 'TELHAM BEAUTY'
Combine it with the rounded, mounding shape and chartreuse flowers of lady's-mantle (*Alchemilla mollis*) or with the ferny foliage and rosy blossoms of painted daisy (*Chrysanthemum coccineum*). Its elegant, bell-shaped blossoms make a nice contrast for the full-blown, petal-filled flowers of shrub roses, garden peonies (*Paeonia lactiflora*), and oriental poppies (*Papaver orientale*). And it's right at home among the spikier profiles of lupines (*Lupinus* hybrids), late-blooming irises, and short-statured, lemony yellow daylilies like 'Little Cherub'.

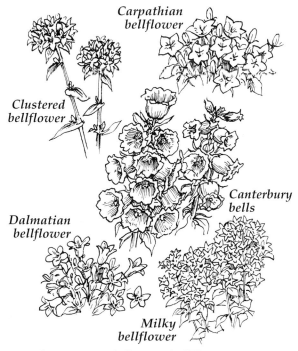

Carpathian bellflower

Clustered bellflower

Dalmatian bellflower

Canterbury bells

Milky bellflower

With so many different bellflowers to choose from, you're bound to find at least one that strikes the right note for your garden.

A Stellar Idea
While plain old peach-leaved bellflower can't quite match the powdery blue-violet shade of 'Telham Beauty', its own lavender-blue bells are quite attractive. Certainly it's a worthy addition to your cutting garden where, with any luck, it will self-sow and spread and keep you well supplied with stems of bell-shaped flowers to bring into your house.

SERBIAN BELLFLOWER

Campanula poscharskyana

SERBIAN BELLFLOWER IS A VIGOROUS, sprawling beauty that grows just about anywhere, from the short seasons of Zone 3 to the warm winters of Zone 8. It even thrives in Zone 9 in coastal California, although it's not happy in the hot, humid Zone 9 of the Gulf Coast.

From a small plant, this all-star spreads quickly to form a central mound of toothed, 1½-inch, heart-shaped, wavy-edged leaves. This mound of foliage may grow to 24 inches or more in diameter and is evergreen in the warmer zones of its range.

In May, Serbian bellflower begins sending out trailing stems that reach about 18 inches long and carry smaller leaves and pretty, inch-wide, starry flowers. Soon the plant is covered in stars—lavender-blue flowers with five narrow, pointed petals and shades of lighter lavender or violet in their throats.

Find a Spot for This Dalmatian

A low-growing relative of note is Dalmatian bellflower (C. portenschlagiana). Similar to Serbian bellflower but smaller, Dalmatian bellflower grows to just 6 inches tall and bears deep violet, trumpet-shaped bells. It blooms in June and July and again later in the season if cut back after its first flush of flowers. Like Serbian bellflower, it's excellent for growing between pavers, in rock gardens, and where it can tumble over walls.

Spotlight on Serbian Bellflower

USDA Plant Hardiness Zones: 3 to 8

Season of Bloom: May to June, again in September to frost

Height × Width: 12 inches × 36 inches

Flower Color: Lavender-blue

Light Requirements: Partial shade to full sun

Soil Requirements: Well-drained gritty soil

Place of Origin: Dalmatian coast

Plant Sources: Bluestone Perennials, Crownsville Nursery, Forestfarm, Milaeger's Gardens, Powell's Gardens, Shady Oaks Nursery, André Viette Farm & Nursery, Weiss Brothers Perennial Nursery, White Flower Farm

HOW TO GROW SERBIAN BELLFLOWER For best success with this charming, well-behaved spreader, plant it in well-drained, sandy or gritty soil. In most of its range, Serbian bellflower prefers filtered light or bright shade. The cooler the region, the more sun it can take. On the cool, foggy coast of California, it prefers full sun, while just a few miles inland, it must have partial shade. In the Midwest and mid-Atlantic states, Serbian bellflower also likes a spot where it gets some afternoon shade. In the South and warmest zones, shade is a must.

If you satisfy these requirements, you'll find Serbian bellflower to be relatively easy-growing. This pretty all-star withstands heat and drought, it harbors no pests or diseases to speak of, and it's long lived and reliably perennial almost everywhere.

After its main flush of flowers finishes in

Atop a low rock wall, Serbian bellflower's lavender-blue stars weave prettily amid the starry yellow flowers of Kamschatka sedum and the white-and-green leaves of variegated rock cress. Serbian bellflower prefers cool climates and appreciates a bit of shade where summer temperatures soar.

late June or July, I gather Serbian bellflower's long stems into my hands. It takes just a fairly gentle tug to break them loose from the central cushion of leaves, leaving the plant looking tidy and neat through the hottest weather of summer. Then, in late August or September, a second flush of flowers appears on shorter stems, and these keep producing flowers—although with less abandon than in spring—right until frost.

PROPAGATING SERBIAN BELLFLOWER
Divide Serbian bellflower in early spring to increase your planting or to reduce the size of a clump. While not invasive, it can expand fairly rapidly by spreading, underground roots. Divide the basal cushion of leaves into four parts. Replant the divisions 12 inches apart and they will fill in to cover a broader area. Serbian bellflower also self-sows and grows easily from seed.

THE RIGHT SITE FOR SERBIAN BELLFLOWER
Its habit of extending long shoots studded with starry flowers makes this low-growing bellflower a great choice for containers. Serbian bellflower looks fine planted where its shoots can tumble over and hang down attractively. And it's a perfect groundcover in shady rock gardens.

Serbian bellflower makes a handsome groundcover in rocky, well-drained soil.

CO-STARS FOR SERBIAN BELLFLOWER
The rich yellow flowers of goldenstar (see page 100) complement the lavender-blue stars of this bellflower, and the two plants make a great groundcovering combo in partial shade. Serbian bellflower also makes an easy-care perennial pal for tender plants like tuberous begonias and potted fuchsias. In the perennial garden, mix its fine texture and low habit with the bold foliage of hostas or the grassy, upright leaves of daylilies. Its starry flowers shine beneath the bright cups of late-flowering red tulips.

CUPID'S DART

Catananche caerulea

CUPID'S DART IS AN UNASSUMING PLANT with sparse slender leaves on 18- to 24-inch wiry stems. Without its flowers, you'd hardly notice it in the garden.

But when it does begin flowering in mid-June, Cupid's dart tops its stems with 2-inch-wide, daisylike flowers. The blunt-tipped petals are lavender-blue and are surrounded by papery, whitish bracts.

One of the features that makes Cupid's dart an all-star is its long season of bloom—starting in mid-June and continuing strong until late August or September. Its impressive bloom time means that Cupid's dart can serve as a companion for early bright perennials like painted daisies (*Chrysanthemum coccineum*) and still be available to calm down the fiery colors of late-flowering plants like cardinal flower (see page 210).

Other Sharp Cupid's Darts

For long-lasting, long-blooming blue flowers, it's hard to top Cupid's dart, although there are a few noteworthy cultivars of this all-star. 'Purple Gem' is a small version that grows to 6 inches and has ¾-inch purple flowers from April until June. 'Bicolor' has blue petals with white tips. The large flowers of 'Blue Giant' have deep blue centers that fade to lighter blue at the edges.

Spotlight on Cupid's Dart

USDA Plant Hardiness Zones: 4 to 9

Season of Bloom: Mid-June to September

Height × Width: 18 to 24 inches × 18 inches

Flower Color: Lavender-blue

Light Requirements: Full sun

Soil Requirements: Loose, well-drained soil of average to poor fertility

Places of Origin: Southern France and Spain

Plant Sources: Carroll Gardens, Daisy Fields, Forestfarm, Garden Place, Greer Gardens, Weiss Brothers Perennial Nursery

Seed Source: Thompson & Morgan

HOW TO GROW CUPID'S DART Its origins in the high, open meadows of the warm (and dry) Mediterranean region provide a good clue as to the conditions Cupid's dart needs to thrive. In this country, too, it makes a fine, trouble-free plant for warm, sunny, dry locations. Pests and diseases aren't a problem.

If this all-star has any drawbacks, it's that the plants produce the most flowers in their second year of growth from seed and aren't particularly long-lived after that. If you try Cupid's dart and find it as useful and pretty as many gardeners do, starting a packet of seeds every couple of years to keep the flower show coming won't seem like much trouble at all. Plants grown from March-sown seed typically will bloom the first year, then put on the big show the following year, and continue to bloom well in their third year.

PROPAGATING CUPID'S DART Seed sown in spring is by far the easiest way to propagate this perennial, although this can lead to color variations in the cultivars. To propagate a Cupid's dart cultivar, divide the fleshy roots or take root cuttings in late fall and overwinter them in a propagation box in cold cellar conditions. The following spring, plant your starts 12 inches apart to make a drift of Cupid's dart in the garden.

THE RIGHT SITE FOR CUPID'S DART

Cupid's darts are champion mixers in the border because of their inconspicuous foliage and stems. The flowers seem to float here and there in groups, resembling lavender cornflowers. They are especially good in masses with brighter colors, as they cool down the feverish, hot summer color displays of lilies and shrub roses.

CO-STARS FOR CUPID'S DART Silvery foliage plants such as artemisias (see page 50) and lavender cotton (see page 274) make good backdrops for Cupid's dart. Its gentle, midsummer blue flower color looks great next to many of the summer pinks, including 'Croftway Pink' bee balm (*Monarda didyma* 'Croftway Pink') and, in warmer regions, 'Ruby Fields' twinspur (*Diascia* 'Ruby Fields').

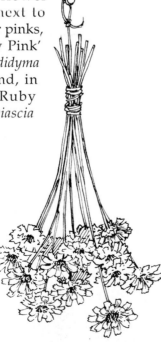

Cupid's dart keeps its lavender-blue color when dried. To dry Cupid's dart flowers, cut them just after their rays (petals) expand and hang them in small bunches in a warm, dry, dark place.

A gardener could easily fall in love with long-blooming Cupid's dart. This easy-care perennial produces 2-inch lavender-blue daisies all summer long and thrives in a dry, sunny site. Individual plants may be short lived, but Cupid's dart is easy to grow from seed and will bloom in its first year of growth.

A Stellar Idea

One of Cupid's dart's chief uses is for cut flowers, so plant enough for cutting as well as for mixing with other perennials in your sunny border. The papery bracts help hold the petals in place when they're dried, and the lavender-blue color holds, too, making them an excellent addition to dried arrangements.

PERENNIAL CORNFLOWER

Centaurea montana

PERENNIAL CORNFLOWER PRODUCES what is un-doubtedly one of the most interesting-looking flowers in the garden. Also known as mountain bluet, it is truly a trouble-free and easy plant to grow.

The 2- to 3-inch flowers are vaguely thistle-like in appearance. Each has a central disk of dark reddish violet florets surrounded by longer, slender, violet-blue ray florets that branch and flare at their tips into four or five points. The result is a bristling whirligig of color. These unique flowers begin to appear in May and continue to July, making a very welcome late spring and early summer display.

Perennial cornflower's stems normally are unbranched, and the flowers are borne singly here and there over the tips of the stems. Stiff bracts hold the elaborate flowers from underneath, and these dry well, making the stems and blossoms excellent cut

More Collectible Cornflowers

Cultivars of perennial cornflower are available, although they offer little improvement over its beautiful flowers and form. 'Caerulea' (sometimes offered as 'Blue') has bluer, less violet flowers. The flowers of 'Rosea' are pink, while those of 'Alba' are white. 'Violetta' bears flowers that are a darker violet shade than those of the species, and 'Grandiflora' has larger, light blue flowers.

Spotlight on Perennial Cornflower

USDA Plant Hardiness Zones: 4 to 9

Season of Bloom: May to July

Height × Width: 24 inches × 24+ inches

Flower Color: Violet-blue

Light Requirements: Full sun to partial shade

Soil Requirements: Average, well-drained, moist soil

Place of Origin: Europe from Belgium to the Pyrenees and east to the Carpathian Mountains

Plant Sources: Kurt Bluemel, Bluestone Perennials, Busse Gardens, Carroll Gardens, Forestfarm, Garden Place, Milaeger's Gardens, Powell's Gardens, Roslyn Nursery, Spring Hill Nurseries, Van Bourgondien, Weiss Brothers Perennial Nursery, White Flower Farm

Seed Source: Thompson & Morgan

flowers. The stems have a fine, spiderweb-like hairiness, and the new foliage is silvered by this same fuzz, although it turns a rough-surfaced green as it matures.

HOW TO GROW PERENNIAL CORNFLOWER

Perennial cornflower thrives without fuss in just about any soil as long as there's adequate moisture and good drainage—it doesn't like wet feet. It's even less picky about light and will grow well in full sun to light shade. Once established, it makes a dense, slowly spreading mass of roots that lends itself to easy division with a shovel.

The stiff bracts beneath perennial cornflower's elaborate blossoms give these showy flowers a long life when they're cut for fresh use or for drying.

In the far north, plant perennial cornflower in a spot where you can confine it or where you don't mind its spreading. Conditions in the coldest part of its range seem to encourage perennial cornflower's somewhat rampant growth tendencies. In most of its range it is well enough behaved, however, and its vigorous growth habit is welcomed by gardeners who don't want to have to laboriously propagate perennials to fill a good-size drift. Other than the occasional slug or snail bite, pests and diseases don't trouble this all-star perennial.

PROPAGATING PERENNIAL CORNFLOWER

Perennial cornflower is a vigorous spreader and self-sower, so it's easy to increase a planting. If you want to establish it elsewhere on your property, divide it every few years and plant the divisions about 12 inches apart. Division keeps it looking its best, too.

In a semishady bed, a mass of casual perennial cornflower contrasts with hybrid lupine's formal spikes and fine-textured catmint.

THE RIGHT SITE FOR PERENNIAL CORNFLOWER

Plant perennial cornflower among woody flowering shrubs in the sunny or lightly shaded part of your landscape, where it will naturalize. Its showy, bristly looking flowers and vigorous growth habit lend themselves to informal gardens, while its long-lasting blooms make it a natural for your cutting garden.

CO-STARS FOR PERENNIAL CORNFLOWER

At the front of the border, perennial cornflower looks fine amid catmints (*Nepeta* spp.) and lupines (*Lupinus* hybrids). Further back in the garden try it in combination with Brazilian vervain (*Verbena bonariensis*). Set off its electric-blue flowers with the summer whites of Shasta daisy (*Chrysanthemum* × *superbum*) or white gaura (see page 146). Or pair it with gooseneck loosestrife (see page 214) and let these two vigorous growers duke it out.

RED VALERIAN

Centranthus ruber

IF EVERY PERENNIAL WERE AS EASY TO GROW as red valerian, we could plant up a garden and forget it. Just give this plant a start and it will self-sow without fail, as its seeds have little dandelionlike parachutes.

And while it's not always invited, it's always a pleasure to see red valerian springing up in out-of-the-way places. European gardeners find that it likes old walls and decayed brickwork—possibly because it loves alkaline soil and finds the limestone mortar to its taste.

But it's the flowers that make red valerian so welcome: Thousands of tiny florets cluster in dense showy heads held above bushy, fleshy, gray-green foliage. The flowers have a nice but not strong fragrance, and the flowerheads will last a full week when cut for an arrangement in the house.

Red valerian is a long-season bloomer, starting in June in the Northeast (earlier farther south) and blooming into October. If the old flowerheads are trimmed off as soon as they finish blooming, the plant will produce new flowers right up until frost.

Shades of Red Valerian

Red valerian's flower color varies from rosy pink to mauve-pink to lilac-red, or even to strong red. The variety coccineus has vivid carmine-red flowerheads, and the white form, C. ruber var. albus, gives a cool look to the garden in the hot days of summer.

Spotlight on Red Valerian

USDA Plant Hardiness Zones: 5 to 9

Season of Bloom: Late June to August, then reblooms to frost

Height × Width: 24 to 36 inches × 24 to 36 inches

Flower Color: Red

Light Requirements: Full sun to partial shade

Soil Requirements: Any soil, but prefers limy, well-drained soil.

Place of Origin: Europe

Plant Sources: Kurt Bluemel, Bluestone Perennials, Carroll Gardens, Daisy Fields, Forestfarm, Garden Place, Milaeger's Gardens, Powell's Gardens, Roslyn Nursery, Shady Oaks Nursery, Spring Hill Nurseries, Van Bourgondien, André Viette Farm & Nursery, Wayside Gardens, White Flower Farm

Seed Source: Park Seed

HOW TO GROW RED VALERIAN Red valerian thrives in just about any soil and condition except wet, boggy shade. It really grows well in a sweet, good, garden soil, but performs nearly as well in poorer soils. As long as the drainage is good—a condition almost always found in limy soils—red valerian will be at home. If your soil is acidic, sweeten a spot for red valerian with ground limestone.

Red valerian is drought tolerant to the point where it naturalizes in many parts of the West where summer water is sparse. Rainfall is usually adequate in the East, but during prolonged hot, dry spells, it will

Red valerian bears dense clusters of red florets at the top of sturdy, branching stems. The plant forms a bushy clump of handsome gray- to blue-green foliage.

Try red valerian in a foundation planting or next to a stone wall. This drought-tolerant plant thrives in the alkaline conditions common to such sites.

appreciate a drink. Water it in the morning, as its leaves can develop mildew if they stay wet overnight. Other than that, red valerian is pretty much pest- and disease-free.

Red valerian struggles in full sun in the heat and humidity of the Deep South, so plant it in light shade in Zones 7 to 9. In the dry heat of the West, however, it seems to do exceptionally well, even in Zone 9. I see it everywhere here in northern California.

PROPAGATING RED VALERIAN Red valerian self-sows readily—just look around existing plants for volunteer seedlings to transplant. You can also divide red valerian by carefully taking basal cuttings from around the outside of the plant in spring. Plant rooted cuttings 18 inches apart in the garden.

THE RIGHT SITE FOR RED VALERIAN Red valerian is a real all-star for difficult places. Use it to bring easy, long-lasting color to steep banks, on rough slopes, or along the roadside. Some people might describe its growth habit as "floppy," but I prefer to call it "relaxed." Either way, red valerian looks lovely growing where it can cascade gracefully—over a wall, for instance.

CO-STARS FOR RED VALERIAN Use the similarly colored flowers of sea-pink (*Armeria maritima*) and ornamental onions (*Allium aflatunense* or *A. giganteum*) to echo the unique pink-to-red-to-mauve color of red valerian's flowers. It also looks good combined with the evergreen gray-green foliage and numerous blossoms of pink- or white-flowered sun roses (*Helianthemum nummularium*). The soft blues of tall bellflowers (*Campanula persicifolia* or *C. glomerata*) and the pink-tinged white flowers of gas plant (*Dictamnus albus*) make fine companions for red valerian, as well. Plant the white-flowered form with large beds of daylilies for a winning combination.

FEVERFEW

Chrysanthemum parthenium

SOME GARDEN PLANTS are immediately noticeable, stunningly beautiful standouts. Not feverfew. This is an unassuming plant of modest appearance. But if you like substance over flash, you will cherish feverfew more and more as the years go by.

Its dainty little flowers—just ½-inch across—are like miniature daisies, with short white petals surrounding yellow centers. They are sprinkled liberally above the ferny foliage from early summer right into October—a blooming season long enough to qualify it for all-star status, even if it didn't have other wonderful qualities to its credit.

In the garden, feverfew gives the impression

Spotlight on Feverfew

USDA Plant Hardiness Zones: 6 to 10

Season of Bloom: June to October

Height × Width: 12 to 36 inches × 12 to 36 inches

Flower Color: White with yellow centers

Light Requirements: Full sun to partial shade

Soil Requirements: Well-drained, moist, light soil

Place of Origin: Southeastern Europe to the Caucasus Mountains

Plant Sources: Carroll Gardens, Daisy Fields, Garden Place, Milaeger's Gardens, Nichols Garden Nursery, Roslyn Nursery

A Doubly Delightful Feverfew

If you want something a bit more elegant than the quaint charm of feverfew's diminutive daisies, try one of the double-flowered cultivars in your garden. Particularly nice is 'White Wonder', a double-flowered selection that produces oodles of long-lasting, tidy white pompons.

For an interesting foliage effect from your feverfew, select golden feather (C. parthenium 'Aureum'). This plant's ferny foliage is bright golden-green to chartreuse, and it produces the same cheery daisies as other feverfews. Other cultivars are not as nice as the species, in my opinion.

of being a very old-fashioned plant, something you might have seen in your grandmother's garden. Indeed, you might have seen it there, and in your great-grandmother's garden, and in her mother's garden, and so on back into antiquity. Feverfew has been a favorite of gardeners and herbalists for centuries and is still used as an herbal medicine for the treatment of migraines. Its aromatic foliage has a sharp, medicinal fragrance that seems to protect it from pests.

HOW TO GROW FEVERFEW It's hard to go wrong with a perennial that's as tough and easy to grow as feverfew. It blooms best in full sun but flowers well enough in shade to qualify for a spot there, too. Feverfew tolerates some dryness, but give it a drink in hot, dry weather and it will reward you with its improved appearance. In the Deep South, keep it very well watered or it will burn out. It's not picky about soil type, although it tends to struggle in dense, wet, clay soil.

You can grow feverfew in Zones 4 and 5, but it needs winter protection there and is probably best grown as an annual. Seed sown indoors early will bloom in midsummer and keep blooming into fall.

PROPAGATING FEVERFEW This all-star self-sows so readily that there's no need to use more elaborate propagation methods. Once you plant it, it will keep popping up here and there in the garden. Seedlings of cultivars like 'White Wonder' revert eventually to the single flowers of the species. Propagate cultivars by division or stem cuttings to retain their desirable characteristics.

THE RIGHT SITE FOR FEVERFEW A cheery, casual plant, feverfew works well in informal gardens. In a sunny to partially shady cottage garden, its clusters of small white daisies make nice counterparts for stronger flower colors. Of course it's a natural for the herb garden where its daisy flowers provide a welcome sight amid the foliage.

If you plant feverfew, you'll eventually find self-sown seedlings in your gardens. Most seedlings will have the single flowers of the species.

The tidy white pompons of double-flowered feverfew make an elegant addition to the herb garden or to your sunny perennial border.

CO-STARS FOR FEVERFEW A diverse collection of garden plants make fine companions for feverfew. For starters, try it with pink garden phlox (*Phlox paniculata*), painted daisies (*Chrysanthemum coccineum*), baby's-breath (*Gypsophila* spp.), or roses. It also looks great with ornamental grasses such as blue fescue (*Festuca* spp.), blue oat grass (see page 162), or fountain grass (*Pennisetum* spp.). Feverfew's tidy little white flowers go with just about everything but look especially pretty growing between and separating strong red-to-yellow colors.

'SNOW LADY' SHASTA DAISY

Chrysanthemum × superbum
'Snow Lady'

LUTHER BURBANK named his prize chrysanthemum the Shasta daisy after the dazzling, snow white presence of Mount Shasta rising 14,000 feet above the floor of California's Central Valley. The clean look of the Shasta daisy's neutral white color has made this chrysanthemum one of the world's favorites for combining with many other flowers. Its long season of bloom and vigorous growth only enhance its usefulness in the perennial border, where it easily earns the title of all-star.

The foliage of the taller types, which may grow to 24 to 36 inches tall, is pretty ragged and rough, making them plants for the back of the border where their foliage is hidden by other plants. But breeding has done wonders with Shasta daisies, and given us 'Snow Lady', a recent All-America Selections winner.

This marvelous plant grows only 10 to 12 inches tall and produces lots of flowers. And while its leaves and stems are smaller than those of other Shasta daisies, its big, white

Other Showy Shastas

Among the standard 24- to 36-inch-tall Shasta daisies, 'Alaska', 'Switzerland', and 'Polaris' are choice single-flowered selections. Desirable double-flowered cultivars, which prefer to grow in some shade, include 'Aglaya' and the creamy yellow-flowered 'Cobham Gold'.

Spotlight on 'Snow Lady' Shasta Daisy

USDA Plant Hardiness Zones: 5 to 9

Season of Bloom: Mid-June through September

Height × Width: 10 to 12 inches × 12 to 18 inches

Flower Color: White with yellow centers

Light Requirements: Full sun

Soil Requirements: Humusy, moist, well-drained garden soil

Place of Origin: Originally hybridized by Luther Burbank

Plant Sources: Garden Place, Weiss Brothers Perennial Nursery, White Flower Farm

Seed Source: Park Seed

flowers aren't. They effectively cover the stems and foliage, which in any case are bushier and more attractive than the lankier types. The pure white flowers of 'Snow Lady' are 2½ inches across, with small yellow centers, and they make a very strong white statement in the garden. They start opening in June and continue blooming for a full three months, right into early fall, and even later if you nick off the spent flowerheads after the first big flush.

Don't be alarmed if you encounter a little confusion when looking for this useful plant by its botanical name: It has more than one. Nobody argues about the cultivar name 'Snow Lady', but you may find Shasta daisy listed as either *C. × superbum* or *C. × maximum*. Still other sources identify it as *Leucanthemum × maximum*. When they get it sorted out, let me know. In the meantime, it remains *C. × superbum* to me.

HOW TO GROW SHASTA DAISY

Plant Shasta daisies in humusy, well-drained, moist garden soil in full sun, and they'll be happy. Don't worry if a few aphids show up— they won't do much harm, and they're food for a whole host of more beneficial garden visitors. If the aphid crowd becomes too large, simply wash them off your plants with the hose. In most cases and in most places, these all-stars are reliably trouble-free.

PROPAGATING SHASTA DAISY

All chrysanthemums benefit from division at least every third year (some gardeners divide them every year, which seems a little excessive to me). Division is necessary because the younger, juvenile plants that form on the outside of

'Snow Lady' Shasta daisy produces full-size white flowers atop compact 12-inch plants.

Divide Shasta daisies in the spring about every three years. Discard the older roots in the center of the clump and replant the younger, outer growth.

the clumps are the best bloomers. Grow them in loose, humusy soil and the occasional spring division is no problem at all. You also can start 'Snow Lady' easily from seed.

THE RIGHT SITE FOR 'SNOW LADY' 'Snow Lady' Shasta daisy is a choice plant for the front of the garden, where it puts on a pretty show all summer. It's great for edging the paths in an evening garden, where it will light the way with its bright white flowers.

Plant some out of the way, too, to cut for summer vases. Gather your Shasta daisies when their petals are just starting to unfold, and they will last and last in the vase.

CO-STARS FOR 'SNOW LADY' In the garden, 'Snow Lady' is one easygoing gal— pretty much any summer-blooming perennial looks good combined with her cheery daisies. Poppies of all kinds, delphiniums, lupines, and lilies all look beautiful with Shasta daisies' pure, clean, white petals. Mix them at the border's edge with a selection of your favorite summer bloomers.

'CLARA CURTIS' CHRYSANTHEMUM

Chrysanthemum zawadskii var. *latilobum* 'Clara Curtis'

LET ME START BY SAYING THAT 'CLARA CURTIS' is no typical chrysanthemum. This pretty all-star shares the many good characteristics for which chrysanthemums are known and adds her own special twists—earlier flowers in a delightful shade of salmon pink.

Whether you find this plant labeled as

A Couple of Captivating Chrysanthemums

If the salmon pink shades of 'Clara Curtis' don't fit into your garden scheme, take a look at her sibling cultivar 'Mary Stoker' (C. zawadskii var. latilobum 'Mary Stoker'). This plant offers the same excellent garden qualities as 'Clara Curtis' and bears soft apricot flowers that fade to straw yellow during an equally long but somewhat later period of bloom.

To narrow the field of fall-blooming mums, I asked Ted King, a grower and exhibitor of hardy garden mums, which cultivar of C. × morifolium (recently renamed Dendranthema × morifolium) he thought was a champion all-star. "There would, of course, be many candidates," he replied. "but I would select the garden mum 'Red Remarkable' as a very good selection." This mum, with brilliant red blooms in September and October, makes compact plants whose flowers resist fading in the bright, hot fall sun of the South and West.

Spotlight on 'Clara Curtis' Chrysanthemum

USDA Plant Hardiness Zones: 4 to 9

Season of Bloom: July to October

Height × Width: 18 to 24 inches × 24 to 48 inches

Flower Color: Bright, warm pink with yellow centers

Light Requirements: Full sun to light shade

Soil Requirements: Rich to average, well-drained garden loam

Place of Origin: Czech Republic and Poland, east to Japan and Korea

Plant Sources: Ambergate Gardens, Busse Gardens, Carroll Gardens, Forestfarm, Milaeger's Gardens, Spring Hill Nurseries, André Viette Farm & Nursery, Wayside Gardens, Weiss Brothers Perennial Nursery

C. zawadskii var. *latilobum* or under the newer name, *Dendranthema zawadskii*, 'Clara Curtis' will give you a new perspective on mums. 'Clara Curtis' begins her display in July or August, erupting in an exuberant burst of warm pink daisies with golden centers. The large, single daisies are 2 to 3½ inches across and are held atop stiff upright stems of deeply lobed, mum-type foliage.

Following a wet spring, 'Clara Curtis' starts blooming in July. Dry spring weather gives her a somewhat slower start and may delay the start of flowering until August. In any case, this plant blooms freely until October.

HOW TO GROW 'CLARA CURTIS' 'Clara Curtis' is remarkably hardy for a chrysanthemum, being reliably winter hardy to Zone 4 and worth trying in Zone 3. The plant's purplish rhizomes spread quickly during the growing season to produce a neat, tidy clump of foliage. In the second year of growth, 'Clara Curtis' may produce dense stands of stems. When these stems reach 4 to 6 inches tall, thin them to at least an inch apart within the stand.

Although most mums are sun-lovers, 'Clara Curtis' tolerates a bit more shade than most. Pests and diseases don't bother this plant, and it's long lived if given frequent division.

PROPAGATING 'CLARA CURTIS' Separate new shoots from the old plant in spring and replant the divisions 12 inches apart. You can also take stem cuttings of 'Clara Curtis' in early summer. Older clumps produce dense stands of stems that need thinning, so divide yearly.

THE RIGHT SITE FOR 'CLARA CURTIS'

'Clara Curtis' is the perfect plant for a border that reaches its peak display in the fall. It also shines when mixed with other perennials in a border that produces flowers all through the garden year, where it will be a late star. And, in addition to its other all-star qualities, 'Clara Curtis' is a butterfly magnet.

'Clara Curtis' opens her first flowers in mid- to late summer, and gets along nicely with summer-blooming annuals like cosmos and cleome.

CO-STARS FOR 'CLARA CURTIS' Perennials with white or blue flowers make excellent companions for 'Clara Curtis'. As 'Clara Curtis' begins to bloom, its flowers look good with the showy white clusters of 'David' summer phlox (see page 248) and the starry blue blossoms of balloon flower (see page 252). A bit later in the season, deep blue monkshood (see page 30), white and pale pink Japanese anemones (*Anemone × hybrida*), blue asters, and rosy purple Joe-Pye weeds (*Eupatorium* spp.) complement the pink daisies of 'Clara Curtis'.

A Stellar Idea

The sturdy stems of 'Clara Curtis' usually need no staking, although they may bow under the profuse flowers—growing the plant up through supporting hoops or twigs will keep them upright.

As fall arrives, 'Clara Curtis' blooms on. Her warm pink daisies brighten up buff-colored grasses and 'Autumn Joy' sedum's rusty fall flowers.

GOLDENSTAR

Chrysogonum virginianum

GOLDENSTAR HAS A MAJOR VIRTUE that might be overlooked because of its unassuming size and modest flowers: It blooms from May to October, one of the few perennials that stays in flower through almost the entire growing season.

Although it's a modest little plant that grows only to about 8 inches tall, goldenstar has some superb qualities as a groundcover. Its roots are stoloniferous runners that send down fibrous roots as they spread. They sprout tidy bunches of neat, dark green, heart-shaped leaves with an embossed surface and toothed or sometimes scalloped margins.

Goldenstar makes a fine, groundcovering mat of leaves, but it isn't rampant or invasive like goutweed (*Aegopodium podagraria*). Starting in May and continuing through the

Stick with Goldenstar

Goldenstar is the only species in the genus <u>Chrysogonum</u>. Apart from finding it called either green and gold or goldenstar, there's little else to confuse you in your search for this all-star and few other plants to steal your affections from it. Some sources do offer cultivars of goldenstar—these are usually very prostrate forms that reach only a few inches tall, even when flowering. In other regards they differ very little from the species.

Spotlight on Goldenstar

USDA Plant Hardiness Zones: 6 to 9

Season of Bloom: May to October

Height × Width: 8 inches × 24+ inches

Flower Color: Yellow

Light Requirements: Full sun to full shade

Soil Requirements: Rich, humusy, moist soil

Place of Origin: Southeastern United States

Plant Sources: Kurt Bluemel, Busse Gardens, Carroll Gardens, Crownsville Nursery, Forestfarm, Greer Gardens, Powell's Gardens, Sunlight Gardens, André Viette Farm & Nursery, We-Du Nurseries

growing season, the plants produce branched, hairy, flowerstalks that emerge from the leaf axils. The starry golden flowers spangle the tips of the flowerstalks. Each 1-inch blossom has a central disk surrounded by five rounded petals; each petal has three ragged teeth on its tip. Goldenstar's flowers are rich, golden yellow, like those of buttercups.

HOW TO GROW GOLDENSTAR Goldenstar is native in the East from Pennsylvania south to Florida and west to the Mississippi River region, although I never personally noticed it growing in the wild in Pennsylvania. In the northern part of its range, Zone 6, it can take full sun as long as there's adequate water, but the farther south you go, the more shade it needs. And in the southern part of its range, its foliage is evergreen.

Wherever it grows, goldenstar likes moist soil. Although it will grow in soil of average

Mix goldenstar with 'Burgundy Glow' ajuga to create a colorful carpet of flowers and foliage that grows well in sun or shade.

fertility, it does best in humusy, compost-enriched soil that resembles that of its native woodlands. In these conditions, goldenstar is rarely troubled by pests or diseases.

PROPAGATING GOLDENSTAR Goldenstar spreads readily, and you can divide its dense mats of creeping roots at anytime during the growing season. Space divisions 12 inches apart and keep the soil moist, and they will grow together to form an attractive, easy-care groundcover. Goldenstar is also easy to grow from seed.

THE RIGHT SITE FOR GOLDENSTAR Not only is goldenstar useful as a continous bloomer in the perennial bed or border, but it also naturalizes well along shady, moist woods edges. Here's a charming plant to tuck into out-of-the-way places in the landscape and in shady corners where it quietly keeps its flowers in view to cheer you as you pass by while walking—or working—in your garden.

From spring until fall, goldenstar produces pretty five-petalled yellow flowers that sparkle amid its tidy, dark green, groundcovering foliage.

CO-STARS FOR GOLDENSTAR Goldenstar's season-long sprinkling of rich yellow flowers goes well with other pretty ground huggers. Mix it with Siberian bugloss' (see page 78) tiny blue flowers, with the showier blues and ferny foliage of blue corydalis (*Corydalis flexuosa*), or with the cheery, tricolored faces of Johnny-jump-ups (see page 320). It also goes great with 'White Nancy' spotted dead nettle (see page 192), Jacob's ladder (see page 254), and navelworts (*Omphalodes* spp.). And it makes a sparkling groundcover beneath taller perennials such as lilies, Solomon's seal (*Polygonatum biflorum*), and summer phlox (*Phlox paniculata*).

BLACK COHOSH

Cimicifuga racemosa

BLACK COHOSH, ALSO CALLED BLACK SNAKEROOT and cohosh bugbane, is one of the finest and most imposing of all garden plants and belongs on anyone's short list of all-star perennials. In spring, it unfurls its pretty, large, deeply divided leaves, making clumps from 24 to 36 inches tall on thin stems. In July, flower spikes emerge and shoot upwards, and then the fun begins.

The florets along the 12-inch-long spikes begin as rounded buds that open into cottony puffs starting from the bottom and progressing upward. Some people say the flower spikes resemble bottle brushes, but that doesn't do them justice. To me they look like creamy white fireworks. The flower spikes are held 24 to 36 inches above the leaves on several branches of a half-dozen spikes each. Although the flower spikes may grow as

More Beautiful Bugbanes

Although they're known by the unlovely name bugbane, other plants in the genus Cimicifuga are worth including in your shade garden. Kamchatka bugbane (C. simplex) blooms in the fall and has somewhat smaller, pleasantly fragrant, white flower spikes. The variety of black cohosh called atropurpurea has purplish foliage, and its white, fall-blooming flower spikes make it a perfect companion for azure monkshood (Aconitum carmichaelii).

Spotlight on *Black Cohosh*

USDA Plant Hardiness Zones: 3 to 8

Season of Bloom: July and August

Height × Width: 4 to 6 feet × 3 feet

Flower Color: White

Light Requirements: Partial shade to full shade

Soil Requirements: Rich, moist, woodsy soil

Place of Origin: Eastern North America

Plant Sources: Kurt Bluemel, Busse Gardens, Carroll Gardens, Forestfarm, Milaeger's Gardens, Powell's Gardens, Sunlight Gardens, André Viette Farm & Nursery, We-Du Nurseries

Seed Source: Thompson & Morgan

high as 7 feet, they need no staking.

The first year you plant it, black cohosh doesn't do much. In the second year, it puts most of its energy into leaves and roots. Finally, in its third year of growth, and for many years after that, black cohosh puts forth an all-star display of flowers during the hot, humid days of July and August.

HOW TO GROW BLACK COHOSH Plant black cohosh in rich, moist, humusy soil like the forest floors of its native woodlands. This plant does best in a site that receives morning sun and afternoon shade but also grows well in both bright shade and full shade. In the northern part of its range, you can grow black cohosh in full sun, as long as you keep the soil consistently moist. In the South, shade is a necessity to keep the leaves from scorching in the sun.

Maple-leaved Japanese bugbane produces many-branched, purple-stemmed flower spikes that bloom in late summer and early fall above broad, lobed foliage.

PROPAGATING BLACK COHOSH It's easy to divide black cohosh in the spring. Separate the clumps and replant the divisions in rich, humusy, moist soil about 12 inches apart in a shady spot. Three divisions planted in a triangular shape make a nice grouping.

THE RIGHT SITE FOR BLACK COHOSH When its flowers are blooming in July and August, black cohosh presides over the shade garden. To enjoy the full effect of the flowers, plant black cohosh against a dark background like deep woodland shade or dark, dense evergreens.

CO-STARS FOR BLACK COHOSH This all-star is such a stately, dominant plant that it can overwhelm smaller perennials. Black cohosh looks great, and completely natural, at the wood's edge or at the back of the shady garden among large foliage plants like ferns and hostas. Companions like Japanese anemones (*Anemone* × *hybrida*) will echo black cohosh's upright form, while rounded, mounding perennials like cranesbills (*Geranium* spp.) provide a nice contrast.

Black cohosh opens its rounded buds from the bottom of each flower spike upward to create creamy bottle brushes that are up to 12 inches long.

A Stellar Idea

Enjoy black cohosh's showy flowers in your garden, but pass by them when you're cutting flowers for a vase in your house. The flowers have a rather unpleasant odor that is said to repel insects—the botanical name, Cimicifuga, has its roots in two Latin words that mean 'bug' and 'to chase away' and the common name, bugbane, is similarly descriptive. Likewise, black cohosh is not a plant you'd choose for a fragrance garden. But its ill scent does serve a purpose—black cohosh rarely is bothered by pests.

'NIOBE' CLEMATIS

Clematis 'Niobe'

WHEN I THINK OF LARGE-FLOWERED hybrid clematis, adjectives like "spectacular," "gorgeous," "stunning," and "outstanding" come to mind, but even these glowing terms don't do this group of plants justice. Clematis vines and flowers are simply indispensible, and are perhaps the most beautiful of all the perennial flowers we grow.

Hundreds of named forms are available, and it's hard to pick just one as an all-star. A hard choice, but not impossible—because there is 'Niobe'.

'Niobe' clematis produces six-petalled, 4- to 5-inch blossoms that open in such a dark shade of red that they're nearly black. These spectacular flowers slowly mature to a rich red color that carries just a hint of blue. Their rich velvety texture only adds to their charm. And in the center of each blossom is a flash of golden stamens. Heart-shaped, somewhat glossy, bright green leaves provide a perfect backdrop for the showy flowers.

A Wealth to Choose From

Choosing from among the many other large-flowered hybrid clematis is largely a matter of taste. Check the catalogs, as there are dozens of good plants available. I like the deep pink bicolored flowers of 'Dr. Ruppel', the white and pink bicolored 'Nelly Moser', and the pale rosy pink blossoms of 'Hagley Hybrid'.

Spotlight on 'Niobe' Clematis

USDA Plant Hardiness Zones: 3 to 9

Season of Bloom: June to September

Height × Width: 8 to 12 feet × 4 to 6 feet

Flower Color: Dark red

Light Requirements: Partial shade to full sun

Soil Requirements: Rich, cool, moist, well-drained soil

Place of Origin: Hybridized in Poland by Wladyslaw Noll

Plant Sources: Greer Gardens, Park Seed, Van Bourgondien, André Viette Farm & Nursery, Wayside Gardens

HOW TO GROW 'NIOBE' Most recommendations for growing clematis say to keep its "feet" in the shade and its "head" in the sun. That is, shade the root zone with tall annuals or shallow-rooted perennials, rather than with a thick mulch that may promote clematis wilt. And let the "head," or uppermost part of the vine, climb up its support into the sunlight. 'Niobe' will do just fine in those conditions, but it prefers partial shade, although it will also bloom in bright shade or partial sunlight.

'Niobe' is a trouble-free clematis. Its care is made easier by the fact that the vine grows only 8 to 10 feet long. Prune in late winter to early spring while the vine is dormant. To enjoy early and late flowers—and 'Niobe' blooms throughout the summer—prune the ends of the vining stems back by less than 12 inches to two large buds. Remove old or dead stems altogether. The vining stems will produce early flowers, and the new growth from the bottom of the plant will bloom later.

If you prune the entire plant back to its lowest pair of healthy buds, 'Niobe' will produce more flowers later in the season.

PROPAGATING 'NIOBE' Clematis hybrids are difficult to reproduce by cuttings, and they're not easy to divide, either. Their seeds are few and unlikely to produce plants that look like the parent plant. Layering the plant, by bending a vine down to the soil and pinning it there to root, is sometimes successful in producing new plants. Otherwise, this is one all-star that is best increased by buying additional plants from a nursery.

THE RIGHT SITE FOR 'NIOBE' Put 'Niobe' where you can look up through its flowers at the sun. When they're backlit, the petals glow like illuminated rubies. 'Niobe' is fairly compact and perfect for a climbing on a fence or for twining around a lamppost or mailbox post.

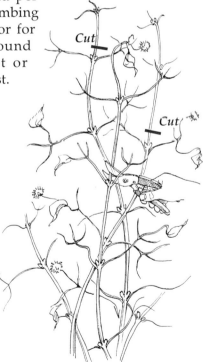

Prune 'Niobe' lightly in late winter to enjoy flowers in both the early summer and early fall. Cut shoot tips back to the first pair of plump buds and remove any old or dead stems entirely.

Dress up a spot in partial shade with the velvety dark red flowers of 'Niobe' clematis. Each luscious blossom is as much as 4 to 5 inches across.

CO-STARS FOR 'NIOBE' The ultimate companion for 'Niobe' is the floribunda rose, 'Gruss an Aachen', whose shell pink roses fairly sparkle next to the dark red of 'Niobe'. 'Gruss an Aachen' enjoys the same conditions, too, since it's one of those choice roses that blooms as well in partial shade as it does in full sun. As with all the large-flowered hybrid clematis, 'Niobe' is so beautiful that it's excellent all by itself, growing up a post, porch support, or latticework.

DOWNY CLEMATIS

Clematis macropetala

BECAUSE MOST PEOPLE THINK OF THE WONDERFUL large-flowered hybrids when they think of clematis, many are puzzled—and delighted—by the sight of downy clematis' blossoms and wonder what the plant might be. Downy clematis is a member of a special group of clematis that bear nodding flowers—delicate blossoms that hang from their compact vining stems like crowds of fairy lanterns or silky ballet skirts.

Downy clematis' fully double flowers are the loveliest of all the small-flowered types of clematis. Each is 4 inches across, with many 2-inch, lavender, petal-like sepals that have blue margins or veining. A cluster of slender, inch-long stamens protrudes from the middle of each flower; the outer stamens are blue and the inner ones are whitish. The vines typically begin blooming in April and continue blooming until early June—or later in the very coldest parts of their range. Showy, bronzy pink, silvery seed clusters follow the flowers.

Additional Classy Clematis

There are several showy cultivars of downy clematis to consider for your garden. Check out the nodding blue flowers of 'Maidwell Hall' and 'Blue Bird', the luscious soft mauve petals of 'Markham's Pink', and the fresh white blossoms of 'Snowbird'.

Spotlight on Downy Clematis

USDA Plant Hardiness Zones: 3 to 9

Season of Bloom: April to June

Height × Width: 6 to 10 feet × 3 to 5 feet

Flower Color: Lavender to powder blue

Light Requirements: Partial sun to light shade

Soil Requirements: Rich, humusy, evenly moist, well-drained soil.

Place of Origin: Northern China, Siberia

Plant Sources: Forestfarm, Greer Gardens, White Flower Farm

HOW TO GROW DOWNY CLEMATIS Like most clematis, this one likes to have its roots in cool, moist shade, while its upper portions grow into bright shade or filtered sunlight. Being a Siberian native, downy clematis survives all but the most arctic conditions. And it's untroubled by pests and diseases.

Because this early-flowering clematis blooms on older stems, pruning is unnecessary except to remove dead or broken stems or to keep the plant compact. If you're pruning to restrict downy clematis' size, remove all of the flowering shoots immediately after they finish blooming.

PROPAGATING DOWNY CLEMATIS Downy clematis is relatively easy to grow from seed. To propagate cultivars of downy clematis, layer them in the summer by bending a vine down to the soil and pinning it there to root.

THE RIGHT SITE FOR DOWNY CLEMATIS Downy clematis produces compact vines that grow 6 to 10 feet long or perhaps a little

Although its flowers are smaller than those of the many large-flowered clematis hybrids, downy clematis can still put on a show. This hardy vine opens dozens of nodding, lavender-blue flowers over a period of several weeks in the spring.

more. One of the plant's quirks is that individual vines will vary in length. But this general compactness is an advantage, as it lets you do fun things with downy clematis. You can grow the vines through a small shrub, up a short post, or even in a large container such as an urn or planting jar. And if it looks good in a container, why not let it scramble over large rocks or trail down a wall from the top of a terrace?

You'll want to touch the delicate nodding flowers of downy clematis to see if their petals are as soft as their fuzzy appearance suggests.

CO-STARS FOR DOWNY CLEMATIS Downy clematis makes a fine combination with its own pink cultivar, 'Markham's Pink' and with a related species, blue-flowered alpine clematis (*Clematis alpina*). It also looks handsome with its white-flowered cultivar, 'Snowbird'. Train the vine up through shrubs such as pieris and photinias, where its nodding blue flowers will look great amid their reddish new foliage.

LILY-OF-THE-VALLEY

Convallaria majalis

LILY-OF-THE-VALLEY IS A TOUGH, ground-hugging all-star that charms everyone who knows it. It was first brought into European gardens in the 16th century, and because of its longevity, reliability, usefulness, beauty and fragrance, it has never left. Meanwhile, early settlers in North America found it growing here, too, and likewise brought it home to perfume their rustic homesteads.

The tradition continued in my family. When I think of my mom, now many years gone, I remember that the first plant she put into the landscape of our new home was lily-of-the-valley along the north side of the garage. I can still see her plucking stems of its flowers for a small vase she placed on the windowsill above the sink, so they were always handy for a whiff while she was elbow-deep in dishwater.

Although its charms are many, lily-of-the-valley is best known for the exquisite, heavy fragrance of its dainty spring flowers. These

Other Lovely Lilies-of-the-Valley

Lily-of-the-valley is such an outstanding performer that its cultivars can hardly improve upon it. A couple worth noting are 'Fortin's Giant', which has extra-large leaves and larger, more abundant bells on its flowerstalks, and 'Rosea', which has pretty pink flowers.

Spotlight on Lily-of-the-Valley

USDA Plant Hardiness Zones: 2 to 8

Season of Bloom: May to June

Height × Width: 8 inches × 24+ inches

Flower Color: White

Light Requirements: Partial shade to full shade

Soil Requirements: Humusy, woodsy, moist, well-drained soil

Place of Origin: Northern hemisphere in Europe, Asia, and North America

Plant Sources: Kurt Bluemel, W. Atlee Burpee, Carroll Gardens, Dutch Gardens, Forestfarm, J. W. Jung Seed, Klehm Nursery, Park Seed, Powell's Gardens, Spring Hill Nurseries, Sunlight Gardens, Van Bourgondien, André Viette Farm & Nursery, Wayside Gardens, White Flower Farm

are petite, waxy white bells with sweetly scalloped hems that arch out and hang along one side of 3- to 4-inch upright flower stems. The flower stems emerge from between lily-of-the-valley's two or three fluted, dark green leaves.

Lily-of-the-valley spreads by creeping rhizomes that grow and root along the soil surface just under the leaf litter. From these rhizomes the crowns, known as pips, send up leaves and flowers in the spring. In the coldest parts of its range, lily-of-the-valley thrives and can make thick, almost impenetrable mats. This vigorous growth usually is welcome in semishady places.

In a cool, shady, woodsy spot, lily-of-the-valley quickly spreads its rhizomes to form a dense groundcover that very few weeds can penetrate.

Lily-of-the-valley's dainty white floral bells fill the air around a planting with their heavenly fragrance. Glossy red berries follow the flowers.

How to Grow Lily-of-the-Valley

Lily-of-the-valley does well in Zones 6 and 7, but is less vigorous and spreads more slowly than it does north of Zone 6. In Zone 8 it struggles and flowers only occasionally. That may be because it's just not cold enough in the winter or because it's too hot in the summer. Plant it here and there around the shady parts of your property, and you'll probably see it grow and spread in some of them and die out in others. In very deep shade, flowering is sparser. And for some reason, once in a while, lily-of-the-valley will grow perfectly happily in full sun.

It's not picky about soil type, although it doesn't like boggy soil or hardpan clays and droughty soil. Treat it like a woodland plant and crumble a shovelful of compost over the beds in spring from time to time to keep it healthy, green, and floriferous. It has no pest or disease problems to speak of.

Propagating Lily-of-the-Valley

As lily-of-the-valley spreads into mats, it becomes crowded and flowering diminishes. Divide the mats into crowns (pips) with their long, thong-like roots in very early spring or in fall and re-plant the divisions 8 inches apart. Or simply carve the mat of roots into chunks with a shovel and replant the chunks elsewhere.

The Right Site for Lily-of-the-Valley

Lily-of-the-valley's low stature, spreading nature, and sweet-scented flowers make it a first-rate groundcover for a shady slope where it can grow to its heart's content. It's also handsome growing beneath shrubs and trees. But be careful about using it in your perennial garden, where its vigorous growth can overwhelm more reserved plants.

Co-Stars for Lily-of-the-Valley

Lily-of-the-valley makes a great carpet for the ground beneath the branches of azaleas and rhododendrons, and it enjoys the same woodsy soil conditions. It's pretty mixed with Grecian windflower (*Anemone blanda*) or other spring-flowering bulbs, and makes a nice shady groundcover combination with periwinkle (*Vinca minor*).

'MOONBEAM' THREADLEAF COREOPSIS

Coreopsis verticillata 'Moonbeam'

WHAT A PERFORMER 'Moonbeam' threadleaf coreopsis is—no wonder it was one of the Perennial Plant Association's first choices for Plant of the Year.

The first thing you notice about this all-star is the beautiful pale yellow color of its 1-inch-wide, daisylike flowers. The color looks good with just about any other color in the garden, making 'Moonbeam' easy to use. The flowers are neat and tidy with dark golden centers, and are produced in upright, wiry-stemmed sprays that cover the tops of the foliage from late June all the way to frost.

In addition to its galaxy of golden flowers, 'Moonbeam' has fine, ferny, threadlike foliage. Given all the large-leaved plants in the perennial garden, what a relief to have an all-star with foliage that can provide some contrast.

Spotlight on 'Moonbeam' Threadleaf Coreopsis

USDA Plant Hardiness Zones: 3 to 9

Season of Bloom: June to frost

Height × Width: 18 to 24 inches × 18 inches

Flower Color: Pale yellow

Light Requirements: Full sun to partial shade

Soil Requirements: Average to poor, well-drained soil

Place of Origin: Eastern United States

Plant Sources: Ambergate Gardens, Kurt Bluemel, Bluestone Perennials, Busse Gardens, Carroll Gardens, Crownsville Nursery, Forestfarm, Garden Place, Greer Gardens, J. W. Jung Seed, Klehm Nursery, Milaeger's Gardens, Park Seed, Powell's Gardens, Roslyn Nurseries, Spring Hill Nurseries, Sunlight Gardens, Van Bourgondien, André Viette Farm & Nursery, Wayside Gardens, Weiss Brothers Perennial Nursery, White Flower Farm

A Couple of Competing Coreopsis

Threadleaf coreopsis has two other cultivars of note. 'Zagreb' is a short, bushy plant with bright yellow flowers, ferny foliage, and the same long-blooming habit as 'Moonbeam'. 'Golden Showers' (also known as C. verticillata 'Grandiflora', and not to be confused with C. grandiflora) grows to 24 inches tall with bright golden daisy flowers.

HOW TO GROW 'MOONBEAM' Don't worry too much about the soil where you're planting 'Moonbeam' coreopsis. It can be average or even poor and as long as it's well-drained, it can even be droughty. 'Moonbeam' will continue to bloom and look fine, so you don't have to worry about a lot of watering during the summer.

Although 'Moonbeam' prefers a sunny spot, it performs well in partial shade. Don't worry about the effects of heat and humidity

Place 'Moonbeam' so its ferny foliage spills gently out of the garden, softening the edge.

'Moonbeam' is an enthusiastic bloomer, to say the least. It flowers reliably all summer long, from June until frost.

if you live in the South—this plant is native from Maryland to Florida and west to Alabama and Arkansas.

Pest or disease problems? It won't have any. It's even mildew resistant. And it comes back reliably year after year, making neat, compact, 3-foot-wide mounds and staying well-behaved forever. About the only thing 'Moonbeam' doesn't do is weed itself.

PROPAGATING 'MOONBEAM' 'Moonbeam' divides easily in the spring, so you can increase it and make drifts of this all-star by replanting the divisions 12 inches apart. The plants do benefit from division every three years or so. You can also propagate 'Moonbeam' by taking basal cuttings from around the roots in the spring.

THE RIGHT SITE FOR 'MOONBEAM' 'Moonbeam' coreopsis' flower color is one of the most versatile in the perennial palette. It contrasts beautifully with rich purples and blues, and is one of the few yellow shades that sets off pink hues to advantage. Create drifts of 'Moonbeam' to tie together stronger flower colors and bolder foliage textures in your perennial garden. 'Moonbeam' makes a great container plant, too, and is tough enough to fill a hanging basket in a sunny spot. Make sure to visit your 'Moonbeam' at twilight or even by (dare I say it?) moonlight, when its pale yellow flowers are positively luminescent.

CO-STARS FOR 'MOONBEAM' COREOPSIS New York aster (*Aster novi-belgii*), cardinal flower (see page 210), red-hot poker (*Kniphofia uvaria*), crocosmia (*Crocosmia × crocosmiiflora*), Stoke's aster (*Stokesia laevis*), daisy fleabane (*Erigeron speciosus*), purple coneflower (*Echinacea purpurea*), spike gayfeather (*Liatris spicata*), prairie mallows (*Sidalcea* spp.), and goldenrods (*Solidago* spp.) look particularly good with 'Moonbeam', but so do hosts of other garden favorites. It's one of the easiest perennials to mix in the border, since just about everything seems to go with it.

YELLOW CORYDALIS

Corydalis lutea

SOME PERENNIALS ARE ALL-STARS because they blow you away with their bold beauty. That could not be said of yellow corydalis. It's an all-star because everything about it is dainty and refined. Its soft gray-green leaves are like the fronds of maidenhair fern—each compound leaf having three smaller lobes with pretty scalloping on the tips. The plant holds its leaves in softly falling tiers, and grows to no more than 12 inches or so tall.

Yellow corydalis begins blooming in May. The slender, ½- to ¾-inch-long, tubular blossoms vary in color from light yellow to rich gold. These flowers are carried in clusters of five or six, joined together at one end, and hanging downward in pretty little groups, like the fingers of a hand held out for a kiss.

Spotlight on
Yellow Corydalis

USDA Plant Hardiness Zones: 3 to 8

Season of Bloom: May to October

Height × Width: 12 to 15 inches × 12 to 15 inches

Flower Color: Yellow

Light Requirements: Partial shade to full sun

Soil Requirements: Rich, moist, well-drained soil

Place of Origin: Southern part of the Alps eastward

Plant Sources: Busse Gardens, Carroll Gardens, Crownsville Nursery, Forestfarm, Powell's Gardens, Roslyn Nursery, Shady Oaks Nursery, White Flower Farm

Seed Source: Thompson & Morgan

A Corydalis of Another Color

If you like the delicate foliage and tubular flowers of yellow corydalis, take a look at its cousin from China, C. flexuosa. Most often available in the cultivars 'Blue Panda' and 'China Blue', this corydalis bears showy clusters of rich blue, fragrant flowers atop clumps of gray-green foliage. It puts on its best display of blue color in cool, moist, acid soil and partial shade. The hotter the climate, the shorter its blooming season. In the warmest zones, C. flexuosa goes dormant in July after blooming for a couple of months.

Yellow corydalis' small clusters of flowers appear here and there over the whole mound of leaves. Flowering continues through the summer and into fall where conditions are not too hot and not too dry. In sunnier, drier spots, it tends to finish its display in August.

HOW TO GROW YELLOW CORYDALIS

Yellow corydalis will grow in full sun (with adequate moisture) or partial shade. It even grows well in full shade, although it's not as thrifty and vigorous there as it is where it gets morning sun and afternoon shade. It prefers a site that's moist but well-drained, and it tolerates limy soil. Yellow corydalis is rarely bothered by pests or diseases.

The buttery yellow flowers and fernlike, gray-green to blue-green foliage of yellow corydalis add refined beauty to the dappled shade of a woodland garden. Yellow corydalis grows best where afternoon shade follows morning sun and where the soil is rich and moist. In favorable conditions, it self-sows and its seedlings may pop up just about anywhere in and around your garden.

PROPAGATING YELLOW CORYDALIS You can divide clumps of yellow corydalis in spring and replant the divisions 8 to 10 inches apart. But it's more easily propagated from fresh seed sown in spring or fall. In sites it likes, yellow corydalis self-sows reliably.

THE RIGHT SITE FOR YELLOW CORYDALIS
Yellow corydalis belongs in the dappled shade garden with its cousin, fringed bleeding heart (*Dicentra eximia*), surrounded by the cheery spurred flowers of columbines. It likes to reseed itself in cracks between stones, between pavers, and in the chinks in walls where there's enough moisture and soil. And why does it appear in these perfect spots? Because something about its shiny seeds is attractive to ants, which carry them off and hide them in crevices, where they later germinate. Although its tendency to reseed means yellow corydalis may pop up anywhere in your garden, you will always welcome it.

CO-STARS FOR YELLOW CORYDALIS Plant yellow corydalis with ferns, columbines, bleeding hearts, primroses, hostas, astilbes, and lungworts (*Pulmonaria* spp.). Blue-flowered cultivars go nicely with yellow-flowered spring- and summer-blooming perennials.

Like yellow corydalis, Corydalis ochroleuca enjoys the alkaline soil next to a stone wall and looks pretty next to the rich blue blossoms of Dalmatian bellflower.

'BLUE MIRROR' CHINESE DELPHINIUM

Delphinium grandiflorum 'Blue Mirror'

WE'D ALL HAVE THE BEAUTIFUL, tall spires of hybrid delphiniums in our gardens—if they didn't take so darn much work. How wonderful, then, that nature has given us Chinese delphinium, a plant that avoids most of the intensive work of the taller delphiniums but still produces the species' characteristic marvelous blue flowers.

Spotlight on
'Blue Mirror' Chinese Delphinium

USDA Plant Hardiness Zones: 3 to 9

Season of Bloom: June to August

Height × Width: 18 to 24 inches × 18 to 24 inches

Flower Color: Rich blue

Light Requirements: Full sun to partial shade

Soil Requirements: Rich, moist, sandy, well-drained, neutral to slightly alkaline soil

Place of Origin: Eastern Siberia to western China

Plant Source: White Flower Farm

Other Delightful Delphiniums

There are other cultivars of Chinese delphinium to consider for your garden. For flowers in other shades of blue, try 'Azure Fairy' or 'Blue Dwarf'. 'Album' is a white-flowered selection.

Another relatively trouble-free delphinium is the wonderful 'Bellamosum' belladonna delphinium (D. × belladonna 'Bellamosum'), a dark blue-flowered plant that does well in hot-weather areas and is the most reliably perennial type. It grows to about 4 feet tall.

If you must have flower spikes, the delphiniums in the Connecticut Yankee series are more compact than most. If you insist on having the big tall ones, choose one of the Pacific Hybrid delphiniums. 'Summer Skies' is a lovely light blue.

Our all-star selection, 'Blue Mirror', grows 18 to 24 inches tall and never needs staking. It's less prone to diseases than its taller cousins. And 'Blue Mirror' Chinese delphinium performs reliably in the South.

While this delphinium tends to be short lived, it's long-blooming. Its spurless, open flowers appear at the ends of branched stems in late June, blooming above finely divided, threadlike leaves. If you remove the spent flowers, 'Blue Mirror' will continue blooming into August, or even to September.

HOW TO GROW 'BLUE MIRROR' Plant 'Blue Mirror' in a site with good air circulation where it will get some shade during the hottest part of the day, especially in the South. An eastern exposure is perfect in all regions that have hot, muggy summers. Amend acidic soil with ground limestone. Add a handful of phosphate rock at planting time to help keep

'Blue Mirror' Chinese delphinium delivers rich blue flowers for most of the summer. Its compact flowerstalks remain upright without staking.

'Blue Mirror' blooming all summer. And don't skimp on the fertilizer—bloodmeal, alfalfa meal, and rich compost are all appreciated by greedy delphiniums.

Pests are few, but slugs find delphiniums especially tasty. Plant your delphiniums in a slug-free zone and circle it with a strip of copper edging or a band of diatomaceous earth. Or arm yourself with a flashlight and handpick slugs as they feed after dark.

PROPAGATING CHINESE DELPHINIUM

Because Chinese delphinium is a short-lived perennial, propagate it by taking stem cuttings from the emerging shoots in early spring every year. Root the cuttings in moist sand in a partially shady site.

THE RIGHT SITE FOR 'BLUE MIRROR'

Plant 'Blue Mirror' where you can enjoy its flowers every time you go into your garden. Because it likes limy soil, 'Blue Mirror' works well in foundation plantings, and its flower spikes stand out against the background provided by a wall, buildings, or shrubs.

CO-STARS FOR 'BLUE MIRROR'

'Blue Mirror' looks good growing amid the bold foliage of blue-green hostas such as 'Krossa Regal' (see page 176), or with the bronzy purple leaves of 'Palace Purple' heuchera (see page 170). Bright red flowers such as Maltese cross (see page 212) and cardinal flower (see page 210) make good companions, too. Mix 'Blue Mirror' with the soft lilac flowers of Yunnan meadow rue (*Thalictrum delavayi*). Or let it shine as the only floral star among silver to gray-green foliage plants like rue (*Ruta graveolens*) or artemisias.

Start seeds or root cuttings every year or so to keep Chinese delphiniums blooming in your garden.

'TINY RUBIES' CHEDDAR PINKS

Dianthus gratianopolitanus
'Tiny Rubies'

THERE ARE MANY WONDERFUL *DIANTHUS* SPECIES and cultivars, but not one of them has charmed me more, been easier to grow, been more reliable, or taken less work than 'Tiny Rubies' cheddar pinks. This plant has qualities that make it a worthy all-star.

Particularly Pretty Pinks

The American Dianthus Society recommends the hybrid Ideal Series pinks (<u>Dianthus</u> Ideal Series). Growing to about 10 inches tall and available in six flower colors—carmine, rose, crimson, violet, deep violet, and cherry with a white edge—Ideal Series pinks are short-lived perennials that are almost always grown as annuals. These All-America Selection winners grow well in zones 2 to 11, and bear a continuous summer crop of clusters of single, 1½-inch flowers with toothed petals.

'Bath's Pink' (<u>D. gratianopolitanus</u> 'Bath's Pink') is another widely known and well-loved selection of cheddar pinks. This rugged beauty tolerates heat, humidity, and drought. At 10 inches tall, 'Bath's Pink' is a bit larger than 'Tiny Rubies', but it performs similarly in the garden, spreading out a handsome carpet of blue-green foliage, and covering itself in fragrant, fringed, single pink flowers from late spring well into summer.

Spotlight on 'Tiny Rubies' Cheddar Pinks

USDA Plant Hardiness Zones: 3 to 9

Season of Bloom: May to July

Height × Width: 4 inches × 18 to 24 inches

Flower Color: Bright rose pink

Light Requirements: Full sun

Soil Requirements: Sandy, well-drained, slightly alkaline soil

Place of Origin: Cheddar Gorge in England, and on the European continent eastward to Poland

Plant Sources: Kurt Bluemel, Bluestone Perennials, Carroll Gardens, Forestfarm, Garden Place, J. W. Jung Seed, Klehm Nursery, Powell's Gardens, André Viette Farm & Nursery, Weiss Brothers Perennial Nursery

In the spring, 'Tiny Rubies' freshens up its 4-inch tall, mounded mat of pretty, grasslike, gray-green foliage. At this stage it looks a lot like sea-pink (*Armeria maritima*), although it's not as coarse. I love its tidy, neat appearance, and the anticipation of the flowers to come.

In May, flowerstalks elongate 1 inch or so above the mound of grassy foliage, giving it a shaggy appearance. Then the tips of these stalks swell and open into ½-inch-wide, double, deep rose pink blossoms that have a clovelike fragrance. The rich color of the flowers really stands out against the gray-green leaves, and the plant blooms heavily.

HOW TO GROW 'TINY RUBIES' Grow 'Tiny Rubies' in well-drained soil in a sunny location. It tolerates partial shade but doesn't grow well in wet, heavy soil. Since cheddar pinks grow naturally on limestone outcroppings, 'Tiny Rubies' will appreciate having some ground limestone added to the soil where you plant it.

In the Southeast, where many lesser plants fade in the heat of the summer, 'Tiny Rubies' is nearly indestructible. It usually starts blooming in March and finishes up in May. But its toughness in southern heat doesn't mean that 'Tiny Rubies' can't take the cold—this all-star gladly grows in gardens as far north as Zone 3.

PROPAGATING 'TINY RUBIES' In summer, after 'Tiny Rubies' finishes blooming, carefully lift the mat of tiny gray-green leaves and pull or cut the outer stems into many small stems with a bit of root attached. Replant these divisions about 8 inches apart. You also can divide the mat into larger sections in the spring. And most cheddar pinks are easy to grow from seed.

THE RIGHT SITE FOR 'TINY RUBIES' Plant 'Tiny Rubies' at the front edge of your border, where its fine textured foliage creates a nice contrast with bolder perennials and where you can enjoy its delightful pink flowers. It's also at home in the rock garden, where it will spill prettily over the stones, and it's just right for brightening up spaces between pavers at the edge of a path.

Whether they're pinks, carnations, or sweet Williams, fragrant *Dianthus* flowers come in an array of colors and sizes to brighten any garden.

'Tiny Rubies' cheddar pinks make up for their petite size by producing lots of rosy pink flowers. These plants thrive in sun and well-drained soil.

CO-STARS FOR 'TINY RUBIES' The bright rose pink flowers of 'Tiny Rubies' look good next to the blue to lavender flowers of perennials such as wild blue phlox (*Phlox divaricata*), bearded iris, balloon flower (see page 252), and Narbonne flax (*Linum narbonense*). Use coral bells (*Heuchera sanguinea*) to echo 'Tiny Rubies' pink flowers while providing round leaves that contrast with its fine-textured foliage. In the rock garden, 'Tiny Rubies' mixes well with the thick, blue-green leaves of sedums and sempervivums, interrupting the sameness of their rounded, fleshy foliage with its grassy leaves and bright flowers.

A Stellar Idea

No matter where you garden, you can keep 'Tiny Rubies' blooming through most of the summer if you remove the faded flowers before they produce seeds. If you don't care to fuss over it that much, 'Tiny Rubies' will still bloom for a good six to eight weeks in most areas. The spent flowerstalks pull away easily from the mat of foliage when flowering is finished.

COMMON BLEEDING HEART

Dicentra spectabilis

EVERY GARDEN SHOULD HAVE A SPOT for this old-fashioned favorite. Its flowers are so charming and pretty that once you've seen them, you'll find it hard to leave common bleeding heart out of your garden.

Common bleeding heart's graceful, long, flowering stems arch in delicate curves above the ground. From these stems, heart-shaped, deep pink buds dangle like charms that open to reveal a drop of white at the tip.

Other Beautiful Bleeding Hearts (and Buddies)

The hybrid bleeding heart 'Luxuriant' (D. 'Luxuriant') has almost as much claim to all-star status as common bleeding heart—although it's not quite as graceful and beautiful in bloom. 'Luxuriant' produces arching, 15-inch sprays of reddish pink, heart-shaped flowers over a very long season: from June until October. Its pretty foliage is deeply divided, soft, blue-green, and more finely textured than that of common bleeding heart.

Dutchman's breeches (D. cucullaria) is a dainty wildflower that's not uncommon in the mid-Atlantic states. In spring it appears in eastern woodlands bearing fernlike foliage and strings of white flowers that look like pantaloons—the Dutchman's breeches—hanging from a clothesline. This plant goes dormant shortly after it flowers.

USDA Plant Hardiness Zones: 3 to 9

Season of Bloom: May to June

Height × Width: 24 to 30 inches × 24 to 30 inches

Flower Color: Rose red and white

Light Requirements: Partial shade to full shade

Soil Requirements: Rich, moist, humusy, well-drained soil.

Place of Origin: Siberia, Japan

Plant Sources: Ambergate Gardens, Kurt Bluemel, Bluestone Perennials, Busse Gardens, Carroll Gardens, Dutch Gardens, Garden Place, J. W. Jung Seed, Milaeger's Gardens, Powell's Gardens, Shady Oaks Nursery, Spring Hill Nurseries, Van Bourgondien, André Viette Farm & Nursery, White Flower Farm

Seed Source: Thompson & Morgan

The foliage is attractive, too—deeply divided, compound leaflets in a soft green to blue-green shade that sets off the pink-and-white flowers perfectly.

HOW TO GROW COMMON BLEEDING HEART Common bleeding heart likes the moist, woodsy soil of a shady garden, although it will grow in full sun where summers are cool and the soil's consistently moist. If you're planting more than one, place them 24 inches apart. When summer heats up or when the soil dries out, common bleeding heart goes dormant until the following spring.

Diseases and insects don't bother common

Common bleeding heart puts on a fine display in a lightly shaded woodland garden, where it makes a great focal point all by itself. Its arching stems of dangling deep pink-and-white hearts and its pretty green to blue-green divided foliage stand out beautifully against a dark background of evergreen trees or shrubs.

bleeding heart unless it's planted in heavy, wet clay soil, where it may rot. South of Zone 6 it tends to be short-lived but makes up for this by self-seeding readily.

PROPAGATING COMMON BLEEDING HEART

Divide common bleeding heart's thick brittle roots with care when the plant is dormant, making sure each division has a root and an "eye" a bud or growth point. You can take cuttings from around the base of the plant in spring or from the fleshy root in late fall or early winter. Hold root cuttings in a bed of compost in a cold frame over winter. Common bleeding heart is also easy to grow from seed.

THE RIGHT SITE FOR COMMON BLEEDING

HEART Use this showy plant in a lightly shaded site where its nicely divided foliage remains beautiful for most of the summer. If dry soil or high temperatures promote dormancy by midsummer, plant common bleeding heart with hostas, ferns, cranesbills (*Geranium* spp.), and other perennials that will hide its empty place in the garden.

CO-STARS FOR COMMON BLEEDING

HEART Common bleeding heart looks pretty growing with a white-flowered cultivar such as 'Alba' (*D. spectabilis* 'Alba'). Surround it with the attractive groundcovering foliage of

When common bleeding heart's flowers are fully open, their inner white petals stick out just a bit from between the outer pink petals at the tip of the heart.

spotted dead nettle (*Lamium maculatum*) or European wild ginger (see page 54), or with hostas, variegated Solomon's seal (see page 256), and ferns. Astilbe (*Astilbe × arendsii*) makes a great companion that enjoys similar growing conditions, as does 'Mrs. Moon' Bethlehem sage (see page 264) with her pink-to-blue flowers and silver-spotted leaves. The clear blue spring flowers of creeping Jacob's ladder (*Polemonium reptans*) and forget-me-nots (*Myosotis* spp.) make an all-time great combination with common bleeding heart's rose-and-white blossoms.

PURPLE GAS PLANT

Dictamnus albus 'Purpureus'

Spotlight on
Purple Gas Plant

USDA Plant Hardiness Zones: 3 to 9

Season of Bloom: May to June

Height × Width: 24 to 36 inches × 24 inches

Flower Color: Mauve-purple

Light Requirements: Full sun

Soil Requirements: Rich, moist, humusy soil

Place of Origin: Europe east to Turkey and the Caucasus Mountains

Plant Sources: Carroll Gardens, Milaeger's Gardens, André Viette Farm & Nursery

Seed Source: Thompson & Morgan

I'VE READ MORE NONSENSE about gas plant than any other perennial, mostly because writers focus on how the plant's volatile oils may be lighted with a match:

Caution: Flammable! "Makes an explosive crack," says one. "The plant's leaves may be set aflame," says another. "Roots and stems exude a flammable gas," says yet another. It's enough to make you wonder if it's safe to grow this pretty all-star in your garden.

To satisfy my own curiousity, I actually took a lighter to the gas plant in my garden, and here's the real scoop: The plant's mauve-purple–veined flowers have a small chamber behind the petal lips in which a lemony smelling volatile oil is produced. On warm days, this flammable oil vaporizes in the chamber, and a flame touched to the flower's lip will produce a small *phffft* of flame. Hence its common name.

But gas plant's odd ability to produce a

When You Want White Flowers

If you prefer white flowers to the purple-veined mauve blossoms of purple gas plant, try either the species (D. albus) or the cultivar 'Albiflorus' (D. albus 'Albiflorus') in your garden. Both of these plants offer the many fine features that make purple gas plant an all-star and are standouts for beauty and long-lasting toughness.

flame is just a novelty. I chose purple gas plant as a perennial all-star because of its sturdiness, hardiness, and trouble-free habits—and because of its exquisite and subtle beauty. Purple gas plant is an upright perennial that grows 30 to 48 inches tall on stems that are so tough they're almost woody. It bears mauve flowers with darker veins on stiff spikes above its dark green leaves.

Its bloom season isn't long—about four weeks—but purple gas plant's flowers are especially welcome because they arrive in early to mid May, before most other perennials get going. The flowers have an airy, graceful look that's enhanced by the cluster of long stamens that extends from the center of each blossom. Attractive seedpods follow the flowers, and purple gas plant's durable foliage looks good all season long. And purple gas plant is long lived. With very little care from you, it will bloom reliably in late spring and early summer for many years to come.

While reports of their flammability are somewhat exaggerated, purple gas plant's pretty, dark-veined mauve flowers can sure warm a gardener's heart.

HOW TO GROW PURPLE GAS PLANT Gas plants are among the longest-lived perennials, especially in the colder parts of their range. Although purple gas plant takes a while to grow to flowering size—three years from seed, and a year to two from purchased plants—once established it's as reliable as any plant in the garden. Site it in a sunny, well-drained spot and leave it there, as its deep roots dislike disturbance. Space plants about 3 feet apart.

PROPAGATING PURPLE GAS PLANT This plant resents being disturbed, but with care you can divide the roots in spring—although you'll notice that it's slow to recover. Purple gas plant comes easily from seed, but it takes three years in the garden before it flowers. Probably the easiest way to get more plants is to buy them from a nursery.

In late spring and early summer, purple gas plant produces a profusion of mauve-to-purple flowers that look great next to the white flowers of the species.

THE RIGHT SITE FOR PURPLE GAS PLANT Purple gas plant is an old-fashioned perennial that looks right at home in cottage gardens and other traditional plantings. But it's equally valuable in the sunny border, where its dramatic spikes enliven the scene before most plants are flowering. It also makes an unusual, fragrant cut flower.

CO-STARS FOR PURPLE GAS PLANT Purple gas plant's mauve-purple color scheme looks nice next to the darker purples of Siberian iris (*Iris sibirica*). It also mixes well with the blue to violet-blues of milky bellflower (*Campanula lactiflora*), peach-leaved bellflower (*Campanula persicifolia*), and scabious (*Scabiosa* spp.), or with the pinks and reds of bee balm (*Monarda didyma*). Daylilies are good companions as well, and it fits in nicely in a planting with roses and flowering shrubs where its roots are less likely to be disturbed by digging than in a perennial border.

YELLOW FOXGLOVE

Digitalis grandiflora

THINK OF A PLEASING ENGLISH COTTAGE GARDEN scene, and you can almost see the charming spikes of foxgloves. Unfortunately, those classic-looking common foxgloves (*D. purpurea*) are biennials that tend to disappear after they flower in their second year.

But not our all-star, yellow foxglove, a true perennial with all of common foxglove's old-fashioned charm and none of its make-work habits. This easy grower asks little of the gardener in exchange for its spikes of creamy, drooping-bell–shaped flowers. In the spring, yellow foxglove produces clumps of large, medium green, toothed leaves. From this clump of foliage, flowering stems elongate in late May or early June to form spikes

A Few Other Fetching Foxgloves

In addition to yellow foxglove, there are a few other more-or-less-perennial foxgloves. The best among them is probably strawberry foxglove (D. × mertonensis), a hybrid plant that comes true from seed and self-sows freely. It's a perennial (that may decide to be biennial) that grows 3 to 4 feet tall, with coppery rose blossoms and attractive foliage. Rusty foxglove (D. ferruginea) is biennial or perennial with long, yellowish flowers that are veined or netted with rusty red and are densely packed on spikes to 6 feet tall.

Spotlight on Yellow Foxglove

USDA Plant Hardiness Zones: 4 to 9

Season of Bloom: June and July

Height × Width: 24 to 36 inches × 24 to 30 inches

Flower Color: Creamy yellowish white with brown markings

Light Requirements: Full sun to partial shade

Soil Requirements: Any moist, well-drained, fertile soil

Place of Origin: Europe to North Africa and east to Central Asia

Plant Sources: Kurt Bluemel, Bluestone Perennials, Carroll Gardens, J. W. Jung Seed, Park Seed, Roslyn Nursery, Sunlight Gardens, Wayside Gardens, We-Du Nurseries

Seed Source: Thompson & Morgan

reaching to 3 feet. The flowers on these first spikes persist well into July.

The blooms appear along the length of the spikes, each one a long tube or bell with a defined lip, like a large gloxinia blossom. They open from the bottom of the spike first, hanging downward and outward at a slight angle. The flowers are a light creamy yellow and their insides are freckled with brown.

HOW TO GROW YELLOW FOXGLOVE Of all the tall, spiky, vertical-accent plants in the perennial garden, yellow foxglove and other perennial and biennial foxgloves are the easiest to grow and care for. Just plant yellow foxglove in any good, slightly acid garden soil

Yellow foxglove's creamy bell-shaped flowers bloom in summer on 3-foot spikes that stand tall without staking.

Excelsior hybrid foxgloves bloom in an array of colors. Sow seeds of these biennials or short-lived perennials outdoors in late summer to keep their showy flower spikes in your garden.

and let it grow. While it performs best in moist, humusy soil in full sun to partial shade, yellow foxglove is fairly durable. I've transplanted it into my garden in hot, dry weather, and while other transplants need pampering, this perennial quickly makes itself at home and gets growing. And other than slugs, pests and diseases don't bother it.

PROPAGATING YELLOW FOXGLOVE Yellow foxglove is a clump-former that's easy to divide in the spring. Separate new rosettes of leaves from the clump and replant them about 24 inches apart. Yellow foxglove grows easily from seed and will self-sow if you leave the stalks of faded flowers on the plants.

THE RIGHT SITE FOR YELLOW FOXGLOVE Because it tolerates some shade, yellow foxglove is perfect for adding a vertical accent in a woodland garden, and its pale flowers show up well in the lower light. It makes a fine display massed in groups of five to seven plants. Plant them in a featured spot by themselves or in the back of the border where they can rise up behind lower-growing perennials. Each plant will have several flowering spikes.

CO-STARS FOR YELLOW FOXGLOVE In a sunny spot, contrast yellow foxglove's subtle flowers with the bright blossoms of oriental poppy (*Papaver orientale*), or echo its upright habit and tubular flowers with peach-leaved bellflower (*Campanula persicifolia*). In partial shade, columbine meadow rue (*Thalictrum aquilegifolium*) makes a pretty companion for yellow foxglove, and fine-textured ferns provide a nice contrast to its large leaves.

A Stellar Idea

When yellow foxglove's creamy flowers are near the end of their bloom and have only a few fresh ones still hanging on at the top of the spike, cut off the flowering spike just above the basal clump of leaves. It takes no time at all to do this, but the results are worth it. Yellow foxglove will respond by sending up several fresh flower spikes—slightly smaller than the first ones— that will bloom on into September.

'CRIMSON STAR' PURPLE CONEFLOWER

Echinacea purpurea 'Crimson Star'

Spotlight on
'Crimson Star'
Purple
Coneflower

USDA Plant Hardiness Zones: 3 to 9

Season of Bloom: Late June to September

Height × Width: 24 to 36 inches × 24 to 36 inches

Flower Color: Rich pink

Light Requirements: Full sun to partial shade

Soil Requirements: Average, moist, well-drained garden soil

Place of Origin: Prairies and eastern woodlands of the United States

Plant Source: André Viette Farm & Nursery

BACK WHEN HERDS OF BISON ROAMED the prairies of North America, wild purple coneflowers bloomed amid the native grasses and other prairie plants. Enhanced by breeding and selection, purple coneflower's pretty lavender-pink daisies now stand proudly in perennial gardens across the country. Although 'Crimson Star' purple coneflower is a relatively new selection of this outstanding perennial, it is undoubtedly the best all-around purple coneflower ever.

Purple coneflower's showy daisy blossoms—soft rosy purple ray petals surrounding a prominent, golden brown center—have earned it the title, "King of the Daisies." But where purple coneflower's color is subtle, 'Crimson Star' is bold—a rich, brilliant crimson pink touched with carmine on the petals, circling a large, dark crimson center. And while the petals of the species droop back toward the stem, so that each flower resembles a large shuttlecock, 'Crimson Star' holds its petals straight out in true daisy fashion. Some purple coneflower cultivars will bleach out in full sun, but not 'Crimson Star'.

HOW TO GROW PURPLE CONEFLOWER

Long life and reliability are among purple coneflower's many good traits. This plant is hardy to Zone 3, so it won't freeze out, yet it's equally able to endure summer heat. Purple coneflower grows best in full sun in average soil, but it won't disappoint you in more difficult conditions. Its taproot lets it withstand periods of drought, and it blooms well—but produces fewer flowers—in a lightly shaded site. And it's easy to care for—pests and diseases don't bother purple coneflower.

Other Pleasing Purple Coneflowers

'Bright Star' purple coneflower (E. purpurea 'Bright Star') is an old standby that's similar to 'Crimson Star' but not quite as showy in flower. 'Magnus' (E. purpurea 'Magnus') is a large-flowered cultivar that carries its petals straight out from the center. If you like purple coneflower in a shade other than purple, try the white-flowered cultivar 'White Swan' (E. purpurea 'White Swan').

Create a display of purple coneflower with drifts of plants spaced 18 to 24 inches apart. Purple coneflower grows gradually to form large clumps that are not particularly in need of regular division. In fact, purple coneflower seems to prefer being left alone, as flowering tends to diminish after it's divided.

PROPAGATING 'CRIMSON STAR' Although it grows into broad clumps, purple coneflower is better left undivided. Take root cuttings in the fall to propagate 'Crimson Star' and other cultivars. If you leave the central cones in the garden, your plants will self-sow, but the resulting seedlings may or may not match the flower color, size, or shape of the parent plants. Purple coneflower is easy to grow from seed sown outdoors in the fall.

THE RIGHT SITE FOR 'CRIMSON STAR'

A planting of this all-star gives you flowers from mid to late June right through Sep-

'Crimson Star' purple coneflower blooms all summer long. Even in full, hot sun, its perky daisies keep their rich pink color.

Add life to your garden with purple coneflower! Butterflies visit it during the summer, and its seeds attract goldfinches during the winter months.

tember in most parts of the country. That's prime perennial time from first to last, and 'Crimson Star' is one of the best perennials to anchor the back of the border with color that associates well with everything from pale yellows to blues to reds. Just don't try to pair it up with anything orange, like crocosmias (*Crocosmia* spp.).

'Crimson Star' is perfect for a cutting garden, too—its flowers will last and last in a vase. Even when they fade and drop their outer rays, the dark centers remain showy and make a great addition to dried arrangements.

CO-STARS FOR 'CRIMSON STAR' Mix 'Crimson Star' with 'Moonshine' yarrow (see page 28) to cool down this purple coneflower's rich pink petals. Or heat things up in your garden with 'Crimson Star' and the pink and crimson flowers of 'Bright Eyes' summer phlox (*Phlox paniculata* 'Bright Eyes'). 'White Swan' purple coneflower gives a touch of elegance to a planting of 'Crimson Star', while the light pink flowers of prairie mallows (*Sidalcea* spp.) contrast nicely with its deeper colors.

'TAPLOW BLUE' GLOBE THISTLE

Echinops ritro 'Taplow Blue'

DESPITE ITS COMMON NAME and its prickly appearance, globe thistle isn't a thistle. It is, however, a perennial all-star that's one of the finest low-maintenance plants in anyone's garden. And 'Taplow Blue' is my choice for the finest selection.

Some plantspeople say it's a selection of *Echinops ritro*, while other sources tie it to *E. bannaticus*, *E. exaltatus*, or even *E. humilis*. I say it doesn't matter unless you're a botanist. What matters is how easy 'Taplow Blue' is to grow and how great it looks in your garden.

Almost everything about this plant is unique and appealing. Its foliage consists of deeply cut, 9-inch lances with lobes that end in thistly looking spines. But these turn out to be all show, for they don't prick you at all. Underneath, the leaves are downy and whitish. They resemble the large bear's-breech (*Acanthus mollis*) leaves that so many would love to grow for foliage contrast but can't because of bear's-breech's frost tenderness. Among all of the round or oval leaves in the garden, globe thistle's foliage provides a welcome, jagged contrast.

Another Great Globe Thistle

For spiky flower balls in a slightly different shade, try 'Veitch's Blue' (E. ritro 'Veitch's Blue'). This cultivar is similar to 'Taplow Blue' but has darker blue flowers.

Spotlight on 'Taplow Blue' Globe Thistle

USDA Plant Hardiness Zones: 4 to 9

Season of Bloom: Late June to September

Height × Width: 48 to 60 inches × 24 to 36 inches

Flower Color: Powdery steel blue

Light Requirements: Full sun

Soil Requirements: Average, well-drained soil

Place of Origin: Spain and southern France eastward to central Asia

Plant Sources: Kurt Bluemel, Busse Gardens, Carroll Gardens, Powell's Gardens, André Viette Farm & Nursery, White Flower Farm

'Taplow Blue' is a large globe thistle, with 2- to 3-inch flower balls at the ends of gracefully curving, branched stems. These flower balls are wonders of nature: Perfectly round, with densely packed, tubular florets that end in sharp-looking points and in a beautiful shade of powdery steel blue.

These unusual flowers begin their show in mid-June in the South, late June in the mid-Atlantic states, and very late June or early July in the Midwest and New England. In California and the Pacific Northwest, they usually bloom in June. Once flowering starts, 'Taplow Blue' blooms for a couple of months.

HOW TO GROW GLOBE THISTLE Once you've planted globe thistle in your garden, you can pretty much forget about it—except to marvel at its nifty round flowerheads. Give it a site in full sun and average garden soil. Established plants are drought tolerant, and they don't need fertilizing either—too much nutrition forces them to bolt (produce seeds) and reduces the blooming season. Pests and diseases are not a problem, and as long as the soil's not too soggy, globe thistle will return reliably every year to add its unusual and attractive flowers to your garden.

PROPAGATING GLOBE THISTLE This plant will grow quite happily in your garden without division. If you leave the seedheads on globe thistle, self-sown seedlings are likely, but not in such numbers as to become invasive. If you want to increase 'Taplow Blue' or other cultivars, separate rosettes of new growth from the base of mature plants in the spring. Replant these divisions 24 inches apart.

THE RIGHT SITE FOR 'TAPLOW BLUE' 'Taplow Blue' globe thistle's powdery steel blue flower color works almost anywhere in the perennial garden but looks especially showy when balanced by a brilliant display of golden flowers, such as goldenrods (*Solidago* spp.). For all its unusual beauty, 'Taplow Blue' is not at its best as a specimen plant—grow it in a big drift where its long stems can flop and toss about and make a spiky splash of blue.

In addition to their uniqueness in the garden, globe thistles make excellent cut flowers and if cut just as they reach full color, they'll last for

Enjoy globe thistle's spiky round flowerheads in your garden or cut them for fresh or dried arrangements.

Use a prickly patch of drought-tolerant 'Taplow Blue' globe thistle to interrupt the sea of rounded leaves in a sunny perennial garden.

months and months when dried. If you let them get too mature, the flower balls will shatter when dry.

CO-STARS FOR 'TAPLOW BLUE' 'Taplow Blue' globe thistle keeps good company with many garden favorites. Try it with summer phlox (*Phlox paniculata*), goldenrods (*Solidago* spp.), daylilies, ornamental grasses, or pink climbing roses. It's useful for backing up early spring-bloomers, whose fading foliage can be covered by globe thistle's toppling stems. Combine 'Taplow Blue' with rose campion (*Lychnis coronaria*) for a startling mix of striking colors.

RED BARRENWORT

Epimedium × rubrum

RED BARRENWORT IS ONE OF THE MOST beautiful groundcovers available for foliage. It gets my nod as an all-star without any hesitation.

Here's a small plant—just 6 to 12 inches tall—that's as happy in the shade under trees as ivy, without ivy's tendency to conquer every scrap of ground. Red barrenwort is not invasive at all and is always well-behaved. In April or May and into June, red barrenwort opens loose clusters of many single, dainty flowers that dangle above the foliage on wiry stems. These flowers, though small, are very beautiful. Four white petals, each wrapped in a rich crimson sepal, form a cross around a

Spotlight on Red Barrenwort

USDA Plant Hardiness Zones: 4 to 9

Season of Bloom: May to June

Height × Width: 6 to 12 inches × 18 to 24+ inches

Flower Color: Crimson and white

Light Requirements: Partial shade to full shade

Soil Requirements: Rich, moist, humusy, deep, well-drained soil

Place of Origin: Hybrid between E. alpinum and E. grandiflorum

Plant Sources: Ambergate Gardens, Kurt Bluemel, Busse Gardens, Carroll Gardens, Garden Place, Greer Gardens, Shady Oaks Nursery, We-Du Nurseries

Enchanting Epimediums and Beautiful Barrenworts

Among the epimediums are several gardenworthy plants that will delight you with their unusual flowers and their long-lasting, attractive foliage. Long-spurred epimedium (E. grandiflorum) grows larger than red barrenwort and has rounded foliage and showy, spurred flowers. The cultivar 'Rose Queen' bears rosy pink flowers; 'White Queen' blooms in white. 'Sulphureum' Persian epimedium (E. × versicolor 'Sulphureum') is a widely offered selection with reddish foliage and yellow flowers. 'Roseum' Young's barrenwort (E. × youngianum 'Roseum') is a smaller plant that has long, narrow leaves and lilac flowers.

central cluster of yellow stamens.

When it opens in the spring, red barrenwort's heart-shaped foliage is a soft, slightly glossy shade of green, touched with pink. In summer the leaves turn darker green and lose their pink tint but remain fresh looking and pretty. Fall frosts turn the foliage rich bronzy red to end the year with a colorful display.

HOW TO GROW RED BARRENWORT Don't be dismayed if your red barrenwort doesn't gobble up the ground in its first season of growth. This well-mannered flowering groundcover takes a while to get going, and needs adequate moisture during that first growing season to get its roots established. But once it gets going, red barrenwort begins a slow, steady spread.

Although its looks are dainty, red barrenwort is a tough plant. Give red barrenwort

Even in dry shade, red barrenwort spreads to form a groundcover of charming spring flowers and showy, long-lasting foliage.

Red barrenwort's new leaves rival the beauty of its flowers. Bearing a pretty mixture of rosy red and green, they cascade over the plant on thin, wiry stems.

what it likes, and it's reliably yours just about forever. What it likes is cool, shady woodland conditions with a rich, humusy, well-drained soil that's evenly moist.

PROPAGATING RED BARRENWORT Red barrenwort's creeping nature makes it easy to divide in spring or fall. Use a sharp shovel or pruning shears to divide the wiry roots— they're tough and a dull tool may squash or damage the plants. Sow seed in the shade garden in fall.

THE RIGHT SITE FOR RED BARRENWORT Red barrenwort is right up there with wild ginger among the elite groundcovers for shade. Use red barrenwort in difficult areas under trees where root competition makes life difficult for other plants. Plant it in big swaths near walkways where you can enjoy its delicate beauty up close.

CO-STARS FOR RED BARRENWORT Red barrenwort makes a fine woodland groundcover. Plant it with rhododendrons, azaleas (*Rhododendron* spp.), and camellias. It's a great groundcover to grow with such garden treasures as nursery-propagated trilliums (*Trillium* spp.), lady's slipper orchids (*Cypripedium* spp.), and trout lilies (*Erythronium* spp.), where its patient growth habits keep it from overtaking its companions. In a moist, shady garden, mix red barrenwort's heart-shaped leaves with the foliage of ferns, hostas, and wild gingers (*Asarum* spp.), and the delicate flower chains of bleeding hearts (*Dicentra* spp.).

A Stellar Idea

In the milder parts of its range, red barrenwort's foliage is evergreen and remains attractive through much of the winter. In late winter to early spring, it's a good idea to cut off the old winter-beaten leaves so that only the colorful new foliage is visible.

'PINK JEWEL' DAISY FLEABANE

Erigeron speciosus 'Pink Jewel'

THE PRETTINESS OF THE FLEABANES commonly sold in nurseries and catalogs belies their toughness and adaptability. They are truly garden workhorses, blooming from June right through the hot summer into

Other Fantastic Fleabanes

In addition to 'Pink Jewel', a few other cultivars of *E. speciosus* stand out for their attractive, long-blooming flowers and durable nature. 'Prosperity' is a popular selection that has lilac-mauve flowers, while 'Sommerneuschnee' covers itself with white blossoms. 'Foerster's Liebling' (a.k.a. 'Foerster's Darling') has pink, almost double flowers.

Gardeners in the warmer zones can take advantage of bonytip fleabane (*E. karvinskianus*, sometimes sold as *E. mucronatus*). From May to frost, this fine-leaved, wiry stemmed plant makes bushy mounds covered with hundreds of little white daisies that gradually turn pinkish mauve. It's always in flower, fills in beautifully anywhere, clashes with nothing, and withstands heat and drought. If it grew in zones colder than Zone 8, it would be my all-star fleabane. The only problem with bonytip fleabane is that if it likes your property, it can self-sow its way to weediness. But if it does start to take over, it's not difficult to simply pull it out.

Spotlight on 'Pink Jewel' Daisy Fleabane

USDA Plant Hardiness Zones: 4 to 9

Season of Bloom: June to September

Height × Width: 18 to 24 inches × 12 to 24 inches

Flower Color: Bright pink with yellow centers

Light Requirements: Full sun

Soil Requirements: Light, sandy, well-drained soil

Place of Origin: Western North America

Plant Sources: Bluestone Perennials, Forestfarm, Weiss Brothers Perennial Nursery

September. Their durability reflects their origins in western North America from the Pacific Northwest down to Mexico, where summers are hot and can be very dry. These trouble-free natives are not used enough in American gardens, and I hope having a recognized all-star among them will help change that.

The daisylike flowers of the daisy fleabane hybrids and cultivars cover a wide range of colors, from pale blue to lilac, mauve, violet, red, and pink. The bushy, compact plants resemble asters.

For our all-star, I've chosen 'Pink Jewel' daisy fleabane. The flowers reach 2 to 2½ inches across, with prominent centers that change from green to yellow as the anthers (pollen-bearing structures) open. A profusion of slender ray petals, resembling finely cut fringe, surrounds the centers. The petal color is a bright, striking pink with a hint of blue in the hue.

Even when the weather's hot and dry, 'Pink Jewel' is a garden gem that produces lots of bright pink daisies all summer long.

HOW TO GROW 'PINK JEWEL' Plant 'Pink Jewel' daisy fleabane in any well-drained garden soil, then relax—this plant can take heat and dry spells without blinking. It's tough enough for full, hot sun but also tolerates light shade. It's pest- and disease-free, too. All this qualifies 'Pink Jewel' as a true low-maintenance plant, with one caveat: Every couple of years, dig the clumps out in the fall, cut off the spent foliage and flower-stalks, and replant the divisions. This will keep 'Pink Jewel' at its peak of flower production and looking daisy fresh.

PROPAGATING DAISY FLEABANE Daisy fleabane is easy to divide in spring or fall, and it benefits from division every two to three years. Replant divisions 12 inches apart. You can also separate new growth from the base of the plant in the spring when it starts growing. Sow seed outdoors in the fall. Mild-climate species like bonytip fleabane (*E. karvinskianus*) readily self-sow.

Daisy fleabanes resemble asters, but they start blooming much earlier. They may still be putting on a show when the fall asters begin to bloom.

THE RIGHT SITE FOR 'PINK JEWEL' 'Pink Jewel' daisy fleabane is a first class border plant. It looks good in front of stone walls, and has a definite place in the sunny perennial garden. The plants hold their flowers atop long stalks that lend themselves to cutting for arrangements in the house.

CO-STARS FOR 'PINK JEWEL' Plant fine-textured 'Pink Jewel' with plants that have dramatic foliage like bearded iris and hydrangeas or with dark evergreens. Its masses of pink daisies look good with a wide variety of flower and foliage colors. Try it with perennials as diverse as horned violet (*Viola cornuta*), snow-in-summer (*Cerastium tomentosum*), basket-of-gold (*Aurinia saxatilis*), cranesbills (*Geranium* spp.), gayfeathers (*Liatris* spp.), and alumroots (*Heuchera* spp.) and with small-leaved groundcovers like thyme and pearlwort (*Sagina* spp.).

ZABEL ERYNGO

Eryngium × *zabelii*

FOR A STARTLINGLY GORGEOUS ACCENT PLANT, it's hard to beat our prickly all-star, Zabel eryngo. I chose this hybrid because, of all the sea hollies I've seen or grown, this is the most beautiful and gardenworthy. Zabel eryngo's foliage is prickly and thistlelike, reaching to about 24 inches, but it's not coarse and large like amethyst sea holly (*E. amethystinum*), or overly rangy like *E.* × *tripartitum*. It's even better looking than its parents, alpine sea holly (*E. alpinum*) and Mediterranean sea holly (*E. bourgatii*)—species that may be easier to find but don't quite match their offspring in visual appeal (although both are striking). Zabel eryngo is

A Selection of Sea Hollies

Two cultivars of Zabel eryngo have been in constant commerce since they were introduced in 1913. 'Jewel' has steely blue flowers and bracts, while those of 'Violetta' are a dark violet shade.

Other sea hollies to try include Zabel eryngo's parents, the highly colored alpine sea holly (E. alpinum) and Mediterranean sea holly (E. bourgatii) with steel blue flowers and white-and-silver-veined leaves. 'Blue Ribbon' flat sea holly (E. planum 'Blue Ribbon') has pale blue flowerheads, and giant sea holly (E. giganteum) is a larger plant that grows to 3 feet tall with blue-green flowers and silver bracts.

Spotlight on Zabel Eryngo

USDA Plant Hardiness Zones: 4 to 9

Season of Bloom: July to August

Height × Width: 24 to 36 inches × 24 to 36 inches

Flower Color: Blue-violet

Light Requirements: Full sun

Soil Requirements: Poor, sandy, well-drained, adequately moist soil

Place of Origin: A hybrid of A. alpinum and A. bourgatii of the Alps and Jura mountains

Plant Source: Busse Gardens

not widely available from American nurseries, but this all-star is worth seeking out and worth asking for in hopes that more nurseries will grow it.

Unlike the spiky looking but texturally soft globe thistle (*Echinops* spp.), sea holly actually is prickly. The flowers are even thornier than the leaves. Steely blue-violet bracts that are tipped with points surround prickly teasel-like centers, themselves collections of tiny spears. These cone-shaped centers are dark with a violet cast, but it's the bracts that steal the show. They glow with a sort of metallic violet-amethyst color that's strange and wonderful. The plants send up sprays of these aggressive looking blossoms on branched stems in July, and the bloom continues well into August.

HOW TO GROW ZABEL ERYNGO Give Zabel eryngo a sunny site with poor, sandy, well-drained soil. Standing water promotes rot problems at the crown of the plant and

The spiky blue-violet flowers of Zabel eryngo contrast handsomely with the dangling pink flower chains of <u>Polygonum</u> <u>campanulatum</u>.

Zabel eryngo's spiny flowers and foliage are eye-catching with the softer shapes of other perennials. This plant is as prickly as it looks, so plant it where you won't brush against it.

can quickly kill it off. Leafminers sometimes invade the leaves. Growing Zabel eryngo in the adverse conditions it likes will probably ward off most problems.

Although they come from the group of plants known as sea hollies, Zabel eryngo's parent plants are native to the mountains of central Europe. In spite of this heritage, Zabel eryngo and its sea holly relatives all will thrive in harsh seaside conditions that prove detrimental to so many other plants.

PROPAGATING ZABEL ERYNGO This prickly perennial grows just fine without division, and in fact, its deep taproots make it difficult—although not impossible—to divide. Plants are best grown from seed and may self-sow in your garden. Move seedlings to where you want them when they're still fairly young—older plants may resent transplanting.

THE RIGHT SITE FOR ZABEL ERYNGO Zabel eryngo's stiff and spiky leaves and stems make it a perfect accent for the many perennials that have ordinary rounded leaves. The metallic blue of the flowers combines wonderfully with lemon yellows as well as with bright pinks. The flowers are everlastings and look pretty much the same when dried as they do fresh on the plant. For drying success, cut them as soon as they reach full color.

CO-STARS FOR ZABEL ERYNGO Zabel eryngo's amazing shade of blue looks stunning with lemon yellow daylilies such as lemon daylily (*Hemerocallis lilioasphodelus*), or with other summer-blooming yellows such as 'Coronation Gold' yarrow (see page 26) or 'Moonshine' yarrow (see page 28). It also mixes well with silver artemisias, and with soft pink or blue flowers like purple coneflower (*Echinacea purpurea*) and Frikart's aster (*Aster × frikartii*).

'GATEWAY' JOE-PYE WEED

Eupatorium 'Gateway'

THE TALL STALKS AND SHAGGY FLOWERHEADS of Joe-Pye weed are a familiar late-summer sight in natural areas across most of the eastern United States. This substantial native perennial can grow to an impressive 7 feet or taller and as summer fades into fall, its rosy purple flowers tower above the other plants that grow in the wet meadows, ditches and streamsides that it loves.

In fact, it's this towering structure—on sturdy, no-need-for-staking stems—that makes Joe-Pye weed a great garden plant. Among the many choices for the perennial garden, there are few plants that serve as very tall, vertical accents that don't need staking and anchor a border like they own it.

More Joe-Pye Gems

The glories of eupatoriums, also called bonesets, don't stop with the various Joe-Pye weeds. Mist flower (E. coelestinum) is also known as hardy ageratum, and like ageratum, it bears puffy clusters of light lavender-blue flowers on 24-inch stems from August until frost. I've combined these with bright orange 'Othello' bigleaf ligularia (Ligularia dentata 'Othello') very successfully.

Plants sold as 'Atropurpureum' spotted Joe-Pye weed (E. maculatum 'Atropurpureum') or as E. purpureum 'Atropurpureum' are probably the same as 'Gateway' Joe-Pye weed.

Spotlight on 'Gateway' Joe-Pye Weed

USDA Plant Hardiness Zones: 4 to 7

Season of Bloom: August to October

Height × spread: 5 to 6 feet × 3 to 4 feet

Flower Color: Reddish purple to mauve

Light Requirements: Full sun to partial shade

Soil Requirements: Constantly moist, neutral, humusy soil

Place of Origin: Eastern North America

Plant Sources: Ambergate Gardens, Busse Gardens, Forestfarm, Garden Place, Milaeger's Gardens, Sunlight Gardens, André Viette Farm & Nursery, Wayside Gardens

The plant gets its name from Joe Pye, an early American Indian healer, who used it in his healing treatments. Our all-star is not the extremely tall wild Joe-Pye weed (*E. purpureum*) of eastern meadows but rather 'Gateway', a probable hybrid between *E. purpureum* and spotted Joe-Pye weed (*E. maculatum*), which is similar to 'Gateway' but slightly smaller with wine red stems and semiflat rather than domed flowerheads.

Although 'Gateway' usually grows to 5 to 6 feet in full sun, it will grow taller in partial shade. What sets it apart is its wine red stems, topped in late summer and early fall by big, puffy, soft-looking flowerheads made up of myriad tiny dusky rose florets. The color description doesn't do the flowers justice. Seen in various lights and times of day, it can be a plain, dull purplish red, a dusky mauve, or a glowing light lilac in the fading light of dusk.

Borne on 5- to 6-foot-tall stems, 'Gateway' Joe-Pye weed's ample mauve flowerheads tower above other perennials in the late summer garden.

'Gateway' spreads gradually to make a big clump several feet across, with strong, stout, colored or mottled stems. Groups of four large, pointed, roughly textured leaves are held in whorls around the stems, giving the plant substance. The stems and leaves make a bold statement in the garden even before flowering begins.

HOW TO GROW 'GATEWAY' Because 'Gateway' Joe-Pye weed's origins are in low-lying meadows, this plant is at its best in con-sistently moist soil. Plant it in sun to light shade (where it will grow a bit taller) in a well-watered border, or along a moist woods edge, or down in a swale where water tends to collect. In the intense heat and humidity of the South, 'Gateway' Joe-Pye weed is not at home. Pests and diseases don't bother this hardy native, but when it's in full flower, swallowtail butterflies and other insects will come to gather its nectar and pollen.

PROPAGATING 'GATEWAY' Divide 'Gateway' Joe-Pye weed's tough crowns in spring or fall to get more of this splendid perennial or to re-duce the size of a large clump. Most Joe-Pye weeds are easy to grow from seed sown out-doors in the fall, and often plants will self-sow if the flowerheads are not removed before seed forms. Plant the seedlings in constantly moist soil.

THE RIGHT SITE FOR 'GATEWAY' Plant 'Gateway' Joe-Pye weed where it can add drama and late summer color to the back of your borders. Let it reign over a meadow garden, or use its rugged character to blend a woodland edge into more landscaped areas nearer to the house. And by all means include it in your butterfly garden.

Be sure to include 'Gateway' Joe-Pye weed in your butterfly garden.

CO-STARS FOR 'GATEWAY' Combine 'Gateway' Joe-Pye weed with the graceful structure of ornamental grasses like maiden grass (*Miscanthus sinensis* 'Gracillimus'), or with other tall perennials such as 'Venusta' queen-of-the-prairie (see page 140), New York aster (*Aster novi-belgii*), milky bellflower (*Campanula lactiflora*), or ornamental rhubarb (*Rheum palmatum*).

CUSHION SPURGE

Euphorbia epithymoides

Spotlight on

Cushion Spurge

USDA Plant Hardiness Zones: 4 to 10

Season of Bloom: April to June

Height × Width: 16 to 18 inches × 18 inches

Flower Color: Yellow

Light Requirements: Full sun to partial shade

Soil Requirements: Average, sandy, well-drained soil

Place of Origin: Eastern Europe from Poland to Greece

Plant Sources: Ambergate Gardens, Kurt Bluemel, Busse Gardens, Carroll Gardens, Crownsville Nursery, Forestfarm, Garden Place, J. W. Jung Seed, Milaeger's Gardens, Park Seed, Weiss Brothers Perennial Nursery

Seed Source: Park Seed

MOST PERENNIALS FLOWER according to the way their stems reach the light, or when conditions are right for the emergence of flowering spikes—that is to say, in a sort of haphazard manner. But cushion spurge (*E. epithymoides*), our choice all-star, makes a neat dome of stems with rich green leaves clustered near the tips. At the tip of each stem, a flat cluster of greenish yellow bracts holds a much smaller cluster of little yellow flowers. These appear in April or May, depending on your latitude. The effect is as if someone has decorated a green cushion with evenly spaced bright yellow flowers.

Cushion spurge is a tough plant, and its yellow bracts will last in the garden for a long time after bloom—even into June. Later

Another Splendid Spurge

While cushion spurge is at its finest in a bright, sunny spot, Robb's spurge (E. robbiae, also sold as E. amygdaloides var. robbiae) is among the few perennials that will thrive in full shade and dry soil. This beautiful plant grows 12 to 24 inches tall and creeps slowly, spreading its thick stems and dark, evergreen foliage into an attractive groundcover. The inconspicuous flowers are surrounded by light yellow-green bracts atop 24-inch stems. Robb's spurge is hardy to Zone 6 if given winter protection.

appearing shoots don't flower. Spurges generally are warm-region or even tropical plants (poinsettia, crown-of-thorns, etc.) but this one is cold hardy to Zone 4, and of all the hardy spurge, it is by far the loveliest.

HOW TO GROW CUSHION SPURGE Give cushion spurge a spot in full sun in the North, since too much shade there will cause it to grow leggy and lose its tidy compact form. In the South, it needs afternoon sun at least, or semishade during the day. Like other euphorbias, cushion spurge tolerates dry soils and prefers a site with well-drained soil. Cushion spurge has no pest or disease problems to speak of. In a favorable spot it will perform

Cushion spurge's chartreuse-yellow flowers create a lovely color combination with the dainty blue forget-me-not–like blossoms of Siberian bugloss. Although cushion spurge starts its display in early spring, its bright flowers (actually long-lasting bracts) keep providing garden interest into June.

reliably year after year and will spread gradually to form a substantial mound.

Over summer the plant will retain its pretty domed shape. You may want to trim it up in July to remove any unsightly shoots and maintain the shape, but this isn't really necessary. And don't trim off the spent bracts, because these age to a rose-bronze color over the summer and continue to look attractive against the dark green foliage. A treat awaits you in the fall, when cold weather turns all its foliage a reddish hue. The plant's milky sap may irritate your skin, so be careful when handling it.

PROPAGATING CUSHION SPURGE Divide cushion spurge's tight clumps in spring, separating smaller sections from the outside of the plant and replanting them 18 to 24 inches apart. Discard any central portion that has become woody. You can also root stem cuttings of cushion spurge in the summer, and it grows easily from seed.

THE RIGHT SITE FOR CUSHION SPURGE As a specimen in its own little featured place, cushion spurge is a standout, but it can also accent a garden of more traditionally shaped perennials. Give it plenty of growing room so the 18-inch-wide dome shape can form without being squished by neighboring plants. It's this

shape that charms those who see it. Because of its tolerance for dry soil, cushion spurge makes a great choice for a large pot.

CO-STARS FOR CUSHION SPURGE Cushion spurge makes a great combination with white tulips. For a hot duo, pair it with the bright red flowers of scarlet avens (*Geum coccineum*). Its bright yellow color shines next to blue flowers like Jacob's ladder (see page 254) and horned violet (*Viola cornuta*). Create a fun, tufted garden by mixing cushion spurge's mounded shape with moss pink (*Phlox subulata*), low-growing pinks (*Dianthus spp.*), rock cresses (*Aubrieta* spp. and *Arabis* spp.) and small ornamental grasses like blue fescue (*Festuca cinerea*).

Drought tolerant and tidy, cushion spurge makes an excellent container plant for a sunny patio.

'ELIJAH BLUE' FESCUE

Festuca cinerea 'Elijah Blue'

BLUE FESCUE is one of the best all-purpose plants in my bag of perennial garden tricks. Its dusty blue-green grassy leaves are a perfect foil for pink-flowering plants and for broad-leaved perennials, and it makes a tough groundcover in areas of poor, dry soil.

'Elijah Blue' is a very blue selection of blue fescue and has some real all-star characteristics. In many areas of the country with witheringly hot summer days—across the South, the Midwest, and the Plains states—blue fescue tends to flower in June and then burn out over summer. But 'Elijah Blue' rarely suffers from such troubles, especially if it gets a bit of light shade in these hot-summer regions. In New England and the Pacific Northwest, and especially in the Mediterranean-like climate of coastal California, it's right at home and gives gardeners no problems.

In June, 'Elijah Blue' extends short flower-stalks above its sea-urchin–like clump of blue foliage. The flowerheads are a soft, pale gold color and fairly inconspicuous.

This Blue Grass Ain't Bluegrass

A similar-looking, but much larger, grass is the evergreen Helictotrichon semper-virens, *commonly called blue oat grass (see page 162). It looks like a 24- to 36-inch clump of blue fescue and likes full sun and regular water.*

Spotlight on 'Elijah Blue' Fescue

USDA Plant Hardiness Zones: 5 to 9

Season of Bloom: June

Height × Width: 6 to 10 inches × 12 inches

Flower Color: Pale gold

Light Requirements: Full sun to partial shade

Soil Requirements: Poor, dry, well-drained soil

Place of Origin: Central to southern France and Pyrenees Mountains

Plant Sources: Ambergate Gardens, Kurt Bluemel, Busse Gardens, Carroll Gardens, Crownsville Nursery, Forestfarm, Garden Place, Greer Gardens, J. W. Jung Seed, Klehm Nursery, Milaeger's Gardens, Powell's Gardens, Shady Oaks Nursery, André Viette Farm & Nursery, Wayside Gardens, Weiss Brothers Perennial Nursery, White Flower Farm

HOW TO GROW 'ELIJAH BLUE' Avoid planting 'Elijah Blue' in rich, humusy, moist garden soil—the kind that nine out of ten perennials prefer. Overabundant water and nutrients make it grow too fast and it loses its pretty tufted shape. 'Elijah Blue' fescue does best in a poor, dry, sandy spot with neutral or slightly alkaline soil.

In early spring, cut the plant back to 1 to 2 inches above the crown, and it will renew its fine-textured-but-tough grassy leaves and pretty shape. After 'Elijah Blue' finishes flowering, you can trim the flowerheads off to prevent self-sowing and to keep the plant looking tidy. If clumps do become lax and overgrown,

When summer gets hot, 'Elijah Blue' fescue keeps its cool, remaining handsome in conditions that drive other blue fescues into dormancy.

divide them in the fall or in early spring. 'Elijah Blue' fescue's foliage wants to be evergreen, even in the coldest parts of its range, so it's easy to find it in late winter.

PROPAGATING 'ELIJAH BLUE'

You can divide 'Elijah Blue' fescue in early spring or in fall, separating the clump into smaller, rooted sections. To create a solid groundcover, replant the divisions 8 to 9 inches apart. Blue fescue may self-sow if you don't remove its seedheads after flowering, and seedlings will vary in color from blue to green.

THE RIGHT SITE FOR 'ELIJAH BLUE'

The color and compact, tufted habit of 'Elijah Blue' make it ideal for edging brick or stone walkways or for growing at the front of the border. Plant it on banks with other soil-holding perennials.

I never seem to give it much care, and yet I'm not afraid to use it frequently in the more unused parts of the perennial garden where a spot of very blue foliage is needed to add some color. Even when it gets a little shaggy after flowering, 'Elijah Blue' still looks better than 99 percent of the rough stuff that grows in these spots.

CO-STARS FOR 'ELIJAH BLUE'

'Elijah Blue' makes an excellent accent plant that goes well with most perennials, especially with clumps of pink-flowered pinks (*Dianthus* spp.) and pink cranesbills (*Geranium* spp.). It looks good mixed with the low, rounded, multicolored leaves of 'Burgundy Glow' ajuga (see page 32) or with annual purple sweet alyssum (*Lobularia maritima*). And its spiky, linear

While they look fine in a natural setting, 'Elijah Blue' fescue's flowerheads give it a wild and crazy look. In a formal garden, you may prefer to trim them off.

texture and blue color contrasts well with round-leaved, red shrubs like 'Crimson Pygmy' barberry (*Berberis thunbergii* var. *atropurpurea* 'Crimson Pygmy'). Actually, there's very little in the garden that it doesn't enhance.

'VENUSTA' QUEEN-OF-THE-PRAIRIE

Filipendula rubra 'Venusta'

FILIPENDULA RUBRA 'VENUSTA' may be called the queen-of-the-prairie, but she's really the queen of any garden she's planted in. The tall, stiff stems grow to at least 4 feet, and reach a lofty 6 or even 7 feet in some locations.

Meadowsweets and More

While 'Venusta' queen-of-the-prairie is the champion all-star of the tall border plants, some of its relatives—mostly known as meadowsweets—offer similarly showy flowers on shorter plants. In small beds or borders where queen-of-the-prairie would be too big and out of scale, Siberian meadowsweet (*F. palmata*) is a lovely substitute that grows 3 to 4 feet tall. Its cultivar 'Elegans' (*F. palmata* 'Elegans') is a bit more compact and has white flowers, while 'Nana' (*F. palmata* 'Nana') bears pink flowers on petite, 10-inch plants.

'Flore Pleno' European meadowsweet (*F. ulmaria* 'Flore Pleno'), also known as queen-of-the-meadow, tops its 48-inch-tall stems with pretty, white, fluffy flowerheads. Double-flowered dropwort (*F. vulgaris* 'Flore Pleno') has shaggy clusters of cream-colored double florets and grows to about 24 inches tall.

Spotlight on
'Venusta' Queen-of-the-Prairie

USDA Plant Hardiness Zones: 3 to 9

Season of Bloom: Mid-June to July

Height × Width: 4 to 6 feet × 4+ feet

Flower Color: Rose pink

Light Requirements: Full sun to partial shade

Soil Requirements: Very moist, deep, rich, humusy soil

Place of Origin: Eastern United States

Plant Sources: Kurt Bluemel, Busse Gardens, Carroll Gardens, Dutch Gardens, Milaeger's Gardens, Powell's Gardens, Shady Oaks Nursery, André Viette Farm & Nursery, Wayside Gardens, White Flower Farm

In mid-June, she opens huge—up to 9-inch-wide—fluffy, cotton-candy plumes made up of jillions of tiny florets of a charming deep rose pink shade. These showy flower clusters persist for four to five weeks, dominating whatever spot this queen is given.

The leaves are exciting, too. They are large, jaggy things that are held stiffly upward, giving the plant a strong vertical energy, even when it's not blooming. Queen-of-the-prairie's tall stems are low-maintenance, too; they never need staking, despite their height.

HOW TO GROW 'VENUSTA' 'Venusta' queen-of-the-prairie is at home in wet soil, where her creeping underground roots will grow outward to make large clumps 4 or more feet across.

Queen-of-the-prairie reigns over the summer garden with stately elegance. She's at her best in moist to wet soil and full sun to partial shade.

Like cotton candy at a summer carnival, 'Venusta' queen-of-the-prairie's deep rose pink flower plumes catch the eye and capture the imagination. Up to 9 inches wide, these showy flower clusters bloom on sturdy, 6-foot stems that never need staking.

In the North, give her a spot in full sun, but as you go below the Mason-Dixon line, increase the shade until she gets partial shade. In the southernmost parts of her range, give 'Venusta' a place in light dappled shade all day.

Because queen-of-the-prairie is native to the eastern United States, she's tough enough to withstand our native pests and diseases. But if you plant this queen in a dry site, she may suffer from spider mite infestations that will pepper the leaves with dead spots, and powdery mildew may coat the foliage. The solution to both problems is a better site where the soil is moist, although you can quick-fix your spider mite troubles by washing them off the plant with a stream of water from a hose.

PROPAGATING 'VENUSTA' 'Venusta' queen-of-the-prairie spreads by creeping roots to form large clumps to 4 feet across. Divide clumps in the fall to increase a planting and to rein in clumps that are crowding other plants in your garden. Replant divisions about 3 feet apart.

THE RIGHT SITE FOR 'VENUSTA' This plant is the ultimate choice for a naturalistic, moist woodland garden, natural border, or sunny woods' edge in a place that stays moist. These conditions are usually suited to darker, heavy plants, and 'Venusta' will open her cheery plumes to lighten the effect. Queen-of-the-prairie's moisture-loving ways also make it a perfect plant for a vertical accent beside a water garden.

CO-STARS FOR 'VENUSTA' Dark rhododendrons and 'China Girl' holly (*Ilex* 'China Girl') make a fine backdrop for 'Venusta' queen-of-the-prairie's pink plumes. Her tall stems and rose pink flowerheads create a common theme with Joe-Pye weed in a moist, woods' edge garden. Or try it with angelicas (*Angelica* spp.), valerians (*Valeriana* spp.), and other moisture-tolerant herbs. You can make an extremely bold garden by planting 'Venusta' queen-of-the-prairie with goat's beard (see page 52), delphiniums, false indigos (*Baptisia* spp.), and the upright pink flowers of obedient plant (*Physostegia virginiana*).

'GOBLIN' BLANKET FLOWER

Gaillardia × grandiflora 'Goblin'

'GOBLIN' BLANKET FLOWER is a prime example of an all-star. This showy hybrid perennial is easy to grow, is a super-long bloomer, and is as colorful as a cowboy on a weekend in town.

Blanket flower is a durable plant, too, with a toughness that comes from its origins in western North America. It can survive in hot, dry soil, in poor soil, and even in seaside conditions.

Its appearance reflects the West, too. The all-star cultivar 'Goblin' has 3- to 4-inch-wide flowers with dark purplish maroon centers and ray petals of rich red tipped with bright golden yellow. 'Goblin' blanket flower's big, bold, bright flowers begin opening in June and continue through the summer usually

Spotlight on
'Goblin' Blanket Flower

USDA Plant Hardiness Zones: 3 to 9

Season of Bloom: June to August

Height × Width: 12 inches × 12 to 18 inches

Flower Color: Red, yellow, and maroon

Light Requirements: Full sun

Soil Requirements: Average to poor, well-drained soil

Place of Origin: Western North America

Plant Sources: Bluestone Perennials, Forestfarm, Greer Gardens, Roslyn Nursery, Milaeger's Gardens, Powell's Gardens, Spring Hill Nurseries, André Viette Farm & Nursery, Wayside Gardens

Seed Source: Park Seed

right up until frost in young, vigorous plants. That's an extra long season of bloom for these welcome flowers, which grow on 12-inch-tall plants to brighten up the spaces between taller perennials.

The lifespan of any individual 'Goblin' blanket flower is variable, and this is perhaps its only flaw. Some may die out after two years, others may live on for many more. Despite this tendency toward quick turnover, 'Goblin' offers so many other advantages that it earns the right to be called a perennial all-star.

HOW TO GROW 'GOBLIN' If you plant 'Goblin' in rich, moist garden loam, it will tend to lose its compact habit and may sprawl, although not unattractively. This plant is more at home in average or even poor soil and asks only for good drainage in order to thrive.

Other Beautiful Blanket Flowers

'Goblin' blanket flower is a hybrid of the perennial blanket flower (G. aristata) and annual blanket flower (G. pulchella), which explains why it's sometimes short lived. This same parentage has produced other garden-worthy cultivars that differ from 'Goblin' mainly in height and flower color. 'Dazzler' has similar flowers—maroon centers and petals with yellow-gold tips—but grows 24 to 30 inches tall. 'Golden Goblin' grows to only 12 inches and has yellow flowers. 'Burgundy' has deep red flowers on 24- to 36-inch plants.

Although the crowns of individual plants may die out, especially in heavy, clay soil, underground roots usually persist to form new crown buds for the next spring. You can ensure that this happens by cutting the flower stems back to the sticky, gray-green foliage before frost kills the plant. This encourages 'Goblin' to form new basal buds that are more winter hardy. In cold regions where snow cover is chancy, a layer of leaf mulch will help it through the winter. Pests and diseases don't bother 'Goblin'.

PROPAGATING 'GOBLIN' Divide 'Goblin' in spring every two or three years to keep it vigorous and growing. Lift the plant and carefully cut it into divisions with a knife. You can also propagate 'Goblin' by taking stem cuttings in late summer or root cuttings in early winter; overwinter cuttings in a cold frame. And you can grow 'Goblin' from seed.

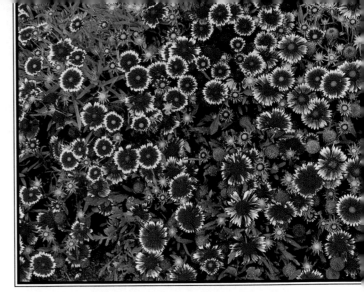

'Goblin' blanket flower thrives where other perennials won't. In dry, poor soil and full sun, 'Goblin' blooms prolifically through the summer.

THE RIGHT SITE FOR 'GOBLIN' This blanket flower's toughness makes it a supremely useful plant on south-facing banks, in thin soils, and in other trouble spots where the more finicky perennials won't grow. Its low habit and masses of warm-colored flowers make 'Goblin' just right for growing at the front of a planting of taller perennials in other warm shades or in cooler blue tones. As a cut flower, its bold color scheme draws the eye and makes it a useful focal point in an arrangement.

CO-STARS FOR 'GOBLIN' 'Goblin' blanket flower's multicolored blossoms look great with other warm-colored daisies, such as large-flowered tickseed (*Coreopsis grandiflora*), threadleaf coreopsis (*C. verticillata*), and purple coneflower (*Echinacea purpurea*). It also goes well with the soft blue flowers of 'Johnson's Blue' cranesbill (*Geranium* 'Johnson's Blue'), with the smaller daisies of white- or lavender-flowered fleabanes (*Erigeron* spp.), and with the rich yellow-golds of goldenrods (*Solidago* spp.). Enhance its southwestern look with ornamental grasses like switch grass (*Panicum virgatum*).

Blanket flower's rich colors bring to mind the bright woven blankets of Mexico and the American Southwest and earn the plant its common name.

SWEET WOODRUFF

Galium odoratum

SWEET WOODRUFF'S ABILITY TO LOOK GOOD and cover lots of territory fairly rapidly makes it perfect for growing under high trees and around understory shrubs—and qualifies it as one of the all-star perennial groundcovers.

One of sweet woodruff's biggest assets is its tidy appearance. Its slender square stems emerge closely spaced from wiry, creeping, underground roots and reach roughly 5 to 8 inches tall. Whorls of six to eight slender, lancelike leaves cover the stems from top to bottom. In May and June, tiny, starlike clusters of ¼-inch flowers open at the tips of the stems. The neat, closely spaced foliage and dainty

Sweet-Scented Slumber

A large patch of sweet woodruff looks inviting, as if a short nap on it would be just the thing. That wouldn't be entirely inappropriate, since another name for this plant is bedstraw. When it's dried, it has a deliciously light and lovely scent with a hint of new-mown hay and a slight note of vanilla. Sweet woodruff flowers give their fragrance to May wine—a German spring tonic so named because you put the May-borne flowers in Rhein wine (sometimes with sweet strawberries), not because the wine is made in May.

Although there are other species of bedstraw (Galium spp.), sweet woodruff is the only one worthy of the garden.

Spotlight on Sweet Woodruff

USDA Plant Hardiness Zones: 4 to 9

Season of Bloom: May to June

Height × Width: 5 to 8 inches × 18+ inches

Flower Color: Pure white

Light Requirements: Partial shade

Soil Requirements: Grows best in moist, humusy soil but tolerates dry and heavier soils

Place of Origin: Europe

Plant Sources: Kurt Bluemel, Crownsville Nursery, Forestfarm, Garden Place, J. W. Jung Seed, Milaeger's Gardens, Roslyn Nursery, White Flower Farm

spring flowers make sweet woodruff a particularly effective and attractive groundcover.

HOW TO GROW SWEET WOODRUFF If you want sweet woodruff to spread widely, plant it in soil that you've loosened and amended with compost, then keep it well watered. To keep it a bit more restrained, let it get by with whatever water the rains bring. In dry summer regions, water it sparingly. Pests and diseases don't bother it.

Sweet woodruff is shallow rooted and may die out in the colder parts of its range if it's not protected by an insulating blanket of snow. In these areas, sweet woodruff benefits from a winter mulch of leaf compost.

PROPAGATING SWEET WOODRUFF Sweet woodruff spreads vigorously and is easy to divide into smaller clumps in spring or fall. It also grows well from seed and will self-sow in your garden.

Sweet woodruff's dainty white spring flowers rest like a late sprinkling of snow above its ground-covering whorls of bright green leaves.

In light shade, fine-textured sweet woodruff creates a pleasing contrast with hosta's bold leaves and with the rounded foliage of creeping Jenny.

THE RIGHT SITE FOR SWEET WOODRUFF

Sweet woodruff is at its best in woodsy areas and natural plantings. In a more formal border, it may spread beyond the bounds you set for it. I've read in various places that in rich, moist soil sweet woodruff will become rampantly invasive, but that hasn't been my experience. I've planted it in a variety of conditions, and it spread to 4 to 5 feet over five to six years.

Here in California, I have some sweet woodruff growing in a fairly sunny, dry spot along the driveway, where it has filled in a few square feet in three years. I wouldn't call that rampantly invasive, and I wouldn't be afraid of using this plant wherever you need a charming groundcover with many assets.

CO-STARS FOR SWEET WOODRUFF

Any number of companions looks good next to sweet woodruff's bright green leaf whorls and clean white flowers. In a shady, woodland setting it covers the ground after spring-blooming wood anemone (*Anemone nemorosa*) goes dormant, and its fine-textured foliage makes a nice contrast for other shade-loving spreaders such as ajuga (*Ajuga reptans*), lily-of-the-valley (see page 108), European wild ginger (see page 54), or yellow archangel (*Lamiastrum galeobdolon*). Wild blue phlox (*Phlox divaricata*) is another excellent woodland companion for sweet woodruff. It also looks great planted beneath and around understory shrubs like azaleas (*Rhododendron* spp.) and rhododendrons. Where there's a bit more sun and moist, loose soil, grow sweet woodruff amid such diverse neighbors as astilbe (*Astilbe × arendsii*), catmint (see page 230), 'Pink Panda' strawberry (*Fragaria* 'Pink Panda'), and daylilies (*Hemerocallis* spp.).

WHITE GAURA

Gaura lindheimeri

WHITE GAURA IS TRULY a plant-it-and-forget-it kind of perennial, with a bloom time so long that once it starts it seems like it's never out of flower. In Sunbelt gardens, white gaura is so tough it's downright essential. This American native readily withstands the heat and drought of the Southeast, the Southwest, and California. I have white gaura growing in several places here in my California property, including a spot that gets very little water in the summer. Laughing at this neglect, white gaura often blooms for me from April through October.

White gaura's flowers are delicate and lovely, and they usually bloom in sufficient numbers to create an elegant display during the summer months and into the fall. Pinkish mauve buds open to reveal white, 1-inch, mothlike flowers that dance and dangle along thin, 3- to 4-foot-tall stems. Typically each stem holds just a few flowers at any one time, but a healthy plant puts up numerous stems that provide a steady supply of flowers.

A Couple of Good Gauras

Two cultivars of white gaura are widely available and gardenworthy: 'Whirling Butterflies' is a bit more compact than its parent and produces more pure white flowers on reddish stems. 'Corrie's Gold' has gold-variegated, willowlike leaves and pale pink-blushed white flowers.

Spotlight on White Gaura

USDA Plant Hardiness Zones: 5 to 10

Season of Bloom: May to October

Height × Width: 36 to 48 inches × 24 to 36 inches

Flower Color: White with a hint of pale pink

Light Requirements: Full sun

Soil Requirements: Average to poor, loose, well-drained soil

Place of Origin: Louisiana and Texas south to Mexico

Plant Sources: Kurt Bluemel, Bluestone Perennials, Busse Gardens, Carroll Gardens, Forestfarm, Garden Place, Milaeger's Gardens, Plant Delights Nursery, Powell's Gardens, Roslyn Nursery, Sunlight Gardens, André Viette Farm & Nursery, Weiss Brothers Perennial Nursery

Seed Source: Thompson & Morgan

White gaura's narrow, lance-shaped leaves are attached directly to the wiry stems and are sparsely spaced along them. The entire plant has an open, airy, fine-textured quality, and when viewed from a distance, the thin stems nearly disappear, leaving the white flowers to float seemingly unsupported over the garden. When a blossom is finished, it drops cleanly from the stem, leaving a tiny seed to ripen behind it.

HOW TO GROW WHITE GAURA This all-star is a tough plant that will grow in heat, humidity, and poor, somewhat droughty soils with little care. But if you treat it better, it will reward you with more stems of its dainty

'Whirling Butter-flies' white gaura's dancing flowers sparkle among the foliage and flowers of darker, denser plants. Plant white gaura where its airy flower stems can spray over the top of perennials around it.

white flowers and a longer season of bloom. White gaura's at its best in a sunny spot with evenly moist, well-drained soil but tolerates more difficult conditions and partial shade. Soggy soils, especially during the winter, can be its downfall. If you remove the faded flowerstalks regularly, it will bloom from late spring until frost.

PROPAGATING WHITE GAURA White gaura grows from a thick taproot and established plants resent being moved or divided. It's best grown from seed and self-sows readily. To propagate cultivars of white gaura, carefully divide mature clumps in spring or take stem cuttings in the summer.

THE RIGHT SITE FOR WHITE GAURA Use white gaura in the middle to back of the sunny perennial border where its tall stems will peek out from amid the rounded shapes of perennials around it. Plant it where its white flowers will dance on the passing breeze as well as in tough sites where you'll appreciate its care-free nature.

White gaura is an excellent choice for Southern gardens, where so many perennials that bloom for a long time and are long lived in the North have short blooming seasons and relatively short life spans in the blazing heat.

Like a kid in a swimming pool, white gaura laughs at summer heat and humidity. Remove its spent flowerstalks to keep it blooming until frost.

And when white gaura stems have a good flush of flowers on them, they make excellent, graceful additions to a vase of cut flowers.

CO-STARS FOR WHITE GAURA Its white flowers make white gaura easy to mix with just about any other plant that enjoys similar conditions. Plant it with dwarf dahlias and cosmos, with blanket flowers (*Gaillardia* spp.), marigolds, yuccas (*Yucca* spp.), or flax lilies (*Phormium* spp.). Ornamental grasses make excellent companions, too, and fleshy sedums give substance to white gaura's airy presence.

A Stellar Idea

As white gaura's flowers fade, they drop from the flowerstalk, leaving a developing seed behind. Cut off seed-bearing stems in September (improving the plant's appearance) and sow the seeds where you want them in the fall.

CRESTED GENTIAN

Gentiana septemfida var. *lagodechiana*

As a group, gentians have earned a certain notoriety among gardeners. Their flowers bloom in some of the richest blue shades perennials have to offer, yet many gentians are difficult to grow and hard to propagate or raise from seed. A lot of gardeners deny themselves those luscious blues and bypass gentians altogether in favor of less finicky plants.

More Gems Among the Gentians

If this crested gentian variety suits you, you may want to try some of the other gentians, even if they can be persnickety. Stemless gentian (G. acaulis) bears exquisite deep blue, bell-shaped flowers and should be one to try after G. septemfida var. lagodechiana.

I have tried (without success) to grow the wildflower bottle gentian (G. andrewsii). Its inch-long, bottle-shaped, closed flowers appear in rich blue clusters atop 18- to 24-inch stems. Oh, the irony when I find a gorgeous stand of this gentian growing wild in an abandoned ditch.

There is another gentian that, like our all-star, is easy to grow. Willow gentian (G. asclepiadea) has 18-inch-long stems, sharply pointed leaves, and late-summer sprays of violet-blue flowers from amid the leaves along the upper half of the stems.

Spotlight on

Crested Gentian

USDA Plant Hardiness Zones: 4 to 9

Season of Bloom: July to August

Height × Width: 8 to 12 inches × 12 to 18 inches

Flower Color: Blue

Light Requirements: Partial shade to full sun

Soil Requirements: Rich, humusy, moist soil

Place of Origin: Eastern Caucasus Mountains

Plant Sources: Garden Place, Milaeger's Gardens, Roslyn Nursery, Shady Oaks Nursery, White Flower Farm

Seed Source: Thompson & Morgan

That's too bad, because there are gentians that are as easy to grow as any other perennial and that bloom in the deep blue color that gardeners covet. One of the easiest of all the gentians to grow, and my choice for a perennial all-star, is a crested gentian variety, *G. septemfida* var. *lagodechiana* (sometimes offered as *G. lagodechiana*).

This mellow crested gentian is a low grower whose 12- to 18-inch stems trail along the ground and turn upward at their ends, reaching from 8 to as high as 12 inches above the ground. Each crown bears several stems that are set thickly along their length with whorls of pretty, bright green, gently pointed oval leaves.

At the ends of the stems and among the leaves near the stem tips, crested gentian's blue flowers appear singly in July, continuing their bloom through August and sometimes even into September. They are an extremely welcome sight, and their rich blue color

Low-growing crested gentian dislikes having its roots disturbed. Plant it in a permanent spot where you can enjoy its rich blue flowers and glossy leaves.

glows against the green of the foliage. Each blossom is a five-petaled open trumpet with slight tufted crests on the petals where they fold outward and a touch of white in its throat.

HOW TO GROW CRESTED GENTIAN

This variety of crested gentian prefers evenly moist soil amended with compost to make it crumbly and rich, and a semi-shady spot. However, as this is one of the few easy-to-grow gentians, it will perform well in sun, in a rock garden as long as it doesn't dry out, and even in a bog garden. It can be an exciting addition to a vaseful of cut flowers, too. In addition to its other advantages, it's not prone to pests or diseases, and it's long lived.

PROPAGATING CRESTED GENTIAN Gentians that aren't clump forming are usually difficult to propagate and this crested gentian variety is no exception. It resents being disturbed for any reason and rarely needs to be divided. But it's fairly easy to grow from seed, although seedlings take a few years to reach blooming size.

THE RIGHT SITE FOR CRESTED GENTIAN Create

small drifts of this charming crested gentian by planting seedlings 8 inches apart in a spot about 3 feet by 4 feet where you can enjoy the rich blue flowers from mid to late summer. Its low-growing habit lets it fit in among rock garden plants and at the edge of a lightly shaded woodland path. Another use is to plant it among bigger perennials near the front of the bed where it can trail among the stems of its taller companions.

CO-STARS FOR CRESTED GENTIAN Plant this crested gentian with other midsummer bloomers. It looks good with the yellow flowers of perennials like threadleaf coreopsis (*Coreopsis verticillata*) and citron daylily (*Hemerocallis citrina*), with the white blossoms of star astilbe (*Astilbe simplicifolia*) and baby's-breath (*Gypsophila paniculata*), or next to the pinks of summer phlox (*Phlox paniculata*) and checkerbloom (*Sidalcea malviflora*). It will trail deep blue flowers at their feet.

In late summer and fall, bottle gentian produces clusters of the showy, closed, bottle-shaped blue flowers that give the plant its name.

'INGWERSEN'S VARIETY' BIGROOT CRANESBILL

Geranium macrorrhizum
'Ingwersen's Variety'

HOORAY FOR THE CRANESBILLS in general and for 'Ingwersen's Variety' bigroot cranesbill in particular! Here's a plant that fills almost every bill I can think of for a perennial all-star. It produces a late spring and summer display of nickel-size, five-petalled, soft rosy pink flowers from May well into June and

Spotlight on 'Ingwersen's Variety' Bigroot Cranesbill

USDA Plant Hardiness Zones: 4 to 9

Season of Bloom: May to June

Height × Width: 12 inches × 18+ inches

Flower Color: Soft rose pink

Light Requirements: Full sun to full shade

Soil Requirements: Just about any soil will suit this plant.

Place of Origin: Found on Mount Koprivnik in Montenegro (formerly part of Yugoslavia) by Walter Ingwersen in 1929

Plant Sources: Kurt Bluemel, Carroll Gardens, Garden Place, Milaeger's Gardens

Consider These Cranesbills

Among the cranesbills, also called hardy geraniums to distinguish them from the tender geraniums (Pelargonium spp.), are many outstanding plants. I asked Robin Parer, director of the International Geranium Society, which kinds she likes. She said that anyone can grow showy geranium (G. × magnificum) with its large violet-blue flowers. And she highly recommends G. phaeum, a clump-forming plant that's hardy to Zone 3. It prefers the shade and blooms in spring with dark maroon to almost black flowers that earn it the common names black widow and mourning widow.

'Wargrave Pink' Endress cranesbill (G. endressii 'Wargrave Pink') is salmon pink and blooms all summer. 'Johnson's Blue' cranesbill (G. 'Johnson's Blue') is a popular cultivar that bears 2-inch muted blue flowers.

even to August at cool elevations and in the North. These flowers have prominent stamens emerging from the darker pink centers of the blossoms. The flowers appear in loose clusters on wiry stems just above the foliage.

The foliage is wonderful, too, even when the plant is out of bloom. The leaves are large—up to 4 inches across—and are rounded and palmately lobed. They are freely produced from creeping underground roots to form a dense clump that smothers out any weeds that may try to germinate beneath them. The leaves are also aromatic—with a heady, slightly citrusy fragrance. In the fall, the foliage turns a rich cherry red and yellow.

HOW TO GROW 'INGWERSEN'S VARIETY'

This durable all-star likes sun, partial shade, and even full shade. It can tolerate drought or be a feature where soil moisture is constant.

'Ingwersen's Variety' bigroot cranesbill is a versatile garden companion with attractive foliage that's easy to mix and match with other leaf shapes, colors, and textures.

In sun or shade, 'Ingwersen's Variety' bigroot cranesbill spreads quickly to form a groundcover any gardener could love. It bears rose pink flowers from spring into summer, above a dense, weed-blocking mat of handsome, fragrant foliage. In fall, the leaves turn from bright green to shades of red and yellow.

And it grows well in that most difficult of garden conditions—the dry shady soil beneath the branches of maples and other thirsty trees.

Gardeners in the country or near forests will appreciate the fact that 'Ingwersen's Variety' bigroot cranesbill is deer resistant, as well as being trouble-free where insect pests and diseases are concerned.

PROPAGATING BIGROOT CRANESBILL
Division in early spring is the best way to increase this vigorous plant. The creeping underground rhizomes are easy to divide with a shovel. Take salad-plate–size pieces and replant them 18 inches apart so they spread to meet.

THE RIGHT SITE FOR 'INGWERSEN'S VARIETY'
'Ingwersen's Variety' bigroot cranesbill is such a pretty addition to the perennial garden that you might overlook its chief garden function as a tightly knit, weed-smothering groundcover that spreads vigorously and easily under almost any conditions. And although it will spread, it's never weedy or invasive. Plant it under shrubs in the shady border, or use it out in the sun wherever you need a pretty, fragrant, easy-care groundcover.

CO-STARS FOR 'INGWERSEN'S VARIETY'
This cranesbill's large leaves and pale pink flowers look charming with larger, woody shrubs as they swirl around their feet. You can use it to shade the roots of clematis and as a low, bushy counterpart to taller perennials such as columbines (*Aquilegia* spp.), lupines (*Lupinus* spp.), and delphiniums if you keep its spreading rhizomes out of their root zones.

BORIS AVENS

Geum × borisii

THE BRIGHT ORANGE TO ORANGE-SCARLET blossoms of Boris avens are a big part of this plant's contribution to the garden. Their eye-catching color attracts your attention to flowers that look like shiny enameled orange jewelry nodding on their little stalks. The other part of the show is Boris avens' lovely, clump-forming leaves. Each cut, frilled leaf is about 6 to 8 inches long, narrow where it attaches to the crown and large lobed at its outward end—making it look like a miniature green ostrich feather. These leaves are very attractive and look good throughout the summer.

In May, branching flower stems appear, rising about 6 inches above the foliage. Each stem opens a small handful (anywhere from two to four or more) of gorgeous, inch-wide (or larger) flowers. The plants bloom well for a good month to five weeks and then the

Spotlight on

Boris Avens

USDA Plant Hardiness Zones: 4 to 8

Season of Bloom: May; intermittently through the summer

Height × Width: 6 to 12 inches × 12 to 18 inches

Flower Color: Orange to orange-scarlet

Light Requirements: Partial shade to full sun

Soil Requirements: Humusy, moist, well-drained soil

Place of Origin: This hybrid's parents are native from the Balkans to northern Turkey

Plant Sources: Kurt Bluemel, Carroll Gardens, Forestfarm, Roslyn Nursery

big floral show subsides. But Boris avens produces flowers intermittently—especially where it gets ample moisture—through August and occasionally even into September.

HOW TO GROW BORIS AVENS Boris avens isn't picky about soil or situation, which means you can pretty much use it where you will. But it does have preferences. It grows best where it gets about three hours of sunlight a day and where the soil is humusy, peaty, rich, and moist but well-drained. Pests and diseases aren't a problem for this all-star. Boris avens and other avens species and cultivars may perform poorly in areas where summer heat and humidity are high.

PROPAGATING BORIS AVENS Since this hybrid will not come true from seed, division in spring or fall is the right way to get an

Additional Admirable Avens

Other avens are worth a spot in the garden, too, especially the larger, deep scarlet-flowered 'Mrs. Bradshaw' avens (G. 'Mrs. Bradshaw') and the soft, pale yellow flowers of 'Georgenberg' avens (G. 'Georgenberg'). Be advised that 'Georgenberg', in particular, is not happy in the intense heat and humidity of the Deep South. Creeping avens (G. reptans) is a low-growing plant with yellow flowers that is usually placed in the rock garden.

increase in your plantings. Boris avens becomes congested and produces fewer flowers after growing for about three years in the garden. When this happens, divide Boris avens in the spring and replant the divisions 12 inches apart.

THE RIGHT SITE FOR BORIS AVENS Boris

avens' bright, red-orange flowers require careful consideration when you're deciding where to plant this all-star. I say place Boris

Boris avens gives you hot color for a cool, moist site. This fiery-flowered perennial grows best in well-drained soil that's moist and rich. That's because hot, dry conditions increase Boris avens' susceptibility to leaf browning and spider mite infestations.

avens where you want the eye to go—that is, at the focal point of your garden design. You won't miss it when it's in bloom. I use Boris avens to relieve and accent large masses of cool colors, such as blue delphiniums, 'Bowles' Mauve' wallflower (*Erysimum* 'Bowles' Mauve'), and low-growing bellflowers (*Campanula* spp.). I find it delightful to look back into a shady garden of soft cool colors and see Boris avens visually ringing like a telephone. If you give it a spot by itself you can be dazzled and charmed simultaneously.

CO-STARS FOR BORIS AVENS Boris avens'

striking, hot colors arrive relatively early in the garden and are best used as an accent to the blues and purples of perennials such as Siberian iris (*Iris sibirica*), Russell Hybrids lupines (*Lupinus* Russell Hybrids), spike speedwell (*Veronica spicata*), Dalmatian bellflower (*Campanula portenschlagiana*), and belladonna delphinium (*Delphinium* × *belladonna*). Other warm-colored flowers like the strong yellow blossoms of large-flowered tickseed (*Coreopsis grandiflora*) and yellow loosestrife (*Lysimachia punctata*), and the reds of Maltese cross (see page 212), Himalayan cinquefoil (*Potentilla atrosanguinea*), and especially sun rose (*Helianthemum nummularium*), create a fine harmony with Boris avens. But keep it away from pink. It also looks good among white flowers or alone, where its strong color can have the floor to itself.

In a sunny spot Boris avens' scarlet-orange flowers sizzle next to yellow-and-green yucca leaves and the yellow daisies of large-flowered tickseed.

'BRISTOL FAIRY' BABY'S-BREATH

Gypsophila paniculata 'Bristol Fairy'

'BRISTOL FAIRY' BABY'S-BREATH is undoubtedly one of the most valuable of all garden plants. It produces 3- by 3-foot mounds of tiny white flowers that look like a frothy cloud is billowing up out of the border. It sets off whatever it's near. There's no question that 'Bristol Fairy' baby's-breath earns its all-star status.

'Bristol Fairy' has slender, inconspicuous leaves. They are scattered and hardly visible below the wiry, many-branched stems that

Spotlight on 'Bristol Fairy' Baby's-Breath

USDA Plant Hardiness Zones: 4 to 9

Season of Bloom: June to August

Height × Width: 24 to 36 inches × 36 inches

Flower Color: White

Light Requirements: Full sun

Soil Requirements: Light, well-drained, alkaline soil

Place of Origin: Central Europe to Siberia

Plant Sources: Bluestone Perennials, Carroll Gardens, Milaeger's Gardens, Powell's Gardens, Van Bourgondien, André Viette Farm and Nursery, Wayside Gardens

A Bouquet of Baby's-Breaths

If you prefer light pink flowers to the white blossoms of 'Bristol Fairy', choose the excellent cultivar 'Pink Fairy' (G. paniculata 'Pink Fairy'), a pink-flowered version of our all-star. 'Flamingo' baby's-breath (G. paniculata 'Flamingo') has large, mauve-pink blossoms. The hybrid 'Rosy Veil' baby's-breath (G. 'Rosy Veil', also offered as G. 'Rosenschleier') is another excellent pink-flowered plant. Grown against gray-green leaves, these pink baby's-breaths make a lovely picture. 'Perfecta' baby's-breath (G. paniculata 'Perfecta') bears double white flowers on plants that are larger and less compact than 'Bristol Fairy'.

Another species worth noting is creeping baby's-breath (G. repens), a creeping form just 8 to 12 inches high. Its cultivar 'Bodgeri' has double, light pink flowers.

work up from the crown, reaching to 3 feet or more and making a pleasing mounded shape. But its flowers are abundant and very much in evidence. Each flower is a ¼-inch, roselike beauty, double and pure white and spangled thickly on the plant.

As 'Bristol Fairy' grows out from its crown in spring, it spreads, and by early summer its white fog buries the fading leaves of Virginia bluebells, spring bulbs, and other summer-dormant plants. The flower show continues into mid-August through most of its range and perhaps even a bit later where summers are cool.

HOW TO GROW BABY'S-BREATH Baby's-breath likes a sweet soil—one with a pH that's neutral to slightly alkaline. To get the most out of this indispensible flower factory, plant it in a light, humusy soil that drains well. At planting, amend the soil with a handful of ground limestone, then give it some more

'Bristol Fairy' spends the summer covered in a cloud of pure white, ¼-inch double flowers. Because the flowers keep their pretty, fresh white look when you dry them, they're a staple in both fresh and dried arrangements.

limestone or a dusting of wood ashes each spring. Don't try to move it once it gets growing; established plants resent being disturbed. Pests and diseases won't bother baby's-breath, but if you plant it in heavy, wet, clay soil, it will soon be gone.

PROPAGATING BABY'S-BREATH Baby's-breath is a taprooted plant, so successful division is unlikely. It's ordinarily grown from seed, but you can take stem cuttings in the spring. Space new plants 24 to 36 inches apart.

THE RIGHT SITE FOR 'BRISTOL FAIRY' 'Bristol Fairy' baby's-breath's fine, airy texture makes it an indispensible foil for large-leaved perennials such as hollyhock (*Alcea rosea*) and common foxglove (*Digitalis purpurea*), and shrubs like hydrangea. Because it's so different from almost every other garden plant, it accents and sets off the spiky leaves of irises and even the huge leaves of ornamental rhubarb (*Rheum palmatum*).

Baby's-breath dries so nicely when cut and hung in a dark, dry, warm room that it looks almost as nice as it does when it's fresh.

CO-STARS FOR 'BRISTOL FAIRY' What isn't a companion to baby's-breath? Plant it with spring plants that will be gone by midsummer,

Baby your 'Bristol Fairy' baby's-breath with an annual spring dusting of lime or wood ash. Baby's-breath grows best in well-drained, alkaline soil.

such as columbines (*Aquilegia* spp.), oriental poppies (*Papaver orientale*), and spring bulbs, so that its sprays will fill the spaces. It goes perfectly with large-leaved perennials, shrubby roses, and with spiky, rich purple salvias (*Salvia* spp.).

A Stellar Idea

In mid- to late summer, when its little blossoms turn brown, baby's-breath can use a little help. A planting of clambering nasturtiums that will cascade over baby's-breath's finished flowers and cover it with bright color late in the season is an idea of famous 19th century British garden designer Gertrude Jekyll's that's as valid today as when she suggested it a hundred years ago.

GOLDEN VARIEGATED HAKONE GRASS

Hakonechloa macra 'Aureola'

A PERENNIAL FOLIAGE PLANT that's fast gaining in popularity—and with good reason—is golden variegated hakone grass, also called Japanese forest grass. Although it has a more limited range than most all-stars, golden variegated hakone grass is a beautiful and useful plant to mix with flowering perennials. The zones where it can grow—Zone 6 (with winter protection) to Zone 9—cover such a large portion of the country that it deserves all-star status.

Golden variegated hakone grass is a lovely, delicate plant, with arching, grassy foliage that grows 12 to 18 inches tall, giving

Spotlight on

Golden Variegated Hakone Grass

USDA Plant Hardiness Zones: 6 to 9

Season of Bloom: August to October

Height × Width: 12 to 18 inches × 18 inches

Leaf Color: Yellow and green

Light Requirements: Partial to full shade

Soil Requirements: Rich, moist, humusy, well-drained soil

Place of Origin: Japan

Plant Sources: Kurt Bluemel, Busse Gardens, Carroll Gardens, Forestfarm, Greer Gardens, Milaeger's Gardens, Roslyn Nursery, Shady Oaks Nursery, Wayside Gardens, Weiss Brothers Perennial Nursery, White Flower Farm

Go Green and White with Gardener's Garters

*Where climate or soil conditions make life tough for golden variegated hakone grass, or where you'd prefer a green-and-white color scheme instead of yellow and green, consider white-striped ribbon grass (*Phalaris arundinacea* var. *picta*). Also called gardener's garters, this durable, rather invasive ornamental grass grows 24 to 36 inches tall and spreads readily on underground rhizomes. While it prefers moist, rich garden soil, white-striped ribbon grass tolerates many soil conditions, grows in light shade, and is hardy in Zones 4 to 9.*

the impression of a small bamboo. Each leaf blade is a soft bronzy yellow striped lengthwise with green.

Tiny, inconspicuous flower spikelets appear in August to October in airy little clusters. The leaves take on a bright pinkish color in the fall before turning a buff color that persists over winter in mild areas.

HOW TO GROW GOLDEN VARIEGATED HAKONE GRASS Plant golden variegated hakone grass in moist, well-drained, rich soil in a lightly shaded site and it will grow well and perform reliably for you. In full hot sun, the leaves may scorch, while too much shade can cause their yellow color to fade. I haven't had any pest or disease problems with it here in California, but I would not plant it where water

Golden variegated hakone grass's cascading, bamboolike foliage takes on bright pink accents as fall arrives. This slow spreader thrives in partial to full shade.

stands in winter, where the soil is clayey and heavy, or where it's likely to dry out.

In Zone 6, mulch hakone grass rather thickly with fall leaves. After the foliage succumbs to frost but before temperatures fall into the teens and single digits, rake the leaves perhaps 12 to 24 inches deep over the stand and hold them in place with branches or with a piece of wire fencing. Given this protection, it should come through the winter just fine. In Zone 7 and southward, hakone grass overwinters with no problems.

PROPAGATING GOLDEN VARIEGATED HAKONE GRASS

As a spreading, stoloniferous grass, hakone grass is easy to divide in the spring or fall. The plain green, unvariegated species is easy to grow from seed.

THE RIGHT SITE FOR GOLDEN VARIEGATED HAKONE GRASS

When dappled light falls on the yellowish bronzy foliage of this cultivar, the gentle reflection helps brighten up a semi-shaded spot. It's great for growing in a shady container, too. Plant it on a hillside where it will cascade gently downward, creating the effect of rushing water flowing over the slope. Hakone grass also looks beautiful draped over rocks, down slopes, and over the edges of walls. In the perennial bed or border, hakone grass looks lovely planted in the front of the garden.

CO-STARS FOR GOLDEN VARIEGATED HAKONE GRASS

This hakone grass looks exquisite with 'Bronze Charm' Batalin tulip (*Tulipa batalinii* 'Bronze Charm'). Its grassy good looks go great with Japanese maple (*Acer palmatum*) and dwarf Alberta spruce (*Picea glauca* 'Conica'), and with other shade-tolerant groundcovers like European wild ginger (see page 54), lady's-mantle (*Alchemilla mollis*), hostas, and epimediums (*Epimedium* spp.). It looks particularly fine with ferns and appreciates much the same growing conditions.

In light shade, mix golden variegated hakone grass's gold-and-green leaves with burgundy-leaved ajuga.

'MOERHEIM BEAUTY' SNEEZEWEED

Helenium 'Moerheim Beauty'

Spotlight on 'Moerheim Beauty' Sneezeweed

USDA Plant Hardiness Zones: 3 to 9

Season of Bloom: August to October

Height × Width: 3 feet × 3 to 4 feet

Flower Color: Red, orange, and gold

Light Requirements: Full sun

Soil Requirements: Any well-drained soil, but does best in moist, rich garden loam

Place of Origin: Eastern North America

Plant Sources: Busse Gardens, Carroll Gardens, Forestfarm, Greer Gardens, Milaeger's Gardens, André Viette Farm & Nursery, White Flower Farm

'MOERHEIM BEAUTY' SNEEZEWEED is one of those stalwart perennials that you can't do without late in the season. Once you grow it and marvel at the strength of its colors and performance, you'll see why it's a shoo-in for all-star status.

Think of sneezeweed as the backbone of your garden from August to frost. It's a hearty bloomer that produces bushels of 1½-inch, daisylike flowers on stout branched stems with pointed, 3-inch leaves. Despite reaching 3 feet or more, they never need staking.

The characteristic that makes 'Moerheim Beauty' stand out from the other sneezeweeds is its color. The flowers open their deep, rich, dark red petals around a raised brown center that's rimmed with gold. The petals fade over time to an orange-gold shade that's as attractive as the initial red and make a fine tapesty of traditional fall colors when planted in large drifts.

HOW TO GROW SNEEZEWEED Because it blooms late in the season, sneezeweed tolerates dryness—although it prefers a moist soil. It favors full sun sites where the soil stays moist, maybe even a little wet. Happy to be out in the heat and sun of August, sneezeweed really takes off in the milder warm days of September, and usually it's still blooming in most northern areas when frost hits.

Root aphids sometimes trouble sneezeweed, but organic gardeners can usually avoid this problem by planting in compost-amended soil.

Other Snazzy Sneezeweeds

'Moerheim Beauty' displays just one of the variations of the yellow-orange-red-brown color scheme covered by sneezeweeds. 'Brilliant' sneezeweed (*H.* 'Brilliant') grows to just 3 feet tall with hundreds of smaller flowers in shades of orange, red, brown, and gold. 'Butterpat' sneezeweed (*H.* 'Butterpat') is a rich yellow and 3 feet tall. 'Crimson Beauty' sneezeweed (*H.* 'Crimson Beauty') isn't crimson—it's bronze-red and grows to 3 feet, and 'Riverton Beauty' sneezeweed (*H.* 'Riverton Beauty') reaches 4 feet tall and bears yellow flowers with maroon centers.

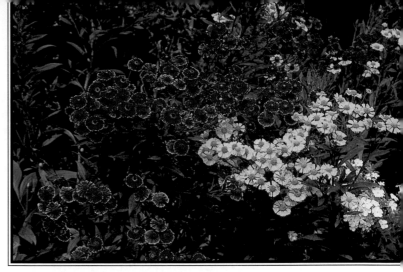

The golden highlights at the petal tips and centers of 'Moerheim Beauty' sneezeweed's flowers shine among yellow sneezeweeds. This all-star looks equally good when you cool off its warm colors with white or blue flowers and silvery foliage.

There is so much soil life in compost that the aphids are soon controlled naturally. Other than that, pests and diseases leave this native alone.

PROPAGATING SNEEZEWEED Sneezeweed is a clump-forming perennial that's easy to divide in spring or fall. The old clumps get crowded after three to four years and need to be divided into several smaller clumps to keep the plants vigorous. Replant divisions 24 inches apart. The species is easy to grow from seed sown outdoors in the fall, but cultivars like 'Moerheim Beauty' need to be propagated by division or by stem cuttings to retain their desirable characteristics.

THE RIGHT SITE FOR 'MOERHEIM BEAUTY'
When everyone else's garden is abandoned to the weeds and is toppling into a mass of overgrown stems and dying foliage, your sneezeweeds will come into their own. They supply an essential color boost just as the apples are ripening.

'Moerheim Beauty' sneezeweed is one of those perennials that looks okay as a small clump, looks better in a small group, and looks absolutely terrific as a large drift—and the larger the area, the better it looks. Fortunately, it's easy to divide clumps of this all-star to get lots more plants quickly.

CO-STARS FOR 'MOERHEIM BEAUTY' From cool-color contrasts to coordinating warm fall colors, 'Moerheim Beauty' looks good with many perennials. Use it to warm up gardens filled with cool blues, silvers, and whites such as Russian sage (see page 242), lamb's-ears (*Stachys byzantina*), 'Snowbank' boltonia (see page 76), asters, summer phlox (*Phlox paniculata*), salvias (*Salvia* spp.), Culver's physic (*Veronicastrum* spp.), and purple coneflowers (*Echinacea* spp.). Or mix and match 'Moerheim Beauty' sneezeweed with the related autumn hues of perennials like 'Goldquelle' shining coneflower (*Rudbeckia nitida* 'Goldquelle'), 'Autumn Joy' sedum (see page 280), 'Moonbeam' threadleaf coreopsis (see page 110), red-hot poker (*Kniphofia uvaria*), goldenrods (*Solidago* spp.), and ornamental grasses.

Plant drifts of 'Moerheim Beauty' sneezeweed with goldenrods and other fall-bloomers to echo the colors of autumn leaves.

DOUBLE-FLOWERED PERENNIAL SUNFLOWER

Helianthus × *multiflorus* 'Flore Pleno'

THIS TOUGH OLD COWBOY OF A PLANT is just what today's gardener needs—something that will make a tall, bold statement at the back of the border, something carefree, easy to grow, reliable, friendly looking, and ready to perform from midsummer to late summer or early fall when many other garden plants have finished up.

The stalks have the large, dark green, pointed leaves typical of sunflowers. Seen from a modest distance, they give the garden some relief from all the busy little leaves in it.

The flowers begin to open in early July to August, depending on the latitude, and they put on a dazzling, six-week show at the

Other Shining Sunflowers

*Among the other the cultivars of perennial sunflower, 'Loddon Gold' (*H.* × *multiflorus* 'Lodden Gold') has substantial 5- to 6-inch flowers in a pretty yellow-gold color. Thin-leaved sunflower (*H. decapetalus*) is one of perennial sunflower's parents and is a single-flowered species with the same bright color but a more slender appearance than perennial sunflower.*

Spotlight on Double-Flowered Perennial Sunflower

USDA Plant Hardiness Zones: 3 to 9

Season of Bloom: July to September

Height × Width: 5 to 6 feet × 5 to 6+ feet

Flower Color: Bright yellow

Light Requirements: Full sun

Soil Requirements: Average, neutral to alkaline, well-drained soil

Place of Origin: A hybrid between annual sunflowers and <u>H. decapetalus</u>, a native of the United States east of the Mississippi

Plant Sources: Bluestone Perennials, Crownsville Nursery, Forestfarm, Milaeger's Gardens, André Viette Farm & Nursery, White Flower Farm

5- to 6-foot level right into September. They are borne in fine profusion and are remarkable for their bright yellow color, their size (3 to 5 inches across), and their double form that resembles dahlias or cushion mums.

HOW TO GROW DOUBLE-FLOWERED PERENNIAL SUNFLOWER Any average, well-drained soil will suit this sunflower, so you don't have to fuss. If you want to treat it well, give it some compost or cow manure in early spring from time to time. It especially welcomes a handful of ground limestone to sweeten the soil. During the summer, perennial sunflower can withstand some dryness, but water it if it begins to look tired. One good soaking will get it through most dry spells in parts of the country that get summer rainfall.

PROPAGATING DOUBLE-FLOWERED PERENNIAL SUNFLOWER 'Flore Pleno' is both a hybrid and a named cultivar, so division is the way to produce more plants while retaining its desirable features. This sunflower needs frequent division to look its best, so divide the clumps every two to three years in the fall and replant the divisions 24 inches apart.

THE RIGHT SITE FOR DOUBLE-FLOWERED PERENNIAL SUNFLOWER Plant double-flowered perennial sunflower wherever you want to make a bold statement in your garden or in the landscape. Not only do these sunflowers do a fine job anchoring the back of the garden, but they also make excellent cut flowers for the house.

Who needs dahlias when double-flowered perennial sunflowers give you flowers like these?

CO-STARS FOR DOUBLE-FLOWERED PERENNIAL SUNFLOWER Mix this quintessential back-of-the-border plant with shorter middle to front of the border late-blooming perennials such as 'Moerheim Beauty' sneezeweed (see page 158), 'Wonder of Staffa' Frikart's aster (*Aster* × *frikartii* 'Wonder of Staffa'), 'Treasure' New England aster (*Aster novae-angliae* 'Treasure') and 'September Ruby' New England aster (*Aster novae-angliae* 'September Ruby'), among many others.

A Stellar Idea

Perennial sunflower's vigor extends below ground, too, where its roots spread easily in good soil. They can outgrow their bounds, which is why it's a good idea to divide them every couple of years. If they get out of hand, dig out the excess and replant or give clumps away as gifts. Or you can define their area with roofing paper or a plastic barrier set into the soil around the roots.

Plant double-flowered perennial sunflowers in a sunny, natural setting and let them grow. They make a hot summer duo with brilliant red salvias.

BLUE ★ OAT GRASS

Helictotrichon sempervirens

IMAGINE A DUSKY, BLUE-GRAY FOUNTAIN of densely packed, slender, stiff leaves that erupt upward to reach 24 inches, then gently arch over in graceful sprays. Now stop imagining and wake up to the reality of blue oat grass, a plant that rates all-star status in everybody's perennial garden. Its narrow, sharply pointed blue leaves form a tidy, dense, 12- to 24-inch tuft that looks good all summer long. In June or July, blue oat grass flowers, sending up slender oatlike stalks with airy, feathery bluish white flowerheads that age to a soft buff color.

HOW TO GROW BLUE OAT GRASS

Plant blue oat grass in a sunny, dry site. Although pests and diseases aren't a problem with this

Spotlight on
Blue Oat Grass

USDA Plant Hardiness Zones: 4 to 9

Season of Bloom: June to July

Height × Width: Leaves 24 inches, with flowers to 48 inches × 48 inches

Flower Color: Buff

Light Requirements: Full sun

Soil Requirements: Average, well-drained, neutral to slightly alkaline soil

Place of Origin: Southern Alps of southwestern France and northwestern Italy

Plant Sources: Kurt Bluemel, Bluestone Perennials, Forestfarm, Garden Place

grass—it resists the rust fungus that can attack other species of *Helictotrichon*—it may rot out if it sits in cold, wet, poorly drained soil.

Blue oat grass is a well-behaved plant. It will spread to make a clump about 24 inches across at the base with a top spray that's about 48 inches across, and stay at that size. In average garden soil, you won't need to baby it with fertilizers, but it will appreciate a little ground limestone in acid soils. In the spring, shake a little compost over the dormant plant.

In late winter, while the plant is still dormant, clean up blue oat grass by pulling out the old seedheads and flowerstalks and any withered leaves, then cut the remaining foliage back by half. Don't trim it back to the ground or it may respond by dying off.

Divide the plant every three years or so in early spring or late winter—perhaps just after you tidy it up. This will expand your numbers of this useful grass and will keep the clumps young and fresh looking.

A Bigger Blue Grass

Where your garden needs a silvery blue boost with a little more visual heft than blue oat grass can provide, check out blue lyme grass (Elymus arenarius 'Glaucus'). This grass's broader blue leaves grow 12 to 36 inches tall and arch over to form a fountain-shaped clump. Blue lyme grass is tough, too, and tolerates conditions that blue oat grass won't: light shade, dry soil, heavy clay soil, and even salt spray. In fact, it can be a bit too tough and can become invasive in good soil. Plant it within a root barrier to keep it from overstepping its bounds.

Blue oat grass sparkles next to the soft yellow flowers of 'Moonbeam' coreopsis. It's equally handsome with rosy pink yarrows and sedums.

PROPAGATING BLUE OAT GRASS

As a clump-forming grass, blue oat grass is easy to divide in spring. Make sure each division has a nice tennis-ball–size group of roots, and re-plant divisions 12 inches apart where you want to create a pretty drift of blue foliage.

THE RIGHT SITE FOR BLUE OAT GRASS

Blue oat grass is not just an all-star in the front of the sunny border, where it makes a beautiful contrast in form and color with the green, broad-leaved perennials around it. It's also indispensible perched on terraces, in a rocky slope garden, and in the open, where it gives a natural look. For fun, use the much smaller but similarly shaped and colored blue fescue (*Festuca cinerea*) with it.

CO-STARS FOR BLUE OAT GRASS

Blue oat grass looks stunning with pink-flowered perennials behind it. Try it with 'Croftway Pink' bee balm (*Monarda didyma* 'Croftway Pink'), 'Bouquet Rose' obedient plant (*Physostegia virginiana* 'Bouquet Rose'), Delavy incarvillea (see page 182), 'Elsie Heugh' prairie mallow (*Sidalcea malviflora* 'Elsie Heugh'), 'Clara Curtis' hardy garden

In summer, slender flowerstalks rise above blue oat grass's frosty blue-gray fountain of leaves.

chrysanthemum (see page 98), and pink phlox. It's also outstanding next to the red-to-purple hues of 'Burgundy Glow' ajuga (see page 32), 'Autumn Joy' sedum (see page 280), and 'Palace Purple' heuchera (see page 170).

A Stellar Idea

For a cool, elegant effect, plant blue oat grass with white-flowered perennials. This color combination is particularly nice for gardens that you enjoy late in the day as the light is fading. Blue oat grass's striking blue-gray foliage really stands out in the evening when its color fairly glows.

'SUMMER SUN' OXEYE

Heliopsis helianthoides 'Summer Sun'

HERE IS TRULY A CARE-FREE PERENNIAL with all the characteristics of an all-star. You really truly can plant 'Summer Sun' oxeye and forget it. It will repay your lack of attention with bushels of 3- to 4-inch golden yellow to yellow-orange daisies from June right into September. That's a summer's worth of golden color that will reliably return for you year after year if you keep the clumps divided every few years so they stay young and fresh.

Some may say, "Not another yellow daisy!" But then they haven't seen the warm, golden yellow—even orange yellow—color of 'Summer Sun'. It has the richest color and choicest form of all the oxeyes, in my opinion. Its blossoms are semidouble, and the centers are a deeper shade of the petal color. The stems

Oxeye Options

If you like 'Summer Sun' oxeye and appreciate its durable nature and cheery good looks, you'll find a few other worthy cultivars to consider for your garden. 'Karat' oxeye (H. helianthoides 'Karat') is a bright yellow single form that is a champion for longevity in the cut-flower vase. 'Incomparabilis' oxeye (H. helianthoides 'Incomparabilis') has warm orange petals. 'Golden Plume' (H. helianthoides 'Golden Plume') is among the best of the double-flowered oxeyes, with oodles of cheery bright yellow blossoms.

Spotlight on 'Summer Sun' Oxeye

USDA Plant Hardiness Zones: 3 to 9

Season of Bloom: June to September

Height × Width: 3 to 4 feet × 3 to 4 feet

Flower Color: Warm golden yellow

Light Requirements: Full sun

Soil Requirements: Good, fertile, well-drained garden loam

Place of Origin: Eastern United States from New York to Georgia and west to the Rockies

Plant Sources: Kurt Bluemel, Bluestone Perennials, Carroll Gardens, Garden Place, Milaeger's Gardens, Powell's Gardens, André Viette Farm and Nursery, Weiss Brothers Perennial Nursery, White Flower Farm

are very branched, with a flower perched at the tip of each branch. The medium green leaves are pointed, toothed ovals set on either side of the stems. And they don't need staking, even when they are 4 feet tall.

HOW TO GROW 'SUMMER SUN' Oxeye is a native, which means it's well-adapted to most of the country, and in this case, especially to the East. Its cultivar 'Summer Sun' performs well as far north as Canada, yet it's one of the best summer-blooming golden daisies for the hot, humid Southeast. There it tolerates the heat, survives drought, and produces plenty of flowers for up to 12 weeks—a remarkable feat in conditions that tend to shorten the bloom times of many lesser perennials.

'Summer Sun' oxeye is rarely bothered by pests or diseases. It thrives in good soil and does well in average soil, although it doesn't like thick, heavy soil. 'Summer Sun' grows best in full sun but tolerates partial shade. It's drought tolerant, too, and it remains compact in heat that turns other perennials leggy. With regular division it remains reliably perennial over its range of hardiness. Bright and cheerful, 'Summer Sun' sets a standard other plants should meet.

'Summer Sun' oxeye's warm golden yellow daisies shine in the midst of orange-red daylilies and rich red bee balms and dahlias.

PROPAGATING 'SUMMER SUN'

Divide 'Summer Sun' oxeye every three years to keep the clumps from dying out in the centers. Division is easy to do in spring or fall. You can also take basal cuttings from new shoots that appear in the spring. It comes fairly true from its seed.

THE RIGHT SITE FOR 'SUMMER SUN'

'Summer Sun' oxeye is perhaps at its best in very large masses used to brighten up an unused area, to bring some color to a seldom-visited outbuilding, to hide the compost pile,

Prolific and pretty, 'Summer Sun' oxeye will give you a summer's worth of showy, 4-inch, semi-double daisies on sturdy compact plants.

or as an edge for the more formal or elaborate flowers of perennial garden beds.

It makes a perfect foil for small ornamental trees with dark foliage such as Myrobalan plum (*Prunus cerasifera*) or purple smoke tree (*Cotinus coggygria* 'Royal Purple'), purple-leaved shrubs like purple barberry (*Berberis thunbergii* var. *atropurpurea*), or as a drift in a meadow planting in a small orchard.

One of its superior uses is as a cut flower. Cut it when the blossoms are almost fully open and it will last for a couple of weeks in a vase in the house.

CO-STARS FOR 'SUMMER SUN' Try masses of 'Summer Sun' oxeye with red, amethyst, or pink daylilies. It also pairs nicely with the dark red-orange sneezeweeds (*Helenium* spp.) and with summer phlox's (*Phlox paniculata*) pastel oranges. Its rich yellow goes great with the blue flowers of 'Wonder of Staffa' Frikart's aster (*Aster × frikartii* 'Wonder of Staffa'), speedwells (*Veronica* spp.), and delphinums, and with the petite yellow-centered daisies of fleabanes (*Erigeron* spp.). Plant it with midsized ornamental grasses for a naturalistic look.

LENTEN ROSE

Helleborus orientalis

LENTEN ROSE DOES SOMETHING that virtually no other perennial can do: It bravely persists through the winter, especially where it's growing in a protected spot. Then it starts to bloom—in January in the mild winter regions and as early as February or March in Zone 6 and northward.

And such flowers! Lenten rose's finely sculpted blossoms are pretty, open-faced, five-petalled bells, 2 inches or more across, that hang in clusters below the leaves. The overlapping petals are white, pink, or rosy purple, with maroon and plum speckles, and they surround a central cluster of showy yellow stamens. Instead of turning brown and wilting as their seeds ripen, the flowers gradually become tinged with green.

Spotlight on Lenten Rose

USDA Plant Hardiness Zones: 4 to 9

Season of Bloom: March to May

Height × Width: 18 inches × 24 inches

Flower Color: White to rosy purple, speckled with maroon

Light Requirements: Partial shade to full shade

Soil Requirements: Rich, moist, woodsy, humusy, loose, well-drained soil

Place of Origin: Bulgaria to Turkey

Plant Sources: Kurt Bluemel, Carroll Gardens, Forestfarm, Garden Place, Greer Gardens, Milaeger's Gardens, Park Seed, Plant Delights Nursery, Powell's Gardens, Roslyn Nursery, Sunlight Gardens, André Viette Farm & Nursery, Wayside Gardens, White Flower Farm

Seed Source: Thompson & Morgan

Other Heavenly Hellebores

Plant breeders have turned their attention to hellebores, and it's worth watching nursery catalogs and the plants at your local garden center to see what wonderful variations in flowers and foliage they come up with. H. atrorubens is a parent to some of the hybrids of Lenten rose and bears rich plum purple flowers. The Christmas rose (H. niger) blooms from January to March in Zones 5 to 9 with greenish white flowers. It's always amazing to see it stand up to the winter weather.

Lenten rose's evergreen foliage—semievergreen in Zone 5—is just as pretty as its shy flowers. Rich, dark green leaves, held out like fingers of the hand, form a handsome mound beneath higher branches of both leaves and flowers. The foliage persists through the summer, although it's less noticable amid the spring and summer flowers of other perennials. But it returns to well-earned prominence when winter arrives.

HOW TO GROW LENTEN ROSE Plant Lenten rose in loose, humusy, neutral to slightly alkaline soil that's amended with leaf mold or compost. If your native soil isn't limy, add

The pretty nodding bells of Lenten rose are a welcome sight in late winter and early spring, when few other flowers dare to show their faces.

some ground limestone to the planting hole. The best place to plant it is in a spot that gets summer shade and winter sun—that is, under deciduous trees. That way it gets winter sun to help it stay healthy and blooming and summer shade to protect its evergreen foliage. In these conditions, Lenten rose grows easily and sturdily, and needs little care other than adequate moisture.

Once your Lenten roses are established, you'll notice that they get along fine without you. They require no cutting back or deadheading, although you'll enjoy their appearance more in the spring if you trim off any old, blackened foliage. You'll find them completely pest- and disease-free, too.

PROPAGATING LENTEN ROSE Lenten rose grows easily from fresh seed sown in loose, humusy, well-drained, limy soil. Self-sown seedlings are likely around established plants. Lenten rose is more agreeable about division than other hellebores, but do this only in the spring, to give the divided plants plenty of time to establish roots to get them through the ensuing winter. Be careful to divide Lenten rose early, before the new foliage emerges.

THE RIGHT SITE FOR LENTEN ROSE The best place for Lenten rose is where you'll be able to see it and enjoy its rare beauty in the winter-to-spring months when flowers are so welcome. Plant it at the base of deciduous shrubs or in front of a sheltering backdrop of evergreens to better show off its early flowers. Its evergreen leaves will look their best where they get a little protection from the elements and will reward you with the sight of something alive and growing just when you start to think that spring will never come.

You'll get lots of flowers for little work from Lenten rose. Just plant it and enjoy it—but don't forget that all parts of this pretty all-star are poisonous, so keep it away from pets and small children.

CO-STARS FOR LENTEN ROSE In late winter and early spring, Lenten rose looks beautiful with spring bulbs such as snowdrops (*Galanthus* spp.) and flowering shrubs like daphnes (*Daphne* spp.), azaleas (*Rhododendron* spp.), forsythias, and others. Later in the season, it's pretty next to ferns and spring-flowering perennials such as columbines (*Aquilegia* spp.), bleeding hearts (*Dicentra* spp.), and astilbes.

'HAPPY RETURNS' DAYLILY

Hemerocallis 'Happy Returns'

YOU COULD EASILY CALL DAYLILIES the greatest perennials of all time. It's almost impossible to find a bad plant among the many daylily species and hybrids—in this century, furious hybridization has resulted in over 40,000 named cultivars listed with the American Hemerocallis Society.

Their blossoms are gorgeous, open-throated trumpets in a rainbow of every color except blue and pure white. Some are delightfully fragrant. They have a long blooming season and never need deadheading.

Spotlight on 'Happy Returns' Daylily

USDA Plant Hardiness Zones: 3 to 9

Season of Bloom: June to October

Height × Width: 18 inches × 24 inches

Flower Color: Soft lemon yellow

Light Requirements: Full sun to partial shade

Soil Requirements: Average, well-drained soil

Place of Origin: Parent species of most hybrids came from China or Japan

Plant Sources: Carroll Gardens, Crownsville Nursery, Klehm Nursery, Milaeger's Gardens, Park Seed, Roslyn Nursery, White Flower Farm

Dozens of Delightful Daylilies

And now a word about 'Hyperion' daylily (H. 'Hyperion'), my runner-up for all-star honors from among the hundreds of daylilies available. 'Hyperion' grows to 4 feet tall and bears lovely, large, graceful, canary yellow flowers that bloom well above the foliage over a six-week season in July and August. In addition to these many charms, 'Hyperion' also has a pretty floral fragrance.

There are too many other daylilies of merit to mention, including many new hybrid tetraploids that I find to be lovely in color but less graceful in form than the diploid and triploid types. If you look through even a few of the many catalogs that feature daylilies, you'll find yourself falling in love over and over again.

It's a humbling task to name a single daylily as the most valuable player of all these all-stars. Yet two hybrid cultivars do stand out among this vast array of outstanding plants: *H.* 'Happy Returns' and *H.* 'Hyperion'. Finally, 'Happy Returns' gets the nod because of its unceasing flower production from mid-June right to the frosts of October.

'Happy Returns' is an offspring of the famous 'Stella de Oro' daylily (*H.* 'Stella de Oro'), introduced a dozen years ago. Like that parent, it blooms in June and reblooms right to frost. 'Happy Returns' also gets its height from 'Stella de Oro', growing to no more than 18 inches tall. Its other parent is 'Suzie Wong' daylily (*H.* 'Suzie Wong'), which gives 'Happy Returns' its soft lemon yellow color. The flowers are small and ruffled, and each one lasts 24 full hours—long for a daylily and nice in the evening when other daylilies tend to close their flowers. But there's no need to worry about the life of each flower; 'Happy Returns' produces them in abundance all season long.

HOW TO GROW DAYLILIES Daylilies are also about the most adaptable perennials. They grow in almost any soil, withstand drought like the word doesn't exist, and spread gently to gradually fill an area, even naturalizing in suitable places. They like sun, they like partial shade, and they'll even grow in full shade—although they'll produce fewer flowers there.

They're not bothered by pests or diseases either, and you can lift and divide them pretty much any time and they'll hardly notice.

PROPAGATING DAYLILIES Daylilies are so easygoing that you can divide them whenever it suits you, even when they're in bloom. Simply unearth the clump and strike through it with your sharp shovel, splitting it into two or more pieces, each with thick, matted roots. For best bloom, divide in spring.

THE RIGHT SITE FOR 'HAPPY RETURNS' In the garden, daylilies are among the most versatile of perennials. They're at home in any

Daylily flower buds are edible, but long-blooming 'Happy Returns' is just too pretty to eat.

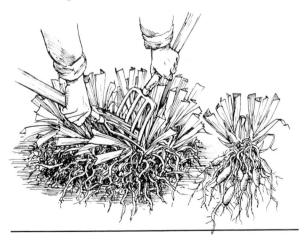

Use the leverage of two back-to-back garden forks to pry apart a clump of thick fleshy daylily roots, or slice through the clump with a sharp shovel.

flowering border, planted in beds of their own, or even used as a flowering, large-scale groundcover in difficult spots. Their foliage is a pretty fountain of green in and out of flower, as useful as an ornamental grass, and excellent for concealing spent bulb foliage.

The short stature of 'Happy Returns' makes it a particularly useful groundcover, and it's a perfect daylily for the front to middle of the garden where its graceful foliage will arch over edging or ground-hugging plants. It's also pretty in a large pot—filling in nicely, blooming prolifically, and suffering not a bit when you're a little forgetful about watering the container.

CO-STARS FOR 'HAPPY RETURNS' The light lemony yellow of 'Happy Returns' mixes well with just about any color, even light pinks. And since it blooms all season, it winds up in combinations with a variety of perennials. It's lovely with Stokes' aster (*Stokesia laevis*), with Russian sage (see page 242), with lavender asters—you name it.

'PALACE PURPLE' HEUCHERA

Heuchera micrantha
var. *diversifolia* 'Palace Purple'

MOST OF US KNOW the common coral bells (*Heuchera sanguinea*), which are pretty enough with their mounds of rounded, green leaves and tiny fire red flowers dangling on tall leafless stems. But then there's 'Palace Purple' heuchera! This astounding plant has dark purplish metallic leaves that show as many colors as there are ways for sunlight to glint off them. It's such a choice plant that it received a Perennial Plant Association Plant of the Year award. 'Palace Purple' is an all-star in every garden where it makes an appearance.

'Palace Purple' was found in England—some say in Kew Gardens, others say at Powis Castle in Wales. Some say this unique plant came from a planting of the West Coast native

Spotlight on
'Palace Purple' Heuchera

USDA Plant Hardiness Zones: 4 to 9

Season of Bloom: May to July

Height × Width: 12 to 18 inches × 18 inches

Flower Color: White

Light Requirements: Full sun to partial shade

Soil Requirements: Humusy, moist, well-drained loam

Place of Origin: Western North America

Plant Sources: Ambergate Gardens, Kurt Bluemel, Bluestone Perennials, Busse Gardens, Carroll Gardens, Crownsville Nursery, Forestfarm, Garden Place, Greer Gardens, Milaeger's Gardens, Powell's Gardens, Roslyn Nursery, Van Bourgondien, André Viette Farm & Nursery

Seed Source: Park Seed

Hail to Heucheras!

A similar and similarly captivating heuchera cultivar is 'Chocolate Ruffles' (H. 'Chocolate Ruffles'). Its leaves are chocolate brown on top and burgundy underneath, with purple flower spikes. Other heucheras of note include 'Pewter Moon' (H. 'Pewter Moon'), which has silvery foliage with pewter-grey veins and maroon undersides and bears ice pink flowers on maroon stems. And regular coral bells (H. sanguinea) now come with crimson, rose, coral, or white flowers, as well as silvered or white-variegated foliage.

small-flowered alumroot (*Heuchera micrantha*), others say it came from American alumroot (*H. americana*), a native of the eastern United States. Still others say that 'Palace Purple' is a separate species all its own, because it does come true from seed.

No matter what its heritage, gardeners everywhere can be thankful for it. The plants form mats or mounds of 4-inch-wide, maple- to grapelike leaves of an odd brown-black-mahogany-purple metallic color that looks slightly different depending on how the light hits it. In any event, it's a dark color and great for associating with light foliage. It looks terrific with light pink and light blue flowers, too.

'Palace Purple' heuchera's glossy bronze-purple leaves contrast handsomely with the gray-green fuzzy foliage and chartreuse flowers of lady's-mantle.

In summer, small whitish flowers bloom on tall, thin stems well above the foliage. Some gardeners cut them off as unworthy or incidental to the leaves, but I like the way they spray over the rather gothic-looking foliage below.

How to Grow 'Palace Purple'
In areas of strong summer sun, plant 'Palace Purple' in partial shade or its dark leaves will green up to some extent—although they'll turn mahogany-bronze again when things cool down in late summer. 'Palace Purple' likes a constant supply of moisture and loose, humusy soil, although some drought won't hurt it. Pests and diseases don't seem to bother it.

A clump of 'Palace Purple' will tend to grow upward on a woody crown above the soil level over time. Every two to three years, lift these clumps and remove the older, woody sections of the crown before replanting the rosettes.

Propagating 'Palace Purple'
Divide the clumps in spring or fall and replant the divisions 12 inches apart. 'Palace Purple' comes true from seed, but be sure to pull out any seedlings that don't show a rich, dark color in the leaves, as there will be considerable variation among seedlings.

Not all gardeners appreciate 'Palace Purple' heuchera's airy sprays of small whitish flowers, but they sparkle like stars against the dense backdrop of the leaves.

The Right Site for 'Palace Purple'
This heuchera performs a function that few other plants do—providing a dark mass of foliage to interrupt the strong sweeps of green typically found in massed garden plantings.

Co-Stars for 'Palace Purple'
The brownish bronze leaves of 'Palace Purple' offer delightful relief from all the garden greens. This all-star looks especially beautiful paired with 'Silver Mound' artemisia (*Artemisia schmidtiana* 'Silver Mound'), pink 'Millstream Laura' summer phlox (*Phlox subulata* 'Millstream Laura'), blue oat grass (see page 162), 'Krossa Regal' hosta (see page 176), and in the warmer zones, blue-gray and mauve echeverias (*Echeveria* spp.).

'BRIDGET BLOOM' FOAMY BELLS

× *Heucherella alba* 'Bridget Bloom'

SUBTLE CHARM IS THE HALLMARK of this perennial all-star. It's one of those plants for semi-shade that you don't notice at first when you stop by a garden. But as you stand there for a minute and begin to look carefully at the plantings, you'll discover 'Bridget Bloom' foamy bells and fall softly in love with it.

Although small, its appeal is large, with quilted-looking, medium green leaves with darker veins. The foliage is quite attractive as it grows into a fine-tufted mat that serves as an elegant, refined-looking groundcover. The

Spotlight on 'Bridget Bloom' Foamy Bells

USDA Plant Hardiness Zones: 3 to 9

Season of Bloom: May to October

Height × Width: 12 to 15 inches × 16 inches

Flower Color: Clear shell pink

Light Requirements: Partial shade to full sun

Soil Requirements: Rich, moist, humusy, well-drained soil

Place of Origin: A rare intergeneric hybrid between Tiarella wherryi and Heuchera × brizoides, made by Alan Bloom in England around 1958

Plant Sources: Ambergate Gardens, Bluestone Perennials, Busse Gardens, Carroll Gardens, Crownsville Nursery, Forestfarm, Milaeger's Gardens, Powell's Gardens, Shady Oaks Nursery

A Couple of Clever Crosses

Look up at the botanical name of this plant and notice the first letter you come to. Yes, the "×" is in the right place, because 'Bridget Bloom' foamy bells is the result of a rare cross between two genera—Heuchera and Tiarella. Her parent species are Heuchera × brizoides and Tiarella wherryi, to be exact. The cross was made and named years ago by the great English plantsman, Alan Bloom.

Another foamy bells (× Heucherella tiarelloides) comes from the cross between Heuchera × brizoides and Tiarella cordifolia, Allegheny foamflower. This plant bears salmon pink flowers and spreads slowly by stolons, unlike × Heucherella alba, which is clump forming.

leaves are very much like a heuchera's (*Heuchera* spp.), but they also resemble the leaves of foamflowers (*Tiarella* spp.).

The flowerstalks are long, branched, leafless wands that open tiny flowers along their length and reach 12 inches or so above the leaves. The flowers are small marvels: Each one has a dark pink tube and calyx and tiny oval petals of a light pink, almost white. The effect from any distance—such as from an adult's height looking down on them—is of an airy spray of tiny, clear shell pink florets. The flowers begin opening in May and flower vigorously through June then taper off and return with more bloom later in the year, even into October. All during this time, the leaves keep looking tidy.

If you like sweet little things, you'll love 'Bridget Bloom' foamy bells. Its dainty pink flowers dance lightly above a mat of triangular, evergreen foliage.

HOW TO GROW FOAMY BELLS

Foamy bells doesn't like being crowded by weeds or other plants, so give it its spot in the border or rock garden and mulch around it with compost or leaf mold. It will enjoy the cooling, moist mulch and will give you years of its dainty little flower wands in return. Be sure to plant it where you'll have no problem keeping it evenly moist during the heat of summer. Few pests or diseases bother it. The leaves are evergreen until you reach the northerly part of its range. A covering of leaf mulch will help pull it through tough winters, especially where snow cover isn't assured.

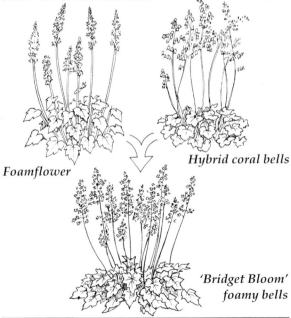

Foamflower

Hybrid coral bells

'Bridget Bloom' foamy bells

The result of a cross between <u>Heuchera</u> and <u>Tiarella</u>, 'Bridget Bloom' foamy bells has sterile flowers that do not produce seed.

PROPAGATING 'BRIDGET BLOOM' 'Bridget Bloom' foamy bells is a clump-forming plant. Because the clumps stay rather small, divide them carefully with a knife or with shears. If it's done in spring and the divisions are replanted 8 to 10 inches apart, you can have a nice stand of 'Bridget Bloom' in just a few years.

THE RIGHT SITE FOR 'BRIDGET BLOOM' Use 'Bridget Bloom' foamy bells as a groundcover beneath shrubs or deep-rooted trees. Plant it at the edge of a woodland path or stairway where you can walk close enough to see its exquisite little flowers. Let big swaths of those precious blossoms dance in the light shade. It also makes an excellent container plant for a shady patio.

CO-STARS FOR 'BRIDGET BLOOM' 'Bridget Bloom' foamy bells makes a lovely groundcover for partial shade. Mix it with pink forms of Bulle's primrose (*Primula × bulleesiana*), dame's rocket (*Hesperis matronalis*), roseroot (*Sedum rosea*), fan columbine (*Aquilegia flabellata*), northern Jacob's ladder (*Polemonium boreale*), hostas, astilbes, and wild gingers (*Asarum* spp.).

'LORD BALTIMORE' HIBISCUS

Hibiscus 'Lord Baltimore'

IF YOU DON'T KNOW THE ROSE MALLOW (*H. moscheutos*), be prepared to be stunned, for you'd never expect this tropical-looking beauty to be able to thrive in cold-winter climates. But thrive it does and in places that are difficult for most perennials.

Our all-star 'Lord Baltimore' hibiscus is a hybrid of the showy but durable rose mallow with many all-star features to recommend it. Chief among them is its huge, 7- to 10-inch-wide, single, saucer-shaped flowers. Each flower consists of five rich, rosy crimson large petals surrounding a prominent elongated cluster of the pistil and stamens.

Here it is in a much more temperate climate, blooming on tall, 4- to 6-foot, erect flowering stems that never need staking. The flowers are spaced evenly along these stems, giving a neat

Spotlight on
'Lord Baltimore' Hibiscus

USDA Plant Hardiness Zones: 5 to 9

Season of Bloom: July to October

Height × Width: 4 to 6 feet × 4 to 5 feet

Flower Color: Rich rose red

Light Requirements: Full sun to partial shade

Soil Requirements: Rich, moist soil

Place of Origin: United States east of the Mississippi

Plant Sources: Ambergate Gardens, Kurt Bluemel, Busse Gardens, Carroll Gardens, Forestfarm, Powell's Gardens, Shady Oaks Nursery, André Viette Farm & Nursery, Wayside Gardens, We-Du Nurseries

Other High-Scoring Hibiscus

In addition to 'Lord Baltimore', some other cultivars deserve recognition. The 'Mallow Marvels' series (H. 'Mallow Marvels' series) delivers assorted red, pink, and white blossoms that are somewhat smaller and more funnel-shaped. The flowers of 'Anne Arundel' hibiscus (H. 'Anne Arundel') are magenta-pink. Among the rose mallows, the 'Southern Belle' series (H. moscheutos 'Southern Belle' series) is dwarfed at 3 feet tall but still opens 10-inch flowers in red, pink, and white.

appearance considering their size. Best of all, 'Lord Baltimore' starts blooming in July and will continue to open its spectacular flowers until frost cuts it down in October. The foliage is maplelike, 6 to 8 inches long, broad and shallowly lobed, soft pale green above and whitish underneath.

HOW TO GROW 'LORD BALTIMORE' Plant 'Lord Baltimore' where it will get full sun or in an area of partial shade that gets sun for at least three to four hours a day. Choose a site with some protection from strong winds, which can tatter the large, delicate flowers. Rose mallow is a marsh plant, and 'Lord Baltimore' prefers consistently moist soil. But don't worry over it too much, this all-star is also fairly drought tolerant and grows well in ordinary sunny garden conditions.

You might expect to find flowers like these only in the tropics, but 'Lord Baltimore' hibiscus blooms happily as far north as Zone 5.

Rose mallow and its hybrids remain relatively unbothered by pest and disease problems. Japanese beetles may feed on the broad leaves. If they do, pick them off and drop them into a can of soapy water to keep them from disfiguring the foliage.

PROPAGATING 'LORD BALTIMORE' Carefully divide the woody clumps of 'Lord Baltimore' hibiscus in the spring and replant the divisions 3 feet apart. You can also take cuttings in the fall for rooting and overwintering in a protected spot. If you can bend a stem to the ground without breaking it, layering is possible in late summer. Rose mallow is easy to grow from seed, although cultivars like 'Lord Baltimore' require vegetative propagation by layering, stem cuttings, or division to retain their hybrid characteristics.

THE RIGHT SITE FOR 'LORD BALTIMORE'
'Lord Baltimore' literally rules in the garden and is as bold a plant as anyone could want. Use its shrublike stature to anchor the back of the border, where it will kick into bloom during the midsummer doldrums, attracting hummingbirds to its red trumpets. Or incorporate it in a waterside planting, where it looks as naturally at home as its marshy origins make it.

CO-STARS FOR 'LORD BALTIMORE' Grow 'Lord Baltimore' with ornamental grasses and boltonia (*Boltonia asteroides*). It's also exceptionally pretty with the finer textures of perennials such as astilbe and clary (*Salvia sclarea*).

The pink-and-crimson flowers of 'Lady Baltimore' hibiscus are at their best in a moist site.

A Stellar Idea

It's helpful to mark the spot where 'Lord Baltimore' or other hibiscus are growing in late fall after the hard freezes hit. These plants awaken from dormancy later in the spring than most other perennials. You don't want to forget where it is and dig into it when putting in new plants in the spring.

'KROSSA REGAL' HOSTA

Hosta 'Krossa Regal'

MOST HOSTAS ARE GROWN for their foliage not their flowers. And of all the beautiful foliage this wide-ranging genus offers the gardener, none is more perfect than that of 'Krossa Regal' hosta.

Krossa Regal leafs out late, as hostas tend to do. The tight mass of fleshy roots sends up many stemless leaves that unfurl from the

Hosts of Hostas

Beautiful though it is, 'Krossa Regal' barely gives you a hint as to the hundreds of hosta selections available with almost any characteristics you'd like. In this well-bred and widely hybridized group of plants you'll find narrow, medium, or large leaves; with yellow or white variegation; in shades of dark, bright, or light green or silvery blues; even with nicely fragrant flowers in the case of August lily (H. plantaginea) and its many offspring. Some other blue-leaved favorites of mine are H. tokudama, a medium-size hosta with deeply puckered and cupped leaves and short stalks of whitish flowers; 'Elegans' Siebold's hosta (H. sieboldiana 'Elegans'), a hefty but re-fined plant with large, round, blue-gray, deeply puckered leaves, and white to pale lavender flowers; and 'Halcyon' hosta (H. 'Halcyon'), a medium-size hosta with deeply ribbed, heart-shaped leaves, and pale lavender flowers.

Spotlight on 'Krossa Regal' Hosta

USDA Plant Hardiness Zones: 3 to 9

Season of Bloom: July to August

Height × Width: 24 to 48 inches × 36 inches

Flower Color: Lilac

Light Requirements: Bright shade or partial shade

Soil Requirements: Deep, rich, moist, well-drained humusy soil

Place of Origin: Hybridized from several species found in Japan, notably H. nigrescens eliator

Plant Sources: Ambergate Gardens, Kurt Bluemel, Bluestone Perennials, Busse Gardens, Carroll Gardens, Crownsville Nursery, Dutch Gardens, Forestfarm, Greer Gardens, Klehm Nursery, Milaeger's Gardens, Plant Delights Nursery, Powell's Gardens, Roslyn Nursery, Shady Oaks Nursery, André Viette Farm & Nursery, We-Du Nurseries

ground like large versions of lily-of-the-valley leaves. Each leaf grows rapidly to about 18 inches, unfurling gracefully into a pointed blade arching gently backward as it exposes its upper surface to the light.

'Krossa Regal' hosta leaves are a wonderful frosty blue-green, lighter on the underside, and about 8 inches across when fully open. The leaf surface bears regular creases that begin in the stalk and flow out toward the tip. When all the leaves have emerged and un-furled, the plant makes a dome about 24

'Krossa Regal' hosta's creased blue-green leaves are its primary attraction. Some gardeners remove its spikes of lilac flowers so they won't detract from the foliage.

Brighten a shady spot with the frosty foliage of 'Krossa Regal'. Its broad leaves provide a pleasing foil to fine-leaved ferns, variegated Solomon's seal, and smaller hostas.

inches tall and 36 inches across. In mid- to late summer, tall, leafless flower spikes shoot up and open pale lilac trumpets that droop from one side of the stalks.

How to grow 'Krossa Regal'

Like most hostas, 'Krossa Regal' is an indestructible plant, but you must give it the conditions it likes for good results. First, it needs a rich, humusy, deep, slightly acid soil that's moist but not boggy. It especially needs good winter drainage or it will die out. Hostas grow slowly; it takes four to five years for them to reach specimen size.

It develops its best shape and frosty blue color in bright shade or semishade (some morning sun, never hot late afternoon sun). Too much shade and it turns a dull green; too much sun, ditto.

And finally, slugs and snails will shred your hostas to the point where you will wish you hadn't planted them. If these mollusks abound where you live, you must put slug- and snail-proof barriers or traps around your hostas. A band of diatomaceous earth will help. A surrounding barrier of copper strips is even better.

Propagating Hostas

Hostas are easy to divide in spring and fall and possible to divide in summer, although this sets them back a bit. After stands fill in and become established, multiply your favorites by taking out wedges from older plants and filling in the holes with fresh humusy soil mixed with compost.

The Right Site for 'Krossa Regal'

Use 'Krossa Regal'—and other hostas—to bring structure and life to areas under trees, along borders, and in beds grouped with other perennials. Brighten up a semishady spot with the silvery blue leaves of 'Krossa Regal' and a few white-flowered companions.

Co-Stars for 'Krossa Regal'

Any semi-shade plants with ferny foliage look fine with large-leaved hostas, among them astilbes, bleeding hearts (*Dicentra* spp.), and ferns. Because hostas are late to leaf out, plant them with very early spring plants like pasque flower (*Pulsatilla vulgaris*), winter aconite (*Eranthis hyemalis*), checkered lily (*Fritillaria meleagris*), and crocuses that will fill their spot until they arrive.

'FRANCES WILLIAMS' SIEBOLD'S HOSTA

Hosta sieboldiana 'Frances Williams'

Spotlight on
'Frances Williams' Siebold's Hosta

USDA Plant Hardiness Zones: 3 to 9

Season of Bloom: July to August

Height × Width: 24 to 36 inches × 48 inches

Flower Color: Pale lavender, almost white

Light Requirements: Sun to shade

Soil Requirements: Rich, moist, humusy, well-drained soil

Place of Origin: Island of Honshu, Japan

Plant Sources: Kurt Bluemel, Bluestone Perennials, Crownsville Nursery, Dutch Gardens, J. W. Jung Seed, Greer Gardens, Klehm Nursery, Milaeger's Gardens, Plant Delights Nursery, Powell's Gardens, Roslyn Nursery, Savory's Gardens, Shady Oaks Nursery, Van Bourgondien, André Viette Farm & Nursery, White Flower Farm

I IMAGINE THERE COULD BE MORE INTERESTING leaves than those of 'Frances Williams' Siebold's hosta, but I have my doubts. Every year, members of the American Hosta Society vote for their favorite among the 600 or so hostas that have been selected or hybridized. And nearly every year for the past 15 years, 'Frances Williams' has been named the favorite or has scored right near the top.

'Frances Williams' has large, 12-inch-long leaves that are 10 inches or so across. They are a rich blue-green, except for an irregular margin of gold-yellow that undulates around the leaf edges. The leaves have long grooves from their stems to their pointy tips, but these grooves are puckered, giving the leaves a textured, seersucker appearance.

Various Variegated Hostas

Some other wonderful variegated hostas include curled leaf hosta (H. crispula), 'Goldbrook' Fortune's hosta (H. fortunei 'Goldbrook'), 'Albo-marginata' Fortune's hosta (H. fortunei 'Albo-marginata'), 'Aureo-marginata' blue hosta (H. ventricosa 'Aureo-marginata'), all with green leaves with whitish margins. 'Gold Standard' Fortune's hosta (H. fortunei 'Gold Standard') is the reverse of 'Frances Williams', with gold leaves edged in green.

HOW TO GROW 'FRANCES WILLIAMS' This is one hosta you can plant in full sun in the North but only in places where it gets plenty of water to keep its roots cool. 'Frances Williams' really prefers bright shade or partial sun, as do most hostas. In the South, shade is all-important or the plants will burn out.

When choosing a spot for 'Frances Williams', avoid frost pockets, as late frosts will injure its tender leaves. This is rarely a problem, since hostas typically leaf out later than most perennials. But that late frost can nip them if they're in a frost-prone spot.

Its pale lavender flowers are pretty, but gardeners love 'Frances Williams' Siebold's hosta for its colorful seersucker foliage.

PROPAGATING 'FRANCES WILLIAMS' Like all hostas, 'Frances Williams' is easy to divide in the spring and fall. Old, established plantings can be hard to unearth and why would you want to move them anyway? The best way to get more plants is to take chunks or wedges out of an established clump, then refill the holes with compost-enriched soil. Replant divisions 24 inches apart.

THE RIGHT SITE FOR 'FRANCES WILLIAMS'
It may take four to five years for a slow-growing clump of this cultivar to plump out to its full size of 4 feet across and 3 feet tall. When it does reach mature size, 'Frances Williams' is magnificent. Use it right at the edge of a bed or border, so its leaves can arch out over the grass. Plant a large group in the shade under tall trees, where its variegations will create the impression of movement among the shadows. Avoid planting 'Frances Williams' under trees that drip sap.

Pair a group of 'Frances Williams' hostas with 'Autumn Joy' sedum. In August, the sedum's small leaves and busy, foamy green flowerheads will look pretty with the hosta and its whitish flowers and later, when the sedum's flowerheads turn to a rich burgundy-brown color, the hosta's fading leaves will splash even more golden yellow to complement the sedum.

CO-STARS FOR 'FRANCES WILLIAMS'
Combine 'Frances Williams' Siebold's hosta with 'Autumn Joy' sedum (see page 280). It also looks good with the dark leaves of its sibling, 'Elegans' Siebold's hosta (*H. sieboldiana* 'Elegans'), with ferns, and with yellow wax bells (see page 188). This substantial hosta also works wonderfully as an unaccompanied specimen.

Use the gold-edged leaves of 'Frances Williams' to echo other yellows in your garden. The broad foliage shines amid fine-textured perennials and ornamental grasses.

'SNOWFLAKE' PERENNIAL CANDYTUFT

Iberis sempervirens 'Snowflake'

AT FIRST GLANCE, 'SNOWFLAKE' perennial candytuft seems like an unassuming little plant, but it is mighty in its own way. The most noticeable feature of 'Snowflake' is the purity of its white flowers. 'Snowflake' begins blooming in late April in the warmer regions and in May in the middle and northern areas and continues its display into June. The 2- to 3-inch flower clusters consist of circular whorls of tiny, flat-bladed petals of a bright, reflective white that puts other garden whites to shame.

The plant is actually an evergreen subshrub, with woody stems and dark green leaves that remain green all winter in the southern part of its range. In the North, cold, dry, winter air may injure the leaves unless you give them some leaf mulch or pine boughs for protection.

Other Sweet Candytufts

Other compact candytuft cultivars include the early blooming 'Alexander's White', which forms dense, 8-inch mounds but doesn't bloom quite as long as 'Snowflake', and 'Pygmaea', a spreading selection that grows to 4 to 5 inches tall. 'Autumn Beauty' and 'Autumn Snow' are two perennial candytuft cultivars that bloom in spring, then again in the fall.

Spotlight on 'Snowflake' Perennial Candytuft

USDA Plant Hardiness Zones: 3 to 9

Season of Bloom: April to June

Height × Width: 8 to 10 inches × 36 inches

Flower Color: Pure white

Light Requirements: Full sun to partial shade

Soil Requirements: Rich, loose, well-drained soil

Place of Origin: Mediterranean region

Plant Sources: Kurt Bluemel, Carroll Gardens, Forestfarm, Garden Place, Milaeger's Gardens, André Viette Farm & Nursery, Weiss Brothers Perennial Nursery

If you live in an area with constant winter snow cover, perennial candytuft will come through fine. 'Snowflake' is a compact cultivar, growing to only 8 inches tall.

HOW TO GROW PERENNIAL CANDYTUFT

Perennial candytuft starts out small but can grow to form a clump as large as 3 feet across, so give it plenty of room to spread out. Perennial candytuft grows best in well-drained, average garden soil. Although it will grow in partial shade, it prefers full sun and is more winter hardy in a sunny spot. You'll also get more flowers from plants growing in full sun. Perennial candytuft's 1½-inch-long leaves remain attractive all through the growing season and even into the winter. Pests and diseases don't bother it.

Give 'Snowflake' a sunny site and well-drained soil, and it will cover itself with a blanket of pure white flowers every spring.

A Stellar Idea

Giving 'Snowflake' a bit of grooming is important because of the plant's tendency to form woody stems. After 'Snowflake' finishes blooming in June, cut it back by at least a third, and preferably by half, to about 4 inches from the ground. This promotes the production of new foliage that looks better for the rest of the year and helps keep 'Snowflake' compact and vigorous.

CO-STARS FOR 'SNOWFLAKE' This all-purpose filler looks beautiful mixed with other spring bloomers like pasque flower (*Pulsatilla vulgaris*), creeping Jacob's ladder (*Polemonium reptans*), hybrid columbines (*Aquilegia* hybrids), wild blue phlox (*Phlox divaricata*), 'Luxuriant' bleeding heart (*Dicentra* 'Luxuriant'), basket-of-gold (see page 70), primroses (*Primula* spp.), rock cresses (*Aubrieta* spp.), and low-growing bellflowers (*Campanula* spp.).

PROPAGATING PERENNIAL CANDYTUFT As perennial candytuft spreads, it produces side shoots that are easy to separate into new divisions. Divide plants after flowering has finished, trimming the tops back to about 4 inches. Replant divisions 18 inches apart. Perennial candytuft is easy to divide but seldom requires it. You can also take tip cuttings after flowering stops. Perennial candytuft grows well from seed sown outdoors in spring or fall; propagate cultivars like 'Snowflake' by division or by cuttings.

THE RIGHT SITE FOR 'SNOWFLAKE' In bloom, this low, frothy white all-star shines when planted atop a terrace, in the front of a border, in a large container with colorful annuals, or mixed with dark-leaved ajuga (*Ajuga reptans*) in a rock garden. 'Snowflake' makes a tidy, low-growing edging along a path, where its white flowers help light the way.

'Snowflake' perennial candytuft's bright white flowers and compact habit make it look exceptionally good cascading over a dark stone or brick wall.

DELAVY INCARVILLEA

Incarvillea delavayi

MOST OF THE INCARVILLEA CLAN are frost-tender, tropical beauties that are rather fussy about their conditions and in no way resemble the kind of hard-working, low-maintenance all-stars we've assembled here. The one magnificent exception is Delavy incarvillea.

This gorgeous perennial is a joy to behold. Its 12-inch-long leaves resemble those of a fern, or better still, a robust Jacob's ladder (*Polemonium* spp.) and form a large rosette of basal foliage. The many glossy, dark green leaflets are prettily toothed and alternate along the leaf stems, becoming smaller toward the tips.

Before the rosette of leaves is fully grown, slender flowerstalks emerge from the centers and reach 24 to 36 inches tall in late May or early June. Bunched at the top of these spikes

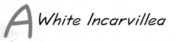

A White Incarvillea

'Snow Top' Delavy incarvillea is a white-flowered cultivar that shares the advantages of the species. 'Snow Top' bears large, white, trumpet-shaped flowers with rich yellow throats, on tall stems above a sizable rosette of dark green, divided leaves. Although its white flowers are less likely to quarrel with other garden color schemes than are the rosy purple flowers of the species; I prefer them to 'Snow Top' Delavy incarvillea's white blossoms.

are several large, 3-inch, trumpet-shaped flowers of a deep rosy red to purplish color with golden yellow throats. The flowers are quite showy and exotic looking, resembling large gloxinias (hence one of its common names, hardy gloxinia) or large versions of the foxglove's flowers (*Digitalis* spp.).

HOW TO GROW DELAVY INCARVILLEA Plant Delavay incarvillea in loose, moist, well-drained soil in full sun to partial shade. In soggy soil, especially in the winter, the plant's deep taproot is prone to rotting.

In Zones 5 and 6, give Delavy incarvillea a thick mulch to protect it from hard frosts and freezes. Dump a few baskets of leaves over it, then pin them in place with branches. Delavy incarvillea is perfectly at home in Zone 7. In Zones 8 and 9 in the South, give it a semi-shady spot and lots of summer water. It does extremely well in Zone 9 in California.

Spotlight on Delavy Incarvillea

USDA Plant Hardiness Zones: 5 to 9

Season of Bloom: Late May to mid-July

Height × Width: 18 to 24 inches × 18 to 24 inches

Flower Color: Rich, rosy red to purple

Light Requirements: Full sun to partial shade

Soil Requirements: Rich, moist, well-drained soil

Place of Origin: Southwestern China

Plant Sources: Dutch Gardens, Forestfarm, Roslyn Nursery, Van Bourgondien

Seed Source: Thompson & Morgan

Large, trumpet-shaped flowers earn Delavy incarvillea its other common name—hardy gloxinia.

Except for marauding slugs, pests aren't a problem for Delavy incarvillea. It suffers no disease problems of note, as long as it's growing in a well-drained location. It's reliably perennial in the majority of its range, struggling only in the intense heat of the Deep South.

PROPAGATING DELAVY INCARVILLEA

Incarvilleas have taproots, which makes division difficult but not impossible. Separate the secondary roots with shoots in early autumn and replant them immediately about 12 inches or so apart. Once established, Delavy incarvillea resents disturbance, so separate these roots carefully. Plants are usually grown from seed, and it may take seedlings two to three years to grow to flowering size.

THE RIGHT SITE FOR DELAVY INCARVILLEA

Of all the garden's perennials, Delavy incarvillea is among the most spectacular and conspicuous, so site it where visitors (and you) can get a good look at it. Delavy incarvillea is so striking it may be best used alone, grouped in drifts of three to five plants. It causes more comment than most other plants, not only for its flowers, but also because the flowers are followed by interesting, elongated seedpods.

CO-STARS FOR DELAVY INCARVILLEA

Delavy incarvillea's rosette of glossy, ferny leaves provides a nice contrast for the spiky foliage of ornamental grasses and Siberian iris (*Iris sibirica*) or for the rounded leaves of lady's-

mantle (*Alchemilla mollis*). Its rosy flowers look good with the blue flowers of perennials such as blue pincushion flower (*Scabiosa caucasica*), creeping baby's-breath (*Gypsophila repens*), great bellflower (*Campanula latifolia*), peach-leaved bellflower (*C. persicifolia*), Dalmatian bellflower (*C. portenschlagiana*), and catmint (see page 230).

Elongated, beak-shaped seedpods follow Delavy incarvillea's showy flowers.

A Stellar Idea

Although it's not hardy in the ground north of Zone 5, you can grow Delavy incarvillea in colder zones if you lift the roots and store them for the winter. Harvest the roots, which are like stubby carrots, after the plant is dormant but before frost penetrates and freezes the soil solid. Store them over the winter in a cold basement under a covering of soil or compost that's moist and never allowed to dry out.

'BEVERLY SILLS' BEARDED IRIS

Iris 'Beverly Sills'

TALL BEARDED IRISES ARE SUCH ALL-STARS that many gardeners stop right there: The garden beds are entirely in irises, in flower in spring, followed by a season's worth of attractive, fanned, swordlike leaves. These irises are the most ubiquitous of garden plants and among the easiest to grow.

As to which is the best, that's a tough question to answer. Bearded irises are so beloved that thousands of new varieties are being introduced each year! It really comes down to a matter of taste, with some help from the American Iris Society.

The Society's top award is the Dykes Memorial Medal, named after one of the world's great iris breeders. To receive this medal, an iris must pass through rigorous

Innumerable Irresistible Irises

Of course there are many other worthy bearded irises. Check the catalogs for starters. And there are many other species of iris that deserve a place in the garden, too: Yellow flag (I. pseudacorus) and Japanese iris (I. ensata) for the wet spots; Louisiana iris hybrids for the Deep South; Pacific Coast iris hybrids for charming small irises; and so many others the list takes pages. But if I were to grow just one iris, there's no doubt which one captures my heart. That's 'Beverly Sills' bearded iris.

Spotlight on 'Beverly Sills' Bearded Iris

USDA Plant Hardiness Zones: 4 to 9

Season of Bloom: May to June

Height × Width: 36 inches × 24 to 36 inches

Flower Color: Coral pink

Light Requirements: Full sun

Soil Requirements: Average, well-drained garden soil

Place of Origin: Hybridized from many species

Plant Sources: Carroll Gardens, Crownsville Nursery, J. W. Jung Seed, Park Seed, Powell's Gardens, White Flower Farm

qualifications first earning the Society's award of merit and then undergoing six years of testing in all American climates and conditions. If you've got a Dykes Memorial Medal winner, you know you've got one of the most superior bearded irises in the world, and one you can absolutely rely on.

Just such a winner is 'Beverly Sills' bearded iris, almost heartbreakingly beautiful in its luscious clear coral pink color, with frilly standards, broad light pink falls, deep pink styles, and a pink beard, or tongue as some call it. It won the Dykes Memorial Medal in 1985 and is unsurpassed for a pink iris in form, color, performance, and all-around beauty.

HOW TO GROW BEARDED IRIS Plant this iris in full sun in average to good garden soil that is loose and well-drained. Because of their fleshy rhizomes, bearded irises are drought- and heat-resistant except in the

A planting of 'Beverly Sills' bearded iris will add beauty and fragrance to your garden. Some gardeners say that irises smell like their colors!

THE RIGHT SITE FOR 'BEVERLY SILLS' Use a patch of 'Beverly Sills' where your garden needs a bit of beauty and drama. Tall bearded irises are so lovely that most gardeners mix their flower colors in beds by themselves. Their bold, spiky leaves make a nice foil for round leaves or fine-texture perennials. Don't forget to smell your bearded irises, as they all are fragrant.

CO-STARS FOR 'BEVERLY SILLS' 'Beverly Sills' certainly can shine on its own but is equally effective mixed with yarrows, blue pincushion flower (*Scabiosa caucasica*), snow-in-summer (*Cerastium tomentosum*), creeping baby's breath (*Gypsophila repens*), bellflowers (*Campanula* spp.), 'Alba' rose campion (*Lychnis coronaria* 'Alba'), and hens-and-chickens (*Sempervivum* spp.).

Deep South. They're hardy through most of the United States, except in the very coldest areas. Pests and diseases aren't much of a problem for well-grown plants, although overly moist soil is an open invitation to rot. If you remove the spent foliage in the fall or early spring, you can avoid the fat pink grubs of iris borers, which travel down through the leaves into the rhizomes, spreading bacterial diseases along the way. If you notice dark streaks in the foliage, squash the larvae in their tunnel, then remove affected leaves.

Every three years, about six weeks after flowering stops, dig up the rhizomes and refresh the plants as described in "Propagating Bearded Iris". Replant them with plenty of room, and cultivate them shallowly, as their roots are near the surface.

PROPAGATING BEARDED IRIS As bearded iris grows, its thick, fleshy rhizome elongates and the new lobes send up leaves and flowers. Dig up the entire rhizome six weeks after bloom and break or cut off the new pieces, each of which should have a fan of leaves and dangling wiry roots. Discard the old part of the rhizome. Trim the leaves back to a couple of inches and replant the fresh pieces 12 inches apart so that the roots are buried but the leaves and a bit of the rhizome from which they arise are above the soil.

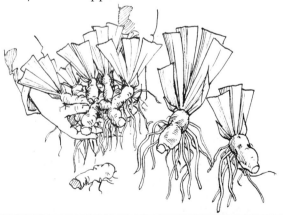

Replant bearded iris divisions with the top half of the rhizome above the soil. Discard the older portions of the rhizomes.

'CAESAR'S BROTHER' SIBERIAN IRIS

Iris sibirica 'Caesar's Brother'

HERE'S TO THE MOST VARIED, useful, beautiful genus in the perennial garden, the irises. And perhaps the most useful and beautiful species of the genus is Siberian iris; and of these, 'Caesar's Brother' must be at the top of anyone's list of all-stars.

There's nothing quite like the flower color of 'Caesar's Brother', a deep, velvety violet that's almost blue-black. The beardless flowers have three standards, as the smaller, upright petals are called, and three larger falls, as the petal-like sepals that arch downward are called. In addition, there are three very narrow, petal-like styles in the center.

Spotlight on 'Caesar's Brother' Siberian Iris

USDA Plant Hardiness Zones: 3 to 9

Season of Bloom: Mid-May to early July

Height × Width: 36 inches × 24 to 36 inches

Flower Color: Deep, velvety violet, almost black

Light Requirements: Full sun to partial shade

Soil Requirements: Moist, well-worked, slightly acid, humusy soil

Place of Origin: Central and eastern Europe to central Asia

Plant Sources: Kurt Bluemel, Bluestone Perennials, Busse Gardens, Carroll Gardens, Dutch Gardens, Forestfarm, Garden Place, Milaeger's Gardens, Powell's Gardens, Sunlight Gardens, Van Bourgondien, White Flower Farm

Other Splendid Siberian Irises

Among the Siberian iris selections currently available, I like the white-flowered 'Alba' (I. sibirica 'Alba'), which makes a spectacular companion for 'Caesar's Brother'. Siberian iris hybrids are many, but I especially admire the bright yellow-and-white flowers of 'Butter and Sugar', the 6-inch white flowers of 'Fourfold White', the pale blue and yellow blossoms of 'Sky Wings', and the medium blue flowers of 'Perry's Blue'. Not coincidentally, all of the hybrids go great with 'Caesar's Brother'.

'Caesar's Brother' looks graceful but is tough and sturdy in performance. Its thick roots plunge deeply into the soil, holding it tightly and making the clumps drought-resistant even though they prefer adequate moisture. The plants tend to be shorter in dry conditions.

Siberian iris

Bearded iris

Siberian iris flowers seem trim and dashing next to the rather open and frilly blossoms of bearded irises.

The leaves are tough, grasslike swords that reach 24 to 30 inches tall. In mid-May, hollow flowerstalks grow from the leaves to various heights, from the leaf tips to well above the leaves. Each flowerstalk produces many of the neat, dainty blossoms.

HOW TO GROW SIBERIAN IRIS

Siberian irises are among the most trouble-free and low-maintenance plants in the garden. They're perfectly hardy, pest- and disease-free (except for thrips when they're grown in too dry a spot), and they never need staking. Plant them in moist, humusy soil in full sun to partial shade for the best results, although they'll endure much more difficult conditions. An established stand needs little more than occasional division and a sprinkling of compost.

PROPAGATING SIBERIAN IRIS

While bearded irises are easy to propagate, Siberian irises tend to be a bit grumpier about the process. Don't disturb them until the centers of the clumps begin to die out. Then, in early spring, lift the clump and divide it by jamming two spading forks back to back into the center of the clumps, then pushing the handles down in opposite directions so the leverage pries it apart. Replant divisions immediately, not allowing them to dry out, at least 18 inches apart.

THE RIGHT SITE FOR 'CAESAR'S BROTHER'

Each clump of 'Caesar's Brother' grows into a dense, weed-excluding mat about 24 inches across, so several plants will anchor a bank or a spot by a large rock or below a tall wall almost like a large groundcover. When the plants finish blooming, the grassy foliage continues to look neat all season, and in the winter it turns brown and lies down neatly,

'Caesar's Brother' adds drama to the landscape with its grassy, swordlike leaves and velvety dark violet flowers.

ready to be cut off just above ground level when spring cleanup comes. 'Caesar's Brother' makes a superb cut flower, too.

CO-STARS FOR 'CAESAR'S BROTHER'

Mix stands of dark-flowered 'Caesar's Brother' with swaths of the lighter colored blossoms of Siberian iris hybrids such as 'Butter and Sugar', 'Fourfold White', 'Sky Wings', or 'Perry's Blue', or with the white flowers of 'Alba' Siberian iris (*I. sibirica* 'Alba'). Use salmon pink oriental poppies as an accent for a large stand of 'Caesar's Brother'. And its spiky, grassy leaves look good fronted with the soft, round foliage of lady's-mantle (*Alchemilla mollis*).

A Stellar Idea

For a showy, upright accent on your deck or patio, try planting 'Caesar's Brother' in a large container. With adequate moisture, this iris will put on a dramatic floral display in a pot and its leaves will remain good looking and healthy throughout the summer.

YELLOW WAX BELLS

Kirengeshoma palmata

YELLOW WAX BELLS DESERVES to be more widely known in the United States. This shrub-size perennial's great beauty can turn the early fall into one of the most eagerly anticipated times of the gardening year.

In April, yellow wax bells produces strong, sturdy green stems that carry large, maplelike leaves of a pleasant medium green. The plant grows 3 to 4 feet tall and almost as wide, forming a striking mass that looks almost tropical. Yellow wax bells looks spectacular planted amid big, blue-green hostas and large shaggy ferns.

As a foliage plant, yellow wax bells anchors the shady garden through the heat of summer and then when temperatures begin to cool off in late August or early September, it starts its captivating flower show, which continues into October. The light of early fall accentuates the lovely, waxy flower's narrow, pale yellow bells that resemble shuttlecocks,

A Korean Cousin

Korean wax bells (K. koreana) is another Kirengeshoma species that you might encounter in nursery catalogs. This plant resembles yellow wax bells in size, shape, and foliage but has upright yellow flowers. The upright form of Korean wax bells is pretty, but not as charming as yellow wax bells' nodding flowers.

Spotlight on Yellow Wax Bells

USDA Plant Hardiness Zones: 5 to 9

Season of Bloom: Late August to October

Height × Width: 36 inches × 24 to 36 inches

Flower Color: Pale yellow

Light Requirements: Semishade or dappled shade to full shade

Soil Requirements: Rich, deep, acid, moist, humusy soil

Place of Origin: Mountains of Japan

Plant Sources: Ambergate Gardens, Kurt Bluemel, Busse Gardens, Carroll Gardens, Crownsville Nursery, Forestfarm, Milaeger's Gardens, Roslyn Nursery, Shady Oaks Nursery, André Viette Farm & Nursery

opening at the tips of the stems and in sprays from the leaf axils. These dainty blossoms nod gracefully on their stems.

HOW TO GROW YELLOW WAX BELLS In the right place, yellow wax bells takes very little maintenance and is not affected by pests or diseases. But you have to plant it in the right place. Think about the misty mountain slopes of Japan, with a deep forest duff that's constantly moist yet well drained and slightly acidic from the decomposing leaf litter. Here the sunlight penetrates in a quiet dappling or there is bright shade under a canopy of high tree branches. If you have a spot with these conditions and you plant yellow wax bells there, you will soon see why it is a perennial all-star.

Yellow wax bells forms a shrub-size clump of attractive maplelike leaves that are a focal point in the shade garden throughout the summer.

Prepare the planting site with old compost or leaf mold dug deeply into the soil. If your soil is alkaline, dig out a large hole about 24 inches wide and as deep and fill it with compost or decayed organic matter with a neutral or acid pH.

After yellow wax bells' flowers fade, rounded, three-horned seed capsules take their place. You can dry these capsules and save them for starting in the late winter to have yellow wax bells seedlings to plant out when spring arrives.

In Zones 5 and 6, mulch yellow wax bells deeply with pine needles. Not only will such a mulch protect the crown of the plant against winter injury, but it will also help acidify the soil as it decomposes.

PROPAGATING YELLOW WAX BELLS Divide yellow wax bells carefully in the spring, making two 12-inch-wide divisions out of a mature 24-inch clump. Replant the divisions about 18 to 24 inches apart. You can also grow yellow wax bells from seed sown indoors in late winter.

THE RIGHT SITE FOR YELLOW WAX BELLS Yellow wax bells adds a dramatic presence to the shade garden and delivers welcome late-season flowers. Combine it with other shade-loving fall bloomers like liriopes (*Liriope* spp.) and azure monkshood (*Aconitum carmichaelii*)

In late summer and into the fall, yellow wax bells produces nodding sprays of pale yellow, bell-shaped flowers that give way to round green seed capsules.

for a stunning display at what can be the least exciting time of the gardening year.

CO-STARS FOR YELLOW WAX BELLS Azure monkshood (*Aconitum carmichaelii*), big blue lilyturf (*Liriope muscari*), 'Elegans' Siebold's hosta (*Hosta sieboldiana* 'Elegans'), 'Halcyon' hosta (*H.* 'Halcyon'), ostrich fern (*Matteuccia struthiopteris*), blue-flowered hydrangeas, and 'Pink Spire' summersweet (*Clethra alnifolia* 'Pink Spire') all are worthy companions for this valuable perennial.

'ROYAL STANDARD' RED-HOT POKER

Kniphofia 'Royal Standard'

Spotlight on 'Royal Standard' Red-Hot Poker

USDA Plant Hardiness Zones: 5 to 9

Season of Bloom: Late July to September

Height × Width: 3 to 4 feet × 3 to 4 feet

Flower Color: Yellow and bright red

Light Requirements: Full sun

Soil Requirements: Good, loose, well-drained, moist soil

Place of Origin: Southern Africa

Plant Source: André Viette Farm & Nursery

ENGLISH PLANT BREEDERS, with their typically English sense of reserve, have been hybridizing cultivars of this hot-colored genus with softened and toned-down colors in recent years. I think that's a shame, because here we have a perennial that's bright and brassy in the garden and proud of it! There's enough elegance in the garden without having to civilize the flamboyant colors of this ruffian.

Of all the red-hot pokers, 'Royal Standard' is the best. Its 3- to 4-foot torchlike flower spikes rise straight up from its grassy leaves in high summer, giving the plant its other common name, torch lily. Each flower spike carries many tubular florets that emerge bright red and turn yellow from the bottom upwards as they open. These florets overlap each other, giving the flowering tip of the poker a shaggy appearance.

Whereas many red-hot pokers have very coarse, ratty-looking foliage that's decidedly unattractive, 'Royal Standard' has slightly narrower, better-looking leaves than most. These leaves appear in dense masses, but frankly, even the best red-hot pokers aren't that wonderful as foliage plants.

HOW TO GROW RED-HOT POKER You can plant this South African native in full sun and just about any kind of soil, as long as it's well drained but not too dry. Pests and diseases aren't a problem. The clumps care for themselves and despite the flowerstalks' height, they need no staking. Division isn't necessary or even desirable unless you need to increase your planting. About all you have to do to keep red-hot poker happy is to shake a little compost over it every year or two.

Other Sizzling Red-Hot Pokers

There are many other red-hot poker cultivars and hybrids worth noting, including 'Early Hybrids' red-hot poker (Kniphofia 'Early Hybrids') which begins producing its red-and-yellow flower spikes in June. 'Primrose Beauty' (K. 'Primrose Beauty') has light primrose yellow blooms, and 'Shining Sceptre' (K. 'Shining Sceptre') bears pokers covered in bold orange florets. 'Little Maid' (K. 'Little Maid') produces light yellow to cream-colored flowers on compact 24-inch plants; and 'Earliest of All' red-hot poker (K. 'Earliest of All') blooms early with coral-rose and yellow flowers.

Many of the new cultivars coming from England are not hardy north of Zone 7. 'Royal Standard', on the other hand, is the hardiest of the available cultivars, and will overwinter in Zone 5 with a light mulch of leaves in late fall and a well-drained site to keep its roots from rotting. If its roots spend the winter in soggy soil, red-hot poker will surely die out.

PROPAGATING RED-HOT POKER If you want to increase your planting of red-hot poker, separate a few crowns and their fleshy roots from the edges of a clump in the fall. Lift the clump and shake or rinse off the soil for easy separation. Trim back the roots a bit and shear off the leaves to about 2 to 3 inches, then replant small divisions about 18 inches apart. But for best bloom, leave it alone; division is not necessary to keep it looking its best.

THE RIGHT SITE FOR RED-HOT POKER Red-hot poker throws fireworks in the garden and makes a spectacular cut flower. You get the greatest color burst when you plant it in drifts of three to five or more plants. Since the 4- to 6-inch flowers are hoisted a good 3 to 4 feet above the leaves, it's possible to place the red-hot pokers behind plants with more graceful foliage and form, such as cushion

The hot colors of 'Royal Standard' red-hot poker echo the blazing heat of the high summer sun.

Plant red-hot pokers amid clumps of variegated moor grass to help hide the pokers' rather average-looking, grassy foliage.

spurge (see page 136), green-and-yellow variegated grasses like variegated moor grass (*Molinia caerulea* 'Variegata'), and the interesting, lime-yellow mounds of 'Limelight' licorice plant (*Helichrysum petiolare* 'Limelight'). I have seen red-hot pokers thrusting up from behind a mound of this pretty rambler to great ornamental effect.

CO-STARS FOR 'ROYAL STANDARD' The yellow and reddish (yielding, from a distance, an orangey effect) color scheme of 'Royal Standard' red-hot poker looks good with yellows and coppery colors, such as variegated moor grass (*Molinia caerulea* 'Variegata'), and perennials like lemon daylily (*Hemerocallis lilioasphodelus*) and 'Moonshine' yarrow (see page 28). Shrubby plants such as 'Limelight' licorice plant (*Helichrysum petiolare* 'Limelight'), Japanese angelica-tree (*Aralia elata* 'Aureo-variegata'), 'Baggesen's Gold' boxleaf honeysuckle (*Lonicera nitida* 'Baggesen's Gold'), purple smoke tree (*Cotinus coggygria* 'Royal Purple'), and cushion spurge (see page 136) make good companions that help to hide 'Royal Standard' red-hot poker's coarse foliage. For relief from all those hot colors, include a mass of cool blue globe thistle (*Echinops ritro*) in the group.

'WHITE NANCY' SPOTTED DEAD NETTLE

Lamium maculatum 'White Nancy'

ONE PERENNIAL STANDS OUT ABOVE ALL OTHERS as a groundcover that reflects and injects light into otherwise solemn, shady places in the garden—'White Nancy' spotted dead nettle. Perennials expert Fred McGourty, says of 'White Nancy', "It's the best introduction among groundcovers for shade that I have seen in the past 25 years." High praise indeed—but well deserved by this all-star.

'White Nancy' blooms for a good 10 weeks in late spring and into the summer—certainly through June and July. Its bright, long-lasting, white blossoms scatter additional light in the shady places and give a cool, clean look to the garden floor in the hottest part of the summer.

The leaves of 'White Nancy' are green with silver mottling, although their overall effect is

Other Sparkling Spotted Dead Nettles

'White Nancy' is a sport of 'Beacon Silver', a worthy cultivar with magenta flowers. 'Pink Pewter' spotted dead nettle (L. maculatum 'Pink Pewter') is almost identical to our all star but bears beautiful, clear pink flowers. For a different foliage effect try 'Beedham's White' spotted dead nettle (L. maculatum 'Beedham's White'), which has bright yellow leaves and white flowers.

Spotlight on 'White Nancy' Spotted Dead Nettle

USDA Plant Hardiness Zones: 4 to 9

Season of Bloom: Late May to August

Height × Width: 12 inches × 24 to 36+ inches

Flower Color: White

Light Requirements: Partial sun to semi-shade

Soil Requirements: Average soil of just about any type

Place of Origin: Europe east to the Caucasus and Turkey

Plant Sources: Ambergate Gardens, Kurt Bluemel, Bluestone Perennials, Busse Gardens, Garden Place, Milaeger's Gardens, Powell's Gardens, Roslyn Nursery, André Viette Farm & Nursery, Weiss Brothers Perennial Nursery, White Flower Farm

silvery—nearly the same as the popular cultivar 'Beacon Silver' (*L. maculatum* 'Beacon Silver'). When the summer gets hot, both 'White Nancy' and 'Beacon Silver' can get a little floppy and open in habit, but 'White Nancy' holds together better.

HOW TO GROW 'WHITE NANCY' 'White Nancy' tolerates almost any kind of soil but dies out in the depths of full, dark shade, especially where the soil is clayey. It grows best in bright shade or in dappled semishade and even tolerates full sun in the cool northernmost part of its range. 'White Nancy' is drought tolerant, too, and it persists in the

In partial shade and well-drained soil, 'White Nancy' shares groundcover duties with deep purple-flowered Dalmatian bellflower.

dry shade under thirsty trees—a difficult assignment for most perennials. This makes 'White Nancy' extra valuable under ornamental maples, for instance.

PROPAGATING SPOTTED DEAD NETTLE

Spotted dead nettle is a running and rooting plant and is very easy to divide in spring or fall. In spring, lift divisions with a trowel and replant them immediately about 8 to 10 inches apart, mulching between them with compost so they fill in over the summer.

THE RIGHT SITE FOR 'WHITE NANCY'

The best use of 'White Nancy' in the garden is as a vigorous, fast-growing, attractive carpet. Although it spreads easily across an open area, 'White Nancy' is not invasive and is easy to remove if it grows into places where you don't want it. By planting 'White Nancy' with other groundcovers such as ajugas (*Ajuga* spp.), aroids (*Arum* spp.), and wild gingers (*Asarum* spp.), you can create a dappled mix of light, silvery foliage with dark leaves.

In a hanging basket 'White Nancy' spotted dead nettle's silvery runners will trail over the sides. This looks especially pretty hanging from the branch of a tree near the house.

CO-STARS FOR 'WHITE NANCY'

This all-star makes a fine companion for little spring bulbs such as glory-of-the-snow (*Chionodoxa* spp.), striped squill (*Puschkinia scilloides*), crocuses, and squills (*Scilla* spp.), and with shade-loving foliage plants such as European wild ginger (see page 54), fringed bleeding heart (*Dicentra eximia*), Lenten rose (see page 166), hostas, and ferns. It's a useful groundcover under azaleas (*Rhododendron* spp.) and in the sometimes-tough conditions under larger ornamental trees and shrubs.

Brighten a shady spot with the white flowers and silvery foliage of 'White Nancy' spotted dead nettle. This vigorous groundcover spreads easily without threatening to take over.

A Stellar Idea

In late July, go over the planting with a string trimmer held a few inches off the ground to cut back the foliage. 'White Nancy' will reemerge within a few weeks looking tighter and more compact for the late summer and fall. It has a persistent habit and will be out there doing its job long after the leaves fall from the trees.

WHITE PERENNIAL SWEET PEA

Lathyrus latifolius 'Albus'

PERENNIAL SWEET PEA IS THE QUINTESSENTIAL plant-it-and-forget-it perennial. Nothing bothers it. It survives despite whatever cruelties nature throws at it. And its white-flowered cultivar, 'Albus', is an exceptionally beautiful plant. All these talents and more make it a perennial all-star for every garden.

Perennial sweet pea is a vine that grows to about 6 to 8 to 9 feet long. It very much resembles its cousin, the annual sweet pea (*L. odoratus*), but it is decidedly perennial and very long lived. It will return reliably year after year, making its spring scramble up whatever support you've provided. And while annual sweet pea is fragrant, white perennial sweet pea is not.

The tough roots of white perennial sweet pea send up stems from the same spot each year and produce new suckers as they slowly spread over the years. Its stems are sturdy and

A Perennial Pea to Plant with Care

Another perennial pea species is everlasting pea (L. grandiflorus) which has larger flowers than perennial sweet pea but fewer color selections—mostly limited to pink-magenta. It is an invasive plant and difficult to eradicate, so plant this species in a confined space where it can cover an ugly wall without escaping into your garden.

Spotlight on White Perennial Sweet Pea

USDA Plant Hardiness Zones: 4 to 9

Season of Bloom: Late June to September

Height × spread: 6 to 8 feet × 5 to 8 feet

Flower Color: White

Light Requirements: Full sun

Soil Requirements: Just about any soil will suit it

Place of Origin: Southern Europe east to Russia and south to the Caucasus

Seed Source: Thompson & Morgan

winged with narrow, lancelike leaves and branching tendrils to grasp its support. Twelve-inch-long flowerstalks emerge from the leaf axils, bearing bunches of white, pealike blossoms. In the species, flower color ranges from light pink to rose-magenta to carmine to white.

HOW TO GROW WHITE PERENNIAL SWEET PEA White perennial sweet pea is tolerant of any soil, as well as extreme drought. It handles California's summer dry spells with ease and asks for nothing but a sunny spot. Hard frosts kill the herbaceous, aerial parts of the vine, and these need to be cleared away during late winter garden cleanup.

PROPAGATING WHITE PERENNIAL SWEET PEA Most gardeners grow white perennial sweet pea from seed, which must be scarified with a nail file or sandpaper, then soaked overnight in water before you plant it outdoors in spring or fall. You can try taking cuttings in the summer, but they are chancy at best. Or try dividing white perennial sweet pea by looking for emerging suckers in early spring and slicing some off from the main roots—also a chancy procedure.

THE RIGHT SITE FOR WHITE PERENNIAL SWEET PEA Magenta is a rather pushy, common color—all right by itself dressing up a waste place or an out-of-the-way fence, but hard to coordinate in a well-thought-out bed or border. On the other hand, the fresh, pure white flowers of our all-star 'Albus' go beautifully with all other colors in the garden, and the vines make a perfect backdrop in the perennial border when trained up the rear fence or wall. White perennial sweet pea has

all the virtues of the species—especially its long season of bloom—and a cool, refreshing look to its flowers, without the color problems posed by the species' strong magenta.

CO-STARS FOR WHITE PERENNIAL SWEET PEA The best companions for white perennial sweet pea are functional, rather than picturesque. Plant it behind oriental poppies (*Papaver orientale*) so that when the poppies finish blooming and turn brown in midsummer, you can use perennial sweet pea's vines to hide them from view. Train white perennial sweet pea up the side of a shed or through a hedge, or let it sprawl down a bank.

Create a cool curtain of green and white over a sunny window: Train white perennial sweet pea up a string or wire trellis to enjoy see-through shade during the hot summer months.

White perennial sweet pea will gladly clamber up any support you provide it. Its sturdy, winged vines climb via branching tendrils to heights of 8 or 9 feet, and they'll trail just as far if you let them grow over the ground.

A Stellar Idea

Mature plants of white perennial sweet pea will tend to sprawl along the ground as well as climbing up any supports you provide. Consider planting it where it can serve as a rough-and-tumble groundcover.

'HIDCOTE' ENGLISH LAVENDER

Lavandula angustifolia 'Hidcote'

GARDENERS WHO LIMIT THEIR USE of English lavender to the herb garden should expand their thinking. This tough plant is one of the most useful of all of the all-star perennials.

Lavender's soft gray-green foliage is perfect for edging any garden. Its classic form lends itself to formal plantings as well as to informal drifts.

Our all-star selection is 'Hidcote' English lavender, a compact form that grows 12 to 18 inches tall. Its slender flower spikes are tipped with a few inches of tightly bunched, dark blue-purple flowers.

HOW TO GROW ENGLISH LAVENDER Plant English lavender in a sunny site where the soil is average to rich and very well drained.

Lots of Lovely Lavenders

There are many other excellent cultivars of English lavender. Other favorites of mine include 'Munstead' (L. angustifolia 'Munstead'), which is also compact and has extremely fragrant, rosy purple flowers; 'Rosea' (L. angustifolia 'Rosea'), which bears rosy pink flowers; and 'Jean Davis' (L. angustifolia 'Jean Davis'), a cultivar with pale icy pink flowers and a compact, perfectly globe-shaped form.

Spotlight on 'Hidcote' English Lavender

USDA Plant Hardiness Zones: 5 to 9

Season of Bloom: June to August

Height × Width: 18 inches × 18 inches

Flower Color: Deep blue-purple

Light Requirements: Full sun

Soil Requirements: Light, sandy-loamy, neutral to alkaline, loose, well-drained, dry soil

Place of Origin: Mediterranean region east to India

Plant Sources: Kurt Bluemel, Bluestone Perennials, Carroll Gardens, Daisy Fields, Forestfarm, Garden Place, Milaeger's Gardens, Van Bourgondien, André Viette Farm & Nursery, Wayside Gardens, White Flower Farm

Seed Source: Thompson & Morgan

Lavender is a tough plant that can withstand dry soil, but too much moisture is its enemy, especially in heavy soils and where winters are cold and wet. Plant it where good drainage will keep it from rotting away during the winter months, and go easy on moisture-holding mulches. English lavender endures even the heat of the Deep South—but is not so long lived there as it is in more temperate regions. Its delightful fragrance comes from volatile oils that tend to keep pests at bay.

PROPAGATING ENGLISH LAVENDER Take cuttings from the new growth around the edges of the plant in early summer. Stick the cuttings in a container of well-drained medium and keep them evenly moist and

A staple of formal gardens, 'Hidcote' English lavender is wonderful planted in less formal drifts at the front of the dry, sunny perennial border.

'Hidcote' English lavender's neat gray-green foliage and upright blue-purple flower spikes make it a good companion for many other garden plants.

covered with a clear plastic tent until they root. You can also divide English lavender in early spring.

THE RIGHT SITE FOR 'HIDCOTE'

Few things are as pretty as a large swath of lavender in full bloom, and the key is to plant plenty of this attractive, aromatic all-star. 'Hidcote' lavender's perfect for separating brighter colored flowers, such as different colors of roses, and its deep blue-purple looks great with rich reds and pale pinks.

Plant enough 'Hidcote' so that you have plenty of flower spikes to harvest and dry for sachets and potpourris. But be sure you leave some in the garden, where you can stand among the plants on a hot summer day and smell the fragrance lifting up to you from the flowerheads.

Lavender's foliage is nicely fragrant as well, with a clean, herbal scent that will have you pinching a few of the slender silver-gray leaves each time you pass the plant. Here's yet another reason for using 'Hidcote' English lavender to edge a pathway or along the side of a deck or patio.

CO-STARS FOR 'HIDCOTE'

English lavender's spiky flowers make it a natural with ornamental grasses such as fountain grass (*Pennisetum alopecuroides*). In the perennial garden, 'Hidcote' looks good with yellow flowers such as 'Coronation Gold' yarrow (see page 26) and 'Moonshine' yarrow (see page 28), as well as with the rosy purples of verbena (*Verbena* spp.). At the front of the garden, give 'Hidcote' an edging of the low-growing, sweet-scented, deep purple flowers of 'Royal Carpet' sweet alyssum (*Lobularia maritima* 'Royal Carpet'). 'Hidcote' lavender's low profile makes it a tidy hedge for around your herb garden, where it looks good planted with herbs such as 'Purpurascens' garden sage (*Salvia officinalis* 'Purpurascens'), catmint (see page 230), rosemary, and lavender cotton (*Santolina* spp.).

A Stellar Idea

As it grows, English lavender's stems tend to become woody. Keep your lavender looking its best by pruning it back by about half its height every two to three years in the spring. This promotes compact, fresh growth and more flowers.

'BARNSLEY' TREE MALLOW

Lavatera thuringiaca 'Barnsley'

IN CASE YOU DON'T KNOW ABOUT THIS PLANT, let me tell you that 'Barnsley' tree mallow is a very superior, easy-to-grow perennial that acts like a shrub. It is gorgeous in its summer-long, nonstop bloom, and easily makes it onto my list of perennial all-stars.

'Barnsley' tree mallow is a soft and elegant plant that grows to about 6 feet tall and almost as wide, with a loosely branching habit much like an open shrub. Its herbaceous parts actually do turn woody over the season but die off in the hard frosts. The entire plant is covered with dusty, pale gray-green, lobed, vaguely maplelike leaves, each one just a couple of inches across.

Here and there along the branches and at their tips, small, furled, pinkish flower buds emerge beginning in June. These open into 2- to 3-inch, saucer-shaped flowers of clear white to a very pale pink with reddish pink

'Barnsley' Tree Mallow

USDA Plant Hardiness Zones: 6 to 9

Season of Bloom: June to October

Height × Width: 6 feet × 4 to 5 feet

Flower Color: White with reddish pink center

Light Requirements: Full sun

Soil Requirements: Good, fertile, moist garden loam

Place of Origin: Southeast Europe to Russia

Plant Sources: Busse Gardens, Carroll Gardens, Forestfarm, Greer Gardens, Milaeger's Gardens, Powell's Gardens, Wayside Gardens, White Flower Farm

Another Terrific Tree Mallow

For West Coast gardeners, there's also malva rosa (Lavatera assurgentiflora), a native of the Channel Islands off the coast of Southern California that's hardy only to Zone 9. This is a superb plant that grows to 12 feet tall and covers itself with a profusion of 2- to 3-inch, rosy lavender, white-striped blossoms through most of the year, with heaviest bloom from April to August.

centers surrounding a pale yellow central cluster of stamens. The flowers look a lot like the blossoms of single-flowered hollyhocks (*Alcea* spp.), prairie mallow (*Sidalcea* spp.), or hibiscus (*Hibiscus* spp.), although 'Barnsley' tree mallow's flowers are daintier than any of these.

You may encounter some confusion as to the true color of 'Barnsley' tree mallow's flowers. I've seen 'Barnsley' with white petals shading to reddish pink in the centers, and then again, I've seen it with pink flowers shading to white centers. And I've seen both these options offered as 'Barnsley' in the catalogs. As to which color scheme is actually 'Barnsley', I defer to the great English plantsman Graham Stuart Thomas, who says 'Barnsley' tree mallow was found in the English village of Barnsley by his friend Rosemary Verey sometime around 1985, and that its flowers are white with red centers.

You'll get the most flowers from 'Barnsley' tree mallow in the early summer, but this all-star will continue blooming with only slightly less enthusiasm throughout the growing season and into fall.

HOW TO GROW 'BARNSLEY' Plant 'Barnsley' tree mallow in a sunny spot in good soil and give it adequate water, and it will reward you by growing into a substantial, beautiful and trouble-free plant. It's not bothered by disesases or by pests, except for Japanese beetles, which love it almost as much as they love roses and grapevines.

In the Deep South, 'Barnsley' appreciates a little shade during the summer months and its foliage is evergreen. In the northern part of its range, give it a deep protective mulch to help it pull through the winter unscathed, and make sure its roots don't spend the winter in soggy soil.

PROPAGATING 'BARNSLEY' To propagate 'Barnsley' tree mallow, you can take stem-tip cuttings in spring or fall, although spring cuttings will be more successful. It's also easy to grow from seed, although seedlings' flowers will revert to the species color of solid pink in most cases.

THE RIGHT SITE FOR 'BARNSLEY' 'Barnsley' tree mallow seems never to be out of bloom once it starts. I have mine planted just where I pull the car into the driveway, and it greets me with continual bloom from June—when the flower show begins—right to October, although the profuse bloom is early and later bloom is dotted here and there over the plant. Because of its stature, it's at home in the shrub border or certainly at the very back of the perennial bed. Wherever you plant it, give 'Barnsley' tree mallow plenty of room to grow, but don't worry about it becoming overpowering—this perennial is large without being bold in either texture or color.

Use 'Barnsley' tree mallow to add shrublike size and a profuse display of delicate, pale pink flowers to a sunny spot in your garden.

CO-STARS FOR 'BARNSLEY' Use 'Barnsley' tree mallow alone as a shrublike accent plant or mix it with other plants of substantial stature. It looks fine amid the tall clumps of ornamental grasses and with stalwart perennials such as white Culver's root (see page 316), mauve-pink 'Gateway' Joe-Pye weed (see page 134), and the blue or white bells of milky bellflower (*Campanula lactiflora*).

'KOBOLD' SPIKE GAYFEATHER

Liatris spicata 'Kobold'

THE SHOWY PERENNIAL KNOWN AS GAYFEATHER or blazing-star likes good, moist, well-drained garden soil, of course; but you can throw it into just about any conditions: Heat like you get in Houston, cold like you get in Minnesota, poor soil that won't support a good crop of weeds, and drought that leaves other plants gasping for water—nothing bothers this sturdy native American. Not only will it survive, it will bloom itself silly for you. From New York to Michigan and south to Louisiana, spike gayfeather (*Liatris spicata*) has to persist through this very wide range of climate and soil conditions. That's why it's such a great performer everywhere. You should have seen mine this summer, enduring the fiery sun of coastal California with ease.

'Kobold' is a compact gayfeather that grows from 24 to 30 inches tall. It makes its appearance in the spring as a short basal tuft

Other Gayfeathers to Gather

*'Floristan White' spike gayfeather (*L. spicata* 'Floristan White') is a pretty cultivar with creamy white flowers on 3-foot spikes. There are also two tall species worth noting: *Liatris pycnostachya* is the Kansas gayfeather, a high plains native with purple flowerstalks that reach 4 feet tall. Tall gayfeather (*L. scariosa*) is similar to Kansas gayfeather but has flower spikes in a deeper*

Spotlight on 'Kobold' Spike Gayfeather

USDA Plant Hardiness Zones: 3 to 9

Season of Bloom: July to September

Height × Width: 18 to 24 inches × 24 inches

Flower Color: Bright rosy lavender-purple

Light Requirements: Full sun

Soil Requirements: Moist, light, well-drained, average soil

Place of Origin: Eastern United States

Plant Sources: Ambergate Gardens, Kurt Bluemel, Bluestone Perennials, Busse Gardens, Carroll Gardens, Forestfarm, Milaeger's Gardens, Park Seed, Powell's Gardens, André Viette Farm & Nursery, Wayside Gardens, Weiss Brothers Perennial Nursery, White Flower Farm

of long, narrow, grasslike leaves. Then in July, a leafy central spire elongates from each tuft. Finally, the green buds at the top of the stalks start opening, from the top of the spike down, into a dense covering of fuzzy, rosy lavender florets. In full bloom the spike resembles a fat mauve bottle brush. The flower show continues through August.

HOW TO GROW 'KOBOLD' Plant this durable all-star pretty much wherever you want—just think full sun—and it will grow and thrive with little or no care. Not only does 'Kobold' perform well just about everywhere, but it's mostly unbothered by pests and diseases. The only thing to watch out for is powdery mildew, which may appear in hot, humid weather and late in the summer. If it becomes a problem, thin your planting of 'Kobold' to improve air circulation and check to see if your plants need water—moisture stress can make plants more susceptible to powdery mildew.

PROPAGATING SPIKE GAYFEATHER

Spike gayfeather will grow happily for years without being divided. But if you want to increase the size of your planting, lift the plants in early fall and divide the corms with a sharp knife. Replant the divisions 12 inches apart to make a drift of a large group of plants. Although cultivars like 'Kobold' won't come true from seed, you can grow the species by sowing fresh seed outdoors in the fall. Seedlings take a few years to grow to flowering size.

'Kobold' spike gayfeather's fuzzy flowers open from the top of the spike down. The resulting lavender-purple bottlebrush is excellent for cutting.

THE RIGHT SITE FOR 'KOBOLD' What a color! 'Kobold' spike gayfeather's flower spike is a striking candle of rosy lavender-purple—a unique color that draws the eye to it. Because of this, use care to place 'Kobold' where its flowers will harmonize with—rather than disrupt—the other colors and flowers around it. I have mine in a bed with just a few other plants chosen for their pale yellow or white neutrality.

When spike gayfeather's showy flower spikes have finished their display, use your pruners to cut them back to their grassy basal leaves.

'Kobold' begins blooming in July, with each cormlike rhizome producing several crowns that each yield a tall bottlebrush of flowers. These are staples of the cut flower trade, and certainly you'll want to plant some where you can cut their blazing flower candles for an indoor arrangement. They dry well, too.

CO-STARS FOR 'KOBOLD' 'Kobold' spike gayfeather has a bright rosy lavender color that can be difficult to combine with other flowers in the garden. Try to avoid planting it with strong orange and orange-red flowers. Its best companions are soft yellows like those of 'Moonbeam' threadleaf coreopsis (see page 110), sundrops (*Oenothera fruticosa*), some of the hybrid goldenrods (*Solidago* hybrids), and even the spiky, yellow-edged leaves of 'Golden Sword' Adam's-needle (*Yucca filamentosa* 'Golden Sword'). The luminous white flowers of 'David' summer phlox (see page 248) and the silvery foliage of 'Silver Mound' artemisia (*Artemisia schmidtiana* 'Silver Mound') and dusty miller (*Senecio cineraria*) are all excellent, cooling counterparts for 'Kobold'.

'CONNECTICUT KING' LILY

Lilium 'Connecticut King'

Spotlight on

'Connecticut King' Lily

USDA Plant Hardiness Zones: 4 to 9

Season of Bloom: June and July

Height × Width: 36 inches × 12 inches

Flower Color: Rich yellow and gold

Light Requirements: Full sun to very light shade

Soil Requirements: Humusy, moist, very well-drained soil of average fertility

Place of Origin: Asiatic Hybrids are crosses of many lily species found throughout Asia to China

Plant Sources: Carroll Gardens, Dutch Gardens, Van Bourgondien, Van Engelen

LILIES REPRESENT A HUGE GENUS of bulbous ornamental plants. There are thousands upon thousands of types, in all colors except blue, and with all sorts of graceful and interesting shapes. So why have I chosen 'Connecticut King' lily as *the* perennial all-star out of all these fabulous flowers?

For starters, I selected 'Connecticut King' because I see no particular reason to wait around for lilies to bloom. As one of the early blooming Asiatic Hybrid lilies—the first of eight divisions to which lily hybrids are assigned by the American Lily Society—'Connecticut King' is just about the first lily to bloom each summer. It opens its first flowers in late June and continues blooming through July, and occasionally even into August. Let other lilies take up where 'Connecticut King' leaves off.

Its flowers are beautiful, too. Across the vast array of lilies there are many flower types to choose from, including many that dangle

Only the Beginning

If you start looking into lilies, you'll find there are only a few jillion (it seems) from which to choose. Peruse the catalogs and you're sure to find some others you like. But start with the all-around easy and lovely 'Connecticut King' and you won't be disappointed.

and nod from their plants, hiding their beautiful faces from view. Not 'Connecticut King'. This all-star bears open, 4- to 5-inch, upward-facing flowers with long, pretty petals, so you can look them in the eye (or down the throat) without having to lift them or bend down to inspect them. Their color is a rich coppery, buttery yellow splashed with gold that's both outstanding on its own and easy to coordinate with other colors in the garden.

'Connecticut King' bears its showy flowers atop sturdy plants covered in whorls of lance-shaped, 4- to 6-inch leaves. While some lilies have slender, tall stems that need staking or at least support from the plants around them, not 'Connecticut King'.

HOW TO GROW 'CONNECTICUT KING' Plant the bulbs of 'Connecticut King' in groups in a sunny site where the soil is well-drained, especially in the winter. If you plant them in heavy soil that stays wet, you can almost count on having problems with rot. Lilies like their roots cool, so place them where the soil is shaded by shrubs or other plants, and mulch around them, too. You'll get the best floral display from bulbs planted in healthy, humusy soil that's amended with bonemeal. Avoid using nitrogen heavy fertilizers such as fresh manures—these will promote lush leaves at the expense of the flowers.

'Connecticut King' is a reliable and tough hybrid lily. When it's well grown and healthy, it suffers few pest or disease problems. However, slugs are known lily munchers, and these slimy pests will gobble your lilies with glee if you don't protect them. Use rings of diatomaceous earth around your lilies, trap slugs in pans of stale beer, or handpick slugs from your plants after dark.

PROPAGATING 'CONNECTICUT KING'

Asiatic Hybrid lilies like 'Connecticut King' grow new bulbs each year, so after a few years, you can carefully divide the bunches in the fall into separate bulbs and replant them to increase your planting. Plant divisions or bulb scales 8 inches apart.

THE RIGHT SITE FOR 'CONNECTICUT KING'

Lilies are a mainstay of the summer border. They look great with delphiniums, bellflowers (*Campanula* spp.), lupines (*Lupinus* spp.), peonies, pink and purple roses, and most other summer flowers. Combine 'Connecticut King' lily's open-faced yellow trumpets with an exuberant collection of summer bloomers to create a lush, cottage garden look. Its rich yellow goes with almost every color except perhaps orange. And even there you can always try a combination. If it doesn't work, lilies are easy to move.

'Connecticut King' is a favorite of florists for two good reasons: its beauty and its longevity as a cut flower. Be sure to plant a few bulbs where you won't mind cutting their blooms for a vase.

'Connecticut King' lily's rich golden-yellow flowers reign over the garden on sturdy stems that never need staking.

CO-STARS FOR 'CONNECTICUT KING' The rich yellow of 'Connecticut King' lily looks particularly nice with light blue flowers. 'Johnson's Blue' cranesbill (*Geranium* 'Johnson's Blue') is a fine companion for the base of the lily plant, for instance, while milky bellflower (*Campanula lactiflora*) makes a good taller companion.

There are several ways to propagate lilies. You can separate bulb scales from the main bulb and replant them or take off and plant some of the bulblets that form along the stem above the main bulb. Bulbils form where the leaves attach to the stems; sow these in a flat to grow for a few seasons before planting them in your garden.

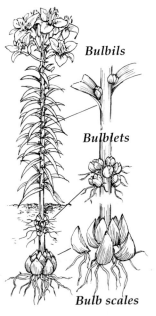

Bulbils

Bulblets

Bulb scales

SEA LAVENDER

Limonium latifolium

DON'T DO ANYTHING SPECIAL for this all-star and it will do something special for you. From late July to September, sea lavender covers itself with clouds of tiny, light, airy, lavender-blue flowers atop stiffly branched stems. These dainty flowers are the perfect filler between the hot-season colors of lilies and other summer-blooming companions.

Sea lavender's flowers get their soft lavender hue from the combination of a whitish calyx surrounding a lavender-blue corolla to form a tiny, trumpet-shaped floret. When it's in bloom, sea lavender looks like a lavender baby's-breath.

While its clouds of flowers are airy, sea lavender's leaves are large: 6 to 10 inches

Spotlight on

Sea Lavender

USDA Plant Hardiness Zones: 4 to 9

Season of Bloom: July to September

Height × Width: 18 to 30 inches × 24 inches

Flower Color: Lavender-blue

Light Requirements: Full sun to light shade in South

Soil Requirements: Light, loose, sandy, well-drained soil of average fertility

Place of Origin: Southeastern Europe to southern Russia

Plant Sources: Bluestone Perennials, Carroll Gardens, Forestfarm, Garden Place, Greer Gardens, Milaeger's Gardens, André Viette Farm & Nursery, Weiss Brothers Perennial Nursery

Seed Source: Thompson & Morgan

long, leathery, and spatula-shaped, with leaf stems that are nearly as long as the leaves. The leaves form a big basal rosette that sprawls fairly low to the ground; above the foliage the flowers bloom in a 24-inch-wide froth.

HOW TO GROW SEA LAVENDER If you try to baby sea lavender by planting it in rich, fertile, garden soil, it will produce taller, weak-flowering branches that will need staking. Find a sunny spot where the soil is average, loose (sandy, if possible), and very well drained—think seaside conditions. That's where sea lavender will do its best producing its sturdiest stems and its brightest flower colors. In the South, it will enjoy a bit of partial shade.

Of Sea Lavender and Statice

If you're looking for a sea lavender with a little more visual impact, try the cultivar 'Violetta' (L. latifolium 'Violetta'), which bears darker, violet-colored flowers. You might also recognize sea lavender's relative, annual statice (L. sinuatum), a popular plant for cutting and for dried arrangements. Easy to grow from seed, annual statice is available in a wide array of colors, including shades of blue, yellow, cream, purple, pink, soft orange, and ruby red. Its flowers hold their rich colors after drying.

Sea lavender's broad, wavy leaves provide a substantial base for its froth of flowers. In well-drained soil, plants are long lived and reliable.

Use sea lavender in the garden like baby's-breath. Its airy cloud of tiny flowers is perfect for blending brighter colors and coarser textures.

Sea lavender has no problems with pests. In cold, wet, poorly drained soils, crown or root rot can be a problem. Plant it in a spot that's sunny with good air circulation and good drainage, then amend the planting area with leaf mold or compost, and you'll avoid most rot problems.

PROPAGATING SEA LAVENDER In late winter to early spring, you can separate new crowns from around the base of the plant without disturbing the main clump. Sea lavender doesn't need regular division and doesn't respond well to disturbance once it's established. You can also grow sea lavender from seed sown outdoors in the fall or started inside in early spring and moved to the garden after the soil warms up. Space new plants or divisions at least 18 inches apart.

THE RIGHT SITE FOR SEA LAVENDER Use sea lavender to add charm and fine texture to a planting of summer-blooming perennials.

Sea lavender's papery flowers are among those known as everlastings. Besides being a great addition to vases of fresh flowers, they dry exceptionally well. Cut and tie several stems together when the flowers are just beginning to show color but before they open fully and are faded by the sun, and hang them upside down in a warm, dry, dark place, such as a garage or attic. They'll persist for many months in dried arrangements.

CO-STARS FOR SEA LAVENDER Plant a mass of sea lavender by itself for cutting. In the garden, combine it with such diverse plants as yellow or gold Asiatic hybrid lilies, Frikart's aster (*Aster × frikartii*), common sneezeweed (*Helenium autumnale*), New England aster (*Aster novae-angliae*), Kansas gayfeather (*Liatris pycnostachya*), fountain grass (*Pennisetum alopecuroides*), Stokes' aster (*Stokesia laevis*), pearly everlasting (*Anaphalis* spp.), yarrows, sea-pinks (*Armeria* spp.), inulas (*Inula* spp.), catmint (*Nepeta* spp.), evening primroses (*Oenothera* spp.), and lavender cotton (*Santolina* spp.).

'CANON J. WENT' PURPLE TOADFLAX

Linaria purpurea 'Canon J. Went'

Spotlight on

'Canon J. Went' Purple Toadflax

USDA Plant Hardiness Zones: 5 to 9

Season of Bloom: June to September

Height × Width: 24 to 30 inches × 18 to 24 inches

Flower Color: Pink

Light Requirements: Full sun to light shade

Soil Requirements: Sandy, well-drained, poor to average soil

Place of Origin: Central and southern Italy and Sicily

Plant Sources: Busse Gardens, Garden Place, Roslyn Nursery

Seed Source: Thompson & Morgan

ALTHOUGH YOU MIGHT DESCRIBE the pink flowers of 'Canon J. Went' purple toadflax as unassuming, this charming plant has many qualities that make it an indispensable addition to the garden. 'Canon J. Went' is extremely easy to grow. It self-sows readily—but never invasively—gently increasing its presence in your garden.

In spring purple toadflax makes pretty tufts of leaves less than 12 inches tall; later, in early summer, the stems elongate. These lithe stems become woody at the base, so they never need staking, even though they grow to reach 30 to 36 inches tall. They're set all around with thin-bladed leaves of the softest grayish blue-green. At the ends of the stems, flower spikes begin to bloom in late June or early July.

The spikes are densely covered with tiny snapdragon-like flowers, which open from the bottom up. In the species these are pur-plish, but the flowers of 'Canon J. Went' are a pretty, soft pink that is the perfect color companion for its cool blue-green leaves. Once 'Canon J. Went' starts blooming, it doesn't want to stop. For several months it puts on its sweet show, continuing to bloom well into September.

A Rock Garden Toadflax

Not many toadflax other than 'Canon J. Went' are widely available in North America. In fact, it's rare to see plain old purple toadflax for sale. For rock garden conditions, you might want to try alpine toadflax (L. alpina). This 3- to 6-inch perennial produces mats of narrow gray-green leaves. It blooms in the summer, bearing sprays of pretty purple snapdragon-like flowers with a blotch of bright orange.

HOW TO GROW 'CANON J. WENT' 'Canon J. Went' will bloom its best for you if you plant it in sandy, well-drained, poor to average soil. If you try to coddle it with very rich, moist soil, you may wind up with lots of leafy growth and few of the elegant, soft pink flowers. So find it a sunny spot where the soil drains well, then don't fuss over this pretty plant. In the hottest places, 'Canon J. Went' appreciates light shade during the summer, but for the most part, it grows best in full sun. In Zones 5 and 6 it will benefit from a winter mulch. Pests and diseases rarely bother 'Canon J. Went'.

While 'Canon J. Went' can be short lived, this pretty toadflax self-sows with ease. Once it blooms, you'll always have some growing in your garden.

The soft pink, spurred flowers of 'Canon J. Went' create a lovely, summer-long color harmony with its narrow blue-green leaves.

PROPAGATING PURPLE TOADFLAX You could divide the clump-forming 'Canon J. Went' purple toadflax, but why go to the trouble when it self-sows so reliably? It's easy enough to find true-to-type, pink-flowered seedlings popping up in its vicinity. Although 'Canon J. Went' doesn't take long to form a large planting this way, it is not at all invasive.

THE RIGHT SITE FOR 'CANON J. WENT' The fact that 'Canon J. Went' purple toadflax's blue-green leaves and soft pink flowers make a color harmony with no help from other plants, along with its preference for poor, well-drained soil, means that this is a plant you can use to your advantage to fill an out-of-the-way or difficult place on your property. And yet this all-star's delicate texture and pretty colors mix attractively and easily with many other perennials in the sunny, dry border.

CO-STARS FOR 'CANON J. WENT' 'Canon J. Went' gets along visually with plenty of other plants. Match its colors and cultural requirements with plants such as cushion spurge (see page 136), Lancaster cranesbill (*Geranium sanguineum* var. *striatum*), 'Silver King' artemisia (*Artemisia ludoviciana* 'Silver King'), common foxglove (*Digitalis purpurea*), pale pink Asiatic lilies, and penstemons (*Penstemon* spp.).

A Stellar Idea

Use your string trimmer or garden shears to whack 'Canon J. Went' purple toadflax back hard once or twice during the growing season. This forces it to produce new stems and the pretty spikes of pink flowers that arise at their tips.

'MAJESTIC' BIG BLUE LILYTURF

Liriope muscari 'Majestic'

OUTSTANDING IS THE PROPER TERM for 'Majestic' big blue lilyturf. Not only is it a flowering perennial all-star for the border or bed, but it's an all-star groundcover as well, and an indispensible foil for your ornamental evergreen shrubs.

Big blue lilyturf's fleshy roots produce dense tufts of ½-inch-wide, tough, dark green, shiny, grasslike leaves that arch gracefully up to about 15 inches tall. These clumps enlarge to colonize their spot so thickly that weeds are unable to compete.

Spotlight on 'Majestic' Big Blue Lilyturf

USDA Plant Hardiness Zones: 6 to 9

Season of Bloom: August to September

Height × Width: 15 inches × 24 inches

Flower Color: Violet-lavender

Light Requirements: Prefers partial shade but will tolerate sun and full shade

Soil Requirements: Average, humusy, well-drained soil

Place of Origin: The Far East from China and Korea to Japan

Plant Sources: Kurt Bluemel, Daylily Discounters, Garden Place, Park Seed, Roslyn Nursery, Van Bourgondien, We-Du Nurseries, Weiss Brothers Perennial Nursery, White Flower Farm

More in the Lilyturf Line

Depending on the effect you're seeking for your garden, there are other useful cultivars of big blue lilyturf, including a couple of variegated selections. Variegated blue lilyturf (L. muscari 'Variegata') has creamy yellow edges on its new foliage and bears violet flowers. 'Silvery Sunproof' (L. muscari 'Silvery Sunproof') is a more sun-tolerant lilyturf with gold-to-creamy white-striped leaves and lilac flowers in early summer.

Creeping lilyturf (L. spicata) grows to about 8 inches tall and spreads widely from underground roots. Its leaves are narrower and more grasslike than those of big blue lilyturf, and its lilac-to-white flower clusters tend to hide down among the leaves. Creeping lilyturf is more cold-hardy (to Zone 5) than big blue lilyturf.

But its success as a grassy groundcover is only part of 'Majestic' big blue lilyturf's appeal. In August and September it sends up tall (to 20 inches), narrow flower spikes covered with tiny, bell-like flowers of a rich violet-lavender color. The catalogs always say the flowers look like those of grape hyacinths (*Muscari* spp.), and they do, but they're much more substantial than grape hyacinths' dainty spring blossoms. And 'Majestic' big blue lilyturf carries its 8- to 10-inch flower clusters in profusion well above the foliage, where they're easy to see. In any event, this all-star puts on a lovely show at a time of year when many of the shrubs it complements are not in bloom.

HOW TO GROW BIG BLUE LILYTURF Big blue lilyturf tolerates everything from full sun to full shade but prefers partial shade.

Flowering may be curtailed in full shade, and full sun may scald the leaves in the hottest regions. Big blue lilyturf sails through drought due to its fleshy roots but performs better where it gets adequate moisture. Its foliage is evergreen, but northern winters will tatter and blast its leaves. Cut all the old winter-weary foliage to the ground in late winter before the new foliage appears, and the plants will reward you with bright green spring foliage that darkens up as summer approaches. Many people think big blue lilyturf isn't winter hardy, but it grows well in Zone 6 and even into the southern half of Zone 5, although it may need winter protection here.

In partial shade, 'Majestic' big blue lilyturf makes a handsome companion to its more sun-tolerant striped sibling, 'Silvery Sunproof'.

PROPAGATING BIG BLUE LILYTURF Big blue lilyturf is a clump-forming member of the lily family with fleshy roots. It divides easily in the spring before new growth starts. Plant divisions 12 inches apart in all directions to increase areas of groundcover.

THE RIGHT SITE FOR 'MAJESTIC' If 'Majestic' big blue lilyturf had no other function but to serve as a pretty-but-tough evergreen groundcover, it would still deserve to be planted widely. But the addition of its showy, dark violet flowers makes it a spectacular companion for all manner of flowering and evergreen shrubs and small trees. 'Pink Spire' summersweet (*Clethra alnifolia* 'Pink Spire') looks great with a surrounding skirt of 'Majestic' big blue lilyturf.

CO-STARS FOR 'MAJESTIC' Use 'Majestic' big blue lilyturf as a groundcover around pots of Cape Colony nerine (*Nerine bowdenii*), or with autumn crocuses (*Colchicum* spp.) and pearly everlasting (*Anaphalis* spp.). 'Majestic' also looks great growing around evergreen shrubs such as holly, sweet boxes (*Sarcococca* spp.), viburnums, yews (*Taxus* spp.), and skimmias (*Skimmia* spp.). In the partly shaded perennial bed, a clump of 'Majestic' will combine its flowers with those of other early fall bloomers like 'September Charm' anemone (see page 42) and 'Bridget Bloom' foamy bells (see page 172).

Underplant a 'Pink Spire' summersweet standard with 'Majestic' big blue lilyturf to create a gorgeous late-season flower show in shades of dark violet and pink.

CARDINAL FLOWER

Lobelia cardinalis

I'LL NEVER FORGET THE FIRST TIME I saw a wild cardinal flower. It was growing in a wet, boggy ditch by a woodsy, shaded lane in rural Pennsylvania. I could see its brilliant scarlet flowers from a quarter of a mile away.

Cardinal flower prefers a soggy site in the garden, too, and even though it's kind of picky about what it likes, it's worth the fuss. The red color of its flowers is so rich and striking that it looks almost unreal.

The plants themselves are elegant and attractive. Cardinal flower's dark green leaves have toothed margins and form a basal rosette from which single, tall, sturdy stems arise. These stems are topped during the blooming season with up to 50 1-inch flowers on a spike. Each flower has a three-lobed,

Other Lovely Lobelias

Cardinal flower has lent its genes to some worthwhile hybrids, such as 'Compliment Scarlet' lobelia (L. 'Compliment Scarlet'). This recent introduction has the same bold color as the species, but its flowers are bigger and its stems taller, to 40 inches. 'Ruby Slippers' lobelia (L. 'Ruby Slippers'), has deep, dark, ruby red flowers on spikes that grow to 3 to 4 feet.

Great blue lobelia (L. siphilitica) is another species that's native to eastern North America. Great blue lobelia bears blue flowers in August and September.

Spotlight on
Cardinal Flower

USDA Plant Hardiness Zones: 3 to 9

Season of Bloom: July to September

Height × Width: 36 to 48 inches × 24 to 36 inches

Flower Color: Red

Light Requirements: Partial shade to full sun

Soil Requirements: Rich, humusy, moist, acid soil

Place of Origin: Eastern North America from Canadian maritimes to Minnesota, and south to Texas and the Gulf States

Plant Sources: Kurt Bluemel, Bluestone Perennials, Busse Gardens, Carroll Gardens, Crownsville Nursery, Forestfarm, Milaeger's Gardens, Plant Delights Nursery, Powell's Gardens, Roslyn Nursery, Shady Oaks Nursery, Sunlight Gardens, André Viette Farm & Nursery, We-Du Nurseries, Weiss Brothers Perennial Nursery

Seed Source: Thompson & Morgan

---

drooping bottom lip. Flowering continues from July into September.

HOW TO GROW CARDINAL FLOWER

Cardinal flower prefers to grow in partial shade but tolerates full sun if it's planted in boggy soil or if it's growing in the cool summers of the North. Plant cardinal flower in a site with rich, moist, acid soil and give it lots of water. Cardinal flower tends to be short lived but can persist in a favorable location—in which case it will need division every three years. The good news is that cardinal flower

Rich red cardinal flower makes a perfect partner for blue flowers like lobelia. Plant cardinal flower in small groups to avoid scarlet overkill.

Illuminate a shady spot with the brilliant flower spikes of cardinal flower. This showy all-star thrives in constantly moist soil and is right at home at the edge of a woodland stream or pond.

self-sows freely, and you are not likely to lose it altogether unless you either let it dry out or bury it under a heavy mulch over the winter. About an inch of leaf litter over the plant usually helps it through northern winters.

PROPAGATING CARDINAL FLOWER Divide cardinal flower in the spring or fall and discard the old, woody, central portion of the plant. Replant the divisions 12 inches apart. Cardinal flower reseeds itself and is easy to grow from seed. Propagate cultivars by division or take stem cuttings after plants finish flowering, leaving one leaf on each section of stem. Sink the stem in a compost-filled nursery box up to the leaf axil. A new plant will form from the leaf axil. Leave rooted cuttings in the rooting box over the winter and pot them up in the spring. Keep the rooting medium constantly moist.

THE RIGHT SITE FOR CARDINAL FLOWER This all-star probably looks its best planted in small groups. Its rare, rich scarlet flowers fairly glow in the shade, where its vivid color can liven up the typically pale flower colors of other shade bloomers. Just don't plant it in deep shade. But do plant it in a boggy spot in full sun, if you like. Then sit back and watch the droves of hummingbirds that will arrive to dine at those scarlet spikes.

CO-STARS FOR CARDINAL FLOWER Heat up your garden by combining cardinal flowers with golden-flowered daylilies in a sunny to lightly shaded spot. White flowers such as pearly everlasting (*Anaphalis margaritacea*), boltonia (*Boltonia asteroides*), and Culver's root (*Veronicastrum virginicum*) look clean and crisp next to cardinal flower's brilliant reds. It makes the perfect partner for the blues of Siberian bugloss (see page 78) and spiderworts (*Tradescantia* spp.).

MALTESE CROSS

Lychnis chalcedonica

THERE ARE A FEW CHOICE PERENNIALS that attract the eye with dazzling color, that accent, disrupt, and add life to otherwise sleepy plantings. A good example of such a plant is our perennial all-star, Maltese cross. Its hemispherical flowerheads are a bright glowing scarlet with enough orange mixed into the color to warm it up and turn it to vermilion, a vivid reddish orange. It's not a common color in the flower garden, but it is a useful one to have.

Here's a fine, old-fashioned, hardy, trouble-free, easy-to-grow plant. Maltese cross forms a clump of straight, unbranched, sturdy, 24- to 36-inch stems clothed in pairs of opposite leaves that look like those of zinnias. In mid-June, it produces rounded clusters of many intensely colored small five-petalled flowers.

A Couple of Campions

Other plants in this genus are given the common name campion, but they share Maltese cross's characteristic brightly colored flowers with five notched petals. 'Vesuvius' Arkwright's campion (L. arkwrightii 'Vesuvius') is a Maltese cross hybrid with similarly brilliant red-orange flowers on more compact, 18- to 24-inch plants. Rose campion (L. coronaria) has gray-green, felty foliage and showy, bright rose pink flowers.

Spotlight on Maltese Cross

USDA Plant Hardiness Zones: 3 to 9

Season of Bloom: Mid-June to early August

Height × width: 30 inches × 12 inches

Flower Color: Reddish orange

Light Requirements: Full sun to partial shade

Soil Requirements: Average, moist, well-drained soil

Place of Origin: Western Russia east to Siberia

Plant Sources: Bluestone Perennials, Busse Gardens, Garden Place, We-Du Nurseries, Weiss Brothers Perennial Nursery

Seed Source: Thompson & Morgan

HOW TO GROW MALTESE CROSS Plant Maltese cross in full sun or in partial shade, especially in the warmer zones. It likes average, adequately moist soil but can tolerate limited drought. It's not bothered by pests or diseases.

Maltese cross is a well-behaved plant, and the clumps seldom grow to more than 12 inches or so across. It is persistent, especially in the North, but Maltese cross won't live forever, so it's a good idea to start fresh seed every few years or to divide it periodically.

PROPAGATING MALTESE CROSS Maltese cross grows easily from seed sown in the spring. If you leave a few spent flower clusters on the plant you'll have self-sown seedlings to transplant where you want them. You can also divide mature plants in the spring. Replant the divisions about 12 inches apart.

Maltese cross gets its name from the shape of its flowers, although a closer look reveals five—not four—deeply notched reddish orange petals.

Don't try to match Maltese cross's vivid reddish orange in the garden! Instead, use it to add zing to whites and yellows, like mulleins or yarrows.

THE RIGHT SITE FOR MALTESE CROSS If you have a spot where you can place three Maltese cross plants in a 12- to 16-inch triangle, surrounded by silvery leaved plants like 'Silver King' artemisia (*Artemisia ludoviciana* 'Silver King') and dark-foliaged evergreens like pines or false cypress (*Chamaecyparis* spp.), you have the best situation for this unusual plant. I've seen Maltese cross growing with dark purple clustered bellflower (*Campanula glomerata*), with which it makes a rousing color statement. It's even more effective planted with white flowers, especially 'Iceberg' roses (*Rosa* 'Iceberg'), where it adds an electric-metallic zing to the sedate whites.

CO-STARS FOR MALTESE CROSS Plant Maltese cross with strong yellows such as 'Coronation Gold' yarrow (see page 26), with darker orange-reds like 'Gibson's Scarlet' cinquefoil (see page 260), with whites like 'Crown of Snow' clustered bellflower (*Campanula glomerata* 'Crown of Snow') or 'Iceberg' roses (*Rosa* 'Iceberg'), with bronzy or purplish leaves like spurge (*Euphorbia* spp.), or barberries (*Berberis* spp.), or with silver-leaved plants like artemisias. Maltese cross makes a useful accent for warm yellow and blue plantings. But keep it away from rosy pink shades and magentas!

A Stellar Idea

To keep Maltese cross blooming in the summer, cut its flowering stems back by a third as the first flower clusters begin to fade. This promotes lateral branching and further flower production on into August.

GOOSENECK LOOSESTRIFE

Lysimachia clethroides

GOOSENECK LOOSESTRIFE IS ONE OF THE EASIEST perennials to grow, and it's one of the most romantic and unique in appearance. But a word of caution is necessary, too. Gooseneck loosestrife is so easy that it can be invasive, especially in the South, if you simply plant it in good, moist garden soil and forget about it.

In Pennsylvania, I developed a perennial garden that was subsequently abandoned. I returned to check on it after a few years, and found that the gooseneck loosestrife had

Spotlight on
Gooseneck Loosestrife

USDA Plant Hardiness Zones: 3 to 9

Season of Bloom: July to August

Height × Width: 3 feet × 3+ feet

Flower Color: White

Light Requirements: Full sun to partial shade

Soil Requirements: Moist, average to humusy soil

Place of Origin: China and Japan

Plant Sources: Kurt Bluemel, Bluestone Perennials, Busse Gardens, Carroll Gardens, Crownsville Nursery, Forestfarm, Garden Place, Milaeger's Gardens, Roslyn Nursery, Shady Oaks Nursery, André Viette Farm & Nursery, Weiss Brothers Perennial Nursery, White Flower Farm

Other Likable Loosestrifes

Although they share the common name "loosestrife" with the aggressive spreaders purple loosestrife (<u>Lythrum</u> <u>salicaria</u>) and wand loosestrife (<u>Lythrum</u> <u>virgatum</u>), gooseneck loosestrife and other <u>Lysimachia</u> species are not related to those infamous wetlands thugs—they're not even in the same plant family. However, they do grow easily enough to be called invasive, particularly in moist soils, so choose a planting site with care.

Yellow loosestrife (<u>Lysimachia</u> <u>punctata</u>) is a prickly looking, sturdy, tall-stemmed plant with spiky golden-yellow flowers along the stem tips in July and August and is remarkably easy to grow. Creeping Jenny (<u>L. nummularia</u>) trails deep green, rounded leaves just an inch or 2 above the ground. It bears cup-shaped yellow flowers from June to August.

pushed the weeds aside and expanded into a 15- by 20-foot patch.

When I ran that garden, however, gooseneck loosestrife gave me no trouble because I kept it in its place. It took no more than a little digging out around the edges of the patch in spring. I grew to love the way its white flower spikes gently curve and recurve to look like the heads of geese.

These drooping spikes of white flowers appear in mid-July and bloom through August to September. The 3-foot, sturdy stems arise in dense stands from creeping, underground rhizomes and are covered in pretty, pointed, medium green leaves. The flowerheads are most curved at the bud stage, straightening up somewhat as the buds open into six-petalled white flowers with yellowish brown centers.

Gooseneck loosestrife's flower spikes tend to all curve in the same direction, creating the cheery effect of a flock of white geese in your garden.

HOW TO GROW GOOSENECK LOOSESTRIFE

Gooseneck loosestrife is vigorous and hardy, care-free, and even weed suppressing. It prefers consistently moist soil of almost any type, in full sun to light shade. Planting it where the soil dries out occasionally will help keep its vigorous growth in check, but it will suffer in periods of extended drought. If you plant it in your garden, you might want to ring its roots with a plastic barrier so its roaming rhizomes will stay in place.

PROPAGATING GOOSENECK LOOSESTRIFE

Gooseneck loosestrife is easy to divide in spring or fall when you'rere starting a new garden area or if you want plants to give away. Division is also helpful as a control measure. Plant divisions 12 inches apart.

THE RIGHT SITE FOR GOOSENECK LOOSESTRIFE

The effect of a patch of these "geese" is charming. They don't look weedy but rather seem neat, friendly, and very much intentional.

In the fall, gooseneck loosestrife will show you its bright yellow-and-red fall foliage—as bright a fall color as any found in the perennial garden. That's a good reason to plant up an area at the back of the property, such as along a woods' edge or by the margin of a pond and let it ramble at will. It naturalizes easily and is good for spots outside of the carefully tended garden. Just because gooseneck loosestrife likes elbow room doesn't mean you have to be afraid of it.

To avoid the effort of digging out stray plants in your garden and to protect neighboring perennials, you may want to circle gooseneck loosestrife's creeping rhizomes with a root barrier.

CO-STARS FOR GOOSENECK LOOSESTRIFE

Choose companions that match gooseneck loosestrife's size and vigor. Plant it with tall gayfeather (*Liatris scariosa*) or Kansas gayfeather (*L. pycnostachya*), 'Pink Beauty' boltonia (*Boltonia asteroides* 'Pink Beauty'), New England aster cultivars (*Aster novae-angliae* cvs.), common sneezeweed (*Helenium autumnale*), bee balms (*Monarda* spp.), heliopsis (*Heliopsis* spp.), and against a backdrop of evergreens.

'CORAL PLUME' PLUME POPPY

Macleaya microcarpa 'Coral Plume'

IS IT THE IMPRESSIVE SIZE OF 'CORAL PLUME' plume poppy that makes it a perennial all-star? It reaches 6 to 7 feet tall, making it one of the largest perennials in the garden.

Is it the beautiful leaves that cover the plant, each 8 inches across, bronzy to cinnamon-toned gray-green above and whitish green beneath, deeply lobed, like big fig leaves, but more rounded and pleasant to look at?

Or is it the coppery pink plumes of loose, fluffy little flowers, each holding a tiny bouquet of stamens, that tower above our heads in airy profusion?

I think any of these advantages would qualify this magnificent perennial as an all-star—and when you put them together, 'Coral Plume' is a surefire winner.

HOW TO GROW 'CORAL PLUME' With 'Coral Plume' plume poppy, it's important to think big and put it in a spot where it will not be out of proportion with the surrounding

Another Pretty Plume Poppy

A sister plume poppy species, M. cordata, grows even bigger than 'Coral Plume', to a towering 9 feet and is topped by plumy white flowers. This is a more invasive plant than M. microcarpa and it needs confinement to keep it within bounds. Once controlled, it is a fine addition to the garden.

Spotlight on

'Coral Plume' Plume Poppy

USDA Plant Hardiness Zones: 4 to 9

Season of Bloom: July to August

Height × Width: 6 to 7 feet × 6+ feet

Flower Color: Coral pink

Light Requirements: Full sun to partial shade

Soil Requirements: Any soil

Place of Origin: Japan, eastern China, and Taiwan

Plant Sources: Busse Gardens, Carroll Gardens, Forestfarm, Garden Place

plants. It likes a moist, well-drained, rich soil—perhaps a bit too much, in fact. Plant 'Coral Plume' in pretty much any soil, in full sun to light shade. If you plant it in good garden soil, you might consider surrounding the hole with a plastic or metal barrier to keep its roots from wandering afield (much as you would for bamboo), as plume poppy can be invasive if allowed to grow unchecked. But I like its vigor, which is in proportion to its size.

In the right spot, 'Coral Plume' will give you no trouble, will be reliably perennial and free of pest and disease problems and will give you that one huge, interesting, and gorgeous perennial to oversee all the others.

PROPAGATING PLUME POPPY Given its nature as a perennial that grows and spreads vigorously from underground running roots, plume poppy is easy to divide in the spring. Root cuttings will quickly send up new tops. You can also propagate the species from seed.

THE RIGHT SITE FOR 'CORAL PLUME' 'Coral Plume' makes a most dramatic statement on its own, without help or interference from any other plants. A perfect spot for a single specimen of 'Coral Plume' might be between a concrete walkway and a wall, where its roots are confined to the space you've allotted for it. It will soften that hard wall edge beautifully.

'Coral Plume' plume poppy's size calls for companion plants of similar stature. You can also plant it in the back of a perennial border where its bronzy

'Coral Plume' towers over the garden without looking coarse. Its lobed foliage makes an elegant backdrop for shorter perennials, while its stature lets it stand alone as a specimen or decidous screen.

In moist, rich garden soil, use a sturdy root barrier to control plume poppy's enthusiasm for spreading its roots beyond its alotted space.

green foliage will help coordinate and calm down hot colors in its own color scheme—the royal 'Gold Plate' yarrow (*Achillea filipendulina* 'Gold Plate'), the fierce colors of crocosmias (*Crocosmia* spp.), the ruddy colors of sunflower hybrids (*Helianthus* hybrids), and cool gray-blue-green lavender cotton (*Santolina* spp.). And 'Coral Plume' works perfectly in the company of large shrubs, where its airy flower plumes can soften dense plants like hollies or its leaves can associate with similar ones, like the substantial foliage of oakleaf hydrangea (*Hydrangea quercifolia*).

CO-STARS FOR 'CORAL PLUME' Plant 'Coral Plume' with other large, impressive plants like shieldleaf rodgersia (*Rodgersia tabularis*, also listed as *Astilboides tabularis*), gunnera (*Gunnera manicata* or *G. tinctoria*), giant hogweed (*Heracleum mantegazzianum*), and ornamental rhubarb (*Rheum palmatum*). Creeping nasturtiums growing at its feet provide a lovely color echo.

HOLLYHOCK MALLOW

Malva alcea var. *fastigiata*

HOLLYHOCK MALLOW IS AN ABSOLUTELY ESSENTIAL plant for the sunny perennial border throughout most of the country. It has all the great traits one associates with a perennial all-star.

For example, once it starts blooming, it won't stop until frost takes it. And since it begins to flower in early July (and even in late June in some locations), that's a wonderfully long period for you to enjoy its blossoms. And they are enjoyable. The pretty, soft pink flowers are 2 to 3 inches across and consist of five carmine-streaked, heart-shaped petals surrounding a little, white, buttonlike center. They grow from the axils where the leaves attach to the stems.

Hollyhock mallow has a deep taproot that gives it a great advantage in dry spells. The

Spotlight on
Hollyhock Mallow

USDA Plant Hardiness Zones: 4 to 9

Season of Bloom: July to October

Height × Width: 48 inches × 24 inches

Flower Color: Soft, rosy pink

Light Requirements: Full sun

Soil Requirements: Average, moist or dry, well-drained soil

Place of Origin: Europe from England to Poland and south to the Mediterranean

Plant Sources: Bluestone Perennials, Busse Gardens, Carroll Gardens, Forestfarm, Garden Place, J. W. Jung Seed, Milaeger's Gardens, Park Seed, Wayside Gardens, Weiss Brothers Perennial Nursery

Seed Source: Park Seed

roots make many crowns that will produce several dozen stems. These are sturdy and never need staking, reaching 48 inches tall in a narrow clump 24 inches across.

After the main flush of blooms, hollyhock mallow continues to dot its stems with flowers for the remainder of the growing season. While mallow looks superficially like a hollyhock (*Alcea* spp.), it is bushier, and its soft green, 2- to 3-inch, veined leaves are deeply cleft into fingers. Still, like hollyhock, hollyhock mallow is tall enough to anchor the back of the border.

Hollyhock mallow is usually offered by nurseries as the variety *fastigiata*, although the plain species shows up occasionally. The latter is similar but not as tall as its variety, and its flowers are a lighter shade of pink.

More Mallows of Merit

Musk mallow (M. moschata) is a casual shrubby plant that grows to 24 to 36 inches tall. It's usually available in either white-flowered ('Alba') or pink-flowered ('Rosea') forms. This medicinal herb is an old-fashioned mainstay of the cottage garden and blooms from July to September. It's hardy to Zone 3.

'Primley Blue' high mallow (M. sylvestris 'Primley Blue') is a showy plant that grows to 5 feet tall. It has bluish hollyhock-type flowers that bloom from May to October.

Proving that tough plants can be pretty, hollyhock mallow blooms through dry spells on sturdy stems that never need staking.

How to Grow Hollyhock Mallow

In Zone 6 and colder, hollyhock mallow is easy to grow and reliable, and it has no real pest or disease problems, save for Japanese beetles. In the heat and humidity of the South, however, spider mites, thrips, and diseases get after hollyhock mallow. While you can grow it there—with a bit of afternoon shade—it may take some work to ward off problems.

Propagating Hollyhock Mallow

Hollyhock mallow's taproot makes it very difficult to divide—but then, it never needs division since it is a very well-behaved plant. Getting more plants isn't usually a problem, as it self-sows freely. You can produce flowering plants more quickly by taking stem cuttings in early summer. Take cuttings from the tips of side shoots; root them in pots; and plant them out in the garden in fall for summer-long bloom next season.

The Right Site for Hollyhock Mallow

Hollyhock mallow's soft pink flowers coordinate nicely with the pale yellow of 'Moonbeam' threadleaf coreopsis. Not only do they look great, but both plants whiz through a dry summer with no problem and continue to bloom together until frost. Make good-size drifts of hollyhock mallow in back with 'Moonbeam' in front of it.

Hollyhock mallow's tall, leafy spikes of saucer-shaped, soft pink flowers make a lovely combination with the rich blue-purple blossoms and feathery divided foliage of annual larkspur.

Co-Stars for Hollyhock Mallow

Hollyhock mallow looks especially good with 'Moonbeam' threadleaf coreopsis (see page 110) but also goes well with sun rose (*Helianthemum nummularium*), borage (*Borago officinalis*), catmint (see page 230), balloon flower (see page 252), 'Summer Snow' obedient plant (*Physostegia virginiana* 'Summer Snow'), and other sunny border perennials.

A Stellar Idea

Shear hollyhock mallow back by about a third after its first flush of flowers. This helps keep the plant blooming through the summer and enhances its appearance by promoting fresh new growth.

VIRGINIA BLUEBELLS

Mertensia virginica

I SUPPOSE EACH OF US HAS A FAVORITE PERENNIAL, and Virginia bluebells is mine. I can't imagine not having its cheery return in the garden each spring, even though I have to baby it here at the edge of its range in California's Zone 9.

In my eastern garden, Virginia bluebells was right at home and flourished. In fact, I first appreciated it when I was driving past a wooded area near Topton, Pennsylvania, and noticed that the floor of the woods—close to half an acre—was a lovely blue. I stopped for a closer look and found the forest floor covered with plants that were putting out loose clusters of the most marvelous flowers.

These were sweetly scented, sapphire blue, inch-long tubes that opened into flaring bells with scalloped edges. Interestingly, the buds were pink. Even the foliage was wonderful—with a tender, fresh texture unlike any other

Beyond Virginia Bluebells

It's unusual to find other bluebells, although they do exist, and some are worth seeking out. M. simplicissima (also listed as M. asiatica) is an asian species. This trailing plant has leathery, curving, gray-green foliage and typical bluebell-type flowers. It grows well by the seaside in partial shade or foggy conditions. Mountain bluebells (M. ciliata) is a Rocky Mountain native with a long, May-to-August bloom season and sturdier foliage than Virginia bluebells.

Spotlight on
Virginia Bluebells

USDA Plant Hardiness Zones: 3 to 9

Season of Bloom: April to May

Height × Width: 12 to 18 inches × 12 to 18 inches

Flower Color: Blue

Light Requirements: Partial shade to full shade

Soil Requirements: Rich, humusy, moist, woodsy, well-drained soil

Place of Origin: Eastern United States

Plant Sources: Kurt Bluemel, Bluestone Perennials, Busse Gardens, Carroll Gardens, McClure & Zimmerman, Milaeger's Gardens, Powell's Gardens, Roslyn Nursery, Shady Oaks Nursery, Sunlight Gardens, Van Bourgondien, André Viette Farm & Nursery

plant I can think of, and a soft gray-blue-green color that perfectly set off the flowers.

Virginia bluebells first appears in April, pushing up mouse-ear–like leaves from its fleshy roots. These swirl rapidly upward and open into the soft and tender foliage that is soon followed by the uncoiling trusses of pinkish lavender buds and hanging blue flower clusters. Enjoy them while they're blooming—once they're done flowering, Virginia bluebells return to dormancy until the next spring.

HOW TO GROW VIRGINIA BLUEBELLS
Virginia bluebells are small plants that rarely grow taller than 18 inches. In favorable growing conditions, they will self-sow and

Virginia bluebells will charm you with pink buds that open to delicate blue bells. Mark their site in spring so you don't dig into dormant plants later.

In moist, woodsy soil, Virginia bluebells spread slowly to form a spring carpet of blue flowers. In your garden, grow them in similar conditions with other shade plants that will fill in when the bluebells go dormant.

slowly colonize an area. What they like is a sunny to shady spot in the typically cool, moist, woodsy forest duff of eastern North America. Pests and diseases don't bother them, but hard, hot sun, dry soil conditions, or alkaline soils will do them in. It's helpful to mark their location in the spring while they're up and blooming, to avoid digging into them later in the season when they're dormant.

PROPAGATING VIRGINIA BLUEBELLS It's possible to divide Virginia bluebells in the spring after they finish flowering, although the process is a bit chancy. You can also expose the plant's roots and take root cuttings. Virginia bluebells will self-sow in a good site where there's not too much mulch in the way, and these volunteer seedlings are the easiest way to increase a planting. Plant seedlings or rooted cuttings 12 inches apart.

THE RIGHT SITE FOR VIRGINIA BLUEBELLS Virginia bluebells are shy and tender beauties and don't take kindly to much handling or insults like dogs or kids running through their bed. They come up, flower, turn yellow, and

are gone by the time the hot weather of summer kicks in. That means it's good to grow them with ferns that arise later in the spring, with hostas, and with other woodland favorites that will fill in for them when they disappear. You can also use Virginia bluebells to underplant small shade-loving shrubs like laurels (*Kalmia* spp.)—the bluebells' show will carry the early spring and be over before the laurel's blossoms appear in June.

CO-STARS FOR VIRGINIA BLUEBELLS Plant Virginia bluebells with spring-blooming wildflowers, such as columbines (*Aquilegia* spp.), with common bleeding heart (see page 118) or other bleeding hearts, and with Jacob's ladder (see page 254), with which it shares similar flowers but different leaves. It's also nice planted amid hostas, ferns, wild gingers (*Asarum* spp.), and other shady plants that will fill its vacant spot for the summer.

'SILVER FEATHER' JAPANESE SILVER GRASS

Miscanthus sinensis 'Silver Feather'

'SILVER FEATHER' JAPANESE SILVER GRASS is undoubtedly one of the most beautiful of all the ornamental grasses. In the summer, 'Silver Feather' is a fountain of gracefully arching, half-inch wide, tough grass blades that grow to 6 feet tall. Each leaf has a showy silver midrib that earns this cultivar its name. The softly upright effect of the long, grassy leaves is especially welcome in gardens that have many large-leaved, mound-shaped perennials.

In late summer to early fall, 'Silver Feather' extends its foamy flowering plumes which rise 12 to 24 inches above the top of the green

Spotlight on 'Silver Feather' Japanese Silver Grass

USDA Plant Hardiness Zones: 5 to 9

Season of Bloom: Late August to December

Height × Width: 6 to 8 feet × 3 to 5 feet

Flower Color: Pale beige-pink

Light Requirements: Full sun to light shade

Soil Requirements: Grows in any type of soil except very wet or boggy soils

Place of Origin: Northern China, Taiwan, to Japan

Plant Sources: Ambergate Gardens, Kurt Bluemel, Bluestone Perennials, Busse Gardens, Carroll Gardens, Crownsville Nursery, Forestfarm, Milaeger's Gardens, Shady Oaks Nursery, André Viette Farm & Nursery, White Flower Farm

Marvelous Maiden Grass

There are many desirable ornamental grasses among the various species and cultivars of maiden grass (M. spp.). Jazz up your garden with zebra grass (M. sinensis 'Zebrinus'), which has alternating horizontal bands of yellow and green on its leaves. Variegated Japanese silver grass (M. sinensis 'Variegatus') has white stripes down the length of its leaf blades, while maiden grass (M. sinensis 'Gracillimus') has narrow, fine-textured leaves with a silver midrib. The broad leaves of giant Chinese silver grass (M. giganteus) form an arching fountain up to 15 feet tall.

grassy fountain. These plumes are arching sprays of shimmering beige-pink, flowing to one side of the flower stem like flags blowing in the breeze. One of the best features of 'Silver Feather' is its reliable flowering. In cold weather, the leaves and flowerstalks of 'Silver Feather' turn to light brown and then to a parchment color. The flowers and leaves persist through the winter.

How to Grow Japanese Silver Grass

This ornamental grass is a very long-lived perennial. It grows well in just about any soil and in full sun to light or partial shade, although full sun and moist, rich soil are its preferred environment. And it has no significant pest or disease problems.

Purple Japanese silver grass displays fall color that earns it another common name, flame grass.

Silver Feather' produces plenty of silky flowerheads, even in cool, moist climates where other maiden grasses flower poorly. Japanese silver grass adds landscape interest for as much as 10 months out of the year.

Large clumps will benefit from division every four years or so. It's also worth your time to cut back Japanese silver grass' faded flowerstalks and leaf blades to just above ground level in March. By May, the new leaves will be growing well, giving you your spring fountain of grass again. About all Japanese silver grass really needs is this yearly shearing and enough water to see it through any droughty periods.

PROPAGATING JAPANESE SILVER GRASS

Divide Japanese silver grass in the spring. Make sure your shovel is sharp enough to cut through the tough roots. If you don't divide it every four years, the center of the clump tends to die out and the roots become woody. Dig up the entire clump and take divisions from the outer ring of live grass, discarding the center. You may need a sharp pruning saw to cut through the roots.

THE RIGHT SITE FOR 'SILVER FEATHER' Mix 'Silver Feather' Japanese silver grass into the back of your perennial garden. It adds a welcome vertical element in gardens where most other perennials are mounding to horizontal in habit. And its fine-textured, linear leaves contrast nicely with broad or rounded foliage. 'Silver Feather' also looks elegant rising in its own spot as a specimen on a lawn. If you can, position 'Silver Feather' where you'll see it with either morning or evening light shining through it. To get full enjoyment from its soft winter colors, plant it against a backdrop of dark bushy evergreens.

CO-STARS FOR 'SILVER FEATHER' 'Silver Feather' makes an excellent companion for big-leaved plants like hydrangeas, plume poppies (*Macleaya* spp.), ornamental rhubarb (*Rheum palmatum*), and rodgersias (*Rodgersia* spp.). It also makes a nice foil for thick stands of phlox and for low, rounded shrubbery. In the perennial garden, plant it with New England aster (*Aster novae-angliae*), 'Snowbank' boltonia (see page 76), azure monkshood (*Aconitum carmichaelii*), and 'Autumn Joy' sedum (see page 280).

'MARSHALL'S DELIGHT' BEE BALM

Monarda didyma 'Marshall's Delight'

THE BELOVED BEE BALMS get their common name because of their attractiveness to bees. They might as easily have been called hummingbird flowers. Many of the most popular cultivars are red, with a crown of tubular florets around the flowerhead—a combination hummingbirds can't resist. And neither can gardeners, for bee balm is a staple in just about every perennial garden.

But our all-star bee balm isn't red—it's a bright, clear pink and is still attractive to both the birds and the bees. 'Marshall's Delight' is

Bunches of Bee Balms

There are many gorgeous bee balm cultivars and hybrids. My personal favorites are 'Croftway Pink' bee balm (M. 'Croftway Pink'), which has very soft, lovely pink flowers, and 'Beauty of Cobham' bee balm (M. 'Beauty of Cobham'), which has very light, almost white, lavender-pink flowers.

A new hybrid, 'Blue Stocking' (M. 'Blue Stocking'), isn't blue, it's violet-purple and quite a departure from traditional bee balm colors. Other mildew-resistant cultivars include 'Purple Mildew Resistant' bee balm (M. didyma 'Purple Mildew Resistant') and 'Gardenview Scarlet' (M. didyma 'Gardenview Scarlet').

Spotlight on 'Marshall's Delight' Bee Balm

USDA Plant Hardiness Zones: 4 to 9

Season of Bloom July to September

Height × Width: 30 to 36 inches × 36 inches

Flower Color: Bright clear pink

Light Requirements: Partial shade to full sun

Soil Requirements: Loose, moist, humusy soil

Place of Origin: Eastern North America

Plant Sources: Ambergate Gardens, Bluestone Perennials, Busse Gardens, Carroll Gardens, Crownsville Nursery, Forestfarm, Garden Place, J. W. Jung Seed, Milaeger's Gardens, Powell's Gardens, Shady Oaks Nursery, Sunlight Gardens, André Viette Farm and Nursery, Wayside Gardens, Weiss Brothers Perennial Nursery, White Flower Farm

its name—for Henry H. Marshall, who hybridized it at the Morden Research Station in Manitoba, Canada. 'Marshall's Delight' has been bred for positive mildew resistance. It's a great improvement over most other types of bee balm, which are notorious for developing disfiguring powdery mildew on their leaves, rendering them tatty and sickly looking instead of chipper and green.

Henry Marshall also deserves praise for coming up with this bright pink, very floriferous bee balm that stays in flower several weeks longer than other types. And

Showy, long-lasting, clear pink flowers crown mildew-resistant 'Marshall's Delight' bee balm. All parts of the plant have a pleasant herbal fragrance.

'Marshall's Delight' seems to have twice the number of tubular flowers arranged around each flowerhead than do the light lavender flowers of the eastern species, wild bergamot (*M. fistulosa*), or the flowers of old-fashioned bee balm cultivars like 'Cambridge Scarlet'.

HOW TO GROW BEE BALM Most bee balms—especially the mildew-resistant selections—are trouble-free and easy to grow. Bee balm spreads via underground roots, although it's just shy of being invasive. Plant it where it will get some sun and some shade during the day.

If you grow bee balms other than 'Marshall's Delight' and its mildew-resistant counterparts, you may find your plants infected with powdery mildew. While thinning the stems to increase air circulation helps, this practice also thins the flowers. A better solution is to make sure the soil stays moist. It sounds odd, given the relationship between fungal diseases and moisture, but plants like bee balm are more susceptible to mildew when they are water stressed.

PROPAGATING BEE BALM Because bee balm spreads from shallow underground roots, it is one of the easiest perennials to divide. Keep plants vigorous by dividing them in spring or fall every three to four years. Plant the divisions 12 inches apart.

'Marshall's Delight' bee balm is just the right shade of pink to make an attractive combination with the rich yellow-and-mahogany-red flowers of 'T&M Originals Mixed' calliopsis. It looks great with blue, purple, or white flowers, too.

THE RIGHT SITE FOR 'MARSHALL'S DELIGHT' 'Marshall's Delight' and other bee balms are large, somewhat shaggy perennials that are well suited to cottage gardens and moist meadow plantings. A large drift of bee balm in bloom is a wonderful sight, so plant it in groups of three or more. Given bee balm's ability to attract hummingbirds (and hummingbird moths, too), it's a good idea to plant it where you can see its visitors from a window of the house.

CO-STARS FOR 'MARSHALL'S DELIGHT' Good companions for 'Marshall's Delight' bee balm include feverfew (see page 94), 'The Pearl' sneezeweed (*Achillea ptarmica* 'The Pearl'), purple coneflower (*Echinacea purpurea*), Russian sage (see page 242), Bukhara fleeceflower (*Polygonum baldschuanicum*), and annuals like purple petunias.

FORGET-ME-NOT

Myosotis scorpioides var. *semperflorens*

WE CAN'T FORGET THE FORGET-ME-NOTS! Almost every gardener, at one time or another, becomes enchanted by these dainty sky blue flowers. And of all the several kinds of this sweetest-of-all little blue flowers, *Myosotis scorpioides* var. *semperflorens* is the prettiest.

Forget-me-not is a plant that likes the water and, like watercress (*Nasturtium officinale*) and yellow flag (*Iris pseudacorus*), it can also be grown in the garden as long as the soil is kept well-moistened and never dries out. Its

Spotlight on
Forget-Me-Not

USDA Plant Hardiness Zones: 3 to 9

Season of Bloom: Late May to frost

Height × Width: 6 to 10 inches × 24+ inches

Flower Color: Bright blue

Light Requirements: Full sun to partial shade

Soil Requirements: Constantly moist gravelly to average soil

Place of Origin: Europe east to Siberia

Plant Sources: Bluestone Perennials, Milaeger's Gardens, André Viette Farm and Nursery

A Few Other Fine Forget-Me-Nots

Garden forget-me-not (M. sylvatica), also called woodland forget-me-not, produces mists of sky blue flowers above somewhat fuzzy, gray-green foliage. More tolerant of garden soil conditions, garden forget-me-not is a short-lived perennial or biennial in most of its range. But it self-sows so freely that it seems perennial, and it's only a matter of getting those volunteer seedlings to come up where you want them or moving them to a desired location. Like Johnny-jump-ups, forget-me-not's cheery flowers are rarely unwelcome, wherever they pop up. 'Victoria' garden forget-me-not (M. scorpioides 'Victoria') is a cultivar that bears deeper blue flowers on plants that grow to just 8 inches tall.

natural habitat is along a stream, pond, or shallow lakeside, in about 3 inches of water. This is also where moving water will deposit gravel, and for that reason forget-me-not prefers a wet, gravelly soil. Most of us don't have that kind of situation in our gardens, but we may have a spot in the garden that's low and tends to be wet, or where it's easy to keep the soil well-watered. That's where to plant the forget-me-nots.

The variety *semperflorens* is our all-star because once it begins flowering in May it will keep blooming into August. Then it continues to produce flowers, at a more sporadic rate, right up until frost—hence its variety name, which means ever-flowering. It's more compact than the species, and produces more flowers, too.

The plants themselves are handsome, with bright green, oblong, fleshy leaves set along stems that sprawl and seldom reach more

Keep the soil moist for forget-me-not and it will supply you with dainty blue flowers from late May until frost. It self-sows, too, and spreads modestly to form compact mats of flowers and oblong leaves.

than 8 to 10 inches tall. From the ends of these stems, small clusters of ¼-inch true blue flowers with yellow eyes keep opening. Under certain conditions, the flowers may be pink, but that's rare. The plants grow easily and flower profusely in the early part of the year, less profusely later on.

HOW TO GROW FORGET-ME-NOT

For best results, plant forget-me-not in full sun to partial shade in wet, gravelly soil, such as you'd find along a small stream. In the garden, give it a spot where the soil is constantly moist. While other species of forget-me-not may have problems with certain insects and diseases, not much bothers *Myosotis scorpioides* except possibly some mildew on the leaves. If conditions get dry, mites may attack. The best defense against both these problems is a healthy plant that gets adequate water.

PROPAGATING FORGET-ME-NOT

Divide forget-me-not's mats of creeping rhizomes in the spring or take summer stem cuttings to increase your planting. Plant the divisions or new plants 12 inches apart. Forget-me-not also self-sows in moist soils and is generally a very easy plant to propagate.

THE RIGHT SITE FOR FORGET-ME-NOT

Forget-me-nots are absolutely stunning growing in a dappled woodland garden by the water. When planting them in the well-watered border, mix them with ferns, hostas, water-loving irises and primroses, plants from the globeflower clan (*Trollius* spp.), and spring bulbs—especially the snowflakes (*Leucojum* spp.). Forget-me-not stays low and adds

sparkle and daintiness to the taller, rougher-looking plants. If given half a chance, they will quickly grow into a pretty flowering ground-cover in a perpetually moist or wet spot.

CO-STARS FOR FORGET-ME-NOT

Plant forget-me-not with summer snowflake (*Leucojum aestivum*) and spring snowflake (*L. vernum*), 'Superbus' common globeflower (*Trollius europaeus* 'Superbus'), marsh marigold (*Caltha palustris*), yellow flag (*Iris pseudacorus*) and other bog irises, primrose (*Primula rosea*), and ferns. In more formal moist-soil plantings, it's enchanting mixed with astilbes.

Forget-me-nots are perfect at the edge of a partly shaded water garden where their blue flowers mix prettily with yellow flags and marsh marigolds.

'ICE FOLLIES' DAFFODIL

Narcissus 'Ice Follies'

I'VE CHOSEN 'ICE FOLLIES' AS THE ALL-STAR daffodil because it's my current favorite. Since it won the American Daffodil Society's top award in 1992, it must be theirs, too.

The real all-star, of course, is the whole genus of *Narcissus*, which includes all those spring-flowering bulbs we call daffodils, jonquils, or narcissus. There are so many kinds in such a profusion of beautiful variations of

Wister Award Winners

The Wister Award is the American Daffodil Society's top honor, named after renowned horticulturist Dr. John Wister, and based on the following qualities: The daffodil must grow well with many blooming stems; the blooms should be long lasting, showy at a distance, and reasonably sun-fast; the foliage should be vigorous and resistant to disease and frost damage; the flower stems should be strong and sturdy, and taller than the foliage; the bulbs should resist basal rot and be slow to divide (too rapid division means the blooms will deteriorate in quality); and the cultivar should be readily available.

The following Narcissus cultivars are recent Wister Award recipients: 'Sweetness' (1993) is an all-yellow, fragrant jonquil; 'Salome' (1995) is a large-cup daffodil with white perianth and a yellow-rimmed, pink cup; 'Peeping Tom' (1996) is a small, all-yellow, cyclamineus daffodil.

Spotlight on 'Ice Follies' Daffodil

USDA Plant Hardiness Zones: 3 to 9

Season of Bloom: April to May

Height × Width: 16 to 18 inches × 6 to 18 inches

Flower Color: White with yellow trumpet

Light Requirements: Full sun to partial shade

Soil Requirements: Good, average, well-drained garden soil

Place of Origin: Europe and northern Africa

Plant Sources: Breck's, Carroll Gardens, Daffodil Mart, Dutch Gardens, J. W. Jung Seed, McClure & Zimmerman, Park Seed, Van Bourgondien, Van Engelen, Wayside Gardens, White Flower Farm

color and form, and they are so useful, that the choice of an all-star really is a personal one.

'Ice Follies' is classified as a large-cup daffodil, which is a large, bold type with a wide cup (or trumpet—the protruding center portion). 'Ice Follies' daffodil's central cup is creamy lemon yellow, surrounded by white petals (the perianth). It's sweetly fragrant, a heavy bloomer, and a vigorous grower in good soil. And while many daffodils are short lived in the warm South, 'Ice Follies' is not.

HOW TO GROW DAFFODILS Plant daffodil bulbs in moist, humus-rich, well-drained soil in full sun to light shade. An ideal location is beneath deciduous trees, where the daffodils will finish blooming before the trees leaf out. Add a bit of compost and a handful

Even in the South, 'Ice Follies' is a reliable performer that returns to bloom each spring. Over time it will spread to fill an increasing area with its sweet-scented flowers.

of bonemeal to the soil at planting and topdress the site with compost or rock phosphate in the spring.

Daffodils will benefit from annual fertilization. Avoid high-nitrogen fertilizers that will promote foliage growth at the expense of the flowers. Daffodils are easier than many other bulbs, because deer won't eat the tops and gophers won't eat the bulbs. And there are few pests or diseases that trouble them.

PROPAGATING DAFFODILS Where they like their spot, daffodils will naturalize, slowly increasing the size of the planting. To promote this benefit, plant them in good soil and full sun, and allow the leaves to thoroughly dry out before cutting them back.

THE RIGHT SITE FOR DAFFODILS There's a grassy bank on the left as you head up my driveway, and we order 100 daffodils of mixed kinds each year and pack them closely, about 12 inches apart or less, over a segment of the slope, increasing the area of the planting each year. I figure that in about another three years, the entire slope will be full of daffodils.

In a more formal setting, plant your daffodils in the garden where daylily foliage or perennial groundcovers will fill in and hide their declining foliage.

CO-STARS FOR 'ICE FOLLIES' Plant 'Ice Follies' with Grecian windflower (*Anemone blanda*), violets and primroses, and early bulbs like glory-of-the-snow (*Chionodoxa* spp.), squills (*Scilla* spp.), striped squills (*Puschkinia* spp.), snowflakes (*Leucojum* spp.), and crocuses. Interplant daffodils with pachysandras, periwinkles (*Vinca* spp.), or daylilies.

Large-cup daffodils like 'Ice Follies' are also called "weatherproofs" because they sail through the hazards of early spring weather—even snow—and maintain their cheery good looks.

A Stellar Idea

When your daffodils have finished blooming, leave their foliage alone. Don't braid it, and don't cut it off until it's almost entirely brown. Those leaves are busy supplying food to the bulbs for next spring's flowers. If the fading foliage bothers you, plant your daffodils with perennials that will fill in and hide the daffodils' leaves.

CATMINT

Nepeta × faassenii

CATMINT IS A GARDEN WORKHORSE, hiding behind the guise of a modest, almost unassuming plant. And yet it has so many uses, has so many nice features, and is such a wonderful companion to so many other plants, that it rates near the top of our list of all-stars.

Catmint's leaves are small, tidy, and neatly toothed all around their margins. The plants form bushy little mounds of foliage. Perhaps catmint's best feature is the cool, gray-green appearance of its leaves, which have a fine, nubbly texture. The stems branch and elongate, and on these flowering stems are a few smaller leaves and a profusion of tiny lavender-blue flowers.

HOW TO GROW CATMINT This perennial grows in just about any soil—although if you asked, it would probably specify a sandy, limy soil as long as it's well drained. It stands up to heat and droughty periods in spite of its mint family heritage and is one of the most

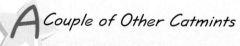

A Couple of Other Catmints

'Snowflake' catmint (N. × faassenii 'Snowflake') is a lovely, white-flowered version of our all-star. Some people swear by 'Six Hills Giant' (N. × faassenii 'Six Hills Giant') as a tougher, larger version of catmint, but it grows to 3 feet tall—and taller when it flowers—and is more prone to flopping over.

Spotlight on Catmint

USDA Plant Hardiness Zones: 3 to 9

Season of Bloom: May to August

Height × Width: 12 inches × 24 to 36+ inches

Flower Color: Lavender-blue

Light Requirements: Full sun

Soil Requirements: Any well-drained soil

Place of Origin: A hybrid of two species that grow in Europe and the Caucasus region

Plant Sources: Kurt Bluemel, Bluestone Perennials, Busse Gardens, Carroll Gardens, Forestfarm, Garden Place, Greer Gardens, Powell's Gardens, Roslyn Nursery, André Viette Farm & Nursery, Wayside Gardens, White Flower Farm

---

highly recommended perennials in this book full of recommended plants. And it has no pest or disease problems to speak of either.

When flowering begins to wane, usually in July, ruthlessly cut catmint way back—by as much as two-thirds of its height. Add the trimmings to your compost pile or use them as mulch under a shrub. After shearing, catmint will produce new shoots that will look fresh and tidy for the rest of the year, and the plants will bloom again from August to the end of summer. If you fail to cut it back, catmint will stop flowering, and its stems may separate and flop over unattractively. This summer shearing is a small price to pay for catmint's continued good looks. Leave the winter-killed foliage on the plants until early spring cleanup. It helps to protect the roots over the winter.

Use 'Six Hills Giant' in spots where you need a larger splash of catmint's lavender-blue flowers and cool, gray-green foliage.

At the front of the garden, catmint's fine-textured flower spikes echo the up-right form of fox-gloves and create a cool color combina-tion with pinks and silvery foliage plants like mullein.

PROPAGATING CATMINT Catmint is among the easiest of plants to divide. Separate rooted sections of the plant in the spring and replant the divisions 12 inches apart. You can also take tip cuttings in the spring.

THE RIGHT SITE FOR CATMINT Here is one of the finest edging plants for a sunny border or walkway in the perennial kingdom. Catmint is also right at home toppling gently over a wall or as a groundcover on a dry, sunny slope. Catmint's cooling effect makes it a ster-ling partner for roses of all colors and for the warm reds and pinks of the June garden.

CO-STARS FOR CATMINT This plant is an ex-ceptionally good-looking companion for roses. Be sure to keep it away from their root zones, however, as the catmint's vigor may over-power that of the roses. Catmint's cool colors make a pleasing foil for the reds and pinks of

perennials such as Delavy incarvillea (see page 182), queen-of-the-prairie (*Filipendula rubra*), sun rose (*Helianthemum nummularium*), 'Prairie Fire' penstemon (*Penstemon* 'Prairie Fire'), prairie mallow (*Sidalcea malviflora*), 'Red Fox' spike speedwell (*Veronica spicata* 'Red Fox'), and ornamental alliums (*Allium* spp.).

A Stellar Idea

If you have a cat, you'll soon find out why this perennial goes by the name catmint. Although this isn't the famous catnip (N. cataria) felines still love to roll in catmint. If you want to dis-courage them, lay a piece of chicken-wire fencing on the ground around the base of your plants, so it's out of sight. Cats dislike the feel of fencing beneath their feet and will leave your catmint alone.

MISSOURI EVENING PRIMROSE

Oenothera missouriensis

MANY PERENNIALS HAVE YELLOW FLOWERS, but only a few deliver the bright, clear lemon yellow of Missouri evening primrose. The blossoms are big and showy—as much as 4 to 5 inches across, lightly fragrant, and cup shaped. They open in the late afternoon

Other Exceptional Evening Primroses

Fremont's evening primrose (O. macrocarpa subsp. fremontii) is a useful perennial with a tangled identity. It's sometimes called O. fremontii and is likely a subspecies of our all-star, Missouri evening primrose, since O. macrocarpa is listed in many sources as a synonym for O. missouriensis. Fremont's evening primrose has narrower leaves than Missouri evening primrose and a somewhat neater habit. Its flowers are pale lemon yellow and its foliage more silvery. Fremont's evening primrose is not as widely available as Missouri evening primrose.

An evening primrose for warmer regions (Zones 7 to 11) is Mexican evening primrose (O. berlandieri). This exceptional plant produces plenty of silvery pink blooms with golden centers over a very long season that stretches from June to October. However, I find that the deer just can't resist it.

Spotlight on
Missouri Evening Primrose

USDA Plant Hardiness Zones: 4 to 9

Season of Bloom: June to August

Height × Width: 8 to 10 inches × 18 to 24 inches

Flower Color: Lemon yellow

Light Requirements: Full sun

Soil Requirements: Average, sandy, light, well-drained soil

Place of Origin: Missouri west to Kansas and south to Texas

Plant Sources: Carroll Gardens, Garden Place, J. W. Jung Seed, Milaeger's Gardens, Van Bourgondien, Weiss Brothers Perennial Nursery

and persist into the evening and are real charmers (not something you can say about many yellow-flowered plants). When they are finished for the night, they close by prettily folding up their petals.

Perhaps part of Missouri evening primrose's charm is the long, tapered, red-blushed green buds from which its flowers open, or the reddish stems that carry them. The red sets off the bright yellow even more. And so do the 3- to 4-inch, lancelike, pointed, glossy, dark green leaves that appear in bunches along trailing stems that tend to toss along the ground instead of standing upright.

The flower buds emerge where the leaves meet the stems, dotting the plant over a very long season of bloom. After the flowers finish their display, they are followed by large, winged seed capsules that are interesting in dried arrangements.

How to Grow Missouri Evening
Primrose Missouri evening primrose likes a warm, sunny spot in soil like that of its southern to southwestern home: sandy, loose, alkaline, and well drained. It isn't that fussy though—I've grown it well in ordinary garden soil. Missouri evening primrose is a tough plant, and it can take heat and drought without missing a blossom. About the only way you can get in trouble with it is to put it where the soil stays waterlogged. In a site with good drainage, established plants will prove to be pest-, disease-, and trouble-free.

Propagating Missouri Evening
Primrose Each spring, Missouri evening primrose's woody roots send out underground stems that you can divide off and plant elsewhere, about 12 inches apart. You can also separate off young shoots that arise from the base of the plant in the spring. Missouri evening primrose grows easily from seed, too, and may, in fact, self-sow.

The Right Site for Missouri Evening
Primrose One of the best ways to use Missouri evening primrose is to plant it atop a sunny terrace, where its loose, somewhat floppy stems can trail down over the wall's face, hanging out its cheerful blooms for all to enjoy. This native of the southern prairies is a first-rate plant for the front of a bed or border or for along a walkway where its gently glowing flowers will light your steps as darkness falls. They don't call it evening primrose for nothing. And they are superb with milky bellflower's blue flowers.

Co-Stars for Missouri Evening
Primrose The clear yellow color of Missouri evening primrose's flowers makes it an easy companion for many other perennials. Its yellow cup-shaped blossoms look superb next to the clusters of open blue bells of milky bellflower (*Campanula lactiflora*), as well as with the blue to lavender flowers of plants

In a sunny, well-drained site, Missouri evening primrose gives you big flowers on compact plants. Each lemon yellow blossom may be as much as 5 inches across, while the plant typically grows only 8 to 10 inches tall.

At the end of the work day, you'll appreciate Missouri evening primrose's habit of opening its flowers during the day and keeping them open into the evening—when you're home to enjoy them.

such as Persian onion (*Allium aflatunense*), Frikart's aster (*Aster × frikartii*), crested gentian (*Gentiana septemfida*), and English lavender (*Lavandula angustifolia*). And Missouri evening primrose won't quarrel with warm yellow and orange flowers like those of butterfly weed (see page 56), common sneezeweed (*Helenium autumnale*), common yarrow (*Achillea millefolium*), orange coneflower (*Rudbeckia fulgida*), hybrid goldenrods (*Solidago* hybrids), lilies, and daylilies.

ALLEGHENY SPURGE

Pachysandra procumbens

Spotlight on
Allegheny Spurge

USDA Plant Hardiness Zones: 5 to 9

Season of Bloom: April to May

Height × Width: 6 to 12 inches × 18+ inches

Flower Color: White to greenish white

Light Requirements: Partial shade to full shade

Soil Requirements: Rich, moist, humusy, well-drained soil

Place of Origin: West Virginia to Kentucky and south to Florida and Louisiana

Plant Sources: Kurt Bluemel, Carroll Gardens, Forestfarm, Powell's Gardens, Roslyn Nursery, Sunlight Gardens, We-Du Nurseries

MOST OF US ARE TIRED AND BORED with *Pachysandra terminalis*, the ubiquitous Japanese pachysandra that you see everywhere under campus trees and around government buildings. Few gardeners know that there is a native American species and that it is a wonderful plant with an easy nature and appearance that far surpasses its Japanese relative. It's our perennial all-star groundcover, Allegheny spurge. Not only is it more beautiful, but it has a true native's ability to ward off the pests and diseases of the shaded, woodsy areas where it likes to grow.

Allegheny spurge is evergreen in the Southeast in Zones 8 and 9 and semievergreen in Zone 7 and the warmest part of Zone 6. In northern Zone 6 and in Zone 5, killing frosts burn back the leaves, and snow and ice push them to the ground.

Some may think of its winter disappearance in the cold climates as a disadvantage

A Pair of Pachysandras

I should mention that the Japanese species has a couple of noteworthy cultivars. 'Green Sheen' Japanese pachysandra (P. terminalis 'Green Sheen') has shiny leaves that look polished, while 'Silver Edge' Japanese pachysandra (P. terminalis 'Silver Edge') has light green leaves with a narrow silver edge around the margins.

compared with the more sturdy evergreen leaves of the Japanese species. Actually, Allegheny spurge's deciduous quality has a solid up-side: When spring rolls around, the plant flowers in April at about the same time that its new foliage is spinning up out of the earth. As a result, the flowers are much more visible than if they were covered with last season's leaves.

These flowers arise from the creeping shoots, usually right at the base of the old leaves, where new leaves are emerging. The flowering stalks are about 4 inches tall in a spike of closely set, narrow, white or greenish white flowers—male above and female toward the bottom.

But it's not really the flowers that provide the show. Rather it's the leaves, which are about 3 to 4 inches long, vaguely oval, and set

Although it doesn't spread with as much vigor as Japanese pachysandra, over time Allegheny spurge forms an attractive, groundcovering clump. It's handsome in fall when frost adds a hint of color to the leaves, emphasizing their silvery mottling.

around with shallow teeth. The leaves come up from the creeping stems in umbrellalike clusters that densely carpet the ground.

Allegheny spurge's leaves are a soft gray-green and sometimes are mottled with silver. A stand of silver-mottled plants is striking, and if you are selecting plants from a nursery, choose ones that show the silvery mottling. This quality is sure to be selected out into a cultivar before too many more years go by. In fall, the leaves acquire reddish tints.

HOW TO GROW ALLEGHENY SPURGE This
plant is an easy grower when it's planted in favorable conditions: humus-rich, moist soil in partial shade to full shade. Once you've got it in the ground, there's nothing more to be done with it but to enjoy its pretty spring flowering and summer-into-fall (and sometimes through-winter) foliage. Allegheny spurge is untroubled by pests and diseases.

PROPAGATING ALLEGHENY SPURGE
Allegheny spurge is a mat-forming plant, and propagation is as easy as lifting divisions in the late spring to early summer, after the plants finish flowering. Plant the divisions 12 to 16 inches apart in well-prepared ground with a mulch of leaf mold so the plants can grow together to form a solid carpet.

THE RIGHT SITE FOR ALLEGHENY SPURGE
Right at home in a woodland garden, Allegheny spurge prefers acid soil and makes a delightful groundcover around rhododendrons and azaleas. Its satiny leaves provide a nice contrast to the glossy foliage of European wild ginger (see page 54), and Allegheny spurge enjoys the same growing conditions.

Allegheny spurge produces feathery spikes of white to greenish white or pinkish flowers that bloom just as its new foliage emerges.

CO-STARS FOR ALLEGHENY SPURGE Plant
Allegheny spurge in large drifts with other shade-loving or shade-tolerant perennials such as 'Luxuriant' bleeding heart (*Dicentra* 'Luxuriant'), Siberian iris (*Iris sibirica*), sweet cicely (*Myrrhis odorata*), ferns, mayapple (*Podophyllum peltatum*), hostas, and daylilies. It keeps good company with many woodland shrubs, including azaleas (*Rhododendron* spp.) and rhododendrons. Around deciduous trees, Allegheny spurge makes a good companion for tall daffodils like 'King Alfred' and for other spring bulbs that will reach higher than Allegheny spurge's foliage.

'BOWL OF BEAUTY' PEONY

Paeonia lactiflora 'Bowl of Beauty'

THE BLOSSOMS OF HERBACEOUS PEONIES have always been the most sumptuous blooms in the garden, but modern breeding work is producing new peonies that surpass anything we've known before. There are now about 900 cultivars offered for sale in the United States, and of them all, 'Bowl of Beauty' is as pretty as anything I've ever seen.

This is one of the new Royal Peony series hybridized in Holland from the common garden peony (*P. lactiflora*) and offered in the United States by Breck's. Each blossom is bowl shaped, from 5 to 7 inches across, with a ring of deep pink petals surrounding an inner puff of frothy, finely cut, ivory-white petals. And they're fragrant, too.

I was so taken with the beauty of these flowers that I called Viki Ferreniea of Breck's to find out more about them. They are a re-

Peonies on Parade

Of course there are hundreds of marvelous garden peony cultivars from which to choose. To enjoy peony flowers with a different foliage effect, you might try the Memorial Day peony (P. officinalis 'Rubra Plena'), which has double, deep red blooms above deeply cut leaves, or fernleaf peony (P. tenuifolia), a popular species with very ferny foliage and small dark crimson blossoms dotted over the surface of the 24-inch-tall plants.

Spotlight on 'Bowl of Beauty' Peony

USDA Plant Hardiness Zones: 2 to 8

Season of Bloom: June

Height × Width: 24 to 36 inches × 24 to 36 inches

Flower Color: Pink and white

Light Requirements: Full sun to partial shade

Soil Requirements: Rich, humusy, well-drained soil

Place of Origin: China

Plant Sources: Breck's, W. Atlee Burpee, Busse Gardens, Dutch Gardens, Van Bourgondien, André Viette Farm & Nursery, White Flower Farm

cent introduction from Holland, where they were bred for cut flowers, meaning they last and last. The flowers are bred to have stronger stems that reach just 24 to 36 inches tall, so they won't flop over.

Not only that, but if old blossoms are quickly deadheaded, the remaining blooms are stronger and larger still. When out of flower, the foliage of 'Bowl of Beauty' remains beautiful and colors up nicely in the fall. And once you plant peonies in your garden, you can enjoy them for a long time, because peonies are among the longest-lived perennials, and plants routinely reach a hundred years old and more.

HOW TO GROW PEONIES Your peony plants will grow and bloom just about forever if you pamper them a bit at planting time. Choose a sunny spot with good drainage and dig a large hole—18 inches wide and as deep. Amend the soil in the planting hole with rotted manure, compost, bonemeal, and some wood ashes. Plant the roots or divisions with the growing points no more than 2 inches below the soil surface. Being planted too deeply is perhaps the most common reason for peonies that fail to bloom. Common garden peony hybrids (*P. lactiflora* hybrids) don't do very well in Zone 9 and warmer because there's not enough winter chill for them.

PROPAGATING PEONIES Division isn't usually necessary with peonies, as they are well behaved and increase slowly in size. But if you want more plants, make divisions or root cuttings with at least three growing points in late August, then replant the divisions 18 to 24 inches apart.

THE RIGHT SITE FOR 'BOWL OF BEAUTY'

Peonies make a fine informal herbaceous hedge along walks and driveways. 'Bowl of Beauty' peony's short stature and sturdy stems make it ideal for this use since it's not as floppy as taller peonies. 'Bowl of Beauty' is at home in the perennial border, too, where it's excellent with spring bulbs. The reddish new foliage looks nice next to the bulbs' flowers and then grows taller to help cover the ripening bulb foliage. You'll probably also want to cut some wonderfully fragrant 'Bowl of Beauty' blossoms for the house.

While ordinary peony blossoms last for a few days to a week, 'Bowl of Beauty' peony's flowers last for an extra four or five days.

CO-STARS FOR 'BOWL OF BEAUTY' Combine 'Bowl of Beauty' with fine-textured perennials such as catmint (see page 230), calamint (see page 80), or 'Canon J. Went' purple toadflax (see page 206). The blue flowers of bellflowers (*Campanula* spp.) are attractive next to its pink-and-white blossoms. Plant it amid fall-flowering asters that will provide a floral display around its still-handsome foliage.

Put a peony ring over the new spring shoots of taller peonies. The leaves will hide the support in just a few weeks.

A Stellar Idea

If you do use peonies for cut flowers, cut them just before the big buds open. They will last for four to six weeks in a plastic bag in the refrigerator, so you can have fresh peonies in the house from June—when the bushes bloom outside and you can take some fresh ones for cutting—right up to August, from buds you've cut and stored in the fridge.

'DEGAS' ORIENTAL POPPY

Papaver orientale 'Degas'

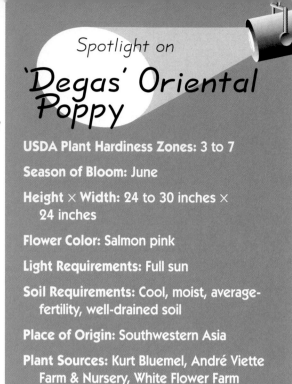

Spotlight on

'Degas' Oriental Poppy

USDA Plant Hardiness Zones: 3 to 7

Season of Bloom: June

Height × Width: 24 to 30 inches × 24 inches

Flower Color: Salmon pink

Light Requirements: Full sun

Soil Requirements: Cool, moist, average-fertility, well-drained soil

Place of Origin: Southwestern Asia

Plant Sources: Kurt Bluemel, André Viette Farm & Nursery, White Flower Farm

ORIENTAL POPPIES DELIVER A COLOR PUNCH that few other garden perennials can rival. A group of three is usually enough to rivet the eye to their part of the garden. The vivid flowers are remarkable both for their rich, saturated colors and for their broad, 4- to 6-inch size.

While oriental poppy's bright reds, pinks, oranges, and whites are useful as accents and as spark plugs for a sedate June garden, none of these brilliant hues has quite the same effect as our all-star. 'Degas' oriental poppy is a stunning soft salmon pink with darker veining in the center of its huge cups. A large group of 'Degas' may remind you of the grace and beauty of a group of the painter's ballerinas.

Oriental poppies have coarse, bristly looking foliage that's not as prickly to the touch as it looks. The foliage persists over the winter in small tufts. In the spring, these tufts grow into a large basal group of leaves from which 24-inch or taller flower stems arise. These are usually leafless but hairy, and topped by big, single blossoms. 'Degas' is an improvement on oriental poppies because it grows only 24 to 30 inches tall and resists toppling or leaning over precariously, a problem that can afflict other cultivars. After 'Degas' blooms in June, the foliage dies away in July and August. Then, in September, you'll notice new little tufts of bristly foliage reappearing.

Other Poppies with Panache

Some of the more popular pink-flowered cultivars of oriental poppy are 'Helen Elizabeth', a pure salmon pink; 'Victoria Dreyfus', which is salmon pink with silver edges; and 'Show Girl', bright pink with white centers. 'Carmine' has bright red flowers with black blotches on the petals, while the flowers of 'Barr's White' are white with black blotches. 'Beauty of Livermore' and 'Brilliant' are both strong reds.

HOW TO GROW ORIENTAL POPPY These poppies are plants for the North. They don't perform very well south of Zone 7, where they tend to break dormancy in the fall and try to grow through the warm winters, only to get hit by recurrent frosts that will destroy or damage them. If new plants are set out early in the spring in the South, they may bloom but will struggle in the subsequent winter, which can be expensive.

Unlike its brazen, red-orange poppy relatives, 'Degas' oriental poppy delivers its crinkly soft flowers in an elegant, easy-to-match shade of salmon pink that looks good with almost anything you plant next to it.

In Zones 3 to 7, plant oriental poppy in full sun in average to rich garden soil that's cool and well drained. Given these conditions, they'll grow healthy and care-free for many years. Not much bothers oriental poppies. If aphids appear, wash them off with a jet of water from the hose. If blight blackens the stems, amend their planting site or move them to where they'll get better drainage and more sun.

PROPAGATING 'DEGAS' To divide 'Degas', wait until the plant is dormant, in midsummer after it's done flowering. Lift the clumps and divide them, replanting the divisions about 24 inches apart. Take root cuttings at the same time. Cut pieces of the deep roots into 3- or 4-inch sections and plant them upright in a nursery box of compost, barely covering the top of the root pieces. When small plants appear, set the box into the garden for overwintering.

THE RIGHT SITE FOR 'DEGAS' Plant a group of 'Degas' oriental poppy where the plants will serve as a focal point for the early June perennial border. You can choose to accent them with a strong red oriental poppy such as 'Carmine'. They also look stunning in combination with plants that have dark violet and blue flowers.

After their flowers fade, gather oriental poppies' bold seedpods to add an interesting touch to dried arrangements. But don't warm up the oven—these are not the poppies that produce tasty seeds for use in baked goods!

CO-STARS FOR 'DEGAS' Baby's-breath (*Gypsophila paniculata*), boltonia (*Boltonia asteroides*), and Russian sage (see page 242) are all good companions for any oriental poppy, because they cover the bare spots left when the poppies fade in July. 'Degas' looks exquisite with dark violet 'Caesar's Brother' Siberian iris (see page 186) and deep blue 'May Night' violet sage (see page 272).

'HUSKER RED' FOXGLOVE PENSTEMON

Penstemon digitalis 'Husker Red'

'HUSKER RED' FOXGLOVE PENSTEMON was named the 1996 Perennial Plant of the Year by the Perennial Plant Association, and this plant definitely possesses all-star qualities. 'Husker Red' is an outstanding, vigorous grower that serves two important functions in the garden. The first is as a colorful foliage plant. Its amazing bronzy, purplish red foliage color was the reason it was selected in 1983 by Dr. Dale

Perusing Other Perfect Penstemons

The genus Penstemon is a fascinating one. It's related to foxgloves (Digitalis spp.), and its flowers are always tubular like foxglove blossoms, only smaller. All penstemons are very attractive to hummingbirds.

Common beardtongue (P. barbatus) is a native wildflower that grows in dry spots. Its hybrid cultivar 'Prairie Dusk' has rosy purple flowers in late May through June, while 'Prairie Fire' has orange-red flowers all summer; both are evergreen in the South. 'Elfin Pink' bears spikes of lipstick pink flowers in early summer and again in late summer if deadheaded.

Foothill penstemon (P. heterophyllus) opens a profusion of small, narrow, tubular true blue flowers from June to August.

Spotlight on

'Husker Red' Foxglove Penstemon

USDA Plant Hardiness Zones: 3 to 9

Season of Bloom: June to August

Height × Width: 30 inches × 24 inches

Flower Color: White

Light Requirements: Full sun to partial shade

Soil Requirements: Well-drained, light, humusy soil

Place of Origin: South Dakota to Canadian maritimes and south to Texas

Plant Sources: Ambergate Gardens, Kurt Bluemel, Bluestone Perennials, Busse Gardens, Carroll Gardens, Crownsville Nursery, Forestfarm, Garden Place, Greer Gardens, J. W. Jung Seed, Klehm Nursery, Milaeger's Gardens, Powell's Gardens, Roslyn Nursery, Shady Oaks Nursery, Sunlight Gardens, André Viette Farm & Nursery, Wayside Gardens, We-Du Nurseries, White Flower Farm

---

Lindgren of the University of Nebraska (home of the Corn Huskers, hence its cultivar name).

In addition, 'Husker Red' is a stunning flowering perennial. From late June into July and August, 'Husker Red' produces about two dozen flowering stalks, each of which opens about 50 bright white tubular flowers in airy sprays above the reddish leaves. The combination is quite striking just by itself, and you can easily see why the Perennial Plant Association chose this perennial above all others as its plant of the year.

'Husker Red' foxglove penstemon's wine red stems and new leaves echo the foliage colors of shrubs like purple-leaved plums and purple barberry.

How to Grow 'Husker Red'

Although it will do best in moist, well-drained, humusy soil, 'Husker Red' tolerates drought and is a tough customer even in average, gravelly soils. Being a native, it's well adapted to pests and diseases and is seldom bothered by them.

Foxglove penstemon (*P. digitalis*) is not the most widely known species of penstemon, but it is much hardier than most of the other species offered in commerce. Native to the northern Great Plains east into the Atlantic provinces of Canada, it survives Zone 4 winters, while other penstemons tend to need protection even in Zone 5. This means you can grow foxglove penstemon just about anywhere in the United States.

Propagating 'Husker Red'

You can take basal or stem tip cuttings from new growth before the plants flower. They'll generally root within 15 days if inserted into a moist potting mixture of 25 percent compost, 25 percent sand, and 50 percent perlite or vermiculite. 'Husker Red' makes clumps that you can divide in early spring before shoots emerge; replant divisions 12 inches apart.

The Right Site for 'Husker Red'

Use the narrow, pointy red leaves of 'Husker Red' to set off the many green-leaved plants in your garden and to make an interesting color combination with blue-green, gray-green, and silver-leaved plants. For example, where artemisias make a light silvery spot in the garden, a nice group of 'Husker Red' foxglove penstemon will provide dark contrast.

Blooming atop tall stalks, 'Husker Red' foxglove penstemon's tubular white flowers carry just the faintest blush of pink.

Co-Stars for 'Husker Red'

'Husker Red' foxglove penstemon looks good with many plants, but it's especially nice combined with blue flowers such as delphiniums, 'Butterfly Blue' pincushion flower (*Scabiosa caucasica* 'Butterfly Blue') and 'Sunny Border Blue' speedwell (see page 314), and with the soft pink blossoms of 'Wargrave Pink' Endress cranesbill (*Geranium endressii* 'Wargrave Pink'). Plant it in groups with 'Moonbeam' threadleaf coreopsis (see page 110), artemisias (*Artemisia* spp.), or 'Moonshine' yarrow (see page 28).

A Stellar Idea

If you want to show off the striking red foliage of 'Husker Red', grow it in full sun. In a shaded site, it tends to turn green.

RUSSIAN SAGE

Perovskia atriplicifolia

RUSSIAN SAGE IS ONE OF THE MOST USEFUL and beautiful of the fillers for any perennial garden. Once you've established it, you can pretty much forget it, for it's a very low-maintenance plant that endures drought without complaint. A mature specimen in full bloom is one of the finest sights in the garden. The Perennial Plant Association named it the 1995 Perennial Plant of the Year.

Russian sage is a shrubby, branching plant with small, narrow leaves, and a loose, open habit. The stems are grayish and the leaves are gray-green with gray-white undersides. A member of the mint family, like garden sage (*Salvia officinalis*), Russian sage is pleasantly fragrant when its leaves are crushed.

In July, Russian sage bursts into a misty froth of small, tubular lavender-blue to violet

Spotlight on
Russian Sage

USDA Plant Hardiness Zones: 4 to 9

Season of Bloom: July to October

Height × Width: 3 feet × 3 feet

Flower Color: Blue

Light Requirements: Full sun

Soil Requirements: Average to dry, well-drained soil

Place of Origin: Southern Russia and Afghanistan east to the Himalayas

Plant Sources: Ambergate Gardens, Kurt Bluemel, Bluestone Perennials, Busse Gardens, Carroll Gardens, Forestfarm, Garden Place, Greer Gardens, J. W. Jung Seed, Klehm Nursery, Milaeger's Gardens, Powell's Gardens, Spring Hill Nurseries, Sunlight Gardens, Van Bourgondien, André Viette Farm and Nursery, Weiss Brothers Perennial Nursery, White Flower Farm

A Russian Sage Riddle

Russian sage's benefits in the garden are much more well documented than its botanical identity. While some horticulturists claim that plants sold as P. atriplicifolia are actually hybrids with P. abrotanoides, others call it P. artemesioides or even P. × superba. The popular cultivar 'Blue Spire' has darker violet flowers and probably is a cross between P. atriplicifolia and P. abrotanoides. My advice is to ignore all this confusion and look for P. atriplicifolia.

flowers. These cover the branching flower-stalks that rise above the leaves. Russian sage has an incredibly long season of bloom. Its flowers will persist for up to 15 weeks, right into October in many places. This long-lasting display makes Russian sage a fine companion for other fall-blooming perennials.

HOW TO GROW RUSSIAN SAGE Plant Russian sage in a sunny spot in well-drained soil of average fertility. Shade and rich soil can make it floppy. Place it where winter moisture can drain away quickly to prevent rotting during dormancy. It's not bothered by pests or other diseases.

Although it's airy, Russian sage is substantial enough to fill the role of a shrub in your garden, while allowing you a peek at what's beyond it.

Although classified as a perennial, Russian sage is really a subshrub, and its stems turn woody by late fall. In the spring, before any new growth starts, trim these stems to a few inches above ground level, leaving some buds on the stubs. This forces new growth of young stems, foliage, and flowers and helps keep the plant compact and tidy.

PROPAGATING RUSSIAN SAGE Russian sage rarely requires division, but you can divide it in the spring to increase the size of a planting. You can also take stem cuttings in late summer to early fall when flowering is finishing up. Some of its stems may sprawl on the ground around it (or you can pull one down). By simply covering a section of a prostrate stem with soil, you can encourage it to root and create a new plant through layering. Plant divisions and rooted cuttings 18 inches apart.

THE RIGHT SITE FOR RUSSIAN SAGE The effect of Russian sage from any distance is of a blue cloud that has settled among more substantial looking plants in the border. As a filler, Russian sage makes an elegant statement, enhancing whatever it's planted with and filling places between the bolder plants around it.

CO-STARS FOR RUSSIAN SAGE Plant Russian sage with red or pink bee balms (*Monarda* spp.), daylilies, pink mallows (*Malva* spp.), and with roses and tree mallows (*Lavatera* spp.). It's also a fine companion for azure monkshood (*Aconitum carmichaelii*), Japanese anemone (*Anemone tomentosa* 'Robustissima'), boltonia (*Boltonia asteroides*), orange coneflower (*Rudbeckia fulgida*), 'Autumn Joy' sedum (see page 280), and ornamental grasses.

In late summer, cool blue Russian sage looks just right with the warm golden daisies of black-eyed Susans. This all-star duo will shine in your garden for several weeks.

JERUSALEM SAGE

Phlomis russeliana

JERUSALEM SAGE IS ONE OF THOSE PLANTS that elicits comments from visitors, the most common remark being, "What is that?"

Its leaves are large, woolly, and gray-green with a sort of pebbly surface. The foliage forms a dense mat held 12 inches or so off the ground on strong, furry, semiwoody stems. The large leaves shade the soil below, so Jerusalem sage is an effective weed-suppressing groundcover.

In June, flowerstalks begin to stretch upward from the leaves. Every 6 inches or so, a pair of opposite leaves form, and just above them, in the leaf axils, the flower buds appear.

Enjoy These Other Jerusalem Sages

A couple of other Jerusalem sage species are available and also make handsome additions to the perennial border with their large woolly leaves and whorls of flowers. P. fructicosa is a good choice for dry, sunny gardens. Hardy in Zones 4 to 8, this 3-foot-tall plant has gray, woolly foliage and whorls of yellow flower buds that bloom in the summer in the North and in the winter in southern California. Prune this shrub-size perennial after it flowers to promote repeat bloom. For purplish pink blooms, try P. tuberosa, a large specimen plant with a bushy habit. It's hardy in Zones 3 to 7.

Spotlight on Jerusalem Sage

USDA Plant Hardiness Zones: 4 to 10

Season of Bloom: June to September

Height × Width: 12 to 42 inches × 24 to 36+ inches

Flower Color: Soft butter yellow

Light Requirements: Full sun to partial shade

Soil Requirements: Average, well-drained soil

Place of Origin: Turkey and Syria

Plant Sources: Carroll Gardens, Milaeger's Gardens, Powell's Gardens, White Flower Farm

The buds completely encircle the stems and open into many hooded, soft buttery yellow flowers. The effect is of a candelabra, set with evenly spaced rings of flowers in a subtle shade of yellow.

These flowering stems keep elongating and producing new rings of yellow flowers right through August and into September in the Northeast. In the mild climate of coastal California, Jerusalem sage flowers in late winter and early spring and is finished by summer.

In California, Jerusalem sage is evergreen, and it looks good when the hellebores and daphnes are blooming. North of Zone 7 in the East, winter kills the tops, but leaves the bare, sturdy stems standing.

HOW TO GROW JERUSALEM SAGE Plant Jerusalem sage in average, well-drained soil in full sun to light or partial shade. In the South and in sunny California, Jerusalem sage does

Jerusalem sage's candalabra-like flowerstalks and bellflowers' purple-blue spires stand tall amid a surrounding skirt of ornamental grasses, lady's-mantle, and astilbe.

best in light shade, while north of Zone 7 it needs a site that gets direct sunlight for at least part of the day. My Jerusalem sage thrives under tall oaks that allow only a little dappled sunlight late in the afternoon. I've never had a problem with any pests or diseases on my planting, and I've never heard of any in other parts of the country. Even the deer don't eat Jerusalem sage.

PROPAGATING JERUSALEM SAGE Jerusalem sage's habit of spreading by underground runners makes it easy to divide in the spring. You can also take stem cuttings and root them in pots. Or you can grow Jerusalem sage from seed. Plant new plants or divisions 18 inches apart.

THE RIGHT SITE FOR JERUSALEM SAGE In my garden, Jerusalem sage is underplanted with 'Beacon Silver' spotted dead nettle (*Lamium maculatum* 'Beacon Silver'). The silvery spotted dead nettle looks beautiful at the feet of the gray-green Jerusalem sage, and 'Beacon Silver' begins producing its lavender-pink flowers just as the Jerusalem sage's bloom season is finishing up. The pink, silver, gray-green, and yellow combination is, I think, one of the more successful medleys in my garden.

Some say that Jerusalem sage makes one of the best specimen plants, to be used on its own in a featured spot. That way, more visitors can see it, notice it, and ask you, "What is that?"

CO-STARS FOR JERUSALEM SAGE Use rounded, mound-shaped plants such as lady's-mantle (*Alchemilla mollis*) and meadow cranesbill (*Geranium pratense*) to balance

Buttery yellow, hooded flowers encircle Jerusalem sage's sturdy flowerstalks above pairs of pebbled gray-green leaves. Although it's not well-known, this all-star is too pretty and useful to remain a garden curiosity.

Jerusalem sage's upright, shrubby stature. Or match its somewhat coarse presence with companions like globe thistle (*Echinops ritro*), amethyst sea holly (*Eryngium amethystinum*), common sneezeweed (*Helenium autumnale*), sunflower cultivars (*Helianthus* cvs.), and 'Six Hills Giant' catmint (*Nepeta* × *faassenii* 'Six Hills Giant'). The upright blue flower spikes of English lavender (*Lavandula angustifolia*), violet sage (*Salvia* × *superba*), and blue spike speedwell (*Veronica spicata*) all look good next to the gray-green foliage and soft yellow flowers of Jerusalem sage.

'CHATTAHOOCHEE' PHLOX

Phlox 'Chattahoochee'

YOU'LL OFTEN FIND THIS DARLING LITTLE PHLOX listed as a cultivar of wild blue phlox (*Phlox divaricata* subsp. *laphamii*), but it is not a cultivar of any species, but rather a hybrid that is quite its own thing. And quite a thing it is. Of all the spring-flowering phlox, 'Chattahoochee' is the most cherished and wonderful to behold. Each flower is an inch across and consists of five petals of a pleasing periwinkle blue with a contrasting reddish maroon eye. These flowers appear in pretty profusion on the trailing, 12-inch-long stems. 'Chattahoochee' begins opening its flowers in April, just in time to join in with the early spring bulb flower show, then it continues to bloom through tulip time. The performance ends in early June, after which its dark green,

Other Spring-Flowering Phlox

While 'Chattahoochee' phlox is one of a kind, there are certainly other low-growing, spring-flowering phlox to try in your garden. Start with wild blue phlox (P. divaricata subsp. laphamii), a parent of 'Chattahoochee' that has loads of sweet-scented light lavender-blue flowers. Its cultivar 'Fuller's White' covers itself with starry, pure white flowers. 'Blue Ridge' creeping phlox (P. stolonifera 'Blue Ridge') is a very beautiful plant for semishade under deciduous trees; its blue flowers bloom from April to June.

Spotlight on 'Chattahoochee' Phlox

USDA Plant Hardiness Zones: 5 to 9

Season of Bloom: April to June

Height × Width: 10 to 16 inches × 18 to 24 inches

Flower Color: Lavender-blue with maroon eye

Light Requirements: Partial shade to full sun

Soil Requirements: Rich, humusy, moist, well-drained soil

Place of Origin: Southeastern United States

Plant Sources: Kurt Bluemel, Bluestone Perennials, Busse Gardens, Forestfarm, Klehm Nursery, Milaeger's Gardens, Powell's Gardens, Roslyn Nursery, Sunlight Gardens

---

opposite, lance-shaped leaves help hide the ripening foliage of nearby bulbs.

There are many gorgeous phlox in this world, but 'Chattahoochee' phlox is undoubtedly my personal favorite. It was originally found in the Chattahoochee River valley that runs from Georgia to the region where Alabama and Florida converge. 'Chattahoochee' phlox is believed to be a natural hybrid of two native species: wild blue phlox (*P. divaricata* subsp. *laphamii*) and downy phlox (*P. pilosa*).

HOW TO GROW 'CHATTAHOOCHEE'

'Chattahoochee' phlox is a slow-growing, ground-hugging, mat-forming phlox with small, narrow leaves that give a bushy appearance to its trailing stems. It's a hardy plant, though, and it is well adapted to the

South and Northeast to at least Zone 5, where it will appreciate a mulch to help it through the winter. Pests and diseases aren't a problem. 'Chattahoochee' likes partial shade—open woodland conditions—regular moisture, and good garden soil. It can take full sun, however, and it responds by making dense mounds of foliage.

PROPAGATING 'CHATTAHOOCHEE'

This hybrid generally does not produce creeping shoots that root, the way other low-growing phlox do, so it is difficult to divide. The best way to get more 'Chattahoochee' is to take stem cuttings in spring or right after flowering finishes.

THE RIGHT SITE FOR 'CHATTAHOOCHEE'

Use 'Chattahoochee' phlox wherever you need a spring carpet of flowers—atop a slope or wall, along a path's edge, or at the front of the perennial border. It's nice beneath deciduous

You'll get a springtime carpet of pretty lavender-blue flowers from 'Chattahoochee' phlox. And it's fun to say, too!

shrubs, too, where it will enjoy spring sunshine before the shrubs' leaves open to give it shade in the summer months. 'Chattahoochee' makes a fine companion for spring bulbs and helps hide their fading leaves when their display is over.

CO-STARS FOR 'CHATTAHOOCHEE'

'Chattahoochee' looks good with spring bulbs, especially tulips, or in the front of the semi-shaded border with fritillaries (*Fritillaria* spp.), snowflakes (*Leucojum* spp.), grape hyacinths (*Muscari* spp.), and 'Jungle Beauty' ajuga (*Ajuga reptans* 'Jungle Beauty'). It's beautiful combined with its cousin 'Fuller's White' woodland phlox (*P. divaricata* 'Fuller's White'). Underplant shrubs such as saucer magnolia (*Magnolia × soulangiana*) with 'Chattahoochee'.

Take cuttings from phlox just below a pair of leaves. Remove the lower leaves, dip the stem in rooting hormone, then stick each cutting in moist potting soil. A plastic bag helps keep things moist.

A Stellar Idea

After 'Chattahoochee' finishes blooming, cut it back, or else it will become loose, shaggy, and not particularly attractive. The trimmed stems will produce new foliage that will look much better than unpruned growth.

'DAVID' SUMMER PHLOX

Phlox paniculata 'David'

Spotlight on

'David'
Summer Phlox

USDA Plant Hardiness Zones: 3 to 8

Season of Bloom: July to September

Height × Width: 3 feet × 3 feet

Flower Color: White

Light Requirements: Full sun to partial shade

Soil Requirements: Rich, humusy, well-drained soil

Place of Origin: Eastern North America

Plant Sources: Ambergate Gardens, Bluestone Perennials, Busse Gardens, Carroll Gardens, Forestfarm, Garden Place, Milaeger's Gardens, Plant Delights Nursery, Powell's Gardens, Roslyn Nursery, André Viette Farm & Nursery, Wayside Gardens, Weiss Brothers Perennial Nursery, White Flower Farm

EVERY GARDEN NEEDS SUMMER PHLOX. While its magnificent flowers are the mainstay of August, summer phlox opens its first blooms in late July and finishes in September. And although it comes in pink, blue, purple, lavender, orange, yellow, and red (and in combinations of these as the petal color is contrasted with darker eyes), I've chosen the white-flowered cultivar, 'David', as the all-star summer phlox.

'David' summer phlox blooms extra early. Its first blossoms begin opening in mid-July in the Northeast, where its wild form is native, and continues blooming into September. Like all the summer phlox, 'David' produces ballooning, 6-inch (or larger) clusters of 1-inch florets in a hemispherical dome that billows up atop the 3-foot stems. In 'David', these stems are sturdier than those of most summer phlox, helping the plant resist wind and rain.

Flocks of Phlox

Cultivars of summer phlox abound, and many deserve a place in the garden. A few of my favorites are 'Bright Eyes', which has pink flowers with crimson eyes; 'Franz Schubert', lilac-pink with purple eyes; cherry red-flowered 'Starfire'; 'Progress', which bears light blue flowers with purple eyes; and 'Orange Perfection', with bright red-orange blossoms.

In addition, 'David' summer phlox's glowing white flowers are wonderfully fragrant.

HOW TO GROW SUMMER PHLOX Plant summer phlox in full sun to partial shade in rich, moist, well-drained soil. Powdery mildew is the bane of this otherwise wonderful perennial and can disfigure a planting, leaving the foliage looking ugly, grayish, and blighted. Plants are particularly at risk during hot, dry weather, although very susceptible cultivars may fall prey to this fungus at almost any time. Maintaining even soil moisture and promoting good air circulation around summer phlox helps to reduce problems with this disease. 'David' is the most mildew resistant of all the summer phlox.

'David' summer phlox's pure white flowers look clean and crisp in the heat. Use them to create cool spots amid the summer garden's hot colors.

The dark leaves and wine red stems of 'Gateway' Joe-Pye weed make a handsome backdrop for 'David' summer phlox's white flower clusters.

'David' will sail through the summer untroubled by powdery mildew. That's one reason why 'David' is good in the hot, humid South, where other summer phlox can struggle.

PROPAGATING SUMMER PHLOX The slowly spreading clumps of summer phlox need division every three to four years to keep a planting youthful and vigorous. Replant young shoots taken from the outside of the clumps 24 inches apart.

THE RIGHT SITE FOR 'DAVID' There's a lot of strong color available under the hot sun of August, and the white of 'David' summer phlox combines beautifully with all of it. Use drifts of 'David' to separate bold colors and to interrupt expanses of dark green foliage. Its white flowers offer cool, crisp relief in the sweltering dog days of August. Plant enough 'David' summer phlox to have some for cutting, too. Gather flowerheads when just half their florets have opened.

CO-STARS FOR 'DAVID' 'David' looks especially good in August with red, pink, and yellow lilies, Russian sage (*Perovskia atriplicifolia*), pink asters, Kansas gayfeather (*Liatris pycnostachya*), leadwort (*Ceratostigma plumbaginoides*), great blue lobelia (*Lobelia siphilitica*), Stokes' aster (*Stokesia laevis*), Culver's root (*Veronicastrum virginicum*), common sneezeweed (*Helenium autumnale*), black-eyed Susan (*Rudbeckia hirta*), and ornamental grasses.

A Stellar Idea

Encourage your summer phlox into extended flowering with a simple trick that's known to most phlox aficionados: Pinch out the main, terminal flowerhead as soon as it shows signs of tiring. This forces the side shoots to produce secondary blooms that will continue on into September.

'VIVID' OBEDIENT PLANT

Physostegia virginiana 'Vivid'

'VIVID' IS AN EXTRAORDINARY SELECTION of obedient plant, with so many nice qualities and good habits that it easily qualifies as a perennial all-star.

Obedient plant's origins are in the wild places of eastern North America. It is superbly adapted to life there and consequently makes a good meadow plant for naturalizing. However, I grow it in my garden here in California with no problems. It is truly at home in most places in the United States. And why is it called "obedient plant?" Because when the flower spikes are in full bloom, you can move one or more of its snapdragon-like flowers, arrayed in vertical rows on the spikes, sideways to another

Spotlight on 'Vivid' Obedient Plant

USDA Plant Hardiness Zones: 2 to 9

Season of Bloom: September and October

Height × Width: 20 to 24 inches × 36+ inches

Flower Color: Deep lilac-pink

Light Requirements: Partial shade to full sun

Soil Requirements: Average, moist soil

Place of Origin: From the Canadian maritimes west to Minnesota and south to Missouri and South Carolina

Plant Sources: Ambergate Gardens, Kurt Bluemel, Bluestone Perennials, Busse Gardens, Carroll Gardens, Crownsville Nursery, Forestfarm, Garden Place, J. W. Jung Seed, Roslyn Nursery, Shady Oaks Nursery, André Viette Farm & Nursery, Weiss Brothers Perennial Nursery, White Flower Farm

Other Well-Behaved Obedient Plants

There's another short obedient plant, the cultivar 'Alba' (P. virginiana 'Alba'), which grows from 18 to 24 inches and blooms from July to September. Its compact size helps it avoid the sagging that can mar the appearance of taller obedient plants planted in overly rich soil. The leaves of 'Variegata' (P. virginiana 'Variegata') have creamy variegation that makes this cultivar showy even when it's not in bloom. 'Variegata' is a less aggressive spreader than the species and has pale pink flowers.

position, and it will stay where you put it rather than spring back.

'Vivid' is a compact form of this durable native plant. And while most obedient plant cultivars and the species grow up to 3 feet tall, sometimes sagging and bending over unattractively when planted in rich, moist garden soil, 'Vivid' is short and compact. It grows just 20 to 24 inches tall on sturdy stems that keep their attractive upright habit. Toothed, lancelike, narrow leaves cover the length of the stems. Obedient plant ordinarily starts blooming in late July or August, but 'Vivid' holds its bright rosy pink flowers for the end of the season, blooming heavily above its dense mats of leaves in September and October.

'Vivid' obedient plant and 'Golden Fleece' gold- enrod combine to end the growing season with an exuberant display of hot colors.

HOW TO GROW OBEDIENT PLANT While it prefers light, partial shade, obedient plant will thrive in full sun. I have it in full sun here in California, and it seems to do fine. Don't worry too much about enriching the soil or fertilizing for obedient plant—it will do fine in average soil and can become floppy if grown in rich soil. Pests don't bother obedient plant, although sometimes rust may spot its leaves. That occurred one year on my obedient plant in Pennsylvania, and I ignored it successfully. On healthy plants it's unlikely to become a problem.

The plant grows in dense clumps from run- ning roots. It's not a truly invasive plant, but obedient plant may outgrow the space you've allotted for it if you ignore it for more than a couple of years. If it spreads too far, simply lift the clumps and divide them with a shovel, replanting as many divisions as you need to refresh the spot. Space them 18 inches apart so they have room to spread. Because it's so pretty so late in the year and such an easy plant to grow, divisions make welcome gifts to gardening friends.

PROPAGATING OBEDIENT PLANT Obedient plant is a vigorous grower with a spreading habit. Division every couple of years is a good way to keep it in bounds and also to get more plants to share or to fill in other areas in your garden. Replant divisions 18 inches apart.

THE RIGHT SITE FOR 'VIVID' This obedient plant's late floral display adds a welcome touch of deep rosy pink-lilac to the garden. Use it to create pretty combinations with the late-season blues and purples of asters and the earthy tones of fall bloomers such as chrysan- themums. 'Vivid' adds a nice upright accent to these mound-shaped plants.

With its straight stems and orderly rows of flowers, obedient plant lives up to its name. Regularly re- move its spent flowers to keep it blooming.

CO-STARS FOR 'VIVID' 'Alba' Japanese anemone (*Anemone × hybrida* 'Alba'), boltonia (*Boltonia asteroides*), purplish New England aster (*Aster novae-angliae*) and New York aster (*A. novi-belgii*), Russian sage (see page 242), blue oat grass (see page 162), and white chrysanthemums all make excellent compan- ions for 'Vivid' obedient plant.

BALLOON FLOWER

Platycodon grandiflorus

BALLOON FLOWER WAS, I BELIEVE, THE FIRST perennial I ever planted. It was a lucky choice, for this plant is absolutely care-free from the gardener's standpoint: easy to grow, pest- and disease-free, long lived, and a very reliable bloomer over a long season.

I consider it to be one of the best perennial all-stars in this book. Balloon flower will repay you handsomely many times over for planting it. When its stems emerge in late spring—be patient—they grow straight up, carrying silvery-backed, green foliage. In summer, the first buds appear at the tops of the stems. Each

Bouquets of Beautiful Balloon Flowers

Balloon flower cultivars offer various options in terms of plant height, flower color, and flower shape. 'Apoyama' balloon flower is a dwarf that grows to only 8 inches tall with purple-blue flowers; the variety mariesii (also sold as 'Mariesii') has violet-blue flowers on compact, 12- to 18-inch stems; and 'Sentimental Blue' is a 6- to 8-inch dwarf with blue flowers. 'Mother of Pearl' balloon flower and 'Shell Pink' balloon flower both have pale pink flowers. The flowers of 'Snowflake' are semidouble and white, while 'Double Blue' bears rich violet-blue double flowers with darker veins. In my opinion, none of these selections rivals the plain blue species for form, color, or beauty.

Spotlight on Balloon Flower

USDA Plant Hardiness Zones: 3 to 9

Season of Bloom: June to September

Height × Width: 24 inches × 24 inches

Flower Color: Blue-violet

Light Requirements: Full sun to partial shade

Soil Requirements: Sandy, well-drained soil of average fertility

Place of Origin: Eastern Asia, Japan

Plant Sources: Kurt Bluemel, Busse Gardens, Carroll Gardens, Dutch Gardens, Forestfarm, Greer Gardens, J. W. Jung Seed, Milaeger's Gardens, Powell's Gardens, Roslyn Nursery, Van Bourgondien, Weiss Brothers Perennial Nursery, White Flower Farm

Seed Source: Park Seed

one opens into a shallow blue-violet saucer with five broad, pointed lobes that form a plump star shape. Slightly darker veins are often visible running the length of the petals. In fall, the foliage turns clear yellow.

HOW TO GROW BALLOON FLOWER Truly one of the most care-free perennials, balloon flower will flourish in almost any soil. However, it does appreciate good drainage and is at its best in well-drained, average to rich soil in full sun to partial shade. It's untroubled by pests and diseases and will pretty much do its thing with little or no effort on your part. But if you're good about removing balloon flower's faded blossoms, it will keep blooming through the summer months and will look nicer than if you don't.

Balloon flower's buds look like little hot-air balloons. In late June and early July, the buds begin opening into rich blue-violet stars,.

Soft peach-colored daylilies make handsome companions for balloon flowers. If you remove its spent flowers, balloon flower will bloom all summer.

Balloon flower's new foliage is slow to appear in the spring but don't be tempted to think the plant has died out. It's one of the last plants to emerge, and it is as hardy and tough as can be. To avoid digging into balloon flowers when putting in new plants, it's wise to mark their spot.

PROPAGATING BALLOON FLOWER

It rarely needs division, but you can divide balloon flower's fleshy taproots to get more of this charming all-star. When the new shoots are an inch tall, gently remove the soil from around the thick roots. Cut off root pieces, dip them in rooting hormone, and replant them about 15 inches apart. You can also grow balloon flower from seed sown outdoors in the fall, although the flower color of seedlings may vary. Seedlings usually take two years to reach flowering size.

THE RIGHT SITE FOR BALLOON FLOWER

This plant's violet-blue color looks beautiful with most other colors in the sunny summer garden. Even an accent of orange isn't out of place as long as it's in moderation. In the evening, when it's dusk and the light from the western sky is growing dim, balloon flower's rich blue-violet blossoms seem to glow.

CO-STARS FOR BALLOON FLOWER

Match balloon flower with flowers in shades of soft yellow, lavender, pink or white. It's also at home next to silvery foliage plants such as artemisias. Lady's-mantle (*Alchemilla mollis*), catmint (see page 230), yellow loosestrife (*Lysimachia punctata*), anise hyssop (*Agastache foeniculum*), summer phlox (*Phlox paniculata*), baby's-breath (*Gypsophila paniculata*), swordleaf inula (*Inula ensifolia*), and obedient plant (*Physostegia virginiana*) all make excellent companions for balloon flower. If you plant Carpathian harebell (*Campanula carpatica*) at balloon flower's feet, the bellflower's open blue-violet stars will echo the shape and color of balloon flower's own starry blossoms.

A Stellar Idea

Use a match to singe the ends of stems of balloon flowers that you cut for use in fresh arrangements. This stops the flow of milky sap and gives them a long life in the vase.

JACOB'S LADDER

Polemonium caeruleum

Spotlight on

Jacob's Ladder

USDA Plant Hardiness Zones: 3 to 9

Season of Bloom: May to July

Height × Width: 30 inches × 18 to 24 inches

Flower Color: Lavender-blue

Light Requirements: Full sun to partial shade

Soil Requirements: Moist, well-drained soil of average fertility

Place of Origin: Western Europe east to Siberia and the Himalayas, to Alaska and down the West Coast to California's Sierra Nevadas and east to the Rockies

Plant Sources: Kurt Bluemel, Busse Gardens, Carroll Gardens, Crownsville Nursery, Daisy Fields, Forestfarm, Milaeger's Gardens, Shady Oaks Nursery, Weiss Brothers Perennial Nursery

JACOB'S LADDER IS A MARVELOUS PERENNIAL. It's a hardy plant that grows wild even in Alaska. But Jacob's ladder grows well in lots of other places, too.

This is a perennial that needs no special care at all. Jacob's ladder reappears reliably for years and always puts on a pretty flower show from May through June and often right into July. Jacob's ladder also has what could be the prettiest foliage of any perennial in the garden. Its attractive leaves provide a pleasant contrast to almost any other foliage in the garden.

In spring, tall, leafy flowerstalks arise from amid the mounds of leaves. These flowering stems grow to nearly 3 feet tall. Clusters of open-faced, nodding, lavender-blue blossoms open in bunches at the tops of the stiffly erect flowerstalks.

HOW TO GROW JACOB'S LADDER Plant Jacob's ladder in moist, average to rich soil in full sun to partial shade. Partial shade is particularly helpful in hot southern regions. Jacob's ladder is at home in the Sierra Nevada mountains and also in coastal California. But the hot, sticky summer weather of the Deep South is not to its liking. Down South, creeping Jacob's ladder (*P. reptans*) may be a better choice.

Insects don't bother Jacob's ladder, and although it may acquire a little mildew as

Other Jacob's Ladders You'll Enjoy

Creeping Jacob's ladder (P. reptans) grows about half as tall as Jacob's ladder, with the same ladderlike foliage, a creeping habit, and a liking for shady, woodsy spots. Its small flower stems produce pink buds that open into sweet little nodding blue bells.

Salmon polemonium (P. carneum) is native to the Cascades of the Pacific Northwest. It likes the East but dies out in the heat of the Southeast. It needs evenly moist, well-drained soil in shade or partial shade. It's hardy only to Zone 5. But it is a pretty plant, with dense foliage and salmon pink blooms that can vary to lavender or even blue, fading to purplish white as they age.

Jacob's ladder gets its name from its lovely compound leaves made up of slender leaflets arranged in tidy rows like the rungs of a ladder.

The ornamental orange stamens of Jacob's ladder set off the lavender-blue shade of the flowers' petals.

summer wears on, it requires no special care. It's not often in need of division either, although you can divide it when you decide your garden needs more of this shining all-star.

PROPAGATING JACOB'S LADDER

Clump-forming Jacob's ladder is easy to divide in spring or fall. Plant divisions 18 inches apart. You can also grow it from seed sown outdoors in the fall or sown in pots in the spring. Keep spring-planted seedlings in their containers through the growing season, mulch them through the winter, then set them out in the garden the following spring.

THE RIGHT SITE FOR JACOB'S LADDER

In partial shade and moist soil, Jacob's ladder's fine-textured leaves make it a worthy companion for the bold foliage of hostas and other large-leaved perennials. In sunnier sites, mix it with the stiffly upright leaves of irises or the broadly grassy foliage of daylilies. A group of Jacob's ladder looks especially pretty planted around the base of flowering shrubs.

CO-STARS FOR JACOB'S LADDER

Mix Jacob's ladder with yellow flowers such as 'Citrinum' basket-of-gold (*Aurinia saxatilis* 'Citrinum'), cushion spurge (see page 136), and 'Golden Queen' globeflower (see page 306), or with yellow-trimmed foliage like that of 'Aureo-marginata' Fortune's hosta (*Hosta fortunei* 'Aureo-marginata') or 'Bowles Golden' sedge (*Carex elata* 'Bowles Golden'). 'Miss Lingard' thick leaf phlox (*Phlox carolina* 'Miss Lingard') looks pretty with it, too. The pink-and-white hearts of common bleeding heart (see page 118) are excellent companions for Jacob's ladder, and it's beautiful with roses.

VARIEGATED SOLOMON'S SEAL

Polygonatum odoratum 'Variegatum'

I'VE JUST COME IN FROM MY SHADE GARDEN, where the beautiful form of variegated Solomon's seal is—as usual—stealing the show. In spring its young green leaves are tinged with pink and maroon, gradually turning a pure, soft light green streaked with pure white, mostly on the outer edges of the leaves. Each leaf is a 2- to 3-inch, pointed oval, held opposite another one in pretty pairs along the length of the stems.

Variegated Solomon's seal's stems arch gracefully, with all stems in a planting usually bending in the same direction. If you straightened them out, each stem would be 18 to 36 inches long. Solomon's seal puts

Other Select Solomon's Seals

Small Solomon's seal (P. biflorum) is a native plant that's common in woods east of the Mississippi. Its 12- to 36-inch stems are angled so that the gray-green leaves are held in a relatively horizontal position. Great Solomon's seal (P. biflorum var. commutatum) has 7-foot stems with dangling clusters of greenish white flowers. P. humile is a charming dwarf Solomon's seal from China, just 6 to 12 inches tall and good for planting in shady spots with lily-of-the-valley (see page 108) and mondo grasses (Ophiopogon spp.).

(see page 108)

Spotlight on Variegated Solomon's Seal

USDA Plant Hardiness Zones: 4 to 9

Season of Bloom: May to June

Height × Width: 18 to 36 inches × 24 inches

Flower Color: White

Light Requirements: Partial shade to full shade

Soil Requirements: Moist, rich, humusy, woodsy, well-drained soil

Place of Origin: Western Europe eastward to Japan

Plant Sources: Ambergate Gardens, Busse Gardens, Carroll Gardens, Crownsville Nursery, Forestfarm, Klehm Nursery, Milaeger's Gardens, Plant Delights Nursery, Powell's Gardens, Roslyn Nursery, Shady Oaks Nursery, Sunlight Gardens, Van Bourgondien, André Viette Farm & Nursery, We-Du Nurseries, White Flower Farm

forth its arching stems from fleshy, creeping rhizomes that expand to make a small clump of anywhere from a half dozen to a dozen or more stems. In the fall, the leaves turn a soft yellow.

Variegated Solomon's seal blooms in May and June. Its narrow, ivory white, bell-like flowers call further notice to this showy shade lover, as they hang in pairs or singly below the points where the leaves join the stems. If you visit your shade garden in the evening, you'll notice their pretty fragrance. And the white variegations of the leaves will seem to light up in the dusk.

HOW TO GROW VARIEGATED SOLOMON'S SEAL

Besides form and fragrance, this perennial all-star has other fine qualities: Its maintenance needs are very low, and although it prefers moist woodland soil, it is very drought tolerant. It is one of the few plants that can thrive among the moisture-greedy roots of maples. Variegated Solomon's seal will take a bit more sun in the North but needs a shady site to grow in the South. Even in Zone 7 and south, it disappears for the winter, but it is long lived and reliable throughout its range. Pests and diseases leave it alone.

Once your variagated Solomon's seal reaches three-year size, consider dividing it so that you can make a stand of about six plants, all spreading toward one another to cover a spot 4 by 6 feet. Mulch the ground between the divisions with leaf litter.

PROPAGATING VARIEGATED SOLOMON'S SEAL

Divide variegated Solomon's seal in late summer when the days are cooling off, so that it may flower the next year. Its creeping underground rhizomes make division simple. Plant divisions 12 to 18 inches apart. You can propagate the species from seed: Remove the seeds from the pulpy blue-black berries in the fall and sow them right away. Seeds are slow to germinate and seedlings are slow to grow to flowering size.

THE RIGHT SITE FOR VARIEGATED SOLOMON'S SEAL

Variegated Solomon's seal is the most visually appealing plant in the shade garden. It's especially pretty dangling its white blossoms, and as a groundcover for shade, it has no peer. Its pale green-and-white leaves light up somber spots and its arching stems help relieve the monotony of low, mat-forming plants.

White flowers dangle from the arching stems of variegated Solomon's seal. Their fragrance brings lilies and hyacinths to mind.

CO-STARS FOR VARIEGATED SOLOMON'S SEAL

Variegated Solomon's seals are the perfect companions for ferns, astilbes, wild gingers (*Asarum* spp.), and hostas. Underplant variegated Solomon's seal with creeping forget-me-not (*Omphalodes verna*), lungworts (*Pulmonaria* spp.), and epimediums (*Epimedium* spp.). It's also at home amid azaleas (*Rhododendron* spp.), rhododendrons, and laurels (*Kalmia* spp.).

In a shady woodland garden, great Solomon's seal makes a dramatic background for fine-textured ferns and golden-green hostas.

'SUPERBUM' HIMALAYAN FLEECEFLOWER

Polygonum affine 'Superbum'

HERE'S A GREAT SPECIAL-PURPOSE PERENNIAL that truly deserves its all-star status. 'Superbum' Himalayan fleeceflower's special purpose is as a ground-covering carpet for difficult sites. But it also stars as a superb perennial for the garden bed.

Some people hear the name *Polygonum* and quake at the thought of the invasive

Spotlight on

'Superbum' Himalayan Fleeceflower

USDA Plant Hardiness Zones: 4 to 9

Season of Bloom: August to October

Height × Width: 10 inches × 24 to 36+ inches

Flower Color: Pink

Light Requirements: Full sun to light shade

Soil Requirements: Average, moist soil

Place of Origin: Afghanistan east to Nepal and Sikkim

Plant Sources: Ambergate Gardens, Busse Gardens, Carroll Gardens

Other Fine Fleeceflowers

You may encounter other cultivars of Himalayan fleeceflower: 'Darjeeling Red' is a commonly found form with deep pink flowers and a vigorous habit. 'Donald Lowndes' is also common and carries double salmon pink flower spikes. It grows to about 8 inches tall and does well in the Southeast.

Another species worth mentioning is snakeweed (P. bistorta), with large leaves that feature white midribs and 4- to 5-inch tubular flower spikes of soft pink. It can be invasive. Like Himalayan fleeceflower, snakeweed also has a cultivar named 'Superbum', just to add to the confusion. In warm regions, pinkhead knotweed (P. capitatum) makes pretty carpets of variegated, pink-tinged leaves and tiny pink flower balls here and there. This plant is attractive but a nuisance if you don't keep it confined.

smartweeds also included within this genus. But Himalayan fleeceflower, while a vigorous grower and a good spreader—desirable characteristics in a groundcover—is easily kept in check and is not an invasive plant.

Himalayan fleeceflower grows only about 10 inches tall in dense mats. Its 4-inch-long leaves seem rather large for the plant's diminutive size. These leaves are evergreen in the mild part of its range, semievergreen in the middle part, and deciduous in the colder part. Where they persist, they turn a pretty bronzy reddish brown in winter.

Our all-star is the cultivar 'Superbum', and it really is superb, with more and larger flowers and less aggressive growth than the species or other cultivars. In late summer and into fall, 'Superbum' Himalayan fleeceflower produces loads of flowers—especially in full sun—on fleecy, nubby, bright pink flower spikes. These spikes are 3 to 4 inches tall and stand straight up from the mass of foliage

'Superbum' Himalayan fleeceflower spreads nicely to carpet an area with its foliage and bright pink flower spikes. Its late-summer flowers look great with purple asters and pink Japanese anemones.

below, emerging at the tips of each leafy stem. The flowers open a pale blush pink, become very bright rose pink and then slowly turn to crimson before fading. They are very eye-catching and appealing and can turn an odd, difficult, or out-of-the-way place into a showy part of the garden.

How to Grow Himalayan Fleeceflower

Himalayan fleeceflower is a vigorous, trouble-free plant. It will certainly help fend off weeds from its spot in the garden. Himalayan fleeceflower isn't picky about the soil where it grows as long as it's not too sandy or droughty—moist, humusy soil is more to its liking. It is not prone to pests or diseases and requires only regular moisture to do its best. Plant it in full sun, or in partial shade in southern regions.

Propagating Himalayan Fleeceflower

This perennial spreads via rhizomes, so it's easy to divide in spring or fall. Simply use your shovel to slice off rooted new growth from the spreading clumps. Plant divisions 12 inches apart to establish a ground-covering carpet.

The Right Site for 'Superbum'

Plant 'Superbum' Himalayan fleeceflower as a groundcover where you can take advantage of its tendency to spread a bit. It's handy for hard-to-tend areas like slopes. Its low habit makes it nice for edging along steps, walkways, or the front of the perennial border. 'Superbum' Himalayan fleeceflower creates an excellent flowering carpet among shrubs and woody plantings, trailing among rocks, and planted with fall-blooming crocuses (*Crocus* spp.) and autumn crocuses (*Colchicum* spp.).

'Superbum' snakeweed holds its pink flower spikes high over its broad leaves, adding color and texture to a planting of hostas.

Co-Stars for 'Superbum'

This Himalayan fleeceflower's showy pink flower spikes are beautiful with 'Honorine Jobert' Japanese anemone (*Anemone × hybrida* 'Honorine Jobert'), Chinese anemone (*Anemone hupehensis*), blue- to purple-flowered New York asters (*Aster novi-belgii*), Japanese silver grass (*Miscanthus sinensis*), and the silvery foliage and misty blue flowers of Russian sage (see page 242).

'GIBSON'S SCARLET' CINQUEFOIL

Potentilla 'Gibson's Scarlet'

FOR THOSE DRY, SUNNY SPOTS in the garden, you can hardly top the mat-forming cinquefoils (*Potentilla* spp.). Out of this useful genus, none has the snap, beauty, and hybrid vigor of our perennial all-star, 'Gibson's Scarlet' cinquefoil.

You may find this plant variously named. I've seen it listed as a cultivar of undersnow cinquefoil (*P. argyrophylla*) and of Himalayan cinquefoil (*P. atrosanguinea*), and of the hybrids *P.* × *russelliana* and *P.* × *menziesii*. But the cultivar name is always listed as 'Gibson's Scarlet'.

Its glory is in the intense scarlet red of its beautiful flowers. Each inch-wide blossom has five petals, and each petal has two soft lobes. In the center of the flower is a dark eye, in which little yellow structures form a narrow five-pointed star. From a standing distance,

Other Select Cinquefoils

Another useful cinquefoil for the garden is staghorn cinquefoil (P. × tonguei), a ground-hugging form that has strawberry-like leaves and exquisite apricot-colored flowers with deep carmine eyes. An old-fashioned favorite is 'Miss Willmot' Nepal cinquefoil (P. nepalensis 'Miss Willmot'), a dwarf, cherry red-flowered cultivar that comes true from seed.

Spotlight on

'Gibson's Scarlet' Cinquefoil

USDA Plant Hardiness Zones: 5 to 9

Season of Bloom: Mid-June to late August or early September

Height × Width: 18 inches × 24 inches

Flower Color: Scarlet

Light Requirements: Full sun

Soil Requirements: Average, loose, well-drained soil

Place of Origin: Hybrid among several species, mostly from the Himalayas

Plant Sources: Bluestone Perennials, Busse Gardens, Carroll Gardens, Garden Place, Milaeger's Gardens, Powell's Garden, Van Bourgondien, Wayside Gardens

the effect is almost entirely one of rich scarlet—a most welcome color to associate with yellows or cooler blues.

It has another glory, and that is its five-fingered, strawberry-like leaves. They are medium green in 'Gibson's Scarlet', although they are silvery underneath and even silver edged in some of its parents. These look pretty planted with fine-leaved or silvery-leaved plants, where their delicate shape can be shown off to advantage. The many loose stems produced by the roots are well-covered by leaves and make dense mats of foliage all summer.

HOW TO GROW 'GIBSON'S SCARLET' This cinquefoil likes full sun and good drainage, although it will tolerate partial shade in the warmer regions. South of Zone 7, 'Gibson's Scarlet' is reputed to have a difficult time, but

In full sun and well-drained soil, you'll get a summer-long display of rich red flowers from 'Gibson's Scarlet' cinquefoil.

Let 'Gibson's Scarlet' grow up through the branches of orange-eye butterfly bush to create a color combination that will catch the eyes of both passersby and butterflies.

here in the West, in Zone 9, it grows perfectly well. In the Deep South, give it a moist, well-drained soil and some shade.

PROPAGATING CINQUEFOIL Cinquefoil spreads to form a shrubby clump that's easily divided in spring or early fall. Plant the divisions 12 inches apart to make a drift of these plants in the perennial bed.

THE RIGHT SITE FOR 'GIBSON'S SCARLET'
'Gibson's Scarlet' cinquefoil makes a nice clump of sprawling stems that spreads about 24 inches across and reaches about 18 inches high. In mid-June, the flowers at the ends of the recumbent stems begin to open. 'Gibson's Scarlet' cinquefoil makes an excellent companion for flowering shrubs. Plant it between stones in the rock garden or to help hold sunny, dry slopes in place.

CO-STARS FOR 'GIBSON'S SCARLET'
'Gibson's Scarlet' cinquefoil provides a terrific strong red foil for the blue flowers of perennials such as Narbonne flax (*Linum narbonense*), peach-leaved bellflower (*Campanula persicifolia*), Dalmatian bellflower (*Campanula portenschlagiana*), balloon flower (see page 252), and woolly speedwell (*Veronica incana*), among others. It makes a hot combination with the yellows of sundrops (*Oenothera fruticosa*), large-flowered tickseed (*Coreopsis grandiflora*) and chaix mullein (*Verbascum chaixii*), as well as with pastel-colored oriental poppies (*Papaver orientale*). Its foliage looks good with the silvery leaves of plants such as lamb's-ear (*Stachys byzantina*), yarrows, and artemisias.

A Stellar Idea

*If you interplant it among open shrubs, 'Gibson's Scarlet' will weave its stems up into them. With careful color coordination for June, July and into August, you can make quite a display. Try its strong red blossoms with the blue or purple flower clusters of orange-eye butterfly bush (*Buddleia davidii*).*

'MIKADO' SIEBOLD'S PRIMROSE

Primula sieboldii 'Mikado'

THERE ARE SO MANY DIFFERENT PRIMROSES, and they all seem so lovely, dainty, and charming in form and flower. How does one choose an all-star from among the many types?

For an answer, I contacted Ann Lunn, a longtime active member the American Primrose Society. This organization will help

Spotlight on 'Mikado' Siebold's Primrose

USDA Plant Hardiness Zones: 4 to 9

Season of Bloom: Mid-April to June

Height × Width: 8 to 12 inches × 12 inches

Flower Color: Rosy purple

Light Requirements: Partial shade to full sun

Soil Requirements: Humusy, moist, neutral, clay soil

Place of Origin: Japan and northern Asia

Plant Sources: Busse Gardens, Roslyn Nursery

Embarking Down the Primrose Path

Siebold's primrose and its all-star cultivar 'Mikado' are excellent primroses, yet they only scratch the surface of this genus. To learn more, you might want to join the American Primrose Society (Addaline Robinson, Treasurer, 41801 S. W. Bugarsky Road, Gaston, OR 97119). Or if you want more information about Siebold's primrose cultivars, check out the American Sakurasoh Association (Paul Held, American Sakurasoh Association, 195 North Avenue, Westport, CT 06880). "Sakurasoh" is Japanese for P. sieboldii.

Ann Lunn also puts in a plug for hybrids of Primula × juliana: "Some of the better named cultivars are 'Wanda' (dark purple), 'Snow White' (white), 'Springtime' (pale lilac), and 'Dorothy' (pale yellow)."

you turn every walkway in your garden into a primrose path.

Ann recommends Siebold's primrose (*Primula sieboldii*) as an outstanding primrose species. Siebold's primrose is a reliable perennial and bloomer. "I believe this is the easiest and most rewarding of the primulas to grow!" Ann says. So from this easy-growing species we get our all-star, the cultivar 'Mikado', selected by world-renowned plantsman Alan Bloom of Bressingham, England. 'Mikado' has especially showy, 6-inch spikes of rich rosy purple flowers. Each of the 10 to 15 flowers on the spike has a small white eye.

HOW TO GROW SIEBOLD'S PRIMROSE

Humusy, moist, neutral, clay soils suit Siebold's primrose best. Dry, sandy, acid soils are not to its liking. And while many primroses need supplemental water in the heat of mid- to late summer making work for the gardener, Siebold's primrose folds its leaves after flowering and disappears by July or August. In this dormancy, it needs no additional water other than that provided by rain.

'Mikado' gives you plenty of reasons to venture down the primrose path. It welcomes spring with clusters of rosy purple flowers, each with a small white eye.

Because of this, Siebold's primrose is heat- and humidity-tolerant and will grow farther into the South than many other primroses. In the very Deep South, along the Gulf, most primroses are chancy at best. After all, they really like the cool, overcast climate of England, the Pacific Northwest, or coastal Northern California, and thrive even in the North. Siebold's primrose grows in Juneau, Alaska, and in northern Minnesota, providing it has snow cover in these colder regions.

Its rhizomatous roots will grow up to the surface over the seasons, so mulch your stands of Siebold's primrose with leaf mold or compost each year to cover the roots. Other than slugs, few pests or diseases bother it.

PROPAGATING SIEBOLD'S PRIMROSE You can divide Siebold's primrose in spring as soon as the foliage begins to emerge but before it blooms. Or better still, wait until the leaves die back and the plants go dormant, then in fall pull back the mulch to expose their rhizomatous roots for easy division. Replant divisions 12 inches apart.

THE RIGHT SITE FOR 'MIKADO' Because 'Mikado' Siebold's primrose will naturalize where it likes its spot, it's good for growing in woodland settings, among rhododendrons, and in shady borders. Under tall trees, it supplies a very effective color splash in early spring with daffodils.

Unlike many primroses, Siebold's primrose doesn't have to grow in the shade. It prefers partial shade but enjoys full sun where the soil stays moist.

CO-STARS FOR 'MIKADO' Combine 'Mikado' Siebold's primrose with shieldleaf rodgersia (*Rodgersia tabularis*), epimediums (*Epimedium* spp.), astilbes, and ferns in the moist, shady garden, and with spring bulbs everywhere.

'Mrs. Moon' Bethlehem Sage

Pulmonaria saccharata 'Mrs. Moon'

Spotlight on 'Mrs. Moon' Bethlehem Sage

USDA Plant Hardiness Zones: 3 to 8

Season of Bloom: April and May, sometimes into early June

Height × Width: 12 inches × 24 inches

Flower Color: Pink fading to blue

Light Requirements: Partial shade to full shade

Soil Requirements: Rich, moist, humusy, woodsy soil

Place of Origin: Southeastern France to Italy

Plant Sources: Kurt Bluemel, Bluestone Perennials, Busse Gardens, Carroll Gardens, Greer Gardens, Powell's Gardens, Shady Oaks Nursery, André Viette Farm & Nursery, White Flower Farm

WOULD YOU RATHER GO TO THE BALL with Mrs. Moon or Margery Fish? I've grown and loved 'Mrs. Moon' Bethlehem sage for years. But rumor has it that 'Margery Fish', a more recent introduction, is more attractive than my beloved 'Mrs. Moon'. Some fickle gardeners even claim that 'Margery Fish' has prettier leaves with more distinct spotting.

Well! Perhaps it's so that 'Margery Fish' is more attractive than 'Mrs. Moon', but I have yet to make Margery's acquaintance (although I see her offered in the Klehm catalog and am tempted). 'Mrs. Moon' Bethlehem sage is still widely sold in nurseries and catalogs and is a thoroughly wonderful perennial, one of the best plants in existence for the shady garden. I'm sure you will be thrilled with 'Mrs. Moon' or with her new rival 'Margery Fish', if you can find it.

The dark green leaves of 'Mrs. Moon' Bethlehem sage are speckled with silvery dots, some of which merge into blotches. These are lovely leaves—wide, elongated ovals with pointed tips and long stems that emerge from the basal clump of roots in early spring. In mid-April, 'Mrs. Moon' puts forth flowering stems—some upright, some sprawling—that carry open clusters of pink buds. As the buds open, the pink petals of the little bell-like flowers gradually age to a rich blue shade.

Loads of Lovely Lungworts

There are almost too many wonderful cultivars of these excellent shade garden plants from which to choose. 'Roy Davidson' lungwort (Pulmonaria 'Roy Davidson') has speckled, narrow, very long leaves and light blue flowers. 'Bertram Anderson' long-leaved lungwort (P. longifolia 'Bertram Anderson') has violet-blue flowers with narrow, cream-spotted foliage. There are many pink-flowered kinds, too, including 'Pierre's Pure Pink' Bethlehem sage (P. saccharata 'Pierre's Pure Pink'), 'Pink Dawn' (P. saccharata 'Pink Dawn'), and 'Leopard' (P. saccharata 'Leopard'). There is also the elegant 'Sissinghurst White' (P. saccharata 'Sissinghurst White') with white flowers.

The leaves of 'Spilled Milk' lungwort (P. 'Spilled Milk') are almost entirely white, just edged with green.

Even without a spring show of attractive pink-fading-to-blue flowers, 'Mrs. Moon' Bethlehem sage would win a place in the shade garden for its striking, silver-speckled leaves.

How to Grow Bethlehem Sage

To keep your Bethlehem sage looking good throughout the summer, make sure it gets sufficient moisture. If it has to struggle through drought, its pretty leaves will take on a wilted, browned, unattractive look, and that would be a shame since this plant is so elegant all season when it receives adequate water. That's not to say that Bethlehem sage has to be in wet soil all summer—established plants are somewhat drought tolerant but may enter dormancy early in extended dry spells. Give Bethlehem sage partial to full shade to protect its pretty foliage from being scorched by hot summer sun. It grows well from the cold regions of the North to the heat of the Deep South. Pests and diseases rarely pose any problems.

Propagating Bethlehem Sage

Divide Bethlehem sage in late spring after it finishes flowering, or in the fall. Separate newer crowns from the clump and discard the older portion of the roots. Replant the divisions 12 inches apart and keep them well watered for the next six weeks.

The Right Site for 'Mrs. Moon'

'Mrs. Moon' Bethlehem sage's combination of silver-spotted leaves and pink-and-blue flower clusters makes a thrilling sight—like a living tapestry on the woodsy garden floor. Planted by itself or mixed with drifts of pastel pink tulips, 'Mrs. Moon' makes an exquisite sight that you'll want to show to friends and visitors when the plants are blooming. But send them into the garden and let them find these treasures themselves.

Co-Stars for 'Mrs. Moon'

Plant 'Mrs. Moon' Bethlehem sage with other spring-bloomers, such as hellebores (*Helleborus* spp.), azaleas (*Rhododendron* spp.), rhododendrons, blue Siberian squill (*Scilla siberica*), and pink tulips. It looks great brightening up a planting of ferns or growing beneath the branches of flowering crabapples, plums, and cherries.

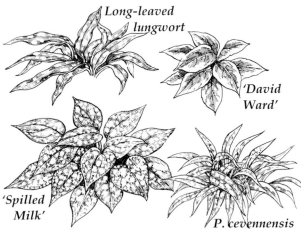

Long-leaved lungwort

'David Ward'

'Spilled Milk'

P. cevennensis

From starry speckles and spots to creamy white margins, shade-loving lungworts offer a lot of different leaf patterns and variegations to love.

PASQUE FLOWER

Pulsatilla vulgaris

Spotlight on
Pasque Flower

USDA Plant Hardiness Zones: 4 to 9

Season of Bloom: April to May

Height × Width: 8 to 12 inches × 12 to 18 inches

Flower Color: Mauve to violet

Light Requirements: Full sun to partial shade in south

Soil Requirements: Rich, gritty, chalky, well-drained soil

Place of Origin: Sweden to England, and east to Finland down to the Ukraine

Plant Sources: Kurt Bluemel, Busse Gardens, Carroll Gardens, Dutch Gardens, Garden Place, Milaeger's Gardens, Van Bourgondien, André Viette Farm & Nursery, We-Du Nurseries

PASQUE FLOWER (*Pulsatilla vulgaris,* also sold as *Anemone pulsatilla*) is one of those small, very beautiful flowers that helps sing the world awake in very early spring. Pasque flower gets its name from the old French word for Easter, because it blooms at about that time. This plant's a little charmer that usually doesn't get much press, but I consider it a perennial all-star for very good reasons.

When the world is bleak and colorless, we welcome any flower. How glad we are, for instance, when the snowdrops (*Galanthus* spp.) open their little white blossoms, but how unimpressed we would be with them if they waited until June or July. That's not the case with pasque flower, whose 2- to 3-inch-wide, cup-shaped flowers of rich violet-purple-mauve-pink (it varies from plant to plant)

Other Pleasing Pasque Flowers

There are other forms and cultivars of this plant, but these are hard to find. Keep your eyes open for them, as a mixture of them with the violet-mauve species is most effective. They include the white-flowered 'Alba' pasque flower (P. vulgaris 'Alba') and 'Rubra' pasque flower (P. vulgaris 'Rubra'), which has magenta to wine red sepals. 'Barton's Pink' pasque flower (P. vulgaris 'Barton's Pink') and 'Mrs. Van der Elst' pasque flower (P. vulgaris 'Mrs. Van der Elst') both have pink blossoms.

can't wait for the leaves to fully emerge before they open. Yes, they'd be showy whenever they bloomed, but here they are to start things off with panache, even when ice crystals still needle the soil on cold spring mornings.

Each flower has six purplish violet petals whose color contrasts vividly with a large, central, golden ring of stamens. Some of these flowers face upwards, while some nod over. Each plant produces a clutch of six, eight, to a dozen flowers in low-growing bunches that are very striking against the winter-worn world. The blossoms appear atop silky-haired stems amid emerging tufts of very finely divided, ferny leaves that remain attractive until mid- to late summer. When the flowers fade, they are replaced by silky, silvery tufts of downy seedheads.

Although flowers like these would be welcome any time of the year, pasque flowers seem especially precious arriving right on the heels of winter.

Plant pasque flower where you'll be sure to see its small but showy soft blossoms in earliest spring. Let its downy flowers, seedheads, and foliage mark the spot for perennials that don't arise until later in the growing season.

HOW TO GROW PASQUE FLOWER
In most of the country, pasque flower grows best in full sun, although a little shade is all right in the Deep South. Pasque flower likes gritty clay soil, especially if the pH is neutral to slightly alkaline. If your soil is acidic, work in some ground limestone as you plant. Good drainage is a must.

Insects don't bother pasque flower, but if the soil is poorly drained, root rot can start. Site pasque flower carefully in a spot where winter and spring water run off quickly and you won't have a problem. Other than that, pasque flower is quite easy to grow.

PROPAGATING PASQUE FLOWER
Pasque flower usually self-sows frequently enough that you can increase your planting by carefully digging up new plants with as much of a rootball as possible and moving them to their new spots. Space transplants 8 inches apart. You can also carefully divide established plants in the fall. If they tolerate this treatment, the divisions will flower the next spring.

THE RIGHT SITE FOR PASQUE FLOWER
Pasque flower is perfect for a border or walkway near the house where you can frequently enjoy the sight of its early blossoms. It can also be successfully interplanted with other taprooted, but later blooming, perennials, such as balloon flower (see page 252) or butterfly weed (see page 56). The pasque flowers will provide you with a trouble-free and pretty reminder of where these late-emerging plants are lurking so you don't dig into them.

CO-STARS FOR PASQUE FLOWER
Spring adonis (*Adonis vernalis*), winter aconite (*Eranthis hyemalis*), Grecian windflower (*Anemone blanda*), and early spring bulbs of all kinds mix well with pasque flower. Its rich flower colors look good next to the textured, multicolored foliage of evergreen 'Purpurascens' garden sage (*Salvia officinalis* 'Purpurascens') and 'Burgundy Glow' ajuga (see page 32).

ORNAMENTAL RHUBARB

Rheum palmatum 'Atrosanguineum'

Ornamental Rhubarb occupies that unique spot as the largest, boldest, most massive perennial in the garden—at least throughout most of the country (gunneras [*Gunnera* spp.] are larger but are perfectly hardy only in Zones 8 to 10).

For years I let common garden rhubarb (*Rheum rhabarbarum*) do double duty in my garden. It was a garden vegetable that I also used in the perennial garden. It had large leaves and a tall flowerstalk, but nothing that compared with the stature and show of its ornamental cousin. When I saw my first ornamental rhubarb, the pie rhubarb went back to the vegetable garden.

Ornamental rhubarb's colorful cultivar 'Atrosanguineum' adds good color to the plant's imposing size. Couple that with its trouble-free habits, resistance to pests (from insects to deer), and its usefulness in the landscape, and it is a worthy perennial all-star.

Another Remarkable Rhubarb

R. palmatum var. tanguticum is another very satisfactory and attractive ornamental rhubarb. It also has reddish leaves in early spring. These are deeply divided and turn dark green later in the year. Its flowers and fruits are also red, and it has enough good qualities to vie with R. palmatum 'Atrosanguineum' for the title of perennial all-star.

Spotlight on Ornamental Rhubarb

USDA Plant Hardiness Zones: 3 to 9

Season of Bloom: May to June

Height × Width: 6 to 8 feet × 5 to 6 feet

Flower Color: Reddish pink

Light Requirements: Full sun to partial shade

Soil Requirements: Rich, humusy, fertile, moist soil

Place of Origin: China

Plant Sources: Forestfarm, Greer Gardens, Heronswood Nursery, Roslyn Nursery

In early spring, ornamental rhubarb's big leaves begin to unfurl. When they first appear, they are crimson-purple, a plummy color that persists into the warm, sunny weather, especially on the undersides of the leaves, before turning mostly green.

As the leaves grow, you also get good reddish color from their stems. Finally they unfurl to their 3-foot-wide, deeply cut and lobed, and extremely ornamental full glory. In late May, the plant sends up a flowerstalk anywhere from 6 to 8 feet high, holding aloft great fluffy clouds of small, rich cherry pink flowers. The flowers are followed by attractive red seeds.

HOW TO GROW ORNAMENTAL RHUBARB

Although this ornamental rhubarb isn't difficult to grow, it does have some very specific needs that must be met if it's to do its best. The first is for adequate moisture through the growing season. Midsummer heat will destroy ornamental rhubarb's robust good looks if it becomes water stressed. It also needs a

Plant ornamental rhubarb in rich, moist soil to sustain its considerable size. Its new leaves are a pretty shade of deep plum red.

good manuring or topdressing with rich compost each spring. Rhubarb's huge growth requires lots of nutrients.

Ornamental rhubarb likes full sun in the North but will do well in partial shade. In the South, some hours of shade during the day will help keep the plants looking good. If properly cared for, ornamental rhubarb is a very long-lived perennial.

PROPAGATING ORNAMENTAL RHUBARB
Divide ornamental rhubarb in the spring or fall. It is a huge plant with big, tough roots that are hard to dig out. Use a hose to expose the top of the root mass in early spring, then slice the root mass into divisions, making sure each one has an eye (bud). Replant divisions 5 feet apart.

THE RIGHT SITE FOR ORNAMENTAL RHUBARB
Two or three of these plants, set in a triangle 5 feet on a side, in full colorful bloom, make an unforgettable sight, even when seen from far across the property. Such a planting can easily anchor an entire garden.

It makes a beautiful and dramatic specimen by itself in a featured spot. It is very effective by a waterside, or at the bottom of an informal rock garden, where it can tie the garden to the surrounding lawn.

CO-STARS FOR ORNAMENTAL RHUBARB
Echo ornamental rhubarb's ruddy colors with the red leaves of 'Husker Red' foxglove penstemon (see page 240)—the rhubarb provides a substantial backdrop for the penstemon's white flowers, as well as for other whites such as 'David' summer phlox (see page 248). 'Burgundy Glow' ajuga (see page 32) also picks up ornamental rhubarb's color scheme and makes a pleasing groundcover to crouch at its

Your pie rhubarb won't do this! In late spring, ornamental rhubarb raises a tall plume of reddish pink flowers high above its deeply cut leaves.

feet. In moist soil and partial shade, match ornamental rhubarb with the equally bold leaves of fingerleaf rodgersia (*Rodgersia aesculifolia*) and the elegant arching stems of variegated Solomon's seal (see page 256).

'GOLDSTURM' BLACK-EYED SUSAN

Rudbeckia fulgida
var. *sullivantii* 'Goldsturm'

SIMPLY PUT, 'Goldsturm' black-eyed Susan is one of the very best perennials in the garden and will be at the top of anyone's short list of all-stars—it's certainly on mine.

'Goldsturm' black-eyed Susan opens its first blooms in late July, continuing in full flower through August, and tapering off through September and up until frost.

Remarkable Rudbeckias

There are many other rudbeckias worth adding to your sunny garden. R. fulgida var. deamii is a very elegant black-eyed Susan with slender petals. 'Gold Drop' ragged coneflower (R. laciniata 'Gold Drop' or 'Goldquelle') is a lighter yellow, double-flowered form. It blooms from July to frost and is hardy to Zone 3. For something completely different, take a look at 'Green Wizard' coneflower (R. occidentalis 'Green Wizard'). Ideal for adding drama to fresh or dried arrangements, 'Green Wizard' has bright green sepals that stick out like rays around a prominent black cone—and it has absolutely no petals.

Imagine a moist, sunny meadow planted with a mix of these various "coneflowers" in a glorious late-summer floral extravaganza!

Spotlight on 'Goldsturm' Black-Eyed Susan

USDA Plant Hardiness Zones: 4 to 9

Season of Bloom: July to October

Height × Width: 24 to 36 inches × 24 to 36 inches

Flower Color: Rich golden-yellow–orange

Light Requirements: Full sun

Soil Requirements: Average, well-drained soil

Place of Origin: United States east of the Mississippi

Plant Sources: Kurt Bluemel, Bluestone Perennials, W. Atlee Burpee, Busse Gardens, Carroll Gardens, Crownsville Nursery, Dutch Gardens, Forestfarm, Garden Place, Greer Gardens, J. W. Jung Seed, Klehm Nursery, Milaeger's Gardens, Park Seed, Plant Delights Nursery, Powell's Gardens, Roslyn Nursery, Sunlight Gardens, Van Bourgondien, André Viette Farm & Nursery, Wayside Gardens, Weiss Brothers Perennial Nursery, White Flower Farm

Seed Sources: Park Seed, Thompson & Morgan

Each of 'Goldsturm' black-eyed Susan's flowers has many raylike petals surrounding a dark brown, almost black, cone in the center. Flowering is supremely reliable, no matter what the summer weather has been. And the plant is very floriferous, opening its 3- to 4-inch daisies all over the tops of the plants' many stiff stems.

The sturdy flowers of 'Goldsturm' black-eyed Susan sparkle like stars surrounded by an airy cloud of soft lavender-blue Russian sage.

'Goldsturm' black-eyed Susan lives up to its German name, which means "gold storm," as it fills the late summer garden with rich golden daisies.

How to Grow 'Goldsturm'

No plant could be easier to grow. 'Goldsturm' black-eyed Susan likes just about any good garden soil and full sun—although it will tolerate some shade. Give it sufficient early moisture to help it reach its usual 24- to 36-inch height, and after that it can take some drought. Pests and diseases don't touch it.

Clumps of 'Goldsturm' black-eyed Susan spread slowly from underground creeping roots, but not invasively, giving you plenty of root mass for many divisions, so you can get more plants without any problem. It's a good idea to divide the clumps every three years to refresh the plantings and to get enough plants to fill a meadow.

Propagating 'Goldsturm'

Propagate 'Goldsturm' black-eyed Susan by division in spring or fall. Spring is the preferred time to allow fall bloom to continue unimpeded. This clump-forming perennial is very easy to divide. Replant the divisions 12 to 18 inches apart. 'Goldsturm' black-eyed Susan also self-sows prolifically.

The Right Site for 'Goldsturm'

This black-eyed Susan is a staple of the "new American garden" look which emulates the prairie with swaths of ornamental grasses and summer-flowering perennials. And its showy flowers look right at home in such a setting. Along with its undemanding yet reliable nature, 'Goldsturm' black-eyed Susan makes a fine cut flower.

Co-Stars for 'Goldsturm'

'Goldsturm' black-eyed Susan's rich flower color and the dark green of its leaves make a fine color combination on their own. A small group of 'Goldsturm' looks pretty planted with flowering tobacco (Nicotiana alata) and ground cherries (Physalis spp.) for a late-season display. Pair 'Goldsturm' black-eyed Susan with vertical plants like tall sunflowers (Helianthus spp.). Heat it up with the rich reds of annuals like zinnias or use a wide planting of Frikart's aster (Aster × frikartii) to cool it down. It makes an excellent companion to large drifts of ornamental grasses like fountain grass (Pennisetum alopecuroides).

'MAY NIGHT' VIOLET SAGE

Salvia × superba 'May Night'

'MAY NIGHT' VIOLET SAGE IS SUCH A CHAMPION performer that it was named Perennial Plant of the Year for 1997 by the Perennial Plant Association.

The genus *Salvia* is a huge one, and many species and cultivars are wonderfully tough, beautiful, and useful plants in our gardens. But 'May Night' stands out for several important reasons. For starters, it has larger flowers than other violet sage cultivars, which gives it more color per square foot of planting. And that color is a rich, dark indigo-violet with reddish purple bracts. The flower display is

Sampling Other Superb Salvias

There are many other cultivars of violet sage (S. × superba) worth planting. 'East Friesland' sage (S. × superba 'East Friesland') is an old standby with deep purple flowers, also growing to just 18 inches. 'Lubecca' (also sold as 'Lubeca') has violet-blue flowers and a longer growing season than 'East Friesland'. It grows about 30 inches tall, making it best for Zone 7 and north.

S. × sylvestris 'Blue Hill', a German introduction, has spikes of pure, light blue flowers that are exceptionally charming. This plant grows only to about 16 inches tall. Its sister is 'Snow Hill', with spikes of white flowers that look lovely with one of the blue-flowered cultivars.

Spotlight on 'May Night' Violet Sage

USDA Plant Hardiness Zones: 4 to 9

Season of Bloom: June to September

Height × Width: 18 inches × 18 inches

Flower Color: Indigo-violet with reddish purple bracts

Light Requirements: Full sun

Soil Requirements: Average, moist, well-drained soil

Place of Origin: Probable hybrid of violet sage (S. nemorosa) and meadow sage (S. pratensis), natives of Europe east to southwest Asia

Plant Sources: Bluestone Perennials, Busse Gardens, Carroll Gardens, Garden Place, Greer Gardens, Klehm Nursery, Milaeger's Gardens, Roslyn Nursery, Sunlight Gardens, Van Bourgondien, André Viette Farm & Nursery, White Flower Farm

made up of typical salvia flowers: small, with a hooded top petal, packed on numerous upright flower spikes that arise from a basal clump of leaves in May and June.

'May Night' also has staying power. Bloom begins in early June—earlier than for most perennial salvias. Given a site with moist soil in full sun, they put on a truly spectacular display. And the show goes on all summer, with the plants staying in bloom until the cool days of September begin to shut them down.

HOW TO GROW 'MAY NIGHT' This super-easy salvia will grow in just about any soil, but like most perennials, it appreciates a nice garden loam. 'May Night' violet sage is basically a full-sun plant and appreciates a steady moisture supply. Insects and diseases don't bother the salvias in general, and that's certainly the case with our perennial all-star.

PROPAGATING 'MAY NIGHT'

To keep the fine, distinctive qualities of 'May Night', you will need to propagate it vegetatively rather than saving seed. Take stem cuttings in spring and root them. Divide the plants in spring or fall. Divisions are easy and root well, especially when you divide the plants in spring. Replant the divisions or new plants 18 inches apart.

'May Night' salvia packs its upright flower spikes with lots of deep indigo-violet blossoms. Light up a dark drift of 'May Night' with the pale yellow daisies and rounded form of 'Moonbeam' threadleaf coreopsis for a spectacular, summer-long display.

THE RIGHT SITE FOR 'MAY NIGHT'

This violet sage deserves a place in every perennial border. Its rich blue-black bloom color is a wonderful foil for pastel pinks, salmons, and lighter blues, as well as for hot colors like reds and yellows. Use them in repeating groups of three in the middle of the border or bed, or bring some to the front to add a bushy break to the lower-growing plants.

It takes lots of small, two-lipped flowers to give 'May Night' its big visual impact. This salvia starts blooming in June and goes for most of the summer.

CO-STARS FOR 'MAY NIGHT'

'May Night' violet sage has two lunar partners that really shine—pale yellow 'Moonshine' yarrow (see page 28) and 'Moonbeam' threadleaf corcopsis (see page 110). Other good partners for 'May Night' are pink flowers and strong orange-yellows like mouse-ear coreopsis (*Coreopsis auriculata*). Silver- and gray-leaved plants like lavender cotton (*Santolina chamaecyparissus*) and artemisias heighten its dark purple flower color.

A Stellar Idea

Gardeners in the South can have problems with salvias in the heat and humidity—the plants tend to grow too tall and flop over. Not 'May Night'! It's a great choice for southern summers because it stands up to heat, humidity, and drought. And since it only reaches 18 inches tall and has sturdy stems, you don't have to worry about 'May Night' falling over.

LAVENDER COTTON

Santolina chamaecyparissus

GARDENERS WHO'VE BEEN TO EUROPE and stepped carefully through precise formal knot gardens have surely seen lavender cotton at work as a low hedge. But here in the States we've allowed it some freedom and found it to be one of the most useful plants in the garden.

Lavender cotton, or santolina, is grown for its handsome foliage rather than its flowers—but it's such a winner in the garden that it deserves to be widely planted. When it comes to adding a bit of silvery gray, nubbly shrubbiness to counteract all the green, wide leaves in the garden, it's a perennial all-star for sure.

The main feature of lavender cotton is the finely divided, rough, scalelike, nubbly, whitish gray foliage that forms a cottony blanket to cover the ground if many plants

Other Classy Lavender Cottons

There are several outstanding cultivars of lavender cotton, including the silver-leaved 'Lambrook Silver', dwarf 'Nana', and lacy 'Plumosus'. Green lavender cotton (S. rosmarinifolia, formerly S. virens) is 24 inches tall, with green thread-like foliage and yellow flowers; it's hardy to Zone 7. It requires the same growing conditions as S. chamaecyparissus. The cultivar 'Primrose Gem' has pale primrose yellow flowers.

Spotlight on Lavender Cotton

USDA Plant Hardiness Zones: 6 to 9

Season of Bloom: August to September

Height × Width: 24 inches × 18 to 24 inches

Flower Color: Yellow

Light Requirements: Full sun

Soil Requirements: Average, well-drained soil

Place of Origin: Spain to North Africa

Plant Sources: Kurt Bluemel, Greer Gardens, André Viette Farm & Nursery, Weiss Brothers Perennial Nursery

Seed Source: Thompson & Morgan

are placed about 12 inches apart in all directions. Like artemisias, all parts of the plant are aromatic if crushed, but the aroma is stuffy rather than pleasant or medicinal. In August, tight little yellow buttonlike flowers splash across the tops of the foliage.

HOW TO GROW LAVENDER COTTON This all-star's needs are simple: good drainage and a warm, sunny spot. Being a native of the warm regions of Spain and North Africa, it doesn't take kindly to really cold weather or wet feet, and Zone 6 is about as cold as it goes. In Zones 6 and 7, winter frost kills its tops back to the ground, but it puts out new growth in the spring just like any other herbaceous perennial.

In Zone 8 and warmer, however, its woody stems live over winter until, after a few years, it's more wood than leaf. That's why even in the warm regions it's a good idea to treat it

In an informal garden, lavender cotton's bright yellow flowers are a cheery bonus. You can shear its pale gray foliage into hedges for more formal sites.

Green lavender cotton bears sulfur yellow flowers and has feathery, dark green foliage. It's great along a sunny path with yarrow, lamb's-ears, and lavender.

like a perennial. Cut it down during the late winter before new growth starts up.

When new growth starts in spring, the plant will reach about 24 inches tall. If you're using it as an informal spot of silver-gray in the garden or to cover and hold a bank or slope, let it run to its full height. If you're using it in a more formal way, to edge a walkway or define a bed, then give it a shearing when it reaches about 14 to 16 inches, cutting it back to 12 inches. It likes this, responding by becoming tighter, denser, and prettier.

Lavender cotton is sturdy, drought resistant, pest- and disease-free and takes little maintenance once you get it going except to keep it trimmed.

PROPAGATING LAVENDER COTTON

Lavender cotton is easy to propagate from cuttings taken from the stem tips and rooted in loose, moist soil. This can be done any time from spring through late summer.

THE RIGHT SITE FOR LAVENDER COTTON In

the perennial bed or border, lavender cotton acts as a peacemaker—one of those silvery gray-leaved plants that separates flowering perennials, forms a backdrop for colorful plants, and provides relief from too many green leaves. It's a perfect plant to grow between perennials with clashing flower colors.

CO-STARS FOR LAVENDER COTTON Plant lavender cotton with low-growing red flowers like 'Tiny Rubies' cheddar pinks (see page 116). Other great combinations are lavender cotton with 'Gibson's Scarlet' cinquefoil (see page 260) and with hot red-orange flowers such as those of sun rose (*Helianthemum nummularium*).

A Stellar Idea

Many gardeners cut off lavender cotton's flowers—I guess they just don't "cotton" to them. (Really, it's because those yellow buttons spoil the formal look of lavender cotton when it's used as a foliage plant.) However, I don't shear off the flowers since I use lavender cotton to cover two banks in informal spots on my property. If you're using it as a silvery separator or backdrop in the perennial bed, you may want to remove them, since they don't add much to the plant's appearance and look tatty when they finish blooming.

ROCK SOAPWORT

Saponaria ocymoides

WHAT ARTIST PLANNED ROCK SOAPWORT'S COLOR scheme so perfectly? The plant makes a low mat of flat, olive green leaves on spreading, many-branched stems of a deep oxblood red. These two colors alone seem to be the perfect pairing of red and green shades, but then the artist goes one better. At the ends of these ruddy branches, five-petaled pink flowers open in loose, blowsy sprays, nearly covering the plant when it's in full bloom. The flowers resemble those of creeping phlox, and their bold pink is a mix of the oxblood of the stems and white.

The color scheme is exquisite—but this perennial all-star doesn't stop there. It's a vigorous spreader and self-sower that will fill an area where weeds are kept down so it can colonize. Yet it's not an invasive plant, just an enthusiastic grower.

Several Sensational Soapworts

If you want rock soapwort in your formal border, find the cultivar 'Rubra Compacta' (S. ocymoides 'Rubra Compacta'), a non-trailing, compact plant with crimson flowers. Other cultivars include 'Alba', with white flowers; 'Carnea', with fleshy pink blooms; 'Splendens', with large, bright rosy pink flowers; and 'Floribunda', with a more floriferous habit. But in my opinion, none of these is as fine as the species.

Spotlight on
Rock Soapwort

USDA Plant Hardiness Zones: 2 to 7

Season of Bloom: May to July

Height × Width: 6 to 9 inches × 24 to 36 inches

Flower Color: Pink

Light Requirements: Full sun

Soil Requirements: Average, sandy, well-drained soil

Place of Origin: Mountains of Spain, plus southern France and northern Italy, and the Alps from Germany to Yugoslavia

Plant Sources: Bluestone Perennials, Busse Gardens, Carroll Gardens, Forestfarm, Garden Place, Milaeger's Gardens, Powell's Gardens, Van Bourgondien, André Viette Farm & Nursery, Weiss Brothers Perennial Nursery,

HOW TO GROW ROCK SOAPWORT

Soapwort is forgiving—it's one of the easiest perennials to grow. And it will grow almost anywhere. It's adaptable to sandy, infertile soils but certainly loves to find a good soil beneath its roots. It likes sun and good drainage, which makes it a great rock garden plant. (Bet you guessed that from its name, rock soapwort.) Wherever you grow it, give it plenty of room to spread out.

Soapwort is a fine plant for the North, but south of Zone 7 it tires easily in the heat and humidity and is short lived.

PROPAGATING ROCK SOAPWORT Take stem cuttings in spring when the plants are in flower. Sow seed of the species in spring. If

After it finishes flowering, cut rock soapwort back to promote fresh growth and another sprinkling of flowers.

A Stellar Idea

Here's a fun trick to try—show your friends how to turn soapwort into soap! The genus Saponaria is called soapwort because if you take some of the roots and scrub them in a little water, you can actually work up a lather. I've done that with bouncing bet (S. officinalis), a European garden plant from Europe that has light pink flowers. Bouncing bet has escaped in the eastern United States and is now a common roadside wildflower.

you want to propagate a named cultivar, make root divisions in spring. (Don't divide plants more often than once every three years.) Plant divisions or started plants 8 inches apart in the garden.

THE RIGHT SITE FOR ROCK SOAPWORT

This soapwort stars in the rock garden, in a tough site where more fussy or tender plants might not grow, and it looks especially fine clambering over rocks, spilling over stone walls, and otherwise disporting itself for our pleasure. I've always found that the sight of my soapwort cheers me up just when I need it.

I also like rock soapwort as a groundcover for full-sun areas. It's especially delightful mixed with the silvery white, little-leaved

Rock soapwort's right at home in the well-drained soil of a raised bed. It can get a bit overgrown and floppy in rich, moist soil.

mats of snow-in-summer (*Cerastium tomentosum*) to form a tapestry of pink and white somewhere near, but not in, the more formal perennial border.

CO-STARS FOR ROCK SOAPWORT Rock soapwort is an excellent choice with snow-in-summer (*Cerastium tomentosum*). I also love to combine it with spring-blooming phlox, pinks (*Dianthus* spp.), and hardy geraniums or cranesbills (*Geranium* spp.).

'FAMA' PINCUSHION FLOWER

Scabiosa caucasica 'Fama'

ONE OF THE MOST POPULAR PERENNIALS worldwide, pincushion flower rewards the gardener with torrents of exquisite blooms on trouble-free, easy-to-grow plants just about all season long.

The flowers of the species are simply marvelous and many of the named cultivars are even better. And 'Fama' is the best of them all. Its flowers are larger and more striking than those of any of the other cultivars, with splashier petals of a richer blue. They really are outstanding.

The flowers of 'Fama' are about 3 inches across, with a 1½-inch disc of silvery white touched with light violet in the center. This disc is stuck all over with indentations and little stamens, giving it the appearance of a

Spotlight on 'Fama' Pincushion Flower

USDA Plant Hardiness Zones 3 to 9

Season of Bloom: June to September

Height × Width: 18 to 24 inches × 18 to 24 inches

Flower Color: Lavender blue-violet

Light Requirements: Full sun

Soil Requirements: Good, humusy, well-drained, neutral to alkaline soil

Place of Origin: Caucasus Mountains

Plant Sources: Carroll Gardens, Forestfarm, Garden Place, J. W. Jung Seed, Milaeger's Gardens, Weiss Brothers Perennial Nursery, White Flower Farm

Seed Source: Thompson & Morgan

A Pocketful of Prizewinning Pincushion Flowers

'Alba' pincushion flower is the white form of 'Fama'. 'Butterfly Blue' (S. columbaria 'Butterfly Blue') is a fine cultivar, with smaller flowers and stature than 'Fama', but with a blooming season from May to November, while 'Pink Mist' (S. columbaria 'Pink Mist') grows just 12 inches tall with lilac-pink flowers from spring to fall.

pincushion. These pincushions are backed with many fine petals of a clear lavender-blue–violet. Each petal is a soft lobe that's finely toothed on the end as it overlaps or is partially covered by the petals near it.

Each flower is borne at the top of a tall, leafless stem that can reach from 18 to 24 inches tall. Many stems arise at any given time from the basal rosette of finely cut leaves, and they keep emerging all summer.

HOW TO GROW 'FAMA' This pincushion flower is easy to grow in any loose, humusy soil with average fertility. In acid conditions, give plants a handful of ground limestone mixed with the soil in the planting hole. To do their best blooming, plants need full sun. 'Fama' is best suited to Zones 3 to 7, and it does poorly in the Deep South, although it is a star in my Zone 9 garden in California, where

With its May-to-November season of bloom, you'll like 'Butterfly Blue' pincushion flower just as much as the butterflies do!

summer heat is not accompanied by humidity, and the nights are always cool.

PROPAGATING 'FAMA' As individual plants get older, they produce fewer blooms over shorter periods of time. Divide them every three to four years, discarding older, woody portions of the roots and replanting the young root sections. Replant the divisions 12 to 15 inches apart.

THE RIGHT SITE FOR 'FAMA' 'Fama' looks wonderful in a sunny bed or border planted near the front in groups of three or more. Its lavender flowers complement other pastel shades, including blue, pink, and white, or you can use it to soften bolder reds, purples, and cobalt blues.

'Fama' pincushion flower is far too pretty to be confined to the garden, so nature has made it an excellent and very long-lasting cut flower. Cut when they're about half opened, and the flowers will last in arrangements for weeks.

CO-STARS FOR 'FAMA' Excellent companions for 'Fama' include woolly yarrow (*Achillea tomentosa*), lady's-mantle (*Alchemilla mollis*), 'Laucheana' sea-pink (*Armeria maritima* 'Laucheana'), 'Olympica' bluebell (*Campanula rotundifolia* 'Olympica'), golden-star (see page 100), 'Spring Beauty' cottage pinks (*Dianthus plumarius* 'Spring Beauty'), 'Pink Jewel' daisy fleabane (see page 130), 'Elegans' Siberian meadowsweet (*Filipendula palmata* 'Elegans'), 'Wargrave Pink' Endress cranesbill (*Geranium endressii* 'Wargrave Pink'), 'Incomparabilis' sunflower heliopsis (*Heliopsis helianthoides* 'Incomparabilis'), and 'Palace Purple' heuchera (see page 170).

Plenty of lavender-blue, 3- to 4-inch flowers—all summer long—give 'Fama' the all-star advantage over other pincushion flowers. Its glossy, deeply divided foliage gives it added interest.

A Stellar Idea

The flower show of 'Fama' is so good, I never want it to end. And luckily, it doesn't! 'Fama' performs from early June until September, producing wave after wave of flowers. But you can help the show along if you pick off the spent blooms. With diligent deadheading, blooming will be continuous. Otherwise, 'Fama' will pause between flushes of flowers, especially during the hottest four to six weeks of summer.

'AUTUMN JOY' SEDUM

Sedum 'Autumn Joy'

'Autumn Joy' sedum is aptly named. Like other sedums, it is a succulent, with thick, fleshy leaves and flowers that are loved by butterflies. This one is very special, however. The most special quality of 'Autumn Joy' sedum is its chameleon-like ability to change flower color. The semidomed, broad flower-heads, composed of many tiny blossoms, appear in August as greenish white ghosts. As August progresses, they change color to a light warm pink. This color deepens in September to a rich salmon pink, then to ruddy burgundy, then to mahogany, and finally, when the flowers die and dry, to dark brown.

HOW TO GROW 'AUTUMN JOY' This hybrid has no real pests or diseases that need taking care of. It will grow in just about any

Some Other Seemly Sedums

There are scores of worthy sedums. Here are some of my favorites. The hybrid 'Vera Jameson' sedum (S. 'Vera Jameson') has blue-green leaves tinged with deep purple. It bears dusty pink flowers in late summer and fall. 'Dragon's Blood' two-row sedum (S. spurium 'Dragon's Blood') is a prostrate groundcover with showy red flowers and dark green leaves that turn red in winter. Whorled stonecrop (S. ternatum) is a native white-flowered species that's an excellent groundcover for shade.

Spotlight on 'Autumn Joy' Sedum

USDA Plant Hardiness Zones: 3 to 9

Season of Bloom: August to frost

Height × Width: 24 inches × 24 inches

Flower Color: Greenish white, changing to light pink, then to salmon pink, changing to red-burgundy, then mahogany and dark brown

Light Requirements: Full sun to partial shade

Soil Requirements: Average, well-drained soil

Place of Origin: Probable hybrid of showy stonecrop (S. spectabile) and orpine (S. telephium)

Plant Sources: Ambergate Gardens, Kurt Bluemel, Bluestone Perennials, W. Atlee Burpee, Busse Gardens, Carroll Gardens, Crownsville Nursery, Forestfarm, Garden Place, Greer Gardens, Milaeger's Gardens, Park Seed, Powell's Gardens, Roslyn Nursery, Sunlight Gardens, Van Bourgondien, André Viette Farm & Nursery, Wayside Gardens, Weiss Brothers Perennial Nursery, White Flower Farm

type of soil, moist or dry—although it prefers a heavy, retentive clay soil that is well drained and never soggy. Too-rich soil creates extra-long stems, which can be weak, causing the big seedheads to flop over.

Although 'Autumn Joy' will grow in partial shade, too much shade promotes long, leggy stems that tend to fall over. You could stake it in the shade, but 'Autumn Joy' won't cause

When they first appear, 'Autumn Joy' sedum's pale broccoli-shaped flowerheads create pools of light next to summer bloomers like black-eyed Susan.

As summer fades, 'Autumn Joy' sedum's flower color deepens to rich pink and burgundy shades that look great with the fall hues of ornamental grasses.

you any work if it's sited correctly. Plants do best in full sun, but make sure they get at least four to five hours of sun a day.

Too much water can make the flower color lighter, too, so keep it fairly dry. Water during dry spells, but otherwise let 'Autumn Joy' fend for itself once it's established.

PROPAGATING 'AUTUMN JOY' 'Autumn Joy' is easy to divide in spring or fall. Replant divisions 15 inches apart. Stem cuttings—the top 4 to 6 inches of the shoots—taken in summer will root in a week to 10 days, allowing you to quickly get a lot of new plants from a single plant.

THE RIGHT SITE FOR 'AUTUMN JOY' Plant 'Autumn Joy' sedum where it can complement other fall bloomers, or let it provide color where early bloomers have finished their show. The thick, succulent leaves make neat masses of light green to gray-green foliage earlier in the year. 'Autumn Joy' looks good all year in a container.

CO-STARS FOR 'AUTUMN JOY' I think 'Autumn Joy' looks just perfect with 'Frances Williams' Siebold's hosta (see page 178). It's also beautiful with leadwort (*Ceratostigma plumbaginoides*), Canadian burnet (*Sanguisorba canadensis*), Kamchatka bugbane (*Cimicifuga simplex*), azure monkshood (*Aconitum carmichaelii*), and chrysanthemums.

A Stellar Idea

'Autumn Joy' is a reliable bloomer, but you can force it to produce even more flowerheads by shearing it back halfway when it's about 8 inches tall. This causes the plants to put up more stems, each of which will bear a flowerhead.

'PARTY GIRL' PRAIRIE MALLOW

Sidalcea 'Party Girl'

IN A WILD LANDSCAPE lush with native flowers, pink-flowered prairie mallow is one of the prettiest. But it was never a great garden plant until recently. Prairie mallow is not for everyone, but where it does thrive, it is a perennial all-star for sure.

'Party Girl' (and all prairie mallows) do best in the parts of the country with cool nights and warm days. That includes coastal California, Oregon, and Washington, up into coastal British Columbia, then into states like Idaho, the warm parts of Wisconsin, Michigan, across into New York State and New England. For folks in the lower Midwest and Middle Atlantic seaboard, the plant can be chancy, depending on the weather. In the Southeast and Gulf States, forget it.

'Party Girl' produces a rounded clump of gray-green foliage in the spring. In July, flowering stems ascend, producing flowers that

Other Preferred Prairie Mallows

Other exciting prairie mallow cultivars include 'Elsie Heugh', light pink; 'Rose Queen', rosy pink; 'Loveliness', shell pink; 'Brilliant', deep rose, and 'Croftway Red', a very deep pink. Like 'Party Girl', these cultivars were developed from hybridizing prairie mallow, S. malviflora, and white prairie mallow, S. candida.

Spotlight on 'Party Girl' Prairie Mallow

USDA Plant Hardiness Zones: 5 to 9

Season of Bloom: July to September

Height × Width: 36 to 42 inches × 24 inches

Flower Color: Bright pink

Light Requirements: Full sun

Soil Requirements: Rich, humusy, moist, well-drained soil

Place of Origin: A hybrid of species native to California and southern Oregon

Plant Sources: Busse Gardens, Daisy Fields, Weiss Brothers Perennial Nursery, White Flower Farm

Seed Source: Thompson & Morgan

look like hollyhocks (prairie mallow is a hollyhock cousin), but they are smaller and more refined. The flowers are 1½ to 2 inches across, wide and saucer shaped and are held vertically against the flower spikes, like hollyhock blossoms. 'Party Girl' prairie mallow's flowers are a bright, rich rose pink with white centers.

HOW TO GROW 'PARTY GIRL' 'Party Girl' grows in full sun to partial shade. It prefers humus-rich, well-drained soil. But "well-drained" doesn't mean "dried out." If you keep 'Party Girl' watered regularly, the plants will bloom for a solid three months. If allowed to dry out, their natural summer dormancy kicks in and they disappear, reappearing with cooler temperatures and fall rains. If you keep them watered and flowering into September, cut them back then to promote new basal growth that will be ready for the next season.

Don't let the name prairie mallow fool you. This pretty 'Party Girl' is refined enough to invite into your perennial border, where she'll put on a late-summer show with her tall stalks of bright pink flowers.

PROPAGATING PRAIRIE MALLOW

Prairie mallows are easy to divide in spring or fall. Division is probably a good idea every four to five years to freshen the plants, more often if you want a lot of plants. Replant divisions 12 to 15 inches apart.

THE RIGHT SITE FOR 'PARTY GIRL'

The informal, hollyhock-like nature of prairie mallow makes it a natural for the cottage garden and wildflower meadow. It also looks great in an informal border or an island bed. Plant it in groups of three in the middle of the bed or border.

The spikes of 'Party Girl' make fine cut flowers, so those folks in areas from Pennsylvania through the upper Midwest should try some

After 'Party Girl' finishes blooming, cut back the flowerstalks to promote healthy growth for next season's display.

in the cut flower garden first to see how they perform. If they like your place, put them in the border, too.

CO-STARS FOR 'PARTY GIRL' Plant 'Party Girl' with Russian sage (see page 242), 'David' summer phlox (see page 248), Missouri evening primrose (see page 232) or Mexican evening primrose (*Oenothera berlandieri*) in Zone 9, lamb's-ears (*Stachys byzantina*), 'Fama' pincushion flower (see page 278) or other blue cultivars of scabious (*Scabiosa* spp.), silvery-leaved artemisias, and lavender cotton (see page 274).

FALSE SOLOMON'S SEAL

Smilacina racemosa

WHEN I FIRST MOVED TO MY PROPERTY in Pennsylvania, false Solomon's seal was one of the wild plants that grew in the place where I wanted to develop a perennial garden.

Looking very much like true Solomon's seal (*Polygonatum biflorum*), false Solomon's seal had made a nice clump on a slope below a group of large boulders. From this clump, many stems rose up a couple of feet and bent over gracefully. The internodes of the stem—the lengths of stem between the leaves—zigged and zagged alternately, adding in-

Other Stellar Solomon's Seals

One other species of false Solomon's seal deserves a place in your shade garden. Shorter than false Solomon's seal at only 12 to 24 inches tall, starry Solomon's seal (S. stellata) has slightly larger (but fewer) flowers and leaves that look like lily-of-the-valley's. True Solomon's seals (Polygonatum spp.) are beautiful plants, with arching stems and bell-like greenish white flowers. Depending on the species, they can range from 6 inches to 72 inches or taller. Like false Solomon's seal, they're great plants for shade and woodland gardens.

Spotlight on False Solomon's Seal

USDA Plant Hardiness Zones: 3 to 9

Season of Bloom: May or June, or even earlier in the southern part of its range, to June or July

Height × Width: 18 to 36 inches × 24 to 36 inches

Flower Color: Creamy white panicles with yellow at the tips

Light Requirements: Full sun to light shade

Soil Requirements: Rich, woodsy, humusy, moist, well-drained soil

Place of Origin: Nova Scotia west to British Columbia but primarily east of the Mississippi, south to Virginia, and west to Missouri

Plant Sources: Busse Gardens, Carroll Gardens, Forestfarm, Greer Gardens, Plant Delights Nursery, Shady Oaks Nursery, Sunlight Gardens, We-Du Nurseries

terest to the plant's appearance. The foliage was delightful—6- to 9-inch-long, deeply grooved, fresh green leaves spaced alternately on opposite sides of the stem.

For a full eight weeks in June and July, each stem produced a puffy panicle of small, creamy white flowers that carried a delicious scent. The very tip of this panicle of flowers seemed to have been dipped in gold. In summer, the flowers of false Solomon's seal give way to a handful of yellowish white berries that will turn a shiny red in fall.

I liked my false Solomon's seal, so rather than dig it out, I grouped it with a clump of

In late spring and early summer, false Solomon's seal brightens lightly shaded woodland settings with its creamy flower clusters. Even without its flowers it makes a useful and pretty groundcover.

dark blue Siberian irises *(Iris sibirica)* accented with salmon pink 'Helen Elizabeth' oriental poppy *(Papaver orientale* 'Helen Elizabeth'). This trio became one of my favorite plant marriages in the whole garden.

HOW TO GROW FALSE SOLOMON'S SEAL

If you give it the kind of soil it likes: rich and humusy, like forest duff, slightly acid, moist, and well drained. False Solomon's seal is very easy to grow, it likes partial shade best but will grow in full sun and full (but not deep) shade. In the Deep South, make sure it gets plenty of water and give it a semishaded spot. It has no pests or diseases and is a tough, reliable perennial. It needs little care other than to cut down the old stems in winter.

After it's planted, keep false Solomon's seal well watered for a month. It spreads slowly and may be shy about flowering for a year or two. Immediately replant any divisions you make, then leave them alone for several years until they're well established.

PROPAGATING FALSE SOLOMON'S SEAL

False Solomon's seal spreads slowly by creeping roots, making division easy. Divide the plants in late summer or early fall. They may bloom the following year, or they may

False Solomon's seal's shiny red berries never last long because birds and small animals love them.

wait an extra year. Replant divisions immediately. Set them 15 inches apart and don't disturb them for three years. Propagation by seed is possible, but it takes several years for the plants to begin blooming.

THE RIGHT SITE FOR FALSE SOLOMON'S SEAL

This all-star is a natural for the shade and woodland gardens—it looks perfectly at home under trees and with other shade-tolerant plants. It's lovely with spring-blooming woodland wildflowers. If you'd like a large patch of false Solomon's seal, let it naturalize under the shade of high trees. Left alone, it can grow to become an effective and very pretty groundcover.

CO-STARS FOR FALSE SOLOMON'S SEAL

Plant false Solomon's seal with Siberian iris *(Iris sibirica)*, peonies, and ferns. It's lovely around shrubs like barberries *(Berberis* spp.), azaleas *(Rhododendron* spp.), and spireas *(Spiraea* spp.). Try it at the woods' edge with bold-leaved plants like ornamental rhubarbs *(Rheum* spp.) and sea hollies *(Eryngium* spp.), and with all-stars like common bleeding heart (see page 118), variegated Solomon's seal (see page 256), and lady's-mantle *(Alchemilla mollis).*

'CROWN OF RAYS' GOLDENROD

Solidago 'Crown of Rays'

WHEN YOU THINK OF GOLDENROD, images of those shaggy plants that gild the ripening meadows of the East in late August and September usually come to mind. But breeders have been at work on this field weed, especially in Europe. They have returned some outstandingly colorful and beautiful forms to us for use in the garden or in semiwild meadow situations.

A perfect example is 'Crown of Rays'. This hybrid, probably of our wild field weed Canada goldenrod (*S. canadensis*) and the European goldenrod (*S. virgaurea*), covers itself in golden flowers just when you need a big splash of color in the late summer garden.

More Solid-Gold Goldenrods

I think 'Crown of Rays' goldenrod is the best of the hybrid cultivars, but there are other good ones. 'Golden Dwarf' goldenrod is just 12 inches tall with deep yellow flowers; 'Peter Pan' goldenrod is 24 inches tall with light yellow flowers; 'Goldenmosa' is 36 inches tall, golden-flowered, and early. The short cultivars are the best and least rampant growers.

'Golden Fleece' dwarf goldenrod (S. sphacelata 'Golden Fleece') is attractive, with golden flowerheads and nice foliage, and it blooms from August to October. It does especially well in partial shade where many goldenrods fear to tread.

Spotlight on 'Crown of Rays' Goldenrod

USDA Plant Hardiness Zones: 4 to 9

Season of Bloom: August to September

Height × Width: 30 inches × 24 inches

Flower Color: Rich harvest gold

Light Requirements: Full sun

Soil Requirements: Average, loose, humusy, well-drained soil

Place of Origin: Probable hybrid of species from the eastern United States and Europe

Plant Sources: Busse Gardens, Carroll Gardens, Powell's Gardens, André Viette Farm & Nursery

'Crown of Rays' is well named. Its stems form an upright column covered with long, pointed, dull green leaves—a rather stiff stance that's topped with a wonderful whirl of flowering plumes. These flower plumes extend outward in graceful undulations, and open into broad, dense rays of tiny, rich golden flowers.

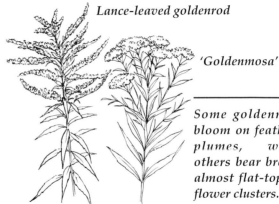

Lance-leaved goldenrod

'Goldenmosa'

Some goldenrods bloom on feathery plumes, while others bear broad, almost flat-topped flower clusters.

'Crown of Rays' goldenrod's flower plumes burst like golden fireworks amid the lavender daisies of 'Mönch' asters. These two all-stars bloom together in the fall garden and create a lovely combination of flower colors and forms.

THE RIGHT SITE FOR 'CROWN OF RAYS'

Mix 'Crown of Rays' goldenrod with other late-summer and fall bloomers like asters, chrysanthemums, and heleniums (*Helenium* spp.), or let it naturalize in a meadow or along a woodland edge. It's a good choice for an area of the property that's semiwild.

CO-STARS FOR 'CROWN OF RAYS'

A fine companion for 'Crown of Rays' is 'Goldsturm' black-eyed Susan (see page 270). Other superb companions include blue and lavender forms of New York aster (*Aster novi-belgii*) and boltonia (*Boltonia asteroides*).

HOW TO GROW 'CROWN OF RAYS'

Our all-star thrives in just about any soil, a virtue it inherits from its tough, wild parents. But 'Crown of Rays' avoids the invasiveness of the species and is a well-behaved, robust grower. Pests don't bother it, and although it may sometimes acquire a little mildew or rust on its leaves, these aren't serious problems.

Plant 'Crown of Rays' in average soil loosened with humus but not overly rich. It needs adequate moisture during the growing season for best bloom, but a soil slightly on the dry side is perfect—just what you find in warm, sunny, out-of-the-way sites away from the rich soil and heavy watering of the flower beds.

'Crown of Rays' is one of those plants, like daylilies, that can be dug out and transplanted anytime, even when it's in full bloom.

PROPAGATING 'CROWN OF RAYS'

There are many ways to increase this easy-to-grow plant. Make divisions in spring or take basal shoots at that time. In summer, take stem cuttings. Plant divisions or new plants 18 inches apart.

A Stellar Idea

'Crown of Rays' isn't just for the garden. Another of its virtues is as a cut flower, either fresh for the vase or to hang and dry. If you cut it to dry when it is just about reaching full bloom, the dried flower plumes will keep their color for winter arrangements. And it's perfectly safe to bring 'Crown of Rays' into the house, even if you or another family member suffers from hayfever. In case you haven't heard, it's ragweed, not goldenrod, that's the culprit.

'SILVER CARPET' LAMB'S-EARS

Stachys byzantina 'Silver Carpet'

IF THERE ARE CHILDREN ANYWHERE NEAR your garden, make sure you plant some 'Silver Carpet' lamb's-ears for them. They will find it irresistible to pull a leaf off this ground-carpeting plant to feel its velvety down and rub its silvery white softness against their cheeks.

Even an inordinate amount of such pulling will hardly harm the plants. They're as tough as an old rooster and just as insistent on having their way. And their way is to spread out and fill a spot with silver-white foliage. So densely do they spread their mats that few weeds will penetrate through them.

Lamb's-ears flowers aren't to everyone's taste (though they're all-stars with bees!). The flowers are borne on 12- to 18-inch flower-stalks. These are upright, downy and silvery white, with a nubbly, knobby "handle" on top that slowly pops open individual, deep magenta flowers, no more than ¼ inch across, at

Another Lovely Lamb's-Ears

*For a bolder foliage effect, there is another nonflowering cultivar, 'Helene von Stein' (*S. byzantina* 'Helene Von Stein'), also sold under the endearing name of 'Big Ears'. As you might guess, its leaves are twice the size of our all-star's 4-inch "ears." This cultivar is very sought after, but I think the foliage seems coarse compared with 'Silver Carpet'.*

Spotlight on 'Silver Carpet' Lamb's-Ears

USDA Plant Hardiness Zones: 4 to 9

Height × Width: 8 to 10 inches × 24 to 36+ inches

Foliage Color: Silvery, whitish gray-green

Light Requirements: Full sun

Soil Requirements: Average to poor, well-drained soil

Place of Origin: Caucasus region to Iran

Plant Sources: Kurt Bluemel, Bluestone Perennials, Busse Gardens, Carroll Gardens, Garden Place, Milaeger's Gardens, André Viette Farm & Nursery, Weiss Brothers Perennial Nursery

an increasing rate until full bloom, at which time the oldest florets are spent. Some people claim to like them. I think they spoil the whole purpose of lamb's-ears, which is to provide a fine silvery carpet under and around other garden plants. That's why I've chosen 'Silver Carpet' lamb's-ears as the perennial all-star. It does not flower—hallelujah! In the past I've spent far too much time pulling or cutting off the flowerstalks, work that has made me doubt the wisdom of planting this evergreen perennial. 'Silver Carpet' avoids the problem entirely.

HOW TO GROW 'SILVER CARPET' Lamb's-ears saves you work as it forms a weed-suppressing groundcover that doesn't need dividing or replanting. It's not choosy about soil, except that it prefers good drainage. It sails through droughts. Pests and diseases don't bother it. About the only problem I know of is stem rot in the Deep South, where

If you don't like lamb's-ears flowers, you'll love 'Silver Carpet'. This all-star forms a tidy mat of foliage that's uninterrupted by gangly flowerstalks.

Soft and silvery lamb's-ears are a popular choice for the front of the garden. They coordinate well with almost everything in the garden and need little care.

summers are hot and steamy. It's not the heat that bothers it, it's the humidity.

In the colder regions, winter will flatten it and turn its leaves to tatters. In the spring, just rake it up and cut off the old stems or take a string trimmer to it before new growth begins.

PROPAGATING 'SILVER CARPET' 'Silver Carpet' is easy to divide in spring, since it spreads by creeping underground roots. If the clump starts dying out in the center, make divisions from fresh outside vegetation and discard the old woody centers. It's also easily propagated by basal cuttings in spring.

THE RIGHT SITE FOR 'SILVER CARPET' It seems to me that 'Silver Carpet' lamb's-ears must be the perfect underplanting for old

roses that spill their rose red flowers onto the silvery carpet below. It's also a great plant for edging the front of the bed or border and for creating a pool of silvery light amid the dark leaves and varied hues of any of the perennials in your sunny garden. Let its pale, silvery leaves light the way alongside a path in your evening garden.

CO-STARS FOR 'SILVER CARPET' Well, I guess it's obvious by now that I think roses are the perfect companions for 'Silver Carpet'. Red-, pink-, and orange-flowered roses are especially good, and lavender to purple blooms aren't bad, either. Lamb's-ears looks good with most perennials, but for a bit of drama, grow it with rose campion (*Lychnis coronaria*). The campion looks like a taller version of lamb's-ears, with its silver stems and leaves—at least, until it sends up its stunning magenta blooms. The hot magenta against the cool silver-gray backdrop is quite a sight, believe me!

'BLUE DANUBE' STOKES' ASTER

Stokesia laevis 'Blue Danube'

'BLUE DANUBE' STOKES' ASTER has all the fine qualities that mark a true all-star. Named for the early nineteenth century botanist, Dr. Jonathan Stokes, the plant is a native of the Southeast, meaning that it's right at home in the region's sweltering summer weather. While many other perennials struggle there and wish they were growing in cool, foggy England, Stokes' aster blooms prolifically.

It just loves to flower, opening blossom after blossom continually from July right through fall to frost, especially if you nick off the dead flowers regularly. In Zone 9, in fact, it will keep producing flowers through the winter if encouraged to do so by deadheading.

True to its all-star status, the blossoms are uniquely beautiful. Each is about 3 inches across, give or take a few millimeters. (I've seen catalogs claim 5 inches for the blossoms, but we'll forgive them a little exaggeration. The truth is that these flowers need no hyperbole—they're exquisite just as they are.) Their

Other Stunning Stokes' Asters

There are at least a dozen other cultivars of Stokes' aster. Try a few to vary your color scheme, or plant them with 'Blue Danube'. Two unusual cultivars are 'Mary Gregory', with yellow flowers, and 'Silver Moon', with large white flowers.

Spotlight on 'Blue Danube' Stokes' Aster

USDA Plant Hardiness Zones: 5 to 9

Season of Bloom: July to frost

Height × Width: 12 to 18 inches × 24 inches

Flower Color: Silvery lavender-blue

Light Requirements: Full sun to partial shade

Soil Requirements: Most soils, as long as they are well drained, especially in winter

Place of Origin: South Carolina to Florida and west to Louisiana

Plant Sources: Kurt Bluemel, Carroll Gardens, Forestfarm, Garden Place, Van Bourgondien, André Viette Farm & Nursery, Wayside Gardens, Weiss Brothers Perennial Nursery, White Flower Farm

color is a lavender-blue, and their shape seems devised by a master jeweler. An inner set of slender, threadlike petals are thickly set in a circle then topped with a dazzle of white stamens that emerge from the center, giving this inner part of the flower a glittery appearance. This disc is surrounded by much longer petals that are deeply divided into four or five lobes at their tips, making a filigreed background setting for the inner part of the flower.

The plants make 18-inch-wide clumps of long, straplike leaves on erect stems. The tops of the stems bear several flowers with staggered opening times, which gives them the long bloom season. Along with all its other good habits, Stokes' aster is easy to divide when you want more of it.

You might just waltz when you see the showy fringed flowers of 'Blue Danube' Stoke's aster. Each jewel-toned blossom is a good 3 inches across.

'Blue Danube' blooms in the heat of the summer and asks for little more than moist, well-drained soil. Regular deadheading keeps the flowers coming until frost.

HOW TO GROW 'BLUE DANUBE' Although it's a southerner, 'Blue Danube' Stokes' aster also does well in the North and is hardy to Zone 5. It's not fussy about the type of soil it grows in, as long as it isn't boggy. This is especially true in the winter, when soggy, wet soil will rot it out. Plants prefer sunny sites. Pests and diseases pass 'Blue Danube' by in search of less adaptable plants. In other words, Stokes' aster is a true low-maintenance garden workhorse throughout most of the country.

PROPAGATING STOKES' ASTER This plant is very easy to divide in spring, with even small divisions rooting readily. Replant divisions 15 inches apart. You can also take stem and root cuttings.

THE RIGHT SITE FOR 'BLUE DANUBE' In the perennial bed or border, 'Blue Danube' Stokes' asters stand out as very decorative and pretty. Place them toward the front where people can stop to see them up close and admire their craftsmanship.

CO-STARS FOR 'BLUE DANUBE' 'Blue Danube' makes a lovely marriage with 'Pink Mist' pincushion flower (*Scabiosa columbaria* 'Pink Mist'), 'Moonbeam' threadleaf coreopsis (see page 110), and 'Moonshine' yarrow (see page 28). Or use pink 'Flamingo' baby's-breath (*Gypsophila paniculata* 'Flamingo') for a spectacular pairing.

A Stellar Idea

When you've got a plant that flowers like 'Blue Danube', it would be a crime not to snip some stems for cut flowers. They last and last, and they are one of the best perennials ever for taking into the house and using in an arrangement. Or bring in an armful from the cutting garden to use all by themselves—they're that beautiful!

CELANDINE POPPY

Stylophorum diphyllum

I LOVE MY SHADY WOODLAND GARDEN, where I have astilbes, ferns, hellebores (*Helleborus* spp.), wild gingers (*Asarum* spp.), Solomon's seals (*Polygonatum* spp.), epimediums (*Epimedium* spp.), and many other plants that like shade and typical deciduous woodland conditions. And I'm always on the lookout for prize candidates to add to the group.

After I read a glowing description of celandine poppy by one of our foremost plantsmen, I thought it looked like it might be a good plant to join this inner circle of woodland friends. And I remembered fondly the perennial weed we called celandine (*Chelidonium majus*) in the East that produced small yellow flowers. (Though I hoped this plant wouldn't be as pedestrian as the weed!) So a few years ago I bought three plants and popped them in near some invasive rehmannia, close by the hellebores (*Helleborus* spp.). Since then, I've been pleasantly surprised at their beauty and reliability (they've even kept the rehmannia at bay!).

I can't make up my mind which aspect of the plant I like more—its flowers or foliage.

Another Pleasing Celandine Poppy

The Chinese version of celandine poppy, S. lasiocarpum, looks much like its American cousin but has bigger leaves.

Spotlight on Celandine Poppy

USDA Plant Hardiness Zones: 4 to 9

Season of Bloom: April to June

Height × Width: 12 to 18 inches × 12 to 18 inches

Flower Color: Yellow

Light Requirements: Partial shade to light shade

Soil Requirements: Rich, humusy, woodsy, moist, well-drained soil

Place of Origin: Pennsylvania west to Wisconsin and south to Tennessee and Missouri

Plant Sources: Carroll Gardens, Powell's Gardens, Shady Oaks Nursery, Sunlight Gardens, White Flower Farm

The nodding flowers are produced relatively sparingly, which adds to its enticement, and they look very much like small Asiatic poppies (*Meconopsis* spp.), with bright, shiny yellow petals and a button of orange-yellow stamens in the center. They are early and charming, and bloom lasts for many weeks in my garden.

Then the leaves mature, and they are very attractive affairs. The 12-inch-long stems carry several of these leaves, which look like deeply lobed and divided oak leaves. They're dark green, tough and slightly hairy to the touch. While they die back in summer in some parts of the country, in my coastal California garden, they stay green into autumn. I am mightily pleased by these unassuming but sturdy little perennials. When I inspected them just now, I noticed their silver-beige seedpods, which are attractive elements themselves.

In a shady spot, celandine poppy's shiny yellow flowers really stand out. This charming woodland native self-sows freely to give you seedlings to share.

Celandine poppy's attractive dark green leaves are lobed like the foliage of the oak trees you might find them growing beneath.

HOW TO GROW CELANDINE POPPY Given moist, humus-rich soil and at least partial shade, celandine poppy is a fuss-free plant. It has no disease or insect problems to speak of.

PROPAGATING CELANDINE POPPY This native is an easy plant to grow from seed, since there are no named cultivars to be preserved by vegetative propagation. It can also be divided in early spring or fall, but do this carefully by lifting the plant and cutting through the crown without damaging the thick roots.

THE RIGHT SITE FOR CELANDINE POPPY Celandine poppy is made for the shade—the shady and woodland gardens, that is. It's also tough enough to hold its own as a border in front of conifers, making a pleasant contrast to the stark, dark green foliage.

CO-STARS FOR CELANDINE POPPY Celandine poppy looks beautiful with just about all other denizens of the woodland garden. Its buttercup yellow flowers are particularly lovely with blue bloomers like Jacob's-ladders (*Polemonium* spp.), Virginia bluebells (*Mertensia virginica*), and pulmonarias (*Pulmonaria* spp.). Its bold foliage contrasts with the fine textures of ferns and bleeding-hearts (*Dicentra* spp.). Other favorite combinations include celandine poppy and variegated Solomon's seal (see page 256), 'Othello' bigleaf ligularia (*Ligularia dentata* 'Othello'), Lenten rose (see page 166), astilbes, hostas, and epimediums (*Epimedium* spp.). And try it with woodland shrubs like azaleas (*Rhododendron* spp.), rhododendrons, mountain laurel (*Kalmia latifolia*), and daphnes (*Daphne* spp.).

A Stellar Idea

Unless you want to spend a part of each spring pulling celandine poppy seedlings, deadhead your plants before the seedpods ripen. But here's a neat fact: If you do have to pull out a plant, you'll see that its roots contain a yellow-orange dye that was used by Native Americans for coloring.

PROSTRATE GERMANDER

Teucrium chamaedrys 'Prostratum'

GERMANDER IS BEST KNOWN as a dark green, little-leaved plant that's widely used as a short hedge or edging around formal herb gardens and flowerbeds. But its role as a boxwood substitute is only the start of germander's uses. In fact, the constant trimming and shoring up of plants used as a decorative edging goes against what we're trying to do in this book, which is to give every gardener a selection of easy-care, high-value, extra-beautiful, multipurpose, grow-anywhere perennials so he or she can create a border that will bloom away while the gardener takes a hard-earned rest in the hammock.

Gardeners have used germander as a hedge in the past, however, because of its shrubby, compact habit and the shiny little ½-inch leaves that are scalloped around the edges and textured on their surfaces. When clipped frequently, it responds by making a

Spotlight on

Prostrate Germander

USDA Plant Hardiness Zones: 5 to 9

Season of Bloom: Mid-July to mid-August

Height × Width: 4 inches × 36 inches

Flower Color: Rosy purplish pink

Light Requirements: Full sun

Soil Requirements: Poor to average, well-drained soil

Place of Origin: Mediterranean region east to southern Russia and Asia minor

Plant Sources: Forestfarm, Nichols Garden Nursery

Seed Source: Park Seed

solid mass of leaves which are aromatic and beloved of cats.

In midsummer, germander's stint as a foliage plant comes to a cheery end as it produces short little flower spikes. The flowers appear on one side of these spikes. They are tubular, with a large lower lip, and are colored a pretty pastel rosy purplish pink. They sprinkle themselves over the surface of the mats made by our all-star cultivar. You can cut the plants back after bloom and they will regrow fresh foliage.

More Gardenworthy Germanders

Wall germander (*T. chamaedrys*) grows to about 12 inches or so and makes clumps smaller in diameter (about 12 inches) than prostrate germander (*T. chamaedrys* 'Prostratum'). Another cultivar, 'Variegatum', has cream-and-green foliage. Cat thyme (*T. marum*) is a lovely, silvery gray plant with pretty, contrasting pink flowers, also beloved of cats and hardy to Zone 5.

Germander's glossy, fine-textured foliage and rosy pink flowers complement many other plants.

Prostrate germander's short stature makes it perfect for edging your perennial border. It's equally at home used as a low hedge for the herb garden.

How to Grow Prostrate Germander

Just give prostrate germander average but well-drained soil in a sunny spot. Well drained is the key here—the better the drainage, the happier prostrate germander will be. Mulch it over winter in Zone 5, where its winter-blasted foliage will need shearing back in areas without consistent snow cover. In Zones 8 and 9, it will be evergreen.

Propagating Prostrate Germander

The creeping roots of prostrate germander are easy to divide in spring. Replant them 12 inches apart. You can also take stem cuttings in summer.

The Right Site for Prostrate Germander

Use prostrate germander as an edging at the front of a bed or border. It's at home as a spreading groundcover on dry, sunny banks, on top of walls, and as a foil for more elaborate perennials in the low border. It's also a good choice to mix into the herb garden—its traditional use—since it looks great with flowering herbs like thymes, oreganos, borage, and others.

Prostrate germander really shines when it's used at the very edge of the border, spilling out onto a path, planted in the dry rock garden along with succulents, or planted on top of a terrace wall, where it can work its way up to the edge of the wall and soften it. But I think that the very best use of prostrate germander is to convert a bare, dry, sandy, sunny site, where even weeds have trouble growing, into a lush green carpet with midsummer flowers.

Co-Stars for Prostrate Germander

Plant this germander with large-leaved plants in a sunny location. Good combinations include prostrate germander as a groundcover under hydrangeas or with plants like foxgloves (*Digitalis* spp.) and cannas (*Canna* spp.). It's especially handsome with light-leaved plants like lamb's-ears (*Stachys* spp.) or groundsels (*Senecio* spp.). Its leaves are glossy enough to glint, so you can use it to contrast with matte-finish or hairy leaves of all kinds. I have placed it under salvias (*Salvia* spp.) and been pleased with the effect.

A Stellar Idea

Breeders have developed the cultivar 'Prostratum' to stay small—growing to just 4 to 6 inches. Thus, you can have the benefit of a low hedge without the work of shearing. You will have to edge it, however, to keep it in place, since given its head, this mat-forming cultivar will grow to fill a circle about 3 feet in diameter.

'LAVENDER MIST' MEADOW RUE

Thalictrum rochebrunianum
'Lavender Mist'

'LAVENDER MIST' MEADOW RUE is a truly majestic perennial, reaching 6 to 8 feet and producing airy mists of tiny lavender-purple flowers with conspicuous yellow centers that jingle along the top third of the tall stems. The whole meadow rue genus is superb, and probably more than one of its members could qualify as a perennial all-star, but I have chosen 'Lavender Mist' meadow rue for several reasons.

First, it's one of the hardiest meadow rues,

Spotlight on 'Lavender Mist' Meadow Rue

USDA Plant Hardiness Zones: 4 to 9

Season of Bloom: July to September

Height × Width: 5 to 8 feet × 3 to 4 feet

Flower Color: Lavender-purple

Light Requirements: Partial shade to full shade, or full sun in the most northerly parts of its range

Soil Requirements: Deep, rich, humusy, woodsy, moist soil

Place of Origin: Japan

Plant Sources: Ambergate Gardens, Busse Gardens, Crownsville Nursery, Forestfarm, Milaeger's Gardens, Powell's Gardens, Roslyn Nursery, Shady Oaks Nursery, Wayside Gardens, White Flower Farm

Other Marvelous Meadow Rues

Some other meadow rues worth planting include the gorgeous 'Hewitt's Double' Yunnan meadow rue (T. delavayi 'Hewitt's Double'). It's similar to 'Lavender Mist' but shorter, with smaller leaves and an even airier appearance. The lilac flowers are double, appearing from August to frost, the stems are purplish, and the plant is exquisite if not as sturdy as our all-star. The species Yunnan meadow rue (T. delavayi) itself is a gardenworthy plant. Columbine meadow rue (T. aquilegifolium) grows 24 to 36 inches tall, with sprays of lavender flowers above columbine-like foliage. It blooms in May and June. Place it at a woods' edge and it will be right at home.

able to withstand the winters even in Zone 4, whereas other types usually freeze out in Zone 5 or colder. Second, whereas some of the other meadow rues can also reach impressive heights, they tend to fall over if planted alone, or their stems will lean together into a tangle if planted in a group. Not so with our all-star, whose stems are sturdy enough to stand up without support, even when they reach a full 8 feet tall, allowing you to make a tidy as well as striking stand.

The foliage usually reaches only about 4 to 5 feet, and it's pretty, resembling the small, three-lobed, flat leaves of the maidenhair fern. Its color is a delicate bluish green, producing a cool effect when combined with its lavender purplish flower sprays. It flowers from July through September—later than most other meadow rues.

You can break some design rules with 'Lavender Mist'—place this tall, airy plant where you can look through it to see shorter, brighter perennials.

HOW TO GROW 'LAVENDER MIST'

'Lavender Mist' meadow rue likes the dappled shade of the woods, so plant it where it can hide from hot afternoon sun. It can take full sun in the northern part of its range. 'Lavender Mist' is happiest in woodland soil conditions—humus-rich soil that's moist but well drained. Diseases aren't usually a problem, but you may notice leaf miners boring twisty channels through the leaves. Pick off and burn the infested leaves.

Meadow rue thrives in the dappled shade and rich soil at the edge of a wooded area.

PROPAGATING 'LAVENDER MIST'

Divide 'Lavender Mist' meadow rue in spring. The best way to avoid root damage is to lift the entire clump and divide it into two to four pieces by slicing down through the roots vertically with a sharp shovel. Replant divisions about 18 to 24 inches apart.

THE RIGHT SITE FOR 'LAVENDER MIST'

The foliage of 'Lavender Mist' is more open and airy than that of most perennials. In fact, you can see through the plant. This openness means you can plant it in front of drifts of shorter perennials with more intense colors and still see the plants behind. Getting a tall plant toward the front of the border means you can interrupt the monotony of plants arranged in neat tiers of heights from front to back. Besides mixing it into the border, try 'Lavender Mist' at the woods' edge, or even plant it farther back in a woodsy place, where it will add some color to all the dark leaves of the understory plantings. Another beautiful combination is 'Lavender Mist' in front of dark green evergreens.

CO-STARS FOR 'LAVENDER MIST'

Mix 'Lavender Mist' with more substantial perennials, such as 'White Pearl' peach-leaved bellflower (*Campanula persicifolia* 'White Pearl'), red valerian (see page 92), and pink turtlehead (*Chelone lyonii*). Or try it with another airy plant like 'Bristol Fairy' baby's-breath (see page 154). It's also lovely with shade-tolerant roses like shell pink 'Gruss an Aachen' (*Rosa* 'Gruss an Aachen').

CRIMSON MOTHER-OF-THYME

Thymus serpyllum 'Coccineus'

CRIMSON MOTHER-OF-THYME may be the smallest of our perennial all-stars, but it's one of the best, with hardly an end to its uses and charms. This creeping thyme forms a dense mat only 4 inches tall or even lower. The mats are made up of tiny, shiny, evergreen leaves on prostrate stems that sometimes root at the nodes, making division a cinch in spring or late summer. These little mats are cute, but the big bonus is the flowers. In late May and June, it's covered over with minuscule bright scarlet flowers. Each flower is just ⅛ inch or so across,

Spotlight on
Crimson Mother-of-Thyme

USDA Plant Hardiness Zones: 3 to 9

Season of Bloom: May to June

Height × Width: 4 inches × 12 to 24 inches

Flower Color: Crimson to reddish purple

Light Requirements: Full sun

Soil Requirements: Average to poor, lime-free, well-drained soil

Place of Origin: Northern France east to the Ukraine

Plant Sources: Bluestone Perennials, Busse Gardens, Carroll Gardens, Powell's Gardens, Sunlight Gardens, André Viette Farm & Nursery, Wayside Gardens, Weiss Brothers Perennial Nursery, White Flower Farm

Other Tempting Thymes

Besides crimson mother-of-thyme, there are other delightful cultivars, including 'Albus' mother-of-thyme (T. serpyllum 'Albus'), with white flowers; 'Carneus', with pale, flesh-colored flowers; and 'Roseus', with pink flowers. Mother-of-thyme (T. serpyllum), with light lavender flowers, is as attractive as almost any of the cultivars except perhaps the bold, striking 'Coccineus'. Woolly thyme (T. pseudolanuginosus), makes a woolly, 2-inch mat of silvery gray-green leaves and produces pink flowers in June. It's a superb companion for mother-of-thyme.

but there are so many that they make a lovely show. The plants may open a few more flowers after the main show is finished, especially in the fall when the weather cools down.

You can use mother-of-thyme as a culinary herb—although common thyme (*T. vulgaris*) will give you more herb flavor per square foot. Its foliage has a lighter version of that delightful thyme fragrance—sharp but irresistible. It's a joy to see the bees happily working amid the flowers.

HOW TO GROW CRIMSON MOTHER-OF-THYME

As a plant of the hot, dry Mediterranean region, crimson mother-of-thyme thrives in spots where other plants would die out. Give it average to poor, very well-drained soil and a sunny site, and it will

thrive. Diseases and pests give it a wide berth. Basically, you plant it and forget it, unless it needs a little tidying up or it's spreading where you don't want it (but it's not invasive).

You may find that crimson mother-of-thyme seeds itself around, which is no bad thing since there are always many places with poor soil that need a little brightening up. Just remember that the seedlings won't necessarily be the same color as the cultivar.

PROPAGATING CRIMSON MOTHER-OF-THYME

The easiest way to propagate crimson mother-of-thyme is to examine prostrate stems for places where they root, then cut and lift these sections, replanting them 8 to 12 inches apart. You can also take stem cuttings in early summer.

THE RIGHT SITE FOR CRIMSON MOTHER-OF-THYME

I think crimson mother-of-thyme is the finest plant for growing among flagstones or pavers in the garden pathway.

Tuck small plants of crimson mother-of-thyme between paving stones. They'll stay low to the ground while spreading to form a fragrant carpet.

Mats of thyme creeping over stones in a pathway is one of my favorite sights in the whole perennial garden, combining the hard cold stone with the soft, fragrant thyme. Rock gardens and crevices in rocks make good places to plant crimson mother-of-thyme, too. And it's the perfect edging plant in any well-drained, sunny garden.

CO-STARS FOR CRIMSON MOTHER-OF-THYME

Crimson mother-of-thyme is beautiful with tulips and other spring bulbs, with ever-blooming daylilies, pussy-toes (*Antennaria* spp.), and the low-growing bellflowers (*Campanula* spp.). I like crimson mother-of-thyme with bluebells (*Campanula rotundifolia*). Also, plant it with woolly thyme (*T. pseudolanuginosus*) for a subtle contrast.

A Stellar Idea

After a while, the stems of crimson mother-of-thyme may turn woody and the foliage may look sparse. Cut it back near ground level when that happens, and the roots will send up a flush of fresh new foliage.

WHERRY'S FOAMFLOWER

Tiarella wherryi

FOAMFLOWER IS ONE OF THE STARS of the shade garden—and its showiest version is Wherry's foamflower, our perennial all-star. Some botanists list *T. wherryi* as its own species, while others say it is actually *T. cordifolia* var. *collina*. You may find it offered in catalogs or nurseries either way.

Allegheny foamflower (*T. cordifolia*) is the most commonly found plant of this genus of native Americans, but I think Wherry's foamflower deserves more attention. While Allegheny foamflower spreads rapidly by underground stolons, Wherry's foamflower makes a compact, stay-at-home clump. And that's important where you want the border to stay pretty much the way you put it in.

Other Fabulous Foamflowers

Allegheny foamflower (T. cordifolia) is very similar in appearance to American alumroot (Heuchera americana), although it's more of a shade lover. Its flowers are puffs of little white stars above medium green maplelike leaves. It blooms from April to June and is a vigorous grower.

Foamflowers are currently the subject of frenzied horticultural selection. You can choose from more than a dozen, including: 'Dark Eye', with burgundy-centered leaves; 'Laird of Sky', with scalloped leaves; and 'Oakleaf', with oaklike leaves and pink flowers. Watch for many more new ones.

Spotlight on Wherry's Foamflower

USDA Plant Hardiness Zones: 3 to 9

Season of Bloom: May to June, with some repeat bloom later in the summer

Height × Width: 6 to 12 inches × 12 to 18 inches

Flower Color: White with pink blush

Light Requirements: Partial shade to full shade

Soil Requirements: Rich, humusy, woodsy, well-drained, acid soil

Place of Origin: Southern Appalachian mountains

Plant Sources: Bluestone Perennials, Busse Gardens, Carroll Gardens, Crownsville Nursery, Forestfarm, Milaeger's Gardens, Powell's Gardens, Shady Oaks Nursery, André Viette Farm & Nursery, We-Du Nurseries, White Flower Farm

Seed Source: Thompson & Morgan

Wherry's foamflower is also the showiest of the foamflowers. The plant sends up thin, wiry stems to 12 inches or taller in May. These are covered for the top 4 to 5 inches with pink buds that open to ¼-inch, fragrant white flowers, each clutching a bouquet of yellow-orange stamens in its center. Each clump produces a handful of these spikes when it flowers in spring, and will produce several more, usually singly, over most of the rest of the summer, even into August.

The spikes retain a pink blush that looks beautiful against the basal clump of emerald green, maplelike leaves. In the fall, the leaves take on a reddish bronze tint.

Pinkish white spires bloom in spring over the maplelike leaves of Wherry's foamflower. Flowering continues at a reduced pace throughout the summer.

HOW TO GROW WHERRY'S FOAMFLOWER

Wherry's foamflower is native to the wooded uplands of the southern half of the Appalachians. As such, it likes humus-rich, moisture-retentive soil, and conditions from dappled to full shade. Being native, it's hardy, pest-free, and untroubled by diseases.

PROPAGATING WHERRY'S FOAMFLOWER

Unlike the stoloniferous species of foamflowers, Wherry's foamflower is a clump-forming perennial, but it's very easy to divide in spring or late summer. Replant divisions 8 inches apart.

THE RIGHT SITE FOR WHERRY'S FOAMFLOWER

No shady garden is complete without a foamy swath of Wherry's foamflower. Plant it near a path where you can appreciate its fragrance. Foamflower is one of the few underplantings that rhododendrons and azaleas (*Rhododendron* spp.) can tolerate around their feet without its diminishing their vigor. And of course, it's perfect for the woodland wildflower garden.

CO-STARS FOR WHERRY'S FOAMFLOWER

Great companions for Wherry's foamflower include wild blue phlox (*Phlox divaricata*), creeping phlox (*Phlox stolonifera*), false Solomon's seal (see page 284), variegated Solomon's seal (see page 256), shieldleaf rodgersia (*Rodgersia tabularis*), lungworts (*Pulmonaria* spp.). Epimediums (*Epimedium* spp.), hostas, ferns, hellebores (*Helleborus* spp.), and trilliums (*Trillium* spp.) also combine nicely with this charmer.

More of a spreader than Wherry's foamflower, Allegheny foamflower makes a pretty woodland partner for Siberian bugloss's blue flowers and pretty pink fringed bleeding heart.

'ZWANENBURG BLUE' SPIDERWORT

Tradescantia 'Zwanenburg Blue'

Spotlight on 'Zwanenburg Blue' Spiderwort

USDA Plant Hardiness Zones: 4 to 9

Season of Bloom: June to September

Height × Width: 24 to 36 inches

Flower Color: Deep blue-violet

Light Requirements: Full sun to partial shade

Soil Requirements: Average, well-drained soil

Place of Origin: North America east of the Mississippi

Plant Sources: Carroll Gardens, Forestfarm, Powell's Gardens, Shady Oaks Nursery, Van Bourgondien, Wayside Gardens, Weiss Brothers Perennial Nursery

'ZWANENBURG BLUE' SPIDERWORT is a hardy, trouble-free, pest- and disease-resistant, grow-anywhere, low-work type of plant. And it has gloriously beautiful flowers that are produced over a long season of bloom, starting in June and continuing for eight weeks in a major flush, and then recurring with less enthusiasm into September. Cutting it back to refresh the foliage in August also encourages 'Zwanenburg Blue' spiderwort to rebloom.

The rich, royal blue of 'Zwanenburg Blue' spiderwort is a lovely sight. White stamens in their centers add a sparkle to their deep coloration. A close look at the flowers reveals a series of variations on the number three: There are three sepals, three petals, and a three-part ovary in the center from which six stamens emerge. Each 2- to 3-inch-wide blossom opens for only a day, but the plant produces many buds that open over its entire eight-week bloom period before slowing down.

Unfortunately, 'Zwanenburg Blue' doesn't have gorgeous foliage to match its flowers. Its stiffly erect, succulent 24-inch stems sheathed in rushlike foliage are rough and coarse looking, although this clump-forming hybrid is more compact and attractive than Virginia

More Superb Spiderworts

Other excellent cultivars include 'Red Cloud', with rosy red flowers, 'Snowcap', with pure white flowers, and 'J. C. Weguelin', with 2-inch light blue blossoms.

Spiderworts' showy flowers bloom amid coarse, grassy leaves that benefit from a late-summer haircut.

Although it tolerates partial shade, 'Zwanenburg Blue' spiderwort does its best blooming in a sunny site. Plant it in the middle of your border, where you can enjoy its gorgeous flowers while hiding its grassy leaves behind more refined-looking perennials.

spiderwort (*Tradescantia virginiana*), its wild cousin. Still, around August, it tends to flop in a haphazard way. As long as you bury it in mid-border or plant it far enough away so you can enjoy the gorgeous flowers without being confronted head-on by the foliage, 'Zwanenburg Blue' more than justifies its place as a perennial all-star.

How to Grow 'Zwanenburg Blue'
'Zwanenburg Blue' is not particular about soil and will grow in some nasty spots where other plants fail. It does better, though, in well-drained soil with a steady moisture supply. Bloom is heaviest in full sun, and becomes sparser in partial shade.

Propagating 'Zwanenburg Blue'
This clump-forming perennial is easy to divide in spring or early autumn. It will also self-sow freely, although seedlings' colors will vary from the cultivar's. Plant divisions or new plants 18 inches apart.

The Right Site For 'Zwanenburg Blue'
Site this spiderwort where it can be seen at a distance, not up close along a path. Or be creative and find neat, tidy, regular companions for it in the border so that its rough habits will make a contrast with them, like a biker at a church social. It's probably best with grasses and grasslike plants that blend well with its foliage. 'Zwanenburg Blue' also looks beautiful naturalized in the landscape or planted on a berm by a pond or stream.

Co-Stars for 'Zwanenburg Blue'
My favorite co-stars for 'Zwanenburg Blue' are grasses and grasslike plants such as daylilies, liriope, and Siberian irises (*Iris sibirica*). Variegated grasses and variegated hostas add extra foliar interest.

A Stellar Idea
Keep spiderwort's floppy foliage looking respectable by cutting it back near ground level in early August when the summer flower flush finishes. It will respond by putting out neater, fresher foliage before frost.

'MIYAZAKI' TOAD LILY

Tricyrtis hirta 'Miyazaki'

I'VE JUST DISCOVERED THE WONDERS of toad lilies in the past few years, and I'm astounded at their performance in my garden! They are like a blessing from heaven, with so many good qualities and charms that they easily qualify as a perennial all-star and even belong in the top rank of all-stars. 'Miyazaki', with its gorgeous flowers, is my favorite of all.

Toad lilies bloom from August to October—a time when much of the garden is falling asleep. And better yet, they flourish in shade. That part of the garden can use all the help it can get in the fall, being basically green, unlike the sunnier areas, which at least have the asters, goldenrods, and chrysanthemums blooming.

The foliage of 'Miyazaki' is beautiful. The stems that emerge from the roots are 24 to 36 inches long, gracefully arching over so they display the ladderlike leaves perfectly to

Spotlight on 'Miyazaki' Toad Lily

USDA Plant Hardiness Zones: 4 to 9

Season of Bloom: August to October

Height × Width: 24 inches × 24 to 36 inches

Flower Color: White and lilac

Light Requirements: Partial shade to full shade

Soil Requirements: Moist, rich, humusy, woodsy, well-drained soil

Place of Origin: Japan

Plant Sources: Ambergate Gardens, Kurt Bluemel, Carroll Gardens, Park Seed, Roslyn Nursery, Shady Oaks Nursery, Wayside Gardens, Weiss Brothers Perennial Nursery

More Terrific Toad Lilies

Interesting cultivars include 'Amethystina' toad lily (T. formosana 'Amethystina'), a rare treasure with blue to blue-violet shading on blossoms speckled with lilac dots and reddish center parts. 'Tojen' toad lily (T. 'Tojen') has white flowers washed with lilac-purple, while T. formosana var. stolonifera has purple and mauve shades and dots on a white background.

passersby. The leaves alternate up the stems, each leaf about 4 to 5 inches long, pointed at the tip, and often edged in lighter green.

The flowers of 'Miyazaki' cluster thickly along the central stem, making a showy display in August. They are orchidlike in appearance, with each 1½- to 2-inch blossom having an intricate central structure and six petals around it. The background color is white to pink, speckled with crimson spots.

Toad lilies are hardy, wintering through here in California with no trouble (many plants find the mild, wet conditions of the California winters difficult). But they also thrive in tough northeastern winters and even in the Midwest, where winters are doubly difficult because temperatures can fluctuate quickly from mild to bitter cold. And the plants return reliably year after year.

'Miyazaki' toad lily's graceful leaves offer an elegant contrast to the fine textures of ferns.

HOW TO GROW 'MIYAZAKI'

Toad lilies do best in partial to full shade in humus-rich, well-drained soil. These plants take no work once sited, other than needing to have their winter-blasted foliage cleared away before spring. Their underground rhizomes allow them to naturalize into large plantings over time, but they're never invasive. We had many days over 100°F here in California last summer and my tricyrtis bloomed their heads off from August right through October. I write this on Halloween, and they still have a few blossoms left.

PROPAGATING 'MIYAZAKI' Toad lilies are rhizomatous plants—with thick, fleshy roots—so they're easy to divide in the spring before growth starts or when you see the first shoots emerging. Replant divisions 12 inches apart.

THE RIGHT SITE FOR 'MIYAZAKI' Place 'Miyazaki' toad lily where its pristine flowers can light up your shady borders. Its distinctive foliage contrasts well with the fine textures of ferns and bleeding hearts, and its dramatic arching form provides welcome relief when planted with a lot of low, mounding plants.

CO-STARS FOR 'MIYAZAKI' Interplant toad lilies with silver- or white-variegated hostas, such as 'Albo-Marginata' wavy-leaf hosta (*Hosta undulata* 'Albo-Marginata'), to give toad lilies a foliage framework worthy of their interesting blooms. Toad lilies are also excellent companions for variegated Solomon's seal (see page 256), Lenten rose (see page 166), and ferns.

Ignore their homely name and plant lovely toad lilies in a spot where you can get a closer look at their orchidlike speckled flowers.

'GOLDEN QUEEN' GLOBEFLOWER

Trollius × *cultorum* 'Golden Queen'

'GOLDEN QUEEN' GLOBEFLOWER provides striking, brightly colored, beautifully structured flowers for the summer shade garden. Because of its beauty and ease of culture (when it gets the right conditions), I'm happy to invite it to join the ranks of our perennial all-stars.

In nature, globeflowers make their homes in the wet bogs, streamsides, and moist areas of northern China and eastern Siberia. For that reason, this all-star is not at home in the southeastern part of the United States but loves the northerly regions, especially Zones 4 through 6. It thrives in the Pacific Northwest and does well along coastal California where the cold ocean water moderates temperatures.

Globeflowers are members of the buttercup family and are closely related to marsh marigolds (*Caltha* spp.). Like marsh

Other Gorgeous Globeflowers

Common globeflower (T. europaeus) has curving, petal-like sepals that produce rounded lemon yellow flower balls borne on long stems. Besides 'Golden Queen', other outstanding cultivars of the hybrid form T. × cultorum, which is a mixture of several species, are 'Canary Bird', with light yellow flowers, and 'Orange Princess', with medium orange flowers. These also have incurved sepals that give the globe shape to the flowers.

Spotlight on 'Golden Queen' Globeflower

USDA Plant Hardiness Zones: 4 to 7

Season of Bloom: July to August

Height × Width: 24 to 36 inches × 24 inches

Flower Color: Yellow-orange

Light Requirements: Full sun to partial shade

Soil Requirements: Constantly moist, rich, humusy soil

Place of Origin: Northern China and eastern Siberia

Plant Sources: Busse Gardens, Carroll Gardens, Dutch Gardens, Forest Farm, Garden Place, J. W. Jung Seed, Milaeger's Gardens, Park Seed, André Viette Farm & Nursery

marigold's, globeflower's leaves are pretty. They're wide, palm-shaped but deeply filigreed and set along the upright, branching 24- to 36-inch stems.

Most members of the globeflower genus bloom in June and July, but 'Golden Queen' flowers a little later, especially in the more northerly part of its range. It may open its first flowers in June or July but continue blooming through July for about six weeks, taking it into August in most places.

You'll be enchanted when it flowers. The plant sends up wiry stems with single flowers at their tips. These are exceptionally large (3 inches wide) and a satisfying yellow-orange color and a beautiful shape: A saucer of petal-like sepals holds an upright clutch of small, slender petals and stamens in the center.

The yellow-orange blossoms of 'Golden Queen' display globeflower's characteristic bowl shape.

Be aware that some nurseries and catalogs list 'Golden Queen' as *Trollius ledebourii*, and some list it as *Trollius chinensis*. When you're plant shopping, the important thing is to look for the name 'Golden Queen'.

How to Grow Globeflower

Globeflower isn't particular about the soil it's planted in, but it must be constantly moist. It actually does well in heavy soils, so if you have clay soil and a wet site, try it. It likes partial shade but will take full sun in the northerly part of its range if there is plenty of moisture.

Propagating 'Golden Queen'

Divide the clumps of globeflower's fibrous roots in early fall when summer's heat diminishes. Replant divisions 12 inches apart. The divisions may take a year to settle in before flowering the following season. 'Golden Queen' comes true from seed, but the seed is hard to germinate.

The Right Site for 'Golden Queen'

Globeflower is a great addition to the moist, shady garden. But if you have a natural area that's shady, or an area with water, or a natural or man-made waterway that gets partial sun, by all means feature it there.

Co-Stars for 'Golden Queen'

In the moist shade garden, showy yellow-orange 'Golden

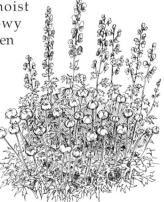

Globeflower's big, bright golden yellow flowers light up a cool, moist, shady spot in front of the deep blue spires of monkshood.

Queen' globeflowers can enliven any of the shade-tolerant plants that have white or blue flowers, such as goat's beard (see page 52) or monkshood (see page 30). It's also nice with Oconee bells (*Shortia galacifolia*), cardinal flower (see page 210), 'Desdemona' bigleaf ligularia (*Ligularia dentata* 'Desdemona'), common rose mallow (*Hibiscus moscheutos*), strawberry foxglove (*Digitalis × mertonensis*), black cohosh (see page 102), hostas, and ferns.

A Stellar Idea

The leaves of 'Golden Queen' will begin to look ratty after flowering, so it's a good idea to cut the plant back at that time. It will then produce a low-growing cluster of leaves that will look good until the plant enters its dormant season.

'FUSILIER' TULIP

Tulipa praestans 'Fusilier'

THERE ARE TULIPS—AND THEN THERE ARE TULIPS. The big mid- to late-season hybrids are wonderful specimens in lovely colors, but they tend not to be perennial, and in the warmer zones, they should actually be treated as annuals. Then there are the species tulips, which are reliably perennial but are now endangered from overcollecting in their native Europe, central Asia, and the Near East.

That's why I recommend our all-star tulip, *T. praestans* 'Fusilier', which is a cultivar of a species tulip. That means it's both perennial and certain to be nursery propagated rather than taken from the wild. This little gem grows only about 8 to 10 inches tall and produces a fusillade of five or six bright scarlet tulips on each bulb's flowering stem.

Other Terrific Species Tulips

Other species tulips and their cultivars have the same perennial habit as T. praestans. Try T. tarda, a very low-growing (only 3-inch-tall) tulip with yellow and white petals; T. turkestanica with yellow and white flowers; the beautiful 'Bronze Charm' Batalin tulip (T. batalinii 'Bronze Charm'), with bronzy salmon flowers; 'Lilac Wonder' tulip (T. bakeri 'Lilac Wonder'), with yellow centers and lilac petals; and T. pulchella 'Violacea', with rich pink flowers.

Spotlight on 'Fusilier' Tulip

USDA Plant Hardiness Zones: 3 to 8

Season of Bloom: April

Height × Width: 8 to 10 inches × 6 to 12 inches

Flower Color: Scarlet

Light Requirements: Full sun to partial shade

Soil Requirements: Rich, sandy, well-drained soil is best, although any good well-drained soil will do

Place of Origin: Europe to central Asia

Plant Sources: Daffodil Mart, Dutch Gardens, Van Engelen

HOW TO GROW 'FUSILIER' Any good garden soil is fine for 'Fusilier' tulips as long as it's well drained. Make sure to site them so that they're in the sun for most of the time their foliage is present. Under deciduous trees is usually okay, since by the time the trees fully leaf out, the tulip foliage is starting to ripen.

PROPAGATING 'FUSILIER' These pretty tulips will naturalize if they get a few hours of sun each day. To divide clumps, just move some of the bulbs to a new site after the foliage has finished ripening.

THE RIGHT SITE FOR 'FUSILIER' Grow 'Fusilier' close to the house where you can appreciate it, since this stunning tulip splashes the ground with the strongest, brightest red imaginable very early in the year, when even the common yellows of for-

There's nothing like spring when 'Fusilier' tulips bloom amid the delicate purple-blue daisies and low, ferny foliage of Grecian windflowers.

'Fusilier' tulips light up a bed of pachysandra with a blaze of brilliant scarlet. Each bulb will produce several flowers on one 8- to 10-inch flowering stem.

sythia and daffodils are welcome and appreciated. Try them in foundation plantings, rock gardens, and flowerbeds and borders where you need a burst of color.

CO-STARS FOR 'FUSILIER' 'Fusilier' tulips never hoist their blooms high above the soil, the way the later tulips do, instead they keep things down near ground level. That makes them exciting companions for other low-growing, early, brightly colored spring bulbs like Siberian squill (*Scilla siberica*) with its intense blue, and some of the strong yellow-orange daffodils.

So many perennials look good with tulips, but all the early spring bulbs are perfect with this bright red tulip. In addition to daffodils and squills (*Scilla* spp.), try 'Fusilier' with striped squills (*Puschkinia* spp.), and glory-of-the-snow (*Chionodoxa* spp.). Plant these brilliant tulips where midspring perennials like pansies, primroses, bleeding hearts (*Dicentra* spp.), and forget-me-nots (*Myosotis* spp.) can grow up to cover the ripening foliage.

A Stellar Idea

Because they are species tulips, 'Fusilier' tulips will be perennial if they get several hours of sun each day they're in leaf. This recharges the bulbs and packs them with food for the next season's display. Not only will they be perennial, but in the right spot—good, loose, well-drained soil with an absence of critters that like to eat them, such as gophers, moles, and other burrowing rodents—they will naturalize and slowly spread.

WHITE NETTLE-LEAVED MULLEIN

Verbascum chaixii 'Album'

AS CHILDREN, WE ALL LOVED the big, wild, weedy common mullein (*Verbascum thapsus*), with its huge flannel-like leaves and towering flower spike dotted here and there with yellow outward-facing flowers. How wonderful, then, to discover as adults that our woolly old friend has cousins that are garden perennials—and great ones at that. White nettle-leaved mullein, for one fine example, is so pretty and useful that it rates as a perennial all-star.

The plant makes a clump of large, 6-inch-long, silvery green leaves that have their own function as a welcome addition to the garden's foliage. In June it sends up a sturdy but slender flower spire that reaches to about 3 feet. Buds all along and around this spire open singly and over a rather long period of time—so that while the spire is not all in bloom at the

Spotlight on
White Nettle-Leaved Mullein

USDA Plant Hardiness Zones: 4 to 9

Season of Bloom: June to August

Height × Width: 24 to 36 inches × 18 to 24 inches

Flower Color: White with mauve or rosy purple eyes

Light Requirements: Full sun

Soil Requirements: Average, well-drained soil

Place of Origin: Southern and central Europe

Plant Sources: Carroll Gardens, Daisy Fields, Forest Farm, Milaeger's Gardens, Powell's Gardens

More Marvellous Mulleins

*Besides nettle-leaved mullein (*Verbascum chaixii*), I enjoy several other mulleins. Good available hybrids include 'Cotswold Beauty', with soft salmon pink flowers; 'Cotswold Queen', with showy amber to salmon-bronze flowers; 'Gainsborough', a very showy mullein with light yellow flowers and silvery foliage; 'Pink Domino', with rose-lavender flowers; and 'Royal Highland', with apricot-yellow spires to 4 to 5 feet that make a strong vertical accent.*

same time, it always has some flowers in bloom from late June right into August.

The flowers are wonderful. They look like white moths that have fluttered to the spire and are sitting on it with their wings open. In the center of each flower is a clutch of wine red or mauve stamens that form an eye, giving the flower a spot of color.

HOW TO GROW WHITE NETTLE-LEAVED MULLEIN Most mulleins tend toward a biennial habit, but nettle-leaved mullein will be perennial if it likes its spot. If you site it in a dry, sunny spot, it will reward you by returning year after year. But if you plant it in rich, moist garden soil, you'll turn it into a biennial if not an annual, for it won't live long there. Like its weedy cousin, 'Album' likes dry, warm soil in full sun, and it especially likes soil that's limy and well-drained.

PROPAGATING WHITE NETTLE-LEAVED MULLEIN

Mullein self-sows, and seed isn't hard to collect, but you may not get the color of the cultivar. The easiest way to propagate the white form ('Album') is to carefully take off secondary basal rosettes if there are any.

You can also take root cuttings during late fall and perpetuate it year after year, even though that means some extra work. It's not hard: Loosen the plant when it's dormant in late fall or early spring and snip off a few long roots. Then replant the parent plant, firming the soil around it. Snip the roots into 3-inch sections, noting which end is toward the root tip and which is toward the plant. Stand these upright in a mix of compost and perlite with the end toward the tip of the root pointing down and the top of the root buried just below the surface. Transplant them to the garden in spring when there's a healthy-looking tuft of four or more leaves on each plant.

THE RIGHT SITE FOR WHITE NETTLE-LEAVED MULLEIN

White nettle-leaved mullein is a perfect plant for a sunny bank with average soil, where it can mingle with other perennials and succulents that like those conditions. It's appealing in an informal planting but also deserves a place in the flowerbed or border if the soil is well-drained.

CO-STARS FOR WHITE NETTLE-LEAVED MULLEIN

This mullein blends beautifully with the tall bellflowers—milky bellflower (*Campanula lactiflora*), great bellflower (*C. latifolia*), and peach-leaved bellflower (*C. persicifolia*). It's also good in a dry, sunny spot with red valerian (see page 92) and cinquefoils (*Potentilla* spp.), and with sedums, hens-and-chickens (*Sempervivum* spp.), and other succulents. I have combined its erect form and color

with 'Miss Willmott' Nepal cinquefoil (*Potentilla nepalensis* 'Miss Willmott') for one of the nicest and subtlest combinations in the high-summer garden.

In a dry, sunny site, white nettle-leaved mullein raises its spikes of flowers next to the yellow flowers of its parent species. Well-drained, slightly alkaline, average soil is what this all-star likes best.

Because they don't open all their buds at the same time, white nettle-leaved mullein's tall spikes of rosy-eyed flowers will put on a display in your garden for several weeks in the summer.

'HOMESTEAD PURPLE' VERBENA

Verbena 'Homestead Purple'

HERE'S A PLANT THAT JUST WANTS TO BLOOM its little heart out, opening clusters of rich purple phloxlike blossoms from May right along through the summer until frost. Plants reach 8 to 18 inches tall. The leaves are glossy green, an inch or so long, and they make the perfect color companion for the purple flowerheads. These flowers are lightly fragrant, too.

No one seems to know the parentage of 'Homestead Purple', which was found growing along a roadside in Georgia by two eminent plantsmen, Allan Armitage and Michael Dirr of the University of Georgia. It's probably a hybrid or variety of rose verbena (*V. canadensis*), the native verbena that is found throughout the Southeast. 'Homestead Purple' is hardy to Zone 6 but needs a good winter

Spotlight on 'Homestead Purple' Verbena

USDA Plant Hardiness Zones: 6 to 10

Season of Bloom: May to frost

Height × Width: 18 inches × 36+ inches

Flower Color: Purple

Light Requirements: Full sun

Soil Requirements: Average, well-drained soil

Place of Origin: Probable hybrid of species native from Virginia west to Colorado and south to Mexico

Plant Sources: Bluestone Perennials, Busse Gardens, Plant Delights Nursery, Powell's Gardens, Roslyn Nursery, Sunlight Gardens, André Viette Farm & Nursery, Wayside Gardens

Other Very Vibrant Verbenas

Brazilian vervain (V. bonariensis) has 4-foot-tall angular stems with puffs of bluish purple flowers at the tips. This great butterfly attractor can be grown as an easy hardy annual in the North, and is perennial in Zones 7 through 10.

Rose verbena (V. canadensis) has several excellent cultivars. 'Gene Cline' grows from 6 to 9 inches tall and produces deep rose red flowers all summer. Then there's 'Lavender', with lavender blossoms, and 'Rosea', with rosy pink blossoms. All are suitable for Zones 6 through 10.

mulch there. From Zone 7 south, it's reliably hardy and also evergreen.

HOW TO GROW 'HOMESTEAD PURPLE' This verbena must have well-drained soil and full sun. It does better in average to poor soil than in rich, moist garden soil, and it thrives even with little water. Make sure you give it plenty of room, though. It's vigorous and will engulf more timid plants. Down South, 'Homestead Purple' thrives in all the heat and humidity that summer can throw at it, blooming happily away for month after month.

PROPAGATING 'HOMESTEAD PURPLE' Take basal cuttings in spring as they emerge, or take root stem cuttings. Check prostrate stems to see if they are rooting, and if they are, make divisions. Plant new starts 18 inches apart.

The Right Site for 'Homestead Purple'

'Homestead Purple' verbena is a great choice for the low-maintenance garden. If the rest of your sunny, dry border is out of flower, 'Homestead Purple' won't be. It's a good plant for the roadside, by the mailbox, or in difficult, dry, out of the way places. It's also perfect for edging a walkway or parking strip, filling a waste space, or adding color to a window box or planter. Incidentally, this verbena is a dual-purpose hummingbird and butterfly plant .

Verbena's ability to spread in dry soil makes it a lively companion for drought-tolerant groundcovers like variegated pittosporum (right).

Co-Stars for 'Homestead Purple'

Grow vibrant 'Homestead Purple' with silver-leaved plants like artemisias, lamb's-ears (*Stachys byzantina*), and dusty miller. Mix it with a white-flowered form of purple coneflower (*Echinacea purpurea*) and your favorite colors of yarrow (*Achillea* spp.). Try it with other verbena cultivars. Or grow it under roses, with species petunias, or with lavender, chives, and silver thyme in the herb garden.

The vibrant flowers of 'Homestead Purple' add pizzazz to plantings of silvery foliage plants and ornamental grasses.

A Stellar Idea

'Homestead Purple' is so care-free and reliable, and it blooms for such a long season, that it's like its annual relatives which are so commonly used as bedding plants. But 'Homestead Purple' verbena is a perennial where it's hardy, so you don't even have to replant it each year. However, gardeners in Zone 5 and northward don't have to pass up this wonderful all-star. If you live in a cold climate, just plant it as an annual and it will outgrow and outbloom any and all "regular" annual verbenas. It only takes a month of hot weather for it to cascade 3 feet over a wall like a purple waterfall.

'SUNNY BORDER BLUE' SPEEDWELL

Veronica 'Sunny Border Blue'

'SUNNY BORDER BLUE' SPEEDWELL is truly a champion performer, even among our perennial all-stars. When you grow it and get to know it, you will see why it was the Perennial Plant Association's Plant of the Year for 1993.

This speedwell combines the best characteristics of its genus with a hybrid's natural vigor. 'Sunny Border Blue' grows into thick clumps about 18 inches tall and up to 24 inches across. Its luxurious leaves are apple green, nicely textured, and fixed oppositely on the straight stems. From the stem tips, the flowering spikes emerge. These explode into thick bloom in late June. The spikes are covered with tiny florets

Some Other Special Speedwells

Woolly speedwell (V. incana) has softly fuzzy gray-green foliage and spikes of blue flowers. Harebell speedwell (V. prostrata) is a low-growing spreader that bears clusters of small blue flowers; several cultivars of this species are available. 'Georgia Blue' speedwell (V. peduncularis 'Georgia Blue') makes a fine evergreen groundcover of about 6 inches tall and bears rich blue flowers with white eyes. 'Blue Peter' spike speedwell (V. spicata 'Blue Peter') has dark blue flowers on 24-inch spikes, and 'Crater Lake Blue' Hungarian speedwell (V. teucrium 'Crater Lake Blue') is an outstanding selection with intense blue flowers.

Spotlight on 'Sunny Border Blue' Speedwell

USDA Plant Hardiness Zones: 3 to 9

Season of Bloom: June to September

Height × Width: 18 to 24 inches × 18 to 24 inches

Flower Color: Deep violet-blue

Light Requirements: Full sun

Soil Requirements: Average, well-drained soil

Place of Origin: Hybrid of speedwell species native to Europe and east through Siberia

Plant Sources: Ambergate Gardens, Kurt Bluemel, Bluestone Perennials, Busse Gardens, Carroll Gardens, Crownsville Nursery, Forest Farm, J. W. Jung Seed, Klehm Nursery, Milaeger's Gardens, Shady Oaks Nursery, Sunlight Gardens, Van Bourgondien, André Viette Farm & Nursery, Wayside Gardens, Weiss Brothers Perennial Nursery

of a rich dark blue-violet color. Some spikes will stand straight up, while others may bend over slightly at the final inch or 2 of their tips.

HOW TO GROW 'SUNNY BORDER BLUE'

Give 'Sunny Border Blue' speedwell a spot in your sunny perennial garden. While it tolerates some shade, it does so at the expense of its flower spikes. To really get the most from it, give it a place in the sun. The soil where it grows is less of a concern, as long as it's well drained and not overly rich. 'Sunny Border Blue' speedwell's fibrous root system needs good drainage, especially in winter when

You'll like the way 'Sunny Border Blue' looks next to the yellow daisies of threadleaf coreopsis. Neither of these perennials minds hot weather or dry soil, as long as it's well drained and not too rich.

cold, wet, waterlogged soil encourages root rots that may kill the plant. Any ordinary soil amended with compost or rotted manure is perfect soil for 'Sunny Border Blue' speedwell.

'Sunny Border Blue' is very long lived, needing division only every five to six years. Its stems will stand straight without any staking unless excessive soil fertility forces it to produce weak, spindly growth. Pests and diseases aren't a problem, and established plants are relatively drought tolerant.

PROPAGATING 'SUNNY BORDER BLUE'
Divide 'Sunny Border Blue' in the spring, or in the fall in the South. You can also take stem cuttings in the spring before plants start flowering. Cuttings root readily, especially if given a dip in rooting hormone before you stick them in a moist, sterile rooting medium. You can also separate off young shoots arising from the base of the plant in summer. Plant divisions and rooted cuttings 12 to 18 inches apart.

THE RIGHT SITE FOR 'SUNNY BORDER BLUE'
Clearly, 'Sunny Border Blue' belongs in the sunny perennial border. Its flower spikes add a vertical accent to gardens filled with rounded, mound-shaped perennials. And its versatile color blends easily with pinks and violets and provides a contrast for hot yellows and reds. Use it as a summer-long source of color for the middle to front of your border or for a sunny, rather droughty spot.

CO-STARS FOR 'SUNNY BORDER BLUE'
'Sunny Border Blue' goes well with the pale yellow daisies of 'Moonbeam' threadleaf

'Sunny Border Blue' speedwell starts blooming in late June and keeps going for up to 18 weeks! Its rich, dark violet-blue flower color mixes easily with most other colors in the garden.

coreopsis (see page 110), the lemony flowers of 'Hyperion' daylily (*Hemerocallis* 'Hyperion'), and bright yellow-gold Missouri evening primrose (see page 232). It's also pretty with White Swan' purple coneflower (*Echinacea purpurea* 'White Swan'), rose pink hollyhock mallow (see page 218), the dusty rose flowers of 'Heidi' yarrow (*Achillea* 'Heidi'), and the white flower clusters of 'Mt. Fujiyama' summer phlox (*Phlox paniculata* 'Mt. Fujiyama').

WHITE CULVER'S ROOT

Veronicastrum virginicum 'Album'

CULVER'S ROOT HAS THE SAME GOOD QUALITIES as speedwells (*Veronica* spp.), to which it's closely related, and it adds the same kind of vertical accent in the garden. But it's on a larger scale than speedwell, and Culver's root adds height to a garden bed so beautifully that it certainly deserves to be welcomed into the select group of perennial all-stars.

For most of the season, Culver's root simply makes a pretty mound of sharp-toothed, lance-like, dark green leaves. The leaves are set in regular whorls along the sturdy, upright stems, giving the plant a clean-cut appearance. As the season wears on, it begins to send up taller stems that—in full sun and with plenty of moisture and rich compost in the soil—can reach up to 7 feet tall, although they are usually in the 4- to 5-foot range. Despite their size, these stems usually don't need staking.

Whorls of 3- to 6-inch-long leaves are set at intervals along the elongating flower stems, but the final 9 inches or so are reserved for a

A Completely Captivating Culver's Root

V. virginicum is the only species of this genus in cultivation today. Within this species, 'Album' is the superior cultivar. There are sometimes lilac-pink or bluish white types available, but these are not as strong visually as white Culver's root.

Spotlight on White Culver's Root

USDA Plant Hardiness Zones: 3 to 9

Height × Width: 4 to 5 feet (sometimes taller) × 3 to 4 feet

Season of Bloom: Early August to late September

Flower Color: White

Light Requirements: Full sun

Soil Requirements: Rich, moist, humusy, well-drained soil

Place of Origin: Massachusetts to Manitoba and south to Texas and Florida

Plant Sources: Busse Gardens, Carroll Gardens, Forest Farm, Milaeger's Gardens, White Flower Farm

myriad of tiny white florets. These flowers open slowly over many weeks in midsummer and early fall, their spikes making a strong vertical statement in the garden. The florets are pure white with prominent stamens, and each is about ¼-inch wide. They tend to open from the bottom of the spire upward.

Tall central spires bloom first, followed by smaller side stems that branch off from the main stem like elegant candelabra. These lateral spires continue the show when the main spires finish, ensuring a good long period of bloom from white Culver's root.

HOW TO GROW CULVER'S ROOT This all-star is easy to grow. It's reliably hardy and you can count on it to reappear year after year, like a good perennial should. This white-spired plant is a native of moist meadows, so it enjoys plenty of water during the growing season.

The tall, branching flower spires of white Culver's root echo the upright, silvery stems of the artemisias growing at its feet.

Water's especially important when Culver's root is putting on major growth in the spring and during the droughty, hot days in July just before it begins to flower. Because it's a heavy feeder, dig lots of finished compost into the soil where you're planting it. This will loosen the soil and improve its drainage. Culver's root isn't bothered by pests and diseases. You can divide it easily in spring.

PROPAGATING WHITE CULVER'S ROOT

Although white Culver's root will self-sow, its seedlings may have creamy flowers, rather than pure white ones like this cultivar. To retain this desirable characteristic, propagate white Culver's root by division or by cuttings. Divide the roots in spring and replant them 18 inches apart. Or take stem cuttings in the spring. Look for new basal shoots to take off and replant in spring.

THE RIGHT SITE FOR WHITE CULVER'S ROOT

Plant white Culver's root wherever you need a strong, architectural vertical accent. 'Album' has darker green leaves than the species. It makes a great plant for the back of the border, especially when backed up by dark evergreens against which the white spires of Culver's root can glow.

CO-STARS FOR WHITE CULVER'S ROOT

Culver's root is a fine plant for the mid- to late season garden. Plant it with 'Pink Beauty' boltonia (*Boltonia asteroides* 'Pink Beauty'), 'Marshall's Delight' bee balm (*Monarda didyma* 'Marshall's Delight'), 'Franz Schubert' summer phlox (*Phlox paniculata* 'Franz Schubert'), purple coneflowers (*Echinacea* spp.), 'Autumn Joy' sedum (see page 280), and asters.

Use your pruners to snip off the fading flower spikes of Culver's root. This helps keep the plant blooming longer and limits self-sown seedlings.

A Stellar Idea

Deadhead Culver's root when it finishes blooming, or you'll be surprised by a squadron of volunteer seedlings next year. Or if you need a few more plants, let your best one go to seed and take advantage of free seedlings. Just dig up the volunteers and move them to where you want them.

'BOWLES' VARIETY' PERIWINKLE

Vinca minor 'Bowles' Variety'

ONCE UPON A TIME, SOMEONE PLANTED periwinkle at the woods' edge on my property in Pennsylvania. It had spread to form a thick, luxurious, dark evergreen mat of trailing stems that colonized an area about 100 × 50 feet, both under the trees' canopy and out in partial sun.

'Bowles' Variety' periwinkle—sometimes also listed as 'La Graveana', 'La Grave', or variety *bowlesii*—is the best of this species by far. It has slightly larger foliage than the plain species, and it's a richer dark green. The flowers are larger and more profuse. These are an inch or more across and a very striking blue-violet or lavender color.

The flowers are borne on short stems that arise from the trailing, woody, permanent stems. Blooms dot the plants here and there from April through May. The amount of flowering depends on how much sun the plants get. The ideal amount of sun for periwinkle is about three to four hours of morning sun, followed by afternoon shade. That's why the eastern edge of a wooded area is such a good

Other Pretty Periwinkles

Besides the superior 'Bowles' Variety' periwinkle, there are other gardenworthy cultivars: 'Alba' periwinkle has white flowers, and the cultivar 'Aureo-variegata' has yellowish leaf margins and veining.

Spotlight on 'Bowles' Variety' Periwinkle

USDA Plant Hardiness Zones: 4 to 9

Height × Width: 8 to 12 inches × 24 inches

Season of Bloom: April to May

Flower Color: Blue-violet

Light Requirements: Partial sun to shade

Soil Requirements: Any good, moist, humusy soil with good drainage

Place of Origin: Europe

Plant Sources: Kurt Bluemel, Carroll Gardens, Forest Farm, J. W. Jung Seed

spot for it. If the plants get full shade, they will still flower, but less profusely.

HOW TO GROW PERIWINKLE Periwinkle is easy to grow and tolerates a wide range of soils as long as the soil has some organic matter. Plants can take heat, drought, rain, and even infertile soil with ease. Periwinkle prefers regular water but doesn't require it. It doesn't like a dry, sunny spot, however. This tough groundcover isn't prone to pests or diseases.

PROPAGATING PERIWINKLE This plant roots from its nodes as it creeps along the ground, making division a simple affair at almost any time during the growing season. Replant divisions 12 inches apart. You can also take tip cuttings in spring and root them.

THE RIGHT SITE FOR 'BOWLES' VARIETY' Periwinkle makes a gorgeous groundcover. Its small leaves have a more refined look than those of the other members of the "big three" groundcovers, English ivy and pachysandra. It's great around a foundation, alongside a

'Bowles' Variety' stands out among periwinkles for its vigorous growth, dense foliage, and showy blue-violet flowers.

CO-STARS FOR 'BOWLES' VARIETY'

In spite of its refined good looks, 'Bowles' Variety' periwinkle is not the best plant to mix with perennials in the formal garden, although it's nice around perennials that can hold their own, like peonies and bleeding hearts (*Dicentra* spp.). Other, less vigorous perennials (and even many shrubs) can lose out to periwinkle's rather competitive nature, which is what makes it so durable in difficult growing conditions. Its best companions are trees and spring-flowering bulbs—both of these seem able to coexist with periwinkle's greedy roots.

path, or in the dry shade under trees and shrubs. Its trailing stems are attractive hanging down from the top of a wall or raised bed or over the sides of a large planter.

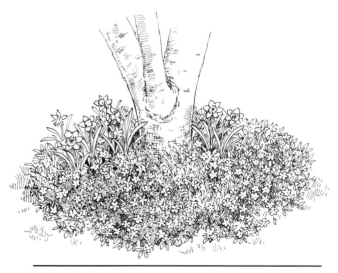

Planted together beneath a deciduous tree, periwinkle and daffodils make a pretty spring combination of blue and yellow flowers. Periwinkle will bloom and spread happily in the dappled shade, helping to hide the daffodils' fading foliage as summer arrives.

A Stellar Idea

A perfect use for 'Bowles' Variety' periwinkle is to plant it over a permanent bed of spring bulbs, especially daffodils. Periwinkle's loose, trailing habit allows the bulb foliage to emerge without trouble, and it can collapse back into the periwinkle's green arms when flowering is finished. The periwinkle's luxurious growth will conceal the unsightly bulb foliage while it yellows and dies, a process called ripening. (Ripening is necessary to give the bulb time to store nutrients for healthy growth and bounteous bloom next season.)

JOHNNY-JUMP-UP

Viola tricolor

OH, THERE ARE BIGGER VIOLETS and more fragrant violets, but no violets are as easy to grow, such prolific self-seeders, as cute and precious, as welcome, or as fun as the little Johnny-jump-up. They're called Johnny-jump-ups because you may plant them here one day, and somewhere down the months or years, they will disappear. And yet over there they'll suddenly appear (jump up) just when you least expect them to and just in time to make a pleasant picture with whatever plant or setting they've decided to bless with their presence. This wonderful tendency to self-sow freely is one of the things that makes Johnny-jump-up a star in the garden. Buy a six-pack of it at the garden center in spring and tuck the plants here and there—under a shrub, in the front of the perennial border, beside the

Varied Vivid Violets

Other pleasing perennials from the genus <u>Viola</u> include tufted pansy (<u>V. cornuta</u>, also called horned violet) and its cultivar, 'Chantreyland', a popular apricot-colored pansy. Sweet violet (<u>V. odorata</u>) is a dainty thing that grows 2 to 8 inches tall and bears sweetly fragrant flowers. Its cultivars include the rich purple flowered 'Royal Robe'; 'Rosina', which has dusky pink flowers; and 'White Czar', which bears white blossoms.

Spotlight on Johnny-Jump-Up

USDA Plant Hardiness Zones: 4 to 9

Season of Bloom: April to June, and sporadically until frost

Height × Width: 3 to 12 inches × 8 to 12 inches

Flower Color: Violet-purple, yellow, and white, in many variations and shades

Light Requirements: Full sun to partial shade

Soil Requirements: Rich, moist, well-drained soil

Place of Origin: Europe to northern Asia

Seed Source: Thompson & Morgan

path…wherever. You will undoubtedly find that you'll now have Johnny-jump-ups in your garden forever. And thank goodness, for they are little marvels of artistic beauty. I've just now gone to my garden, where they are still flowering in November (having started their bloomathon in April).

Here's one flower: Two petals of the richest, most velvety royal purple stand up behind three forward petals. These are ivory white, two petals on top and a larger third petal below. This third petal is notched in the center of its lower edge, and there at the notch is a blotch of deep violet color. In the center, where the three petals come together, is a glowing pool of yellow-orange. From this pool of gold emerge 12 dark violet stripes that ray out from the center, like beams from the disk of the sun.

Here's another flower: The form is the same, except the three forward petals are a glowing lavender-violet backed by rich burgundy petals and striped with the deepest

In a moist, cool container, Johnny-jump-ups strike a note of rich color amid the greens of moss and foliage. Next season they'll bloom around the base of this planter, too!

midnight violet rays from the golden center. You could spend considerable time just looking at the variations of these blossoms.

Johnny-jump-up blooms most heavily from April to mid-June, then it flowers sporadically all summer to frost. As it blooms, it's like pansies or petunias in that the stems keep elongating as they blossom. Over the course of a season, the stems may reach 12 to 24 inches long, with tufts of leaves and flowers arising upright from the flopping stems at their tips and here and there along their lengths.

How to Grow Johnny-Jump-Up Johnny-jump-up does best in rich, moist garden soil, in full sun to partial shade. Other than that, it isn't at all particular. It has no pest or disease problems. And despite its habit of popping up here and there, Johnny-jump-up is not invasive and is always welcome as it adds that just-right spot of color.

Propagating Johnny-Jump-Up Sweet Johnny-jump-up will reseed prolifically. If you need some in a new spot, just look for volunteers and move them to the places you choose.

The Right Site for Johnny-Jump-Up Where can't you use Johnny-jump-ups in your garden and landscape? These small plants are great for planting around and under shrubs, anywhere along paths or walkways, and in the front of the perennial bed with any other plants that won't grow over and shade them. Their tendency to "jump up" lets them add little spots of color here and there where you may least expect it.

Cheery Johnny-jump-ups will bring color to un-expected spots in your garden. Even though they tend to pop up in surprising spots, these jewel-toned flowers are de-lightful and not at all invasive.

Co-Stars for Johnny-Jump-Up With its tricolored flowers, Johnny-jump-up has the advantage of being the perfect companion for itself. But it also looks sweet with the bigger faces of pansies (*V. × wittrockiana*), with the frothy white flowers of perennial candytuft (*Iberis sempervirens*) or the annual sweet alyssum (*Lobularia maritima*) or with the yellow flower clusters of basket-of-gold (see page 70). In the spring it makes a good accompaniment for yellow or yellow-and-white daffodils, too.

ADAM'S-NEEDLE

Yucca filamentosa

Spotlight on
Adam's-Needle

USDA Plant Hardiness Zones: 4 to 11

Season of Bloom: July to August

Height × Width: 3 to 5 feet × 3 to 4 feet

Flower Color: White

Light Requirements: Full sun

Soil Requirements: Sandy, dry, well-drained soil

Place of Origin: Southern New Jersey to Florida then west to Mississippi

Plant Sources: Kurt Bluemel, Bluestone Perennials, Busse Gardens, Carroll Gardens, Forest Farm Garden Place, J. W. Jung Seed, Shady Oaks Nursery, André Viette Farm & Nursery

ADAM'S-NEEDLE LOOKS LIKE A DESERT PLANT, with its long, swordlike leaves spraying up and out of a central clump. It acts like one, too, cruising through summer drought without trouble. But our perennial all-star Adam's-needle isn't a desert plant. It grows naturally in the sandy, dry, heat-struck soils of the southeastern seaboard and Gulf states. The leaves are tough, with filamentous hairs splitting off along the leaf margins. And the roots are tough, too, growing as thick as a baseball bat and obstinately clinging to the ground, so that in time they become hard to remove. A thick stem emerges from these roots. It's short, and set all around with whorls of gray-green leaves, which are about an inch wide and 24 to 36 inches long. Their effect is like an explosion of outward-facing swords.

In July and into August, Adam's-needle

Attractive Adam's-Needles

Adam's-needle has handsome, gray-green leaves, but there may be places in your landscape that call for something more. For those spots, you might consider one of our all-star's variegated cultivars: 'Color Guard' has leaves with creamy white centers edged with gray-green; 'Golden Sword' has yellow centers with green margins. 'Bright Edge' has green centered leaves with cream-colored margins, while 'Variegata' has leaves striped green and creamy yellow.

sends up a stout, tough, tall flowerstalk that opens like a big asparagus frond. But instead of tiny leaves and little flowers, it hangs out many 2-inch, white, sweetly fragrant, drooping bells that bloom several feet above the leaves. These are followed by seedpods with interesting, regular rows of seeds that you can sow after curing them overwinter.

HOW TO GROW ADAM'S-NEEDLE This yucca will thrive in any dry, loose, well-drained soil, but it really needs full sun all day to produce its best flower show. Although some of its older evergreen leaves may get blotchy and patchy, these can be easily removed. Not much in the way of pests or diseases bothers it.

PROPAGATING ADAM'S-NEEDLE Remove offsets from the base of the plant in spring or fall and replant them elsewhere—24 inches

Variegated Adam's-needles such as 'Golden Sword' really make a stir in the garden. Their spiky yellow-and-green leaves create a bright spot between dark shrubs and masses of fine-textured foliage.

Adam's-needle may grow for several years before it flowers, and each crown produces just one flowerstalk. But there are always younger crowns waiting to fill in as the older crowns fade.

apart if you are massing them. You can also divide the roots, but that is hard with established plants because their tough roots resent moving. It's better—and easier—to expose some roots on one side of the plant and cut off a few, then cut them into 6-inch pieces, planting them upright just under the surface of a box full of compost. Overwinter them, then plant them out in the spring. You can also grow Adam's-needle from seed.

THE RIGHT SITE FOR ADAM'S-NEEDLE

Adam's-needle's explosion of swordlike leaves offers a fine contrast to all the broad leaves in the typical perennial garden. Its gray-green foliage goes well with most other foliage colors and textures, as well as with most perennials' flowers. Plant it in a group by itself on a sunny, dry bank or a rocky outcropping, or in a waste place. Its tall tower of bell-like white flowers also mixes with large, broad-leaved shrubs. Planted with succulents and cacti, Adam's-needle gives a desert appearance to the landscape. Place it where you won't be watering, and forget it.

CO-STARS FOR ADAM'S-NEEDLE

Although it's classed as a perennial, Adam's-needle works best among shrubs such as juniper and broom (*Genista* spp.) and with plants that suggest desert-dry conditions, such as sedums, hens-and-chickens (*Sempervivum* spp.), echeverias (*Echeveria* spp.), spurge (*Euphorbia* spp.), cabbage palm (*Livistona australis*), and cacti. A large, dry, rocky outcropping is an ideal place for Adam's-needle. In the north, from Zones 4 to 6, Adam's-needle makes a bold statement with fine-leaved shrubs like spireas (*Spiraea* spp.), barberries (*Berberis* spp.), and hedges.

A Stellar Idea

While most of Adam's-needle's narrow, linear leaves will grow straight out from the plant's thick stem, a few of them will bend over somewhere along their length. This can make the plant look less tidy than it otherwise might. Where Adam's-needle is in a frequently seen spot, snipping off any floppy leaves can improve its appearance.

Sources of Perennials Found in Perennial All-Stars

LOOK TO YOUR LOCAL NURSERIES and garden centers when seeking perennial all-stars for your garden—you're sure to find many of these excellent plants there. However, some may be easier to find from mail-order sources, and you'll enjoy the wealth of other fine perennials these companies offer.

Contact these businesses to find out how to get a copy of their catalog. Some catalogs are free, while others may be available for a small fee; this fee is often credited toward your first order. Plant societies and smaller companies often appreciate receiving a self-addressed, stamped business envelope enclosed with your inquiry.

The following mail-order companies identified themselves as sources of perennials listed in this book at the time of its publication. Supplies of perennials can fluctuate in response to increases in demand or unfavorable weather conditions, so be patient. If a company doesn't have the perennial you're looking for, ask them why. They may be planning to offer it again in their next catalog, or they may have a newer cultivar to offer in its place.

Ambergate Gardens
8730 County Road 43
Chaska, MN 55318-9358
(612) 443-2248

Bloomingfields Farm
P.O. Box 5
Gaylordsville, CT 06755-0005
(860) 354-6951

Kurt Bluemel
2740 Greene Lane
Baldwin, MD 21013-9523
(410) 557-7229

Bluestone Perennials
7211 Middle Ridge Road
Madison, OH 44057
(800) 852-5243

Breck's
U. S. Reservation Center
6523 North Galena Road
Peoria, IL 61632
(800) 722-9069

W. Atlee Burpee & Company
300 Park Avenue
Warminster, PA 18991-0001
(800) 888-1447

Busse Gardens
5873 Oliver Avenue, SW
Cokato, MN 55321-4229
(800) 544-3192

Carroll Gardens
444 East Main Street
Westminster, MD 21157
(800) 638-6334

The Crownsville Nursery
P.O. Box 797
Crownsville, MD 21032
(410) 849-3143

The Daffodil Mart
7463 Heath Trail
Gloucester, VA 23061
(800) 255-2852

Daisy Fields
12635 SW Brighton Lane
Hillsboro, OR 97123
(503) 628-0315

Daylily Discounters
One Daylily Plaza
Alachua, FL 32615
(904) 462-1539

Dutch Gardens
P.O. Box 200
Adelphia, NJ 07710-0200
(800) 818-3861

Forestfarm
990 Tetherow Road
Williams, OR 97544-9599
(541) 846-7269

Garden Place
6780 Heisley Road
P.O. Box 388
Mentor, OH 44061-0388
(216) 255-3705

Goodness Grows
Highway 77 North
P.O. Box 311
Lexington, GA 30648
(706) 743-5055

Greer Gardens
1280 Goodpasture Island Road
Eugene, OR 97401-1794
(800) 548-0111

Heronswood Nursery
7530 NE 288th Street
Kingston, WA 98346
(360) 297-4172
(360) 297-8321 (fax)

Hildenbrandt's Iris Gardens
1710 Cleveland Street
Lexington, NE 68850-2721
(308) 324-4334

J. W. Jung Seed Company
335 South High Street
Randolph, WI 53957-0001
(800) 247-5864

Klehm Nursery
4210 North Duncan Road
Champaign, IL 61821
(800) 553-3715

McClure & Zimmerman
108 West Winnebago
P.O. Box 368
Friesland, WI 53935-0368
(414) 326-4220

Milaeger's Gardens
4838 Douglas Avenue
Racine, WI 53402-2498
(800) 669-9956

The Natural Garden
38W443 Highway 64
St. Charles, IL 60175
(630) 584-0150

Nichols Garden Nursery
1190 North Pacific Highway
Albany, OR 97321-4580
(541) 928-9280

Park Seed Company
1 Parkton Avenue
Greenwood, SC 29647-0001
(864) 223-7333

Plant Delights Nursery
9241 Sauls Road
Raleigh, NC 27603
(919) 772-4794

Powell's Gardens
9468 U.S. Highway 70 East
Princeton, NC 27569
(919) 936-4421

Roslyn Nursery
211 Burrs Lane
Dix Hills, NY 11746
(516) 643-9347

Savory's Gardens
5300 Whiting Avenue
Edina, MN 55439-1249
(612) 941-8755

Shady Oaks Nursery
112 10th Avenue SE
Waseca, MN 56093
(800) 504-8006

Spring Hill Nurseries
110 West Elm Street
Tipp City, OH 45371
(800) 582-8527

Sunlight Gardens
174 Golden Lane
Andersonville, TN 37705
(800) 272-7396

Thompson & Morgan
P.O. Box 1308
Jackson, NJ 08527-0308
(800) 274-7333

Van Bourgondien
245 Route 109
P.O. Box 1000
Babylon, NY 11702-9004
(800) 622-9997

Van Engelen
23 Tulip Drive
Bantam, CT 06750
(860) 567-5323

André Viette Farm and Nursery
P.O. Box 1109
Fishersville, VA 22939
(540) 943-2315

Wayside Gardens
1 Garden Lane
Hodges, SC 29695-0001
(800) 845-1124

We-Du Nurseries
Route 5 Box 724
Marion, NC 28752
(704) 738-8300

Weiss Bros. Perennial Nusery
11690 Colfax Highway
Grass Valley, CA 95945
(916) 272-7657

White Flower Farm
P.O. Box 50
Litchfield, CT 06759-0050
(800) 503-9624

Recommended Reading

THE AMERICAN HORTICULTURAL SOCIETY. *The American Horticultural Society Illustrated Encyclopedia of Gardening: Perennials.* Mount Vernon, VA: The American Horticultural Society, 1982.

ARMITAGE, ALLAN M. *Herbaceous Perennial Plants.* 2nd ed. Champaign, IL: Stipes Publishing, L.L.C., 1997.

BAILEY, LIBERTY HYDE, et al. *Hortus Third.* New York: Macmillan Publishing Co., 1976.

BIRD, RICHARD. *The Propagation of Hardy Perennials.* London B.T. Batsford, Ltd., 1993.

BRADLEY, FERN MARSHALL, ed. *Gardening with Perennials.* Emmaus, PA.: Rodale Press, 1996.

CLAUSEN, RUTH ROGERS, AND NICOLAS H. EKSTROM. *Perennials for American Gardens.* New York: Random House, 1989.

COX, JEFF, AND MARILYN COX. *The Perennial Garden.* Emmaus, PA.: Rodale Press, 1985.

HEBB, ROBERT S. *Low Maintenance Perennials.* New York: Quadrangle/New York Times Book Co., 1975.

HERITEAU, JACQUELINE, et al. *The American Horticultural Society Flower Finder.* New York: Simon & Schuster, 1992.

HOBHOUSE, PENELOPE. *Color in Your Garden.* Boston: Little, Brown & Co., 1985.

HUDAK, JOSEPH. *Gardening with Perennials Month by Month.* 2nd ed., rev. and expanded. Portland, OR.: Timber Press, 1993.

JELITTO, LEO, et. al. *Hardy Herbaceous Perennials.* 3rd ed. 2 vols. Portland, OR.: Timber Press, 1990.

KÖHLEIN, FRITZ, AND PETER MENZEL. *Color Encyclopedia of Garden Plants and Their Habitats.* Portland, OR.: Timber Press, 1994.

MCGOURTY, FREDERICK. *The Perennial Gardener.* Boston: Houghton Mifflin Co., 1989.

PHILLIPS, ELLEN, AND C. COLSTON BURRELL. *Rodale's Illustrated Encyclopedia of Perennials.* Emmaus, PA.: Rodale Press, 1993.

PHILLIPS, ROGER, AND MARTYN RIX. *The Random House Book of Perennials.* 2 vols. New York: Random House, 1991.

STILL, STEVEN M. *Manual of Herbaceous Ornamental Plants.* 4th ed. Champaign, IL.: Stipes Publishing, 1994.

SUNSET BOOKS AND MAGAZINE STAFF. *Western Garden Book.* 6th ed. Menlo Park, CA.: Sunset Publishing Corp., 1995.

THOMAS, GRAHAM STUART. *Perennial Garden Plants, or The Modern Florilegium.* 3rd ed. Portland, OR: Timber Press, 1990.

WILSON, HELEN VAN PELT. *The Fragrant Year.* New York: William Morrow & Co., 1967.

Photo Credits

© **Allan Armitage**
18 (bottom), 173, 207 (left), 279 (bottom)

© **C. Colston Burrell**
13 (bottom), 29 (top), 99 (top), 123 (right), 141 (left), 157 (bottom), 159, 181 (bottom), 189 (top), 249 (right), 251(top), 253 (right), 269 (top), 281 (right), 301 (bottom), 311 (left)

Robert Cardillo/ Organic Gardening
13 (second from top), 19 (second from top), 22-23, 61, 83 (top), 119 (bottom), 229 (both), 271 (left)

© **David Cavagnaro**
35, 213 (bottom), 239

© **R. Todd Davis**
4, 11 (second from top), 16 (third from top), 20 (top), 49, 67 (bottom), 111 (left), 125 (top), 135 (top), 141 (right), 187, 211 (right), 215 (top), 237, 265, 277 (top), 293 (right)

© **Alan & Linda Detrick**
14 (top), 21 (second from top), 33 (right), 63 (bottom), 211 (left), 213 (top), 225 (right), 271 (right), 273, 287

© **Ken Druse**
103 (left), 305 (bottom)

© **Derek Fell**
41 (bottom), 45 (bottom), 69, 85, 89, 131 (bottom), 135 (bottom), 139 (top), 165 (bottom), 185, 233 (bottom), 255 (left), 269 (bottom), 283, 289 (left), 323 (left)

T. L. Gettings/ Rodale Images
16 (top), 53 (right), 55, 67 (top), 87 (top), 93 (left), 95, 101 (left), 125 (bottom), 197 (right), 221 (right), 231 (left), 241 (bottom), 245 (bottom), 279 (top), 289 (right), 315 (bottom), 321 (bottom)

© **John Glover**
10 (second from top), 11 (top), 12 (third from top), 15 (bottom), 19 (top), 20 (second from top), 27 (left), 39 (bottom), 45 (left), 79 (left), 107 (both), 109 (left), 111 (right), 113 (bottom), 121 (right), 123 (left), 129 (both), 133 (both), 137, 157 (top), 167 (top), 171 (right), 181 (top), 197 (left), 199 (top), 217, 231 (right), 233 (top), 259 (top), 261, 267 (left), 285, 309 (left), 311 (right), 321 (top)

John Hamel/ Rodale Images
1

© **Pamela J. Harper**
191, 195

© **judywhite/ New Leaf Images**
161 (both), 175 (bottom), 219 (left)

© **Dency Kane**
99 (bottom), 165 (top), 225 (left), 243 (top), 291 (right)

© **Jay G. Lunn**
14 (third from top), 263 (both)

© **Charles Mann**
10 (third from top), 14 (second from top), 17 (bottom), 21 (top), 57 (left), 59 (top), 71 (top), 83 (bottom), 87 (bottom), 91, 93 (right), 109 (right), 117, 145 (left), 147 (left), 163 (right), 167 (bottom), 201, 251 (bottom), 275 (left), 277 (bottom), 301 (top)

© **David McDonald**
79 (right), 199 (bottom), 281 (left), 313 (bottom)

© **Clive Nichols**
2 (The Anchorage, Kent), 3 (The Priory, Kemerton, Worcs), 5 (EastGrove Cottage, Worchester), 6 (Old Rectory, Berkshire), 7

© **Plant Pics**
205 (right)

Park Seed Company
149, 183, 221 (left)

© **Jerry Pavia**
11 (third from top), 17 (top), 43 (top), 73 (bottom), 113 (top), 119 (top), 129 (left), 131 (top), 177 (both), 189 (bottom), 193 (top), 219 (right), 257 (bottom), 275 (right)

© **PhotoSynthesis**
19 (third from top, and bottom), 33 (left), 63 (top), 235

© **Susan Roth**
10 (bottom), 13 (third from top), 18 (second from top), 29 (bottom), 43 (bottom), 127, 155 (left), 241 (top), 247, 295, 297, 305 (top), 309 (right)

© **Richard Shiell**
11 (bottom), 12 (top), 15 (second from top), 16 (bottom), 17 (second and third from top), 18 (top), 20 (third from top), 21 (third from top), 25, 27 (right), 31 (both), 37 (bottom), 47 (both), 51, 57 (right), 71 (bottom), 73 (top), 77, 105, 121 (left), 139 (bottom), 143 (top), 155 (right), 163 (left), 169, 175 (top), 179 (top), 193 (bottom), 203, 209, 253 (left), 307, 313 (top), 319, 323 (right)

Delilah Smittle/ Rodale Press
205 (left)

© **Aleksandra Szywala**
13 (top), 37 (top), 53 (left), 151 (both), 171 (left), 223 (left), 243 (bottom), 257 (top), 267 (right), 293 (left), 317

© **Connie Toops**
12 (bottom), 16 (second from top), 59 (bottom), 101 (right), 143 (bottom), 291 (left)

© **Paddy Wales**
ii, 8–9, 15 (top), 18 (third from top), 39 (top), 65, 103 (right), 145 (right), 147 (right), 179 (bottom), 215 (bottom), 223 (right), 245 (top), 259 (bottom), 315 (top)

Wayside Gardens
10 (top), 41 (top), 75, 97, 153, 207 (right), 227, 249 (left), 255 (right), 299, 303

White Flower Farm/ Michael H. Dodge 81, 115

On the cover:
'Ice Follies' Dafffodil: Robert Cardillo
Balloon Flower: Connie Toops
'Goblin' Blanket Flower,
'Connecticut King' Lily, Music Series Hybrid Columbines: Richard Shiell
'E. C. Buxton' Marguerite: John Glover

Index

Note: Page numbers in *italic* indicate illustrations. **Boldface** references indicate photographs.

(continued)

USDA Plant Hardiness Zone Map

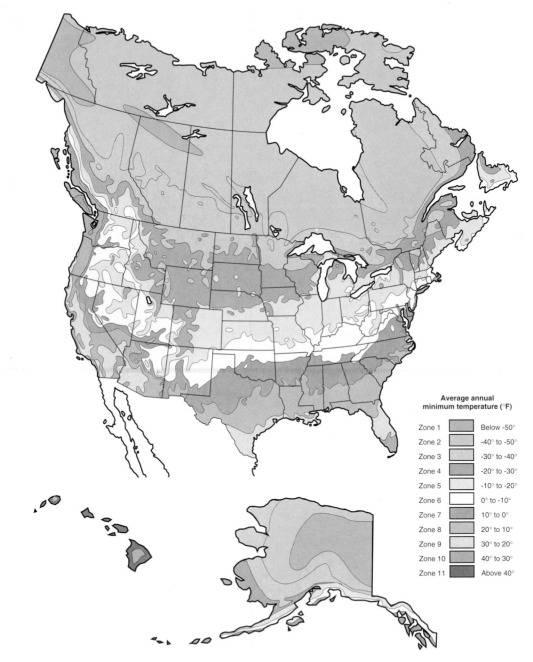

Average annual minimum temperature (°F)

Zone		Temperature
Zone 1		Below -50°
Zone 2		-40° to -50°
Zone 3		-30° to -40°
Zone 4		-20° to -30°
Zone 5		-10° to -20°
Zone 6		0° to -10°
Zone 7		10° to 0°
Zone 8		20° to 10°
Zone 9		30° to 20°
Zone 10		40° to 30°
Zone 11		Above 40°

This map was revised in 1990 to reflect the original USDA map, done in 1965. It is now recognized as the best indicator of minimum temperatures available. Look at the map to find your area, then match its color to the key at the right. When you've found your color, the key will tell you what hardiness zone you live in. Remember that the map is a general guide; your particular conditions may vary.